Educational contributions
of associations

ONTARIO'S EDUCATIVE SOCIETY / VII

Educational contributions of associations

W.G. FLEMING

UNIVERSITY OF TORONTO PRESS

© University of Toronto Press 1972
Toronto and Buffalo

Printed in Canada

Volume VII
ISBN 0-8020-3273-7

Complete set (8 volumes)
ISBN 0-8020-3284-2
Microfiche ISBN 0-8020-0079-7
LC 77-166928

Preface

Volume VII, the last in the series ONTARIO'S EDUCATIVE SOCIETY, is designed to give some impression of the educational contributions of a fairly comprehensive selection of those associations which have had a primary or an incidental interest in some aspect of education. To speak of the educational system of the province is ordinarily to underestimate the influence of most of these organizations, since they tend to operate in a semiformal or an informal fashion. Even a more general reference to education often ignores the importance of their work. One reason is that there has been an unrealistic tendency to equate education with schooling, and to think of it as the exclusive responsibility of institutions specifically maintained for the purpose. Such an attitude would of course be absurd in a society that recognized itself as truly educative. A second reason for the neglect of the educational contribution of associations is that the educational element in their purposes and activities is often inextricably bound up with cultural, recreational, philanthropic, self-protective, and other components. A third reason is that many of these associations demonstrate little interest in publicizing their work beyond their members.

As has been indicated in earlier volumes, ONTARIO'S EDUCATIVE SOCIETY attempts to adhere to a very broad definition of education. In recognizing the development of mental powers, the stimulation of intellectual curiosity, the cultivation of aesthetic interests, and other purposes that nearly everyone would regard as educational, it does not exclude the acquisition of skills, some very complex and others of a simple, mechanical nature, required for occupational success. The greatest difficulties are perhaps found in the area of attitudes. It is easy to agree that education should inspire the individual to love the good, the true, and the beautiful. The matter can be put more specifically in terms of helping him to appreciate certain great works of literature or to feel a sense of awe in the face of a complex mathematical structure. Somewhere along the way toward persuading him of the superior value of some firm's soap flakes or cigarettes, education no doubt ends and something else begins, whether promotion or, in less agreeable language, propaganda. Since the dividing line must be drawn in terms of values, and since these are to a considerable extent an individual matter, the decision is inescapably subjective.

The policy followed in ONTARIO'S EDUCATIVE SOCIETY might perhaps be defined as "When in doubt, call it education."

The problem of definition was evident in the responses received from many of the associations to our requests for information. Some showed no equivocation whatever in describing publication and the holding of conferences, seminars, and meetings as educational activities. A considerable number did not hesitate to include the preparation of briefs for submission to government officials, commissions, committees, and other agencies under the same heading, whether the subject had anything to do with the educational process or not. It is clear that many association officers feel that effective social service must entail, not only relief from the problem or handicap involved, but also measures to enable the victim to improve his own lot. That is, he can be effectively helped in the long run only if he is to some extent educated. Similarly, the encouragement of cultural activities often involves training performers, whether amateur or professional, and educating others to appreciate excellence of achievement. A certain number of respondents indicated in a fairly decisive manner that their associations had nothing to do with education, despite information from other sources that they were involved in many activities that others had no hesitation in calling educational. A few took an intermediate position, and generously supplied material that they doubted would be considered relevant.

Some limitations have had to be placed on the treatment of the theme of volume VII. It might have seemed desirable to try to locate all the associations making some perceptible contribution to education under the broadest of definitions, to describe their structure and the constitution and by-laws under which they operated, to trace all the significant events in their history, to explore the full range of their activities to show the context in which their educational contributions were made, and to evaluate their impact on education. Such a task would, however, have been far too great for the limited human resources with which this project was executed. If it could have been effectively undertaken, the results would probably have taken seven volumes to record. In accordance with the more restricted objectives actually pursued, what was regarded as a reasonably representative selection of associations was made within each category. The choice, rather than being entirely systematic, has been strongly affected by the ability and willingness of officials to supply information. Further, the treatment of historical origins and events and the description of activities not closely connected with education were severely limited. Little is said about the structure and operational procedures of most of the associations, for such matters are not relevant to the major purpose of the volume.

In one sense the term "voluntary" is applicable to all the associations dealt with. Although some of them operate under statutes which require that all those in a particular professional or other occupational category belong in order to practise or continue in employment, the extent to which any individual member will contribute is nearly always a matter of his own choice. Thus effort on behalf of the association may be considered voluntary, even though membership is not. The whole group of associations may be regarded as a kind of counterweight to government bureaucracy or officialdom.

It is difficult to exaggerate the extent to which the strength of a democratic society depends on the willingness of citizens to work together outside governmental structures for the advancement of a wide range of causes. It is no discredit to members of associations to observe that their motives are far from being exclusively altruistic. The beneficial social effects of their efforts are not destroyed because in the process they gratify their desire for companionship and personal recognition. While it is not always true that what is good for the individual is good for society, it is comforting to observe how often the two areas of interest overlap.

There is a tendency in increasingly complex societies for voluntary efforts to prove inadequate to handle many aspects of social need. There comes a point where public resources must be employed to cope with the magnitude of the task and to ensure reasonably fair treatment for all. Few would dispute the desirability, for example, of having publicly supported schools replace those maintained as an act of charity. It is possible that some urgent reforms have been delayed because of the existence of voluntary agencies whose valiant but inadequate labours have provided an excuse for official inaction. In Ontario, at least, it would appear that the more common tendency has been for such agencies to develop an awareness of a need and to fill it during the transitional stage before government intervention. In certain areas their efforts have obviated the need for governmental assumption of responsibility, and thus helped to prevent the weight of the official bureaucracy from becoming overwhelming. Where the major responsibility has passed to the government, associations have often found a supporting role for themselves and thus ensured that the rendering of service retains an air of humanity.

Voluntary participation in an association is an excellent means of preparing for the exercise of democratic responsibility. Knowledge of parliamentary rules may often be inexact and their application rather free and easy, but it is difficult to take an active and effective part in the proceedings without acquiring a certain amount of tolerance for and patience with varying points of view.

The use of the past tense to refer to most aspects of the associations' activities, and even to their very existence, will be noted. This practice does not usually mean that the associations will have vanished by the time this volume is read, although in some that in fact will be the case. It merely emphasizes the impossibility of keeping track of and recording changes during the long interval between the submission of the manuscript to the publisher and the date of publication. Where the expression "at the time of writing," or some similar phrase, is not explicitly used, it should be understood.

It was the writer's original intention to make a much more definite distinction between associations with purely provincial interests and those operating on a national scale. However, for the most part it appears that an organization has remained narrowly provincial in scope only if its major functions have consisted in exercising some power, such as licensing, that comes within purely provincial jurisdiction. Even in these cases there has been an almost inevitable tendency for a national co-ordinating body to be formed. There are many cases of provincial associations acting as chapters or divisions of national associations, and performing complementary functions. Anyone who has difficulty finding links among the different geographical regions of Canada would do well to examine the very real unifying influence exerted by associations. Even in education, where provincial authority is so dominant, it is surprising how much interchange of information and opinion can be ascribed to these bodies. In view of the national character of so many of the associations, no special effort has been made to restrict a discussion of their influence to Ontario alone, although examples of their activities have been selected from that province where convenient and applicable.

One warning about the selection of content in this volume is perhaps in order. There were a few associations, of which the Metropolitan Educational Television Association was an example, whose activities tied in so closely with themes dealt with in earlier volumes that they were given complete treatment there. Further, some of the major associations, such as the teachers' federations, were involved in so many events and developments of major importance that the story of their activities and contributions is to some extent scattered through most or all of the volumes. An attempt at anything like complete treatment in volume VII would involve an undue amount of repetition.

Acknowledgments

I am deeply indebted to the Honourable William G. Davis, Minister of Education and of University Affairs at the time of writing, for providing me the full co-operation of his departments in the production of the series of volumes constituting ONTARIO'S EDUCATIVE SOCIETY. In this task I was given access to all pertinent material in the two departments under his direction. His officials at the time of writing, headed by Dr J.R. McCarthy, Deputy Minister of Education, and Dr E.E. Stewart, Deputy Minister of University Affairs, were also extraordinarily co-operative and helpful. I am particularly grateful to these officials for enabling me to pursue the work in a way that most appeals to a member of the university community: that is, I was completely free to choose, present, and interpret the facts according to my own best judgment. I did not feel the slightest pressure to adapt or modify the material in any way so as to present an "official" version of educational developments in Ontario. As a consequence, I am completely responsible for any opinions or interpretations of the facts that the work contains. The generous assistance for the project provided by the Ontario government, without which publication would have been impossible, does not involve any responsibility for the contents.

I would like to express my particular gratitude to those who assisted me so devotedly in the project: Miss L. McGuire, my loyal secretary, who served from the time the work began in the spring of 1968, Mrs E. West, who also served with extraordinary devotion and competence during most of the same period, and Mrs S. Constable, Miss D. Mc-Dowell, and Mrs G.J. Moore, each of whom participated during an extended period. Mr C.H. Westcott, who served as Executive Assistant to the Minister of Education and University Affairs, gave me continuous encouragement and helped to deal with practical problems relating to production and publication. Particularly helpful advice and information were given by Dr C.A. Brown, Professor E.B. Rideout, and Dr J.A. Keddy. Arrangements by Dr G.E. Flower to relieve me of the majority of my other professional obligations during most of a three-year period are also greatly appreciated. In addition, I would like to acknowledge my general indebtedness to the hundreds of people who supplied information so willingly in a variety of forms. That I am unable to name them all individually does not mean that I am any the less grateful for their contributions.

W.G. FLEMING
July 1971

Contents

Educational contributions of associations

ONE

Broadly based education associations

What were labelled "broadly based education associations" for the purposes of this volume were associations concerned with a wide variety of issues cutting across educational levels. Some were supported or sponsored by a number of other associations, while others acted as umbrellas under which constituent associations operated. Both provincial and national organizations are included. The Ontario Educational Association (OEA) and the Canadian Education Association (CEA) are given relatively detailed treatment in recognition of their preeminent status in the field of voluntary educational effort.

ONTARIO EDUCATIONAL ASSOCIATION

Origin and early history
The first meetings for Ontario teachers were organized as a result of the initiative of the provincial authorities. Egerton Ryerson encouraged the holding of county school conventions beginning in 1846, mainly for the purpose of dealing with administrative matters. At first these conventions were held at five-year intervals, but later they became annual events. The origin of the OEA dates from the first meeting on a provincial scale in 1861.

The official historian of the organization is E.C. Guillet, who wrote a centennial history, *In the Cause of Education*,[1] covering the period between 1861 and 1960. This book contains not only the facts about the origin and development of the association, but also many observations about the evolution of educational practices and the changing outlook of educators during the hundred-year interval. In his preface the author identifies the work as a summary of the educational thought of a century. By its nature ONTARIO'S EDUCATIVE SOCIETY must rely heavily on the original research undertaken by Guillet to produce this account.

Guillet identifies Robert Alexander as the one man who might with justice be called the founder of the OEA. In 1860, when he was teaching at Newmarket, the Teachers' Association of North York appointed him as a delegate to the New York State Teachers' Association. He returned from Buffalo convinced of the desirability of forming a provincial association. A committee was set up, with him as secretary, to press for the necessary action. Egerton Ryerson co-operated by publishing in the *Journal of Education* an appeal to teachers to attend a preliminary meeting at Toronto in January 1861. If they were not chosen as delegates from their cities, towns, townships, or counties, the teachers were urged to attend as individuals.

There was some initial antagonism among the approximately 120 teachers and normal school students who assembled in the County Court Room. This feeling was based, according to Guillet, on the fact that the initiative had come from graduates of the normal school who were employed in North York, while many leading Toronto teachers and principals were "County Board men." At the meeting the proprieties were observed by seating the men in the body of the court room and the women in the jury box. After the passage of a resolution that a constitution be drawn up, and at the conclusion of an appropriate adjournment to work out the details, a draft was presented and dealt with clause by clause. The first clause recognized the eligibility for membership of ladies and gentlemen engaged in any department of instruction, members of the Council of Public Instruction, members of county boards of instruction, superintendents of schools, editors of educational journals, and ex-teachers. A motion to include acting trustees was presented but defeated. The annual membership fee was fixed at $1, or $10 for life membership. The new organization was called for the time being "the Teachers' Association of Canada West."

Further consideration was given to the constitution later in the year when the first regular meeting was held. The four main aims of the association were defined thus:

(1) to secure the general adoption of the most approved methods of instruction; (2) to secure the improvement of textbooks in use in the schools of the province; (3) to enlarge the views of teachers and stimulate their exertions for the advancement and diffusion of knowledge; and (4) to encourage the interchange of ideas and stimulate friendly intercourse in the profession.[2]

During the first decade nearly all the annual conventions were held at one location or another in Toronto. The exception was the one held in Hamilton in 1862. The original intention of meeting successively in Toronto, Hamilton, Kingston, and London was defeated in 1863 when the Kingston members showed little interest in acting as hosts. Among topics dealt with by major speakers during the early 1860s were the advancement and diffusion of knowledge, the duties of teachers, school rewards and punishments, the importance of teachers and the desirability of raising the status of the profession, the need for better remuneration to reward improved service, content and methods in various school subjects, the problem of truancy, compulsory education, and the quality of textbooks. Although the discussions were often characterized by the moralizing tone so typical of the Victorian era, many of the arguments advanced had a surprisingly modern ring. For example, although the opponents of corporal punishment were far from strong enough to prevail, they saw in physical brutality many of the undesirable consequences that were later confirmed by psychological research. On the other hand, it was safer in those days to affirm that children often learned to love the hand that struck them.

By 1865 the relative timidity of the initial conventions gave way to sharper criticism of existing practices and the treatment of more controversial topics. Not only the clergy, but even the Superintendent of Education himself, was subjected to attack. That teachers were not yet prepared to be too belligerent was, however, demonstrated by the defeat of a motion that disputes between trustees and teachers be settled by committees consisting of a representative of each plus a third member acceptable to both, rather than by a representative of each and the local superintendent, according to existing practice. Much of the criticism was directed at the deficiencies of the grammar schools and the inadequacies of school inspection. At that time inspectors were commonly clergymen with no special background for understanding education. There was considerable sentiment in favour of better educational opportunities for girls.

Some suggestions for the strengthening of the association emerged in 1866 when a committee recommended that there be a secretary in each county to work for the establishment of a local association and to maintain liaison with the provincial body, that a circular be distributed to promote the association, that the association be incorporated, and that the two-week summer vacation be extended to enable teachers to attend both local and provincial meetings. There was considerable support for the proposal that the vacation include the last two weeks in July and the first two in August.

In the 1870s the conventions of what was then called the Ontario Teachers' Association produced an increasing number of resolutions and recommendations on various topics. These tended to reflect the growing role of committees in conducting preliminary explorations and discussions. The publication of an educational journal was proposed as a means of supplanting dime novels and other such loose and mischievous literature. The establishment of industrial schools was urged to look after vagrant and incorrigible pupils. Recommendations were made for higher qualifications for teachers and supervisors. Amendments to educational legislation were suggested. Pressure was exerted in favour of salary improvements.

In 1871 the Grammar School Association and the Ontario Teachers' Association united under the name of the latter. The beginning of a permanent pattern became evident in the creation of three sections, one for teachers in public schools, one for teachers in high schools, and one for inspectors. General subjects were henceforth considered by the whole group, while more specific ones were dealt with in the sections. The Board of Directors was to settle disputes over the classification of a subject. Each section had a standing committee consisting of four of its own members and one from either of the other sections. Further organizational changes in 1892 led to the formation of six sections: University and College, High School, Public School, Training School, Inspectors, and Kindergarten.

The conditions for membership were liberalized in the 1880s. One of the most important changes was a provision for membership by trustees. A first attempt, apparently blocked by the minister, was made in 1886 to change the date of the annual conference from August to the three days prior to Good Friday, with attendance counting as teaching days. A proposal of similar nature was made in 1888, but it was not until 1892 that the Easter date was accepted.

There was no convention of the association as such in 1891 because the National Teachers' Association of the United States held its meetings in Toronto during that year. Ontario teachers attended, and a number of prominent members of the Ontario Teachers' Association gave addresses. The year was memorable in that the foundations were laid for the Dominion Educational Association, later the CEA.

Guillet reviews a large number of addresses by leading speakers on a great variety of topics. No doubt these addresses varied as much in quality as in range of subject matter. One of the many recurrent themes had to do with the need for raising standards in schools and the procedures that might be employed in the pursuit of this objective. It is easy to see how educators were tempted to advocate more numerous and in some cases more exacting examinations. Yet they demonstrated considerable awareness of the dangers of placing too much reliance on these devices. As might well be imagined, speakers in those days often attempted to raise teachers' morale by assuring them of the great importance of their calling. After the establishment of six sections in 1892, the relative importance of general addresses tended to decline in importance, while the proportion of those of a technical nature increased.

A particularly interesting insight into the major educational issues at the turn of the century is provided in an address given by the Honourable Richard Harcourt immediately after his assumption of the education portfolio in the provincial government. He predicted six major educational changes for Ontario: 1 / an increase in technical education, which would be encouraged by grants-in-aid, 2 / reforms in the county model schools, which were considered to be too numerous and to have too short a term, 3 / permissive legislation enabling municipalities to grant retirement allowances equal to a year's salary to compensate for benefits from the superannuation fund, which was being phased out, 4 / relief from the burden of examinations by such devices as a teacher's report on the pupil's standing, 5 / the addition of at least a year to the minimum age at which a person could begin to teach, and 6 / permissive legislation enabling municipal councils to make grants to colleges and literary, scientific, and historical societies.

Some of the concern for protective measures which later characterized the teachers' federations was demonstrated in 1906. A committee which had been appointed earlier reported in favour of establishing an Ontario Teachers' Union, which would concern itself with mutual improvement and protection. As a means of achieving its objectives, such an organization would need some control over teachers' qualifications. There were recommendations for equitable superannuation, a recognition of teachers in appointments to higher educational offices, and the compilation of a register of all teachers. The report was not adopted, but referred back to the directors for further study. The convention did, however, pass resolutions bearing on teacher status and welfare: that school boards be discouraged from using the "state salary expected" approach, that the government be asked to establish minimum salaries for teachers, that minimum qualifications of teachers be materially increased, that the principal of a school with two to five rooms have at least a Senior Leaving certificate, and that public school grants be substantially increased.[3] Despite the initial hesitation, the Ontario Teachers' Union was soon established, and registered rapid membership gains.

During the first two decades of the nineteenth century perhaps the most persistent concern of the association was superannuation. Committees formulated proposals, meetings were sought with elected and appointed officials, and speeches were made on the subject. Year after year the response was discouraging and frustrating. There were difficulties in arranging meetings with the authorities and vague assurances of sympathy that never led to positive action. Only the more fortunate teachers were under any degree of protection through schemes organized on a local basis. Success in getting a provincial plan established was finally achieved in 1917.

The formation of federations of women public school teachers, men public school teachers, and secondary school teachers at the end of the First World War had important implications for the association. One of the speakers at the convention in 1920 pointed out the advantages of a federation of all Ontario teachers, which he thought should be affiliated with the OEA. The federations, however, continued their separate existence, remaining independent both of one another and of the association. The result was that the latter paid less attention to protective concerns than would otherwise have been the case.

Financial and other difficulties faced by teachers were nevertheless so serious during the depression of the 1930s that many speakers at the annual conventions alluded to them or chose them as major topics. As President of the Ontario Secondary School Teachers' Federation (OSSTF),

A.C. Lewis spoke in 1936 of the deplorable salary levels then prevailing. He declared that there were more than a score of university graduates receiving $900 a year or less. The surplus of teachers at that time was seriously undermining the security of those who were employed, and there were appeals for better tenure arrangements.

The prestige of the OEA appears to have been very high during that period. Among the speakers of current or later prominence were university presidents, cabinet ministers, premiers, Prime Minister R.B. Bennett, and, a few years later, the Governor-General, Lord Tweedsmuir. It was reported, however, that the general calibre of presidents of the association was lower than it had been during the early years of the century. The quality of the addresses was not, moreover, closely related to the importance of the speaker.

For the association itself the period of the 1930s was one of financial crisis. Arrangements had been made in 1928 to appoint a full-time secretary at an annual salary of $3,000. When the incumbent, A.E. Bryson, resigned in 1935, he was re-employed on a part-time basis without responsibility for field work. The office of field secretary was established a short time later, but could not be maintained after 1939 because of the inadequacy of funds. Printed proceedings were dropped for a six-year period until a government grant made it possible to resume them in 1942. The following year C.W. Maedel began a long period of service as treasurer of the association.

A significant development between 1943 and 1945 was the holding of eight one-day regional conferences. Resolutions produced at these meetings, dealing with such matters as changes in school finance, teacher preparation, administrative units, and other aspects of educational activity, were forwarded to the Department of Education. In view of the large number of resolutions submitted by the sections of the association year after year, it seems safe to assume that they suffered from over-abundance.

Guillet provides a summary of the characteristics of educational thought and procedure during the 1950s, presumably as reflected in the addresses and discussions of OEA conventions during that decade.

The sociological aspects of education are given increasing stress, and one finds an emphasis upon the psychoanalytic way of looking at things; the tendency to grant greater responsibility and dignity to pupils, sometimes with a corresponding decline in the status of the teacher; and always a voice here and there asking for return to fundamental disciplines, and to plain English that is readily understood.[4]

Structure

A formal change of some significance occurred when the association was incorporated by letters patent dated January 1, 1966. Much of the existing structure was approved, while advantage was taken of the opportunity to make certain constitutional changes. W.E. Bayes was reconfirmed in the office of executive-secretary, to which he had succeeded after the resignation of G.W. Finlayson.

According to the by-laws in force at the time of writing, the affairs of the association were in the hands of the Senate, which consisted of members elected annually and eligible for re-election. Part of the membership consisted of representatives of the sections. The Senate also chose five additional members, along with a past president, a president, a first vice-president, and a second vice-president. The first three of these had to have service in the offices of president, first vice-president, and second vice-president respectively. The Nominating Committee thus needed to make a real choice only for the last of these offices. There was provision for three regular meetings a year and for special meetings which might be called by the president or on the request of five members.

The Executive Committee, elected by the Senate from among its own members, consisted of the four chief officers plus one member for every twelve sections and corporate members of the association. Those in the second category were to be chosen in such a way as to ensure representation from each area of education represented by the sections and corporate members. The committee performed the type of functions usually assigned to such bodies.

The actual administration of the affairs of the organization was in the hands of a full-time executive secretary. His duties were to keep minutes of meetings of the Senate, of the Executive Committee, and of members of the association, to give required notices of meetings of these bodies, to prepare agenda for meetings and produce records on request, to act as custodian of the corporate seal and of all books and other documents belonging to the association, and to safeguard the financial assets of the association and transact business as required.

There were several categories of membership. Associate members, who were exempt from the payment of membership fees, consisted of students registered at Ontario teacher training institutions. Ordinary members, who paid fees, belonged to one of the sections of the association. Fees were shared between the section and the association. Life members were those who had served as past president or who, in the opinion of the Senate, had made an outstanding contribution to education in Ontario and to the activities of the association or of a section or a corporate member thereof. Honorary members, who were exempt from fees, were designated by the Senate for a maximum period of one year. Corporate members included named associations such as the Ontario Federation of Home and School Associations and others that might be designated by the Senate and paid the prescribed fee. Special members were representatives of the corporate members. All except associate members were entitled to vote at annual or general meetings of the association.

Sections, which might be formed with the approval of the Senate, could adopt their own constitutions with the permission of the same body, and could choose such officers as they considered necessary for the transaction of their business. The secretary of each section was expected to supply a copy of the record of business proceedings to the executive secretary on request. If special services were provided for the members, a section could collect an amount in addition to the annual fee prescribed by the Senate. Certain restrictions existed to ensure reasonable co-ordination of the activities of the sections. They could not, for example, hold meetings that conflicted with those of the association. They also had to announce their meetings in the official program issued at least three weeks before the annual convention of the association. In order to win approval for its initial formation, a potential section had to present a petition signed by no fewer than twenty-five members of the association. It had also to maintain its membership at this level to avoid the threat of dissolution.

The sections which offered programs at the 1970 convention were as follows: the Ontario Business and Commerce Teachers' Association, the Ontario Association for Counselling and Attendance Services, the Teacher Education Section, the Elementary Teachers' Association, the Ontario School Library Association, the Educational Media Section, the Ontario History and Social Science Teachers' Association, the Science Teachers' Association of Ontario, the Ontario Council of Teachers of English, the Home Economics Section, the Ontario Personnel and Guidance Association, the Ontario Geography Teachers' Association, the Ontario Society for Education through Art, the Ontario Association of Teachers of Mathematics, the Ontario Principals' Association, the Ontario Modern Language Teachers' Association, the Ontario Physical and Health Education Association, the Special Education Section, the Ontario Association for Continuing Education, the Ontario Music Educators' Association, the Technical Section, the Occupational Teachers' Association, the Ontario Industrial Arts Association, the Vice-Principals' Section, the Ontario Technical Directors' Association, the Canadian Textbook Publishers' Institute, the Ontario Federation of Home and School Associations, the Ontario Association for Teachers of Retarded Children, the Ontario Municipal and Provincial Education Officers' Association, the Professional Social Workers in Education, and the Teachers of the Young.

In 1968 the Senate approved a proposal to invite firms to become business corporate members, paying a fee of $200 a year. In return, each firm would have the privilege of sending an observer to Senate meetings at its own expense, where he would be permitted to speak on matters under consideration, but not to vote. At least one separate session of each Senate meeting would be devoted to the interests of business members. These members would receive the publication of any section or association that interested them, with the cost borne by the central OEA office. They would be invited to plan a session or group of sessions at the annual convention in co-operation with the OEA Convention Committee. They would be encouraged to hold an annual one-day conference in conjunction with the Senate to focus attention on a particular aspect of their common areas of educational concern. A certain number of places would be reserved for them in any educational tour that the association sponsored.

The sections and corporate members of the OEA have been responsible for an impressive number of publications. In the late 1960s the list included the *Elementary Teachers' Bulletin*, issued twice a year by the Elementary Teachers' Association; the *Home Economics Newsletter*, issued twice a year by the Home Economics Section; the *Ontario Society for Education Through Art Journal*, issued three times a year by the Ontario Society for Education through Art; the *Bookmark*, issued from one to three times a year by the Library Section; the *Commercial Newsletter*, issued twice a year by the Ontario Business and Commercial Teachers' Association; the *Recorder Magazine*, issued four times a year by the Ontario Music Educators' Association; the *Ontario Industrial Arts Bulletin*, issued twice a year by the Ontario Industrial Arts Association; the *Monograph*, issued four times a year by the Ontario Geography Teachers' Association; the *Crucible*, issued three times a year by the Science Teachers' Association of Ontario; the *Occupational Teachers' Association Bulletin*, issued three times a year by the Occupational Teachers' Association; an information sheet issued nine times a year by the Educational Media Section; the *Indian Education Bulletin*, issued four times a year by the Indian Education Section; the *Ontario Principals' Association Newsletter*, issued two or three times a year by the Ontario Principals' Association; *Primary Pathways*, issued once a year by the Primary Section; the *Kindergarten Newsletter*, issued twice a year by the Kindergarten Section; the *Ontario Personnel & Guidance Bulletin*, issued three times a year by the Ontario Personnel and Guidance Association; the *Bulletin*, issued by the Ontario Physical and Health Education Association; the *Ontario Mathematics Gazette*, issued by the Ontario Association of Teachers of Mathematics; the *Headmaster*, issued by the Ontario Secondary School Headmasters' Council; *Classical News and Views*, issued by the Ontario Classical Association; the *Canadian Journal of History*, issued by the Ontario History and Economics Teachers' Association; the *Ontario Modern Language Review*, issued by the Ontario Modern Language Teachers' Association; and newsletters issued by the Ontario Association for Continuing Education and the Ontario Council of Teachers of English. The official OEA publication was the *Ontario Education Review*, of which nine issues were published in 1968–9.

Regional conferences
Toward the end of the 1960s the holding of regional conferences constituted one of the major efforts of the OEA to extend its influence over a wider terrain and to maintain a high level of interest throughout the year. Conferences involving the co-operation of the Elementary Teachers',

Kindergarten, Primary, and Library Sections and the Ontario Principals' Association were held at Barrie, Kitchener, and Oshawa in the fall of 1968. The Friday evening session was devoted to a discussion of the recommendations and implications of the Hall-Dennis report, the Saturday morning meetings were led by people selected by the section representatives, and Saturday afternoon was devoted to a display of audio-visual equipment. A major effort was made to publicize the conferences through prepared programs, through contacts with teachers, administrators, school boards, and Home and School Associations, and through the newspapers and other media. The report to the Senate for 1968–9 suggested that other sessions held in the future should include leaders of the elementary and secondary schools, the universities, and the teacher-training institutions, members of school boards and administrative staff, representatives of the colleges of applied arts and technology, members of the Continuing Education Section, and leaders of the Ontario Federation of Home and School Associations. There was said to be a need for conferences focusing attention on particular subjects such as language and communication, mathematics and science, social studies, and the arts, while others should deal with such topics as the administration of schools and the future of education in Ontario. Plans were made for conferences to be held at Peterborough, Sudbury, and Stratford.

Section meetings throughout the year
In addition to regional conferences involving several sections, a growing number of section meetings were held in addition to the annual convention. In 1967–8, for example, the list of such gatherings included a three-day workshop held in August by the Home Economics Section to enable two hundred teachers to learn about the curriculum for grades 7 and 8 and to study improved methods of teaching; a Centennial Conference for Science Teachers held in November, which attracted over 2,300 delegates from across Canada and the northeastern part of the United States; a one-day conference organized by the Ontario School Counsellors' Association to bring members the latest information about the role of the guidance counsellor in the changing educational scene; a three-day symposium held by the Ontario Music Teachers' Association in Toronto in January; and a two-day session organized by the Ontario History Teachers' Association in London in February. Some of these gatherings were considered particularly valuable in that they gave teachers from kindergarten through grade 13 a chance to mingle and to overcome misunderstandings and misconceptions.

Relations with the OSSTF
In 1965, when the OSSTF established subject councils, there appeared to be a possibility of overlap, duplication of effort, and even of conflict between these councils and the OEA subject sections. An OEA-OSSTF Joint

Committee was established to try to ensure that these eventualities would be avoided. Discussions made it clear that the OSSTF subject councillors were mainly responsible for assisting district branches, schools, and individuals with problems, for planning conferences, and for acting as resource people at seminars. The OEA subject sections concentrated on producing good convention programs and on publishing subject journals. These were activities that the OSSTF was unable to undertake on a comparable scale. The committee agreed on four main types of co-operation. 1 / There would be consultation between the two organizations over dates and other aspects of proposed conferences. 2 / A list of subject councillors would be made available to the OEA each year, with an indication of changes as they occurred. 3 / There was a trend toward the organization of OEA subject divisions to correspond to the thirty-two districts of the OSSTF, thus facilitating close liaison in the planning of development work. 4 / Results of the organization by the OSSTF of all updating courses for secondary school teachers would be reported to OEA Senate members.

Study tours
In 1966 the OEA began to organize study tours of educational institutions outside Canada for teachers, trustees, academic and business administrators, and architects. The tour for 1970 lasted from May 1 to 15, and included visits in the Netherlands, Germany, and England. The OEA contribution consisted chiefly in making the arrangements, and did not involve any great expense.

Appraisal
At the end of his term of office as president in 1969, Walter Pitman offered a candid appraisal of the recent achievements of the organization. In his remarks he went beyond the progress made during a single year to evaluate the entire position and status of the OEA in the educational system of the province. While finding certain causes for satisfaction, he made it clear that there was a great deal of room for improvement.

Pitman felt that the age of the association and the prestige won in a previous era were not sufficient to ensure its survival and growth. It could be "either an element of the energy release or a part of the debris." During 1968–9 several avenues of development had been explored. The OEA had recognized the importance of the report of the Hall-Dennis Committee by organizing major conferences around its themes. Pitman had hoped to see the beginning of a research thrust that would have enabled the association to articulate its position more effectively, but no such initiative had materialized. He had hoped that, through its publications and section regional conferences, it might have become a bridge between the Ontario Institute for Studies in Education and the teachers of Ontario, but here again there had been no success.

A second initiative, which had shown some signs of producing results, had entailed an attempt to involve students in the conference. Some had participated in the St Lawrence Hall program and in other activities. Pitman believed, however, that there must be more continuous and meaningful exchange of views. Students would have to find a place within the structure of the organization, take part in section and intersection workshops and conferences, and contribute to publications. There remained critical steps to be taken.

Pitman thought it was time for the OEA to follow several of the sections and adopt a regional organization. He also considered it necessary to combat the particularism of the sections by emphasizing fall conferences involving several sections such as those of the primary, kindergarten, and elementary teachers, as well as the Educational Mosaic program. A move to strengthen the role of the Senate as a policy-making body offered prospects of bringing the sections together. This body had recently gone beyond organizational details to study the community college program, educational television, and leadership techniques.

To Pitman there was great significance in the fact that the OEA was the only organization that had within its ranks teachers, principals, administrators, parents, trustees, and representatives of the business world. He found the lack of interchange of views among these groups of increasing concern. Certain educational developments, such as the establishment of larger units of administration, were making communication more difficult. Particularly serious was the widening gap between parents and the educational system. Pitman felt that this system, which purported to increase understanding and build bridges between people, was actually widening the gulf. As compared with his parents, the child now thought and reacted differently and argued from different premises. There was a prospect of a society in conflict and a continuing confrontation between young and old. The OEA seemed called upon to increase the activities of parents in the association. Steps were already underway to give trustees a more conscious, useful, and active role.

THE CANADIAN EDUCATION ASSOCIATION

Status

During the period under review the CEA has had a unique role because of the peculiar distribution of governmental responsibility for formal education in Canada. In the absence of any effective co-ordinating agency at the federal level or, until the establishment of the Council of Ministers of Education in the 1960s, of any body devoted to interprovincial co-operation, it bore the main burden of linking the provincial systems. It had to operate with caution in order to avoid any impression of interfering with policy making, which was a provincial function. It concentrated, rather, on providing services designed to facilitate intelligent policy making by provincial authorities.

Finances and membership
Financial support was provided by the provincial departments of education, which made grants in proportion to the population of their respective provinces. A considerable number of the larger urban school systems across the country made contributions on the same basis. At the end of the 1960s these two sources accounted for about 90 per cent of the budget of the association. Some additional funds were supplied by individual memberships, which were open to professional educators and others having an interest in education. Since these memberships entitled the holders to receive the association's two publications, *Canadian Education and Research Digest* and the *CEA News Letter*, the net gain was not very great.

Structure
As of 1969 the affiliates of the CEA included the Canadian Association for Adult Education, the Canadian Home and School and Parent-Teacher Federation, the Canadian School Trustees' Association, l'Association canadienne des éducateurs de langue française, and the Canadian Association of School Superintendents and Inspectors. The Board of Directors consisted of the ten deputy ministers of education serving *ex officio*, others elected from among senior departmental officials, superintendents of large local school systems, representatives of teacher-training institutions, and still others representing affiliated organizations. The Executive Committee consisted of the president, the past-president, the vice-president, and four directors. In 1969 the secretariat consisted of a staff of fourteen under the supervision of F.K. Stewart who, during a long period of service as executive secretary, had come in a sense to personify the organization.

History
The early development of the CEA, or the Dominion Educational Association, as it was at first called, was recorded in an MEd thesis submitted to the University of Toronto by F.K. Stewart in 1956.[5] In it he gave an account of the issues that concerned those who assembled at the first convention in Montreal in 1892. Some of these issues were of importance only at the time, while others continued to challenge the educators of the 1970s. In a series of resolutions relating to the universities, the delegates expressed appreciation of university extension work, but deplored the practice in certain universities of giving instruction in secondary school work. They thought it desirable for the universities to agree to adopt a common standard of matriculation. Resolutions referring to the school system dealt with the overlapping of the work of elementary and high

schools, the importance of thorough inspection of public and high schools, the need for uniform nomenclature among the provinces in designating schools, the prevalence of truancy and irregular school attendance and the need for more exacting laws to counteract these tendencies, and the desirability of establishing kindergartens as part of the school system in all provinces. There was a modern ring to the view that adequate facilities should be provided for teacher training, although the concept of adequacy was no doubt somewhat different in those days. An issue that has not ceased to cause concern had to do with the problems experienced by pupils in transferring from one province to another. It was also felt that an effort should be made to equalize the requirements for teachers' certificates and to provide for their recognition throughout the country.

Stewart judged the inauguration of the new organization impressive, but found little in the records of the second convention, held in Toronto three years later in conjunction with the annual meeting of the OEA, to show that the original enthusiasm was immediately sustained. The misgivings of some observers of the initial events appeared to be well founded when nothing of any consequence was done about the earlier resolutions and no new ones were recorded. There was, however, a revival of interest by the end of the century. In 1898 a recurring theme was introduced when a committee was formed to consider and report on the establishment of a central bureau of education for Canada. The main positive achievement seems to have been a move to have Empire Day observed by suitable exercises in the schools. Attendance at these early conventions was overwhelmingly from the immediately surrounding area, since the cost of travel was too great for more than a handful of people from distant provinces to attend.

At the meeting in 1901 a committee was established to consider the possibility of having a dominion registration of teachers, with implications for interprovincial recognition of teachers' certificates. The proposal to have a federal education bureau along the lines of the U.S. Bureau of Education was presented at the same gathering in stronger terms than previously. The Quebec Superintendent of Education made it perfectly clear on that occasion that the Catholic Committee of the Council of Public Instruction was irrevocably opposed to any such scheme. During much of the history of the CEA Quebec spokesmen tended to be suspicious of the organization, as this and other centralizing moves were discussed, if not actually advocated. In fact, the Catholic system of Quebec was not even represented at conventions between 1901 and 1917.

Some of the other causes that were promoted during the early years of the twentieth century were the provision of education in frontier, railway construction, and lumbering areas, the desirability of improving moral instruction in the schools, the need for more generous financial aid to education, the importance of emphasizing patriotism in the school program, the need for statistics on teachers' salaries, and the importance of industrial and agricultural education. It would be impossible to assess the effect of the resolutions adopted. In some cases they referred to developments that probably would have occurred in any event. In others they were little more than expressions of benevolent sentiments.

An attempt was made in 1909 to improve the effectiveness of the organization. To this end a committee made a series of proposals: 1 / that a permanent, full-time secretary be appointed at a fixed salary; 2 / that a systematic effort be made to enrol in the association every teacher in Canada and every other person with a vital interest in education; 3 / that a convention be held at least every two years; 4 / that a special committee be formed to prepare a convention program for every department of the association; 5 / that each provincial government send at least one special representative to every convention, and pay all his expenses; 6 / that an effort be made to keep members informed about educational matters at home and abroad through the publication of a full report of the proceedings of the conventions of the association and of the addresses delivered there, the publication of an annual report summarizing educational progress in each province, and the publication of an educational monthly or quarterly discussing national problems of education from a national point of view; 7 / that revenues be increased through annual fees from an increased membership and increased annual grants from the provinces; 8 / that a strong and united effort be made to induce the dominion government to establish a bureau of education similar to the Bureau of Education at Washington; 9 / that changes be made in the constitution in harmony with the preceding proposals; and 10 / that a committee be formed to assist in carrying out the proposals.

The proposals led to the establishment of a committee to indicate which clauses should be accepted as the basis for future action. This committee concluded that the crucial step would be to secure and pay for the services of a permanent secretary. A further committee was thereupon appointed, consisting of one member from each province, to consider the financial and other aspects of the matter and to report at the next meeting. The time was not ripe for the proposed development, and no decisive action was taken.

The perennial proposal for a national bureau of education received a great deal of attention once again at the meeting in 1917. Views on the role and functions of this bureau varied considerably. One proponent emphasized the importance of collecting educational statistics. Another thought an effort should be made to combat parochial tendencies in education, and that the flood of foreigners likely to enter Canada after the war should be instructed in Canadian ideals. A third suggested a national clearinghouse that might be administered by the provincial departments of education and the provincial and dominion educational associations. The Superintendent of Education for Quebec was not enticed by any of the proposals, and the representative of Ontario observed that, in view of this disagreement, the matter should not be pressed. One result was that the Dominion Educational Association was forced to rely on its own efforts for the performance of liaison functions.

At the 1917 convention a committee made proposals for a change in the nature of the association. A resolution was passed to make it representative of provincial departments of education, school inspection and supervision and other phases of school administration, associations of trustees, and normal schools and university departments of education. Also, as a less controversial alternative to a national bureau of education, a suggestion was made to federal government authorities that provision be made for the collection of educational statistics.

The meeting held in 1918 saw the adoption of a new constitution and a change in name to the Canadian Education Association. The period immediately following was not, however, characterized by any great increase in influence or effectiveness. The next convention, which was not held until 1922, might have been missed altogether if it had not been scheduled to follow a meeting of ministers of education and officials of provincial departments. In the meantime a National Council of Education had developed from a conference held in Winnipeg in 1919 to consider the relationship of Canadian education to character and citizenship. The organizers hoped to make departments of education more effective by arousing public support for their efforts. The conference was attended by approximately 1,500 delegates from all parts of the country. The National Council which emerged consisted of fifty members, of whom thirty-six were elected by the conference and fourteen by the council. Among those serving were some of the leading figures in the OEA. The new organization made an effort to establish the long desired national bureau under its own direction, with voluntary financial support and assistance from the federal and provincial governments. Although early progress seemed promising, and there appeared to be a good prospect that an interprovincial bureau would be established, the idea was eventually abandoned. After 1926 the organization engaged in a number of ill-defined activities, and no further conferences were held after 1929. The ball was thereupon tossed back to the CEA.

No annual meetings were held between 1929 and 1934, although the constitution specified that they be called at least every second year. Stewart suggests as possible reasons the lassitude of the twenties, the hope that the National Council of Education would establish a central education office, and the onset of the depression.[6] The delegates were unhappy enough about the situation to rebuke the officers for the delay and to instruct them to act in accordance with the constitution in the future.

The convention made a concerted effort to give more point and direction to the affairs of the association by appointing committees with the responsibility of solving certain specific educational problems in which all the provinces had an interest. One resolution proposed the establishment of a committee to investigate the courses of study in the provinces in order to select the best elements in each and transmit the information to the various departments of education. Another committee was to investigate the conditions required for entrance to the normal schools in the various provinces and the length of professional training required in each. A third committee would investigate the practices and procedures of various examination systems. A fourth committee was to examine the standards required for graduation from the high schools of the various provinces and for admission to the universities. These committees took their assignments seriously, and prepared reports for the next meeting.

An interesting development occurred in 1936 when a representative of the Canadian Teacher's Federation suggested that that organization co-operate with the CEA in establishing a bureau of educational research. A motion to this effect was discussed and carried. In an attempt to implement the proposal a committee was set up with wide representation from the different provinces, and a report was prepared for the 1938 conference. The main responsibility for organizing and supporting the projected Canadian Council for Educational Research was left to the CEA directors.

At this conference a representative from Newfoundland expressed the desire of his constituency to be associated with the Canadian provinces in the CEA. The name of the organization was accordingly changed, temporarily as it turned out, to the Canada and Newfoundland Education Association, along with the appropriate modifications in the constitution.

At the conference in 1941 a new effort was made to secure the appointment of a permanent, full-time secretary. Action on the part of the executive was to be contingent on the availability of the necessary funds. According to a resolution of the directors, the secretariat would have four main purposes: 1 / to serve as a medium of expression for the departments of education and the major national educational organizations in matters of common educational concern; 2 / to advise and co-operate with federal government agencies in matters of common educational concern; 3 / to act as a central agency for the dissemination of information among the departments of education and the national educational organizations; and 4 / to promote the cause of education throughout the country. After the convention the directors set up a committee with the authority to establish a permanent secretariat, subject to the approval of the Executive Committee. The time did not, however, prove to be propitious for these plans to come to fruition.

As a result of the efforts of a committee of prominent educators from several provinces, a report was submitted to the convention of 1943 under the title *Report of the Survey Committee Appointed to Ascertain the Chief Educational Needs of the Dominion of Canada*. Perhaps no one would dispute F.K. Stewart's view that possibly no other single activity had a greater effect on the future development of the association than the publication of this report. The extent to which it served as a blueprint for

Canadian education following the end of the Second World War is somewhat more open to question. At least there is doubt about its widespread circulation.

The beginning of an important development occurred in 1943 when R.S. Lambert proposed the establishment of a national advisory committee on school broadcasting. Action taken on this proposal resulted in an important educational contribution extending over many years. The same convention demonstrated a continued interest in a theme which had received attention in the 1930s: the textbooks used in Canadian history. Other matters of interest to the association at this stage were revealed in the president's report for 1944: a report on larger units of school administration; the promotion, through provincial departments of labour and education, of advanced legislation to protect young people against occupational exploitation; the securing of concessions in parcel post rates on visual aids; the securing of concessions to educational publishers for priorities in obtaining materials for production; the establishment of priorities for departments and boards of education for the purchase of radio receiving sets and for the acquisition of equipment used by the armed services after the war; steps taken to ensure that the association would be consulted about a proposed United Nations organization for educational and cultural reconstruction; the establishment of a Canada–United States Committee on Education; and the efforts of a committee to facilitate arrangements for pension credit for teachers for service in more than one province.[7]

In 1945 the money required for the employment of a full-time secretary-treasurer was secured, and an appointment seemed imminent. This development was temporarily interrupted by the withdrawal of support by the Quebec authorities, who feared that the formation of a secretariat would constitute a threat similar to that posed by a federal bureau. The executive decided to proceed with its plans in any case despite the less favourable conditions that appeared to have emerged, while at the same time working for a reversal of the Quebec decision. There was considerable gratification when it succeeded in achieving the latter objective. The first full-time secretary, C.E. Phillips, assumed his new responsibilities on September 1, 1945.

A number of important developments occurred just at the end of the war, even though no convention was held in 1945. A decision was made to publish a journal, *Canadian Education*. Approval was given for the establishment, in conjunction with the Canadian Public Health Association, of the National Committee for School Health Research. A policy was defined whereby money for educational research might be accepted from government bodies or private sources, with certain qualifications. The Canadian Council for Educational Research was disbanded and a Canada and Newfoundland Education Association Research Council formed in its place. In 1946 a new constitution was adopted and the earlier name of the association was restored by dropping the reference to Newfoundland, although the continued participation of the latter was not questioned. A key provision of the constitution was the restriction of voting rights to representative delegates.

The constitution of 1946 was the first one that stated the aims of the association in any detail. There were four items:

To bring about a better understanding on the part of each province and of Newfoundland of the educational ideals of each, to the end that with due regard to constitutional rights the cause of education may be promoted in all.

To collect and make available to educators in Canada and Newfoundland information on educational developments in Canada and elsewhere.

To foster educational research in Canada and Newfoundland and to publish reports of selected research studies.

To collaborate with other educational organizations and to function as a co-ordinating agency.[8]

The CEA demonstrated a continued interest in educational research, with somewhat spotty results. In addition to the program carried out by the National Committee for School Health Research, it sponsored the Canadian Research Committee on Practical Education between 1947 and 1951. Although the establishment of a CEA Research Department was delayed for some years, resources were found to extend information services. A news letter was first issued in 1946 and became a regular publication in 1948. From time to time, reports appeared on topics of particular interest to school boards and departments of education. The Research Council was the vehicle by which grants-in-aid were distributed for individual projects. In 1953 this council co-operated with the Canadian Teachers' Federation and l'Association canadienne des éducateurs de langue française in establishing the National Advisory Committee on Educational Research, which served a useful purpose until the formation of the Canadian Council for Research in Education in 1961. The existence of this body did not prevent the supporting organizations from continuing their independent research and information service programs. Its particular functions were to make an annual survey and review of the research efforts in all fields of public education, to prevent overlapping of research efforts, to identify research areas not touched by any group, and to suggest projects on which joint action might be taken.

During the early 1900s provision was made for meetings of special interest groups within the association, but this arrangement was eventually abandoned. A new movement in this direction began in the late 1940s and early 1950s. Meetings of supervisors and teachers of art led in 1955 to the formation of the Canadian Society for Education through Art.

Directors of visual education met as the CEA–National Film Board (NFB) Advisory Committee. Directors of radio education met as a Canadian Broadcasting Corporation (CBC) advisory committee. Directors of curriculum found the conventions a good place to exchange ideas. Those involved in teacher education also held meetings as part of the convention program. Through the CEA–Kellogg Project in Educational Leadership encouragement was given to the organization of a Canadian Association of School Superintendents and Inspectors.

The directors were not enthusiastic about seeing the association break up into sections in the pattern of the National Education Association and the OEA. According to Stewart, the country was too extended and the number of officials too small to contemplate the formation of many small groups. It was also thought desirable for all members to share points of view with those in other specialties. Another factor militating against the formation of sections was the fact that only a limited number of officials could attend the conventions in any particular year.

Sponsorship in the late 1940s of the research projects already mentioned led the executive to request the executive secretary to explore with foundations in the United States the possibility of obtaining funds for educational research. While a number of research areas were mentioned, the executive apparently had no particular project in mind. The W.K. Kellogg Foundation demonstrated an interest, but rejected the idea of supporting a research project in favour of an action program. Stewart, who had been appointed executive secretary after Phillips had resigned in 1947, was in a position to suggest such a program. He had been engaged in a study of post-war developments in Canadian education which showed that the establishment of larger school areas was one of the most significant of these. Further, J.G. Althouse, Chief Director of Education for Ontario, had proposed that some Ontario school inspectors meet their western counterparts to exchange ideas about problems in the administration of larger school areas. Plans were therefore worked out for a project in school administration and supervision. There was some initial difficulty over whether or not the director would be responsible to the executive secretary. The foundation settled the matter, however, by making it clear that funds would be provided only for a project that constituted an integral part of the CEA program, and not one that operated in relative independence. The support of the foundation was very substantial; an initial commitment of over $230,000 for the five-year period dating from January 1, 1952 was raised to $266,000 before that time had elapsed. Further substantial sums were also granted to the CEA for the expansion of its activities beginning in 1957, and to the University of Alberta for an expanded graduate program in school administration and supervision.

The additional grant made it possible to continue to hold annual interprovincial short courses for school superintendents and inspectors. About eighty of these officials assembled annually for intensive study at the Banff

School of Fine Arts. The program has certainly done a great deal to break down the parochialism and complacency that earlier characterized some of the provincial school systems. It has also produced a kind of fraternal feeling among an important category of Canadian educators.

The research division
The prospect that the CEA might be able to establish a research division with a full-time director seemed rather remote until Imperial Oil Limited came forward in 1957 with a large grant for the purpose. The division that took shape as a result had the following aims:

(a) to collect and disseminate information on research now being carried on (there is considerable – locally, provincially, and at universities);
(b) to publish, through printing of summaries or articles of greater length where warranted, research findings useful to educators generally, and to provincial departments of education and local school authorities in particular;
(c) to publicize, through personal visits by a CEA research staff member and through the printing of brief semipopular leaflets and pamphlets, interesting developments and practices evident in educational experiments under local school authorities;
(d) to serve as a liaison agency in educational research for local, provincial and university research workers; for instance, as a liaison agency on the studies now being carried on at the Ontario College of Education and the University of Alberta in the identification of outstanding secondary school pupils, so that the findings of each might be better known to the other, and the findings of both made better known to educationists and school trustees generally. Such a service could be performed for other research activities as well, in order that the widest and best utilization may be made of significant discoveries in Canadian education;
(e) to serve as a library and reference centre to which local and provincial authorities could turn for prompt and reliable sources of information on research data (agencies, books, research magazines) in various countries;
(f) generally to act as a clearing house for information on educational research, and as a stimulating and co-ordinating agency in research.[9]

Activities associated with the Short Course
Certain activities related to the Short Course in Educational Leadership were supported by funds from the W.K. Kellogg Foundation. In 1957–8, for example, $400 was granted for courses for school principals in each of Alberta and British Columbia, $1,000 for a principals' workshop in Newfoundland, $1,000 for a special inspectors' conference in Nova Scotia, and $200 for a conference on supervisory practices for a group of exchange teachers held by the League of the British Commonwealth in Toronto.

Specialized conferences

In 1961 locally employed directors and superintendents of education in cities having a population of more than 100,000 began to meet annually under CEA auspices. The association made the general arrangements while the participants defrayed their own expenses. As an example of the program offered at these meetings, participants in the sessions at Vancouver in 1965 discussed the utilization of staff, the selection and training of principals for elementary schools, and Canada's responsibility to developing countries. Arrangements were made for visits to schools in the area and all delegates were taken on a tour of the Simon Fraser University campus. The 1969 meeting, held in Saskatoon, dealt with such matters as the drug abuse problem, austerity in education, and the role of the school board.

A two-day seminar on the drug problem in Canadian schools was held in June 1970. Most of the participants were representatives of local education authorities, supplemented by a number of provincial officials. During the two days before the annual convention of the same year there was a meeting of senior school board officials and administrative officers to discuss means of communicating with the public. It seemed likely that this aspect of the work of the CEA would tend to increase.

Research and information

The president announced at the annual convention in 1957 that Imperial Oil Limited would donate $100,000 over a period of five or six years to enable the CEA to establish a research office. One of the actions taken by the executive in response to this action was to recommend a revision of the constitution of the Research Council to provide for its enlargement from four to six members, one of whom would be from British Columbia to allow more complete geographical representation, and one an urban superintendent, because much of the work would be done with urban school systems. As now constituted the council was to receive applications for grants-in-aid, to recommend to the CEA directors payment of grants-in-aid, to supervise the research, and to pass upon final reports. With respect to the Research and Information Service and the Research Department, when established, the council was to advise the directors on the services to be given, on the skilled researchers to be employed, and on the operation of the service in general. Where the association proposed to sponsor research projects jointly with other bodies, it was to advise the directors of the desirability and practicality of any suggested project, to help in the planning of any approved project, and to advise on the research procedures to be employed in carrying out the project. It was to receive progress reports and final reports on research projects undertaken or sponsored by the association, to evaluate these reports, and to submit the evaluations to the committees in charge of the projects.

In May 1958 C.P. Collins, who had had a number of years' service as a school superintendent in Saskatchewan and had just completed his Ph D work at the University of Alberta, was employed as research officer. Among the first activities of the small supporting staff was the classification of certain books and reports relevant to research acquired during previous years. A comprehensive series of visits and interviews by the research officer revealed a widespread recognition of the need for a clearinghouse on educational research in Canada. Canadian educators were reported to be interested in what was going on and where, in what problems were being investigated and by whom, in what educational problems were most common in Canada, in what had been published in books and periodicals that was pertinent to education in Canada, and in ways in which research findings could be made available to administrators so that they would be of practical value. Clearinghouse functions received strong emphasis during the next few years. In order to further the dissemination of information, the publication of the *Canadian Research Digest* was begun in 1959. A decision was soon made to integrate this publication with *Canadian Education* to produce *Canadian Education and Research Digest*.

An eagerness to get involved in actual research led the executive and the Research Council to consider a rather lengthy list of possible projects. A decision was eventually reached to engage in one on teaching load and related factors. Questionnaires were thereupon sent to the ten provincial departments of education and to sixty urban administrators requesting information on regulations in force which determined teacher load and on studies on the matter being currently conducted. A pilot study was undertaken, involving about 150 teachers, to pre-test a questionnaire, which was expected to be perfected and distributed to a sample of some 1,200 teachers in all Canadian provinces early in 1962. In March of that year the executive decided that the project was too expensive to carry out as planned, and it was accordingly dropped. Meanwhile, other activities had been undertaken. For example, questionnaires were circulated in cities of over 100,000 to people in central office positions, who were asked to identify the job specifications for resident administrative and supervisory staff such as principals and consultants, and people with a reputation for a high degree of competence who held such positions within a system. Reports were then issued on the consultant, the supervisor, the principal, and the vice-principal in schools at different levels. Data were also compiled and reports issued on such topics as prohibitive limitations on school bus transportation as imposed by the various departments of education; grouping to provide for individual differences; requirements for teaching certificates in Canada in 1962; vocational guidance services in Canadian schools; and the status of school librarians.

An Invitational Conference on Educational Research was held in conjunction with the annual convention at Saskatoon in 1959. It was judged so successful that a committee of representatives of the CEA and the National Advisory Committee on Educational Research (NACER) was formed to plan a second conference in 1961. By the time it was held the Canadian Council for Research in Education had been established, and assumed the role assigned to NACER. The CEA took the responsibility for printing and distributing the proceedings.

The Research Office was very active in preparing and issuing reports, most of them rather brief, on various topics of interest. Matters dealt with in these reports in the single year between September 1961 and September 1962 concerned salary schedules for administrative and teaching staff in selected Canadian systems; the organization and management of school cafeterias in secondary schools in selected urban centres; terms used in school administration (a glossary); policies and practices followed in textbook rental services to secondary school students; the cost to parents of school textbooks; safety measures for rural children boarding or leaving school buses; changes in school laws and regulations; summaries of graduate theses in education and abstracts of staff studies; education studies in progress in Canadian universities; community use of school facilities; school attendance regulations; educational, social, and cultural activities conducted for adults by urban school boards; problems related to the employment of teachers; and authorization of school textbooks. The topics indicate that most of this material was of a highly utilitarian nature, rather than representing an attempt to contribute to educational theory.

Collins left his position as research officer in March 1962 to become Director of Teacher Training in Saskatchewan. His departure, along with the exhaustion of the Imperial Oil grant, signalled a decline in the relative importance of the research program. For a few months C.E. Phillips, who retired from his position of Director of Graduate Studies at the Ontario College of Education in June 1962, gave part-time assistance in directing and co-ordinating the activities of the Research and Information Division. For a somewhat longer interim period C.B. Routley, retired Superintendent of Professional Development in the Department of Education, carried on as research officer. A regular appointment was made in 1964, when H.A. Peacock assumed the office for what was to be a four-year period. Routley acted as executive secretary of the CEA in 1963–5 while F.K. Stewart was on leave in England, where he served as Secretary of the Commonwealth Education Liaison Committee and Director of the Commonwealth Education Liaison Unit.

Referring to the collection and dissemination of information on current educational policies in Canada as the main function of the CEA Research and Information Division, the annual report of the executive secretary for 1964–5 pointed out that the improvement of the service depended both on an increased flow of information to the CEA office and on an up-to-date method of storing it. Some progress toward this end had resulted from the adoption of a simple information storage and retrieval system involving the use of needlesort cards. The reference library was expanding each year, particularly in the vertical file, which contained clippings on a wide variety of educational topics. Department of Education, university, and school board officials were finding it an increasingly useful reference source. During the year the Research and Information Division conducted eight surveys and issued twelve major reports, as well as responding to requests from various agencies.

After the resignation of H.A. Peacock as research officer in 1968, the Research and Information Division was renamed the Information Division to indicate that more emphasis would henceforth be placed on surveys and on the dissemination of educational information. The information officer was made responsible for the supervision of *Canadian Education and Research Digest* and the *CEA News Letter*. It was decided that the publication of *Education Studies in Progress in Canadian Universities* would be discontinued, and that only *Education Studies Completed in Canadian Universities* would be published in the future.

Changes in emphasis were further signalled in 1969 when *Canadian Education and Research Digest* was renamed *Education Canada*. It was to attempt henceforth to be an authoritative forum on current issues and problems in education, with some movement away from its earlier research orientation. The *CEA News Letter* was also given a format and style designed to improve its effectiveness in giving a quick overview of current educational activities and developments. The publication *Education Studies Completed in Canadian Universities* became the *Directory of Education Research in Canada*, which undertook to cover a wider range of studies than its predecessor, including projects covered by national, provincial, and local bodies.

Teacher exchange

The CEA continued to handle the teacher exchange program, which attracted a considerable number of teachers annually throughout the postwar period. Imperial Oil Limited made several grants of $5,000 a year during the late 1950s and early 1960s. Most Canadian exchanges were with the United Kingdom, although smaller numbers were arranged with Australia, New Zealand, and the United States, and among different provinces. A recurrent problem was the difficulty in matching applicants from different countries. The report of the executive secretary in 1960 indicated that an increasing number of school boards seemed to be willing to make adjustments within their systems to permit teachers to participate in the scheme with slightly changed subjects or grades.

During the early 1960s the program covered provision for visits by members of staffs of teacher training colleges to comparable institutions in other parts of Canada. Members of university faculties also received assistance for travel at home and abroad. Some faculty or departmental staff members were given grants to attend the CEA Short Course at Banff. In 1962–3 provision was made for a special travel grant of $1,000 to enable a faculty of education staff member to conduct a study of some subject in which he had an interest.

In 1962 Imperial Oil began providing an extra $500 to help meet the administrative expenses of the program. As the number of teachers and of staff at teacher training colleges and faculties of education increased, the number of applications for exchange grew correspondingly. As a result of a request from the CEA the company raised its contribution in 1966–7 to $7,500, plus $500 for administrative costs.

A program of exchange between English-speaking and French-speaking teachers in Canada was undertaken on the initiative of the CEA and l'Association canadienne des éducateurs de langue française as a Ministers' Project for Centennial Year in 1967–8. During that year twenty-one teachers were chosen from each language group, and the results were regarded as encouraging. The Council of Ministers accordingly agreed to continue the project, and contributed a yearly grant of $45,000. Interest subsequently declined, however, and only thirteen pairs of teachers were matched out of a total of thirty-three applicants. One reason for this development was thought to be the growing number of exchange programs of other types. In any case, the Council of Ministers decided to terminate the plan after 1970–1.

Involvement in international matters
From the time of the formation of the Canadian National Commission for UNESCO in 1958, the CEA had three members on the executive. Arrangements were also made to have the CEA executive secretary attend commission meetings to promote continuity of representation and to act as a convenient channel of communication between the commission and the departments of education. The commission shortly undertook what was known as the Major Project in Mutual Appreciation of Eastern and Western Cultural Values. The CEA hoped for the support of the Canadian government to enable it to participate in certain affairs of the International Bureau of Education (IBE). When this support was not granted, the Canadian National Commission for UNESCO made contributions to assist two CEA representatives to play some part in conferences sponsored by that body.

The CEA continued to send representatives to the UNESCO-IBE conferences in accordance with this arrangement until 1965–6. At that time fresh representations were made to the Honourable Paul Martin, Secretary of State for External Affairs, asking that Canada join the IBE. This request was acted upon, and the representatives of the CEA were included in the Canadian delegation, thus attaining official status for the first time. Information about Canadian education was supplied to the conference in the form of books, statistical information, and a collection of photographs of Canadian schools.

Commonwealth Conferences on Education were held successively at Oxford in 1959, New Delhi in 1962, and Ottawa in 1964. The delegates, who were representatives of governments, considered existing methods of co-operation and ways of expanding and improving them. The third of these conferences meant a great deal of extra work for the CEA. Requests for information received by the Department of External Affairs from citizens of foreign countries were usually referred to the association. The report of the acting executive secretary for the year mentioned some of the more unreasonable and absurd of the inquiries. At the fourth conference, held in Lagos, Nigeria, in 1967, the Canadian government was responsible for leading papers on four topics: 1 / basic vocational education, 2 / standards in technical and vocational education, 3 / technical and vocational teacher education, and 4 / training administrators of technical and vocational programs in Canada.

Reference was made in the annual report of the executive secretary for 1965–6 to the increasing number of international conferences in education. There also appeared to be a greater willingness on the part of the Canadian government to send delegations to such conferences. During the year the CEA sent representatives, not only to the IBE Conference in Geneva, but also to the World Congress of Ministers of Education on the Eradication of Illiteracy, held in Teheran; the Organisation for Economic Co-operation and Development (OECD) Meeting on Educational Investment and Planning, held at The Hague; the OECD Meeting of the National Directors and Representatives of the Educational Investment and Planning Program, held in Vienna; the Special UNESCO Intergovernmental Conference to Examine a Draft Recommendation to Member States on the Status of Teachers, held in Paris; the Commonwealth Conference on the Education and Training of Technicians, held at Huddersfield, England; and the General Conference of UNESCO, held in Paris. In some cases these representatives were nominated by the CEA to serve on a Canadian government delegation.

Scholarships and fellowships

The CEA was involved in a variety of ways in awards for study. The Imperial Relations Trust Fund Fellowship was granted for study at the London Institute of Education until after 1961–2. The CEA persuaded various industrial donors to provide the funds for fellowships for study in the program in school administration at the University of Alberta. Assistance was offered by a number of Canadian textbook publishers, by Imperial Oil Limited, and by the International Nickel Company of Canada. The CEA also assumed the responsibility for publicizing the Queen Elizabeth Scholarship and for selecting a winner. This award enabled the recipient to study kindergarten and nursery school work at the Eliot-Pearson School of Tufts University. For many years small sums were made available for studies, mostly conducted by graduate students in colleges or faculties of education. In the mid-sixties $1,500 was distributed among four or five students each year for this purpose.

Awards were introduced in 1964–5 to enable senior educators from various parts of the Commonwealth to visit Canada to discuss educational matters and to exchange information relating to their own particular interests. The visits were intended to be of benefit to the fellowship holder and his country as well as to Canada. The CEA executive was given the right to nominate two members to serve on the Canadian Commonwealth Scholarship and Fellowship Committee. The fellowship holders in 1965–6 included one from Australia, one from England, one from Scotland, and one from India. The following year awards were made to H.S. Wyndham, Director of Education in New South Wales, Sir Alec Clegg, Chief Education Officer for the County Council of the West Riding of Yorkshire, and K.J. Revell, Chief Education Officer for the London Borough of Croydon. There were some subsequent complications over procedures for handling nominations for the fellowships.

Involvement with other agencies
Many of the contributions of the CEA have been made through representation on and co-operation with other agencies. These have included the Canadian Council for Research in Education in its original form as established in 1961 and after its reconstitution in 1966, the Canadian Conferences on Education, the Canadian Conference on Children, the National Employment Committee, the Canadian Education Week Committee, the National Technical and Vocational Training Advisory Council, the National Advisory Council on School Broadcasting, the CEA–NFB Advisory Committee, and the National Junior Red Cross Advisory Committee. In 1965 the CEA was invited by the l'Association canadienne des éducateurs de langue française to name a representative on its Board of Directors. This invitation, which was eagerly accepted, meant that representation between the boards of directors of the two organizations was reciprocal.

Further moves toward co-operation between l'Association canadienne des éducateurs de langue française and the CEA were made in 1969, when the two executives met to discuss the roles of their respective associations. An *ad hoc* committee, consisting of four members of each organization, including the executive secretaries, was established to study possible areas of co-operation. Among the suggestions made were that a joint convention might be held as soon as it could be arranged, possibly in 1971; that a joint newsletter be published or some other means of joint communication be adopted; and that joint seminars be held to deal with specific topics. Study of these and other matters indicated that there was a substantial difference in the aims and objectives of the two organizations. A positive recommendation was made with respect to the proposed joint convention, and no difficulty was seen in arranging for joint meetings on special topics. The idea of producing a joint publication, however, did not appear to be practical.

Miscellaneous projects
In 1965 a grant of $25,000 from the Ford Foundation enabled forty-nine Canadian educators to visit school systems in the United States where special projects were being conducted for the culturally deprived child. Each participant prepared a report summarizing his observations and impressions of the schools he visited. The reports of the English-speaking observers were edited by E.J. Quick and published under the title *New Opportunities for the Culturally Deprived*, while those of the French-speaking observers were published as *Nouveaux horizons pour les enfants désherités*.

The year 1965, the twentieth anniversary of the United Nations, was designated International Co-operation Year. In response to a request for the appointment of a representative, the CEA named the executive secretary to serve on the National Executive Council of International Co-operation Year. One specific outcome was the stimulus given to the pairing of Canadian secondary schools with those in other parts of the world. In accordance with proposals made at the Third Commonwealth Conference, emphasis was placed on pairing within the Commonwealth, and contacts were made through the Commonwealth Education Liaison Unit in London.

Constitutional revision
During 1959–60 the constitution of the CEA underwent substantial modification. The qualifications for membership were presented in considerable detail in Article III. Individual membership applied to 1 / any professional educator employed in an educational institution or school system controlled or recognized by any provincial department of education, 2 / anyone interested in education who was a member of a group or association entitled to be represented by a delegation, 3 / any other person engaged in education or in work connected with education in Canada, subject to the approval of the directors, and 4 / all life members and honorary presidents of the CEA. Representative delegates were designated as follows: 1 / a maximum of seven from each of the departments of education in the ten provinces; 2 / a maximum of four chief executive officers or superintendents employed by school boards in each province; 3 / a maximum of four representatives of teacher-training institutions in each province; 4 / one representative of each of the following institutions engaged in educational research: the Department of Educational Research of the Ontario College of Education, the Education Branch of the Dominion Bureau of Statistics, l'Institut pédagogique St-Georges, and any

other research institution approved by the Board of Directors; 5 / a maximum of four representatives of the supervisory or inspectoral staffs of each province; 6 / two representatives of the Canadian Teachers' Federation and two representatives of each provincial federation of teachers; 7 / one representative of the Canadian School Trustees' Association and one representative of each provincial association of school trustees; 8 / one representative of the Canadian Home and School and Parent-Teacher Federation and one representative of each provincial Federation of Home and School; 9 / one representative of the Canadian Association for Adult Education and one representative of each of such provincial associations for adult education as might be approved by the Board of Directors, up to a maximum of two representatives from each province; 10 / one representative of each university in Canada; 11 / one representative of each additional national or provincial educational association or agency whose application for representation was approved by the Board of Directors; and 12 / all life members and honorary presidents.

In 1969 organizational representation on the Board of Directors was dropped and the number of directors was reduced from thirty-three to thirty. Ten of the positions were reserved for the senior permanent official of each provincial department of education, or his deputy, and twenty were to be filled by majority vote of the members. Further changes in 1970 involved a minor alteration of the statement on aims, a revision of voting procedures, and a provision for the replacement of a vice-president who proved unable to complete his term.

*Establishment of Council of Ministers of Education
and aftermath*
Of great significance to the CEA was the establishment of the Standing Committee of Ministers of Education in 1960. Initiative for this development has been attributed to J.P. Robarts, then Minister of Education for Ontario. Robarts is said to have shown great diplomatic skill in producing co-operative action without drawing too much attention to difficult constitutional issues. The story of what developed into the Council of Ministers in 1967 has been recounted in volume II, chapter 14. In a sense the potential importance of the CEA as a national co-ordinating body could not help but be substantially diminished with the establishment of this council as a separate body.

During a period of uncertainty in 1967–8 the executive of the CEA met the Chairman of the Council, W.G. Davis, to discuss the probable future role and function of the association. Davis expressed the view that the council would be mainly concerned with certain areas of interprovincial co-operation and with relationships between the provinces and the federal government in the fields of manpower, post-secondary education, audio-visual media, and related problems. It might take several years for the role of the council to emerge. He thought that, in the meantime, the CEA should proceed with its current and contemplated projects. The executive then asked the secretary to prepare a working paper that would serve as a basis for a review of the future role of the CEA.

In 1968 the directors asked the executive to appoint a committee to examine the role, structure, and financial support of the CEA over the succeeding decade. After deliberating the issue, the members of the executive decided to constitute themselves as such a committee, and to obtain the aid of consultants, who would travel widely, interview those whose opinion might be helpful, and prepare a report. The results of the inquiry of this "task force" were considered in 1969. All the consultants had found that the CEA was held in very high regard across the country. The opinion had frequently been expressed that, if the organization were to be disbanded, another would soon have to be formed to take its place. One of the recommendations of the task force was that the CEA continue to undertake special projects or studies under *ad hoc* committees or commissions, with financial support from foundations or corporations. The executive secretary noted in this connection that there had been a recent trend toward provincial self-examination and appraisal, and that the conduct of projects on a national scale would involve struggling against a rather strong tide. He expressed the view, however, that there was still a great need for more and better information about activities, developments, and trends in Canadian education.

A change in financing policy adopted by the Quebec government in 1969–70 had ominous implications for the future of the CEA. Grants would be paid to the CEA and l'Association canadienne des éducateurs de langue française on the basis of the proportions of English-speaking and French-speaking populations in that province. The reduction in the contribution to the CEA was to be spread over a four-year period. The implication that the association represented only the English-speaking educators of Quebec was recognized by a postponement of plans to expand services in the French language. There was some apprehension about the consequences of a breach in the practice of contributing in proportion to population, which all the provinces had followed since 1945.

L'ASSOCIATION CANADIENNE DES ÉDUCATEURS
DE LANGUE FRANÇAISE

L'Association canadienne des éducateurs de langue française (ACELF) was formed in Ottawa in 1947 on the initiative of the Conseil de vie française en Amérique. It consisted of a group of French-speaking educators devoted to the cause of French culture and education in all parts of Canada. As stated in 1968, its purposes were as follows: 1 / to serve the cause of French-language education and culture; 2 / to arouse interest and stimulate action in favour of French-language education and culture; 3 / to co-operate with all agencies, institutions, groups, or departments pursuing similar objectives; 4 / to engage in activities relating to its aims, particularly to place an information service concerning French-language education and culture at the disposal of educational associations and institutions, to encourage the distribution of any publication that might contribute to the cause of French-language education and culture, and to facilitate the exchange of ideas and experiences designed to promote French-language education and culture; 5 / to maintain relations with Canadian, international, and other associations and to co-operate with them in matters relating to French-language education and culture.

According to the structural arrangements existing in the late 1960s, there were three classes of members: accredited, associate, and individual members. Accredited members consisted of 1 / the department of education in each province; 2 / any Canadian university where instruction was given in French; 3 / any local, regional, or provincial board or association administering a French-language school system; 4 / any corporate body or association in a province with an English-speaking majority which had as its main purpose the improvement and spread of the "French fact"; 5 / any local, regional, or provincial association of French-speaking professional educators; 6 / any national organization consisting of associations in categories 3, 4, and 5; and 7 / any other organization, institution, or association recognized by the Board of Directors. Associate membership was open to any organization with a majority of French-speaking members, but for which teaching or the pursuit of an educational objective was subordinate to its main purpose. Individual membership was open to any professional educator or anyone interested in education. Members had the right to be elected to the various positions within the association, to attend all meetings of the association, both general and special, to participate in discussions, to receive the bulletin and other communications of the association, and to request of the secretariat any information that was within its competence to provide. Only delegates of accredited members or their alternates and directors of the association had the right to vote at annual general assemblies or at special meetings.

THE ONTARIO ASSOCIATION FOR CURRICULUM DEVELOPMENT

The Ontario Association for Curriculum Development originated in a motion passed by Ontario delegates to a meeting of the Association for Supervision and Curriculum Development of the National Education Association in Detroit in February 1951 to the effect that the Ontario Teachers' Federation call a meeting of various groups to consider establishing a similar conference in Ontario. The result was the formation of a committee to organize a conference for the fall of the same year. In addition to the Ontario Teachers' Federation, the sponsoring groups were the Ontario Federation of Home and School Associations, the Ontario School Trustees' Council, the Ontario Department of Education, the Urban School Inspectors' Association, the Civil Service School Inspectors' Association, the School Business Administrators' Association, the Parent-Teacher Associations, the teacher training institutions, the Canadian Education Association, the universities of Ontario, and the Committee on Practical Education of the CEA.

The purpose of the association was to provide a forum for the discussion of curricular issues on which all points of view might be heard. At the three-day annual conferences people representing a wide variety of positions and interests in education engaged in such discussion. The term "curriculum" was defined so broadly that there was room for a great range of topics. It became established policy at the beginning for participants to decide before the conference which group they wished to join, and to remain with it except when conference speakers were addressing the entire gathering or general meetings were being held. With the assistance of a chairman, a "resource person," and a recorder, the discussions were adapted to suit the interests of the group. Although reports of the discussions were circulated after the conference, the process was the matter of primary concern rather than the conclusions reached. Resolutions were not expected, although an exception was made in 1957 for the one which led eventually to the founding of the Ontario Educational Research Council.

Each sponsor sent a certain number of delegates who, along with those invited to attend in order to make a specific contribution, and others with an interest in the proceedings, usually ensured a stimulating exchange of opinions. Contrary to intentions, however, it sometimes happened that a large proportion of the participants in a discussion group registered in order to learn about the topic rather than to make a contribution, and, as a result, the proceedings turned into an informal lecture by the chairman or the resource person, or on occasion a question and answer session, with most of the group asking the questions and these two individuals supplying the answers.

Although the Ontario Association for Curriculum Development flourished through the 1960s, it made its maximum impact during the 1950s when the number of conferences and meetings competing for the attention of the participants was much smaller. A brief outline of the program for 1955 will give some idea of the ground typically covered. At the first general session N.V. Scarfe gave an address entitled "Finding a Personal Philosophy of Education." There were nine discussion groups dealing with the following topics: Supply and Training of Teachers (Elementary); Supply and Training of Teachers (Secondary); Standards in Ontario Education (two groups); Finding a Personal Philosophy of Education; Supervision of Education (two groups); Preparation for University; the Relationship of the Home and the School; the Teacher and the Board; the Teaching of English (Primary and Junior Divisions); and the Teaching of English (Intermediate Division). These topics indicate how far the conference departed from any narrow view of curriculum.

The conference for 1956 repeated some of the same themes and introduced new ones. Discussion groups dealt with topics listed as follows: Clarifying the Roles of the Supervisors, Inspectors, and Principals; the Superintendents, Inspectors, and Principals at Work in Urban Centres; Improving the Teaching of English (Grades VII to XIII); Improving the Teaching of Mathematics; Improving the Teaching of Science (Grades VII to XIII); Mental Health and Its Place in Education; How to Treat the Gifted Children; How to Treat the Gifted Child; Classroom Management to Cope with Mental and Physical Changes in Children; the "How" Group; Research in Ontario Education; the Place of the Humanities; and the Contentious Issues in Education. There were two general addresses, one by C.E. Phillips on Curriculum Development in Ontario and the other by J.A. Gibson on the Imagery of Education.

In 1961 the usual session was merged in the larger Ontario Conference on Education, held at Windsor, to which reference is made in several volumes of ONTARIO'S EDUCATIVE SOCIETY. The theme of the 1962 conference was Learning to Learn, with twenty discussion groups dealing with the teaching of various subjects such as mathematics, science, history, geography, English, second languages, and technical and commercial subjects, as well as broader topics such as Society and the School, Independent Learning and Intellectual Growth, Research in Education, Developing a Personal Philosophy of Education, and Evaluation and Standards. A keynote address was given by Jerome Bruner.

The discussions in 1966 centred on the theme of decentralization of authority from the Department of Education to the local school areas. The topics for discussion were largely defined in terms of questions. Some examples were Who Decides Aims and Objectives in Education? Who Determines Curriculum Change and for What Reasons? How Are Changes in Curricula to be Evaluated? Do Media Determine the Curriculum or Does the Curriculum Determine the Media? How Do We Relate Children's Needs to Curriculum Design? What is the Effect of Local Environment on Curriculum? and How May Local and Provincial Agencies Co-operate in Curriculum Development? These examples provide clear evidence of the trend toward more general discussions.

The conference in 1969 demonstrated the same interest in broad topics, examples of which were About Human Relationships, About Being Human, About Values, What Do We Do About Individuality in Children? What Do We Mean By "Continuous Progress"? and How May Teacher-Candidates be Taught About Children? There were also some topics inviting quite specific discussion, such as the Consultant, Among Principal and Staff, and Among the Staff. The opening speaker, D. Bakan, Professor of Psychology, dealt with education and the future of human relations.

Reports of the discussions indicate a high degree of awareness of the issues and problems of education. The degree of imagination demonstrated in selecting topics and the success of the association in securing outstanding and provocative speakers give promise of a major role for the association in the future. Perhaps its chief influence has been and will be in the area of attitude shaping.

THE ONTARIO ENGLISH CATHOLIC
EDUCATION ASSOCIATION

The Ontario English Catholic Education Association (OECEA) was established in 1943 through the initiative of the Roman Catholic bishops of Ontario. It represented an effort to unite individuals, school boards, teachers, Catholic societies, and parishes in the cause of improving Catholic education. Through a constitutional change in 1965 greater emphasis was placed on lay responsibility and initiative. Teachers, trustees, and parents were given representation through their chartered organizations, while the bishops maintained an appointee on the governing council.

According to the constitution, the association pursued the following objectives:

(a) To promote and strengthen the principles of Christian education among Catholics in the Province of Ontario.
(b) To foster, unite and co-ordinate all efforts to provide Catholic education in Ontario.
(c) To provide a medium which will effectively express and encourage Catholic thought and action on questions affecting education.
(d) To develop a standard of excellence in education, particularly among Catholic youth, by stimulating among member bodies and other responsible educational groups the exchange of beneficial ideas and factual information.
(e) To provide an annual forum where the objectives of the Association may be discussed.

The association was extremely active in campaigning for better financial provisions for the separate schools and for the extension of the Roman Catholic separate school system beyond the grade 10 level. In 1946 a comprehensive statement was submitted to the Royal Commission on Education by the Ontario Catholic Education Council, which had representatives from the OECEA, as well as from a number of other organizations. Evidence was presented to show the financial difficulties under which the separate schools functioned, and efforts were made to counter some of the arguments used by the opponents of separate schools.

Among the many statements and documents prepared over the years with respect to these issues was a *Brief Presented to the Prime Minister of Ontario and to the Members of the Legislative Assembly by the Catholic Bishops of Ontario* in October 1962. Reference is made to this submission in volume II, chapter 6. In it the bishops expounded the view that the separate schools were a true part of the public school system. They explained why they regarded it as essential that a Roman Catholic child be educated in an atmosphere that was consistent with his religious beliefs. They appealed for greater freedom of action in formulating the curriculum used in the separate schools. While they disclaimed any intention of asking for a separate curriculum or separate textbooks in all subjects, they requested "serious consideration of the needs of the Catholic schools in the framing of the curriculum in a number of subjects." They expressed the view that, although Catholic teachers graduated from teachers' colleges adequately trained to handle the methodology and administration of the classroom, they were not satisfactorily prepared to take up positions in Catholic schools. They suggested as the best solution the establishment of a number of Catholic teachers' colleges, although they did not take an adamant position on the issue.

The bishops' brief was not, to say the least, welcomed by the government of Ontario. Continuation of long-standing policy demanded that a negative position be taken with respect to most of the requests. On the other hand, as noted in volume II, effective steps were instituted to reduce the discrepancy between the financial resources available to the two elementary school systems.

The position of the OECEA remained constant during the 1960s. It was expressed emphatically by the executive president, E.J. Brisbois, at the Twenty-fifth Annual Catholic Education Conference in Toronto on March 22, 1969.

Notwithstanding what one may hear to the contrary from editorial writers who have their personal point of view, from well-meaning and sincere critics, and from individual Catholics who tend to be self-appointed spokesmen, the vast majority of the Catholic community intends to maintain and to improve the Catholic Public Schools, and to work for extension and completion of the Separate School System through the remaining secondary grades.

Such is the declared policy of this Association.

Many found it difficult to understand the extreme fervour with which Roman Catholics, working through the OECEA and affiliated organizations as well as individually, waged their campaign for the extension of a system that seemed to have served them reasonably well, despite their continual expressions of dissatisfaction, for many years. In fact, however, there was a growing feeling that despite the greatly improved financial position of the separate schools resulting from the operation of recently devised school grant plans, the separate school system was in serious and increasing danger from another quarter. Partly because of the impetus given by the Hall-Dennis Committee, there promised to be a rapid move toward the integration of elementary and secondary education, in terms both of organization and of curriculum. Apprehensive Roman Catholics feared that parents might be tempted to avoid the hiatus between elementary education in the separate school and secondary education in the publicly supported secondary school by starting their children in the public elementary school in the first place. Thus it seemed increasingly imperative to provide a continuous program of Catholic education to the end of high school. The urgency of the issue was reinforced by the fact that rapidly rising education costs threatened to close the Roman Catholic private secondary schools, which were at best able to accommodate only a small proportion of the graduates of separate schools.

The issue reached a high point of interest in the provincial election of 1971, when the Liberal and New Democratic parties campaigned for an extension of the separate school system while the Conservatives held their ground against such a move. The resounding victory of Prime Minister Davis and his followers seemed to ensure that there would be no immediate change in the status quo.

TWO

Federations of elementary and secondary school teachers

Ontario school teachers were organized in a manner unique among Canadian provinces, with recognition given to the four distinguishing features of level, sex, religion, and language. Despite these differences, the five federations and the Ontario Teachers' Federation (OTF), in which they found unity in diversity, had most of their purposes and activities in common. They were all concerned with the protection and welfare of their members, giving continuous attention to salaries, job security, superannuation, and other such matters. They made an extremely important contribution to education through the upgrading of their own membership. Mainly operating through the OTF, they exerted steady pressure on education officials and legislators to improve their own status and to ensure that schools were operated under the best possible conditions. Since formal education was largely a provincial matter, the Canadian Teachers' Federation (CTF) did not provide a close parallel to the provincial federations. Besides filling a co-ordinating role, it engaged in a number of distinctive activities. The teachers' federations at both levels had much in common with other professional associations. They are given separate treatment here because of their special relationship to the schools.

THE FEDERATION OF WOMEN TEACHERS' ASSOCIATIONS OF ONTARIO

Purposes
According to the constitution of the Federation of Women Teachers' Associations of Ontario (FWTAO), as revised at the annual meeting in 1968, the objects of the association were as follows:

a) to advance and safeguard the teaching profession in Ontario both through the efforts of FWTAO as an affiliate and in co-operation with the Ontario Teachers' Federation;
b) to promote and protect the interests of public elementary school women teachers;
c) to promote a high standard of professional ethics;
d) to influence public attitudes concerning the professional aims and activities of women teachers;

e) to maintain and improve the professional competence of our members;
f) to promote the cause of education throughout the world.

Membership
The revised constitution of 1968 defined five categories of membership.
1 / Statutory members were members of the OTF who were legally qualified
to teach in an elementary public school and were under contract to teach
in such a school or in a Protestant separate school and were not active
members of any other teachers' organization affiliated with the OTF.
2 / Voluntary members were women, other than inspectors or persons
employed to teach in a school for a period up to one month, who held a
teacher's certificate, were engaged in an educational capacity, or were
employed by the FWTAO, and had been accepted by the Board of Governors of the OTF for membership in that organization. 3 / Associate members were women who were formerly members of the FWTAO and had
retired from the teaching profession but wished to maintain contact with
their professional organization, and whose applications had been approved; or who were formerly members in good standing who were temporarily not employed by any school board, and whose applications had
been approved; or who were teachers-in-training attending teachers'
college; or who were guest teachers on exchange. 4 / Affiliate members
were women who were qualified as elementary school teachers, were
members of other affiliated bodies of the OTF, and were approved for
membership by the Board of Directors. 5 / Honorary membership might
be conferred on anyone who had given outstanding or meritorious service
to education, to the profession, or to both.

Structure
For federation purposes the province was divided into regions, associations,
and units. The officers included an honorary president, an immediate past
president, a president, a first vice-president, and a second vice-president.
The Board of Directors appointed a treasurer for a one-year term from
among the members of the FWTAO executive, an Advisory Board consisting of the three former presidents, an executive secretary, and executive
assistants. The Board of Directors consisted of four officers (the past
president, president, first vice-president, and second vice-president), the
five FWTAO members elected to the Board of Governors of the OTF, other
directors from each region, and the executive secretary, who might vote
on all except financial matters. The executive assistants and members of
the Advisory Board were non-voting members of the Board of Directors.
The executive consisted of the four elected officers serving on the Board
of Directors, the executive secretary, and the five members elected to the
Board of Governors of the OTF. The non-voting members of the Board of
Directors were also non-voting members of the executive.
The officers of the associations were a past president, a president, a

first vice-president, a second vice-president, and a secretary-treasurer or a secretary and a treasurer. The officers of the units were a president and a secretary and such other officers as the association and the unit considered necessary. Each association had an executive consisting of the association officers, the presidents of the units within the association, and the members of the Board of Directors who belonged to the association. The executive of a unit consisted of the officers, the president of the association, and any FWTAO directors belonging to the unit.

There were three groups of committees. The elected standing committee were those dealing respectively with educational finance, legislation, goodwill, superannuation, and status. The appointed standing committees dealt with the emergency fund, honorary membership, awards, teacher education and certification, teachers' college liaison, research, and executive staff personnel. The Board of Directors and the executive were empowered to appoint special committees when the circumstances warranted.

Rules governing professional conduct
The rules governing professional conduct were stated in By-Law 6, Section 1.

a) A member shall strive at all times to achieve and maintain the highest degree of professional competence and to uphold the honour, dignity, and ethical standards of the teaching profession.
b) A member shall not
   i) break a contract of employment with a Board of Trustees, or
   ii) violate a written or oral agreement to enter into a contract of employment with a Board of Trustees, or
   iii) while holding a contract of employment with a Board of Trustees make application for another position the acceptance of which would necessitate her seeking the termination of her contract by mutual consent of the teacher and the board, unless and until she has arranged with her board for such a termination of contract if she obtains the other position.
c) A member shall
   i) on making an adverse report on another member, furnish her with a written statement of the report at the earliest possible time and not later than three days after making the report.
   ii) refuse to accept employment with a Board of Trustees whose relations with the FWTAO are unsatisfactory.
d) When a member of the FWTAO has failed to comply with a), b), or c) of Section 1, the FWTAO Executive shall have the authority to recommend disciplinary action be taken by the Ontario Teachers' Federation; or to concur, or not concur with recommendations regarding disciplinary action

made by the Department of Education or the Ontario Teachers' Federation.

The FWTAO asserted the right to refuse membership to any woman teacher who became eligible by accepting employment with a school board, and to expel any member, who

i) upon being notified of an alleged breach of professional conduct, refuses without adequate cause or excuse, when requested in writing, to appear before the executive of the FWTAO.
ii) accepts a position with a Board of Trustees whose relations with the FWTAO have been declared unsatisfactory by the FWTAO Executive.

Procedures were outlined in the by-laws for an inquiry into the conduct of a member, with expulsion as a possible outcome.

Origin and early history

The FWTAO is fortunate in having a historical record of its origin and development up to 1968 in the form of a book by Doris French entitled *High Button Bootstraps*.[1] This account does full justice to the hopes, ideals, and aspirations of the members during the first fifty years of the life of the organization. The factual basis for the story is derived from a very large number of original papers, as well as a variety of secondary sources. Important contributions were also made by actual participants in the events through their personal recollections.

French identifies the formation of the Lady Teachers' Association of Toronto in 1888 as the first move to organize women teachers. She describes the depressed position of members of her sex in these terms.

In Toronto in those days the public schools were crowded far beyond their capacity: some luckless women had as many as 100 pupils to teach in a single classroom. Naturally the women were given the youngest children – and salaries were based on the grade taught. Few women advanced to the higher grades so long as there were men teachers about to fill the posts, and of course the differential between men's and women's salaries held good even when they taught at the same level. The women teachers always took a back seat. When a deputation of teachers went to the Board on a matter of salaries, even when women's salaries were being considered, the Board agreed to hear only the men.[2]

The primary objective of the Toronto association was to set up a fund to help women teachers who were ill. The idea spread during the next twenty years to such places as London, Galt, and Ottawa. During this period Lady Aberdeen, wife of the seventh Governor-General, who held office from 1893 to 1898, inspired the organization of an Educational Union, which held monthly meetings where papers on educational matters were read. This venture proved premature, and was disbanded in five years. The associations formed in the major cities continued, however, to progress. The one in Ottawa took the lead in considering salary matters, a rather risky activity in those days when school boards could readily demonstrate their displeasure by firing teachers who dared to show dissatisfaction with their lot. Most of the teachers, although prepared to benefit from the efforts of others, were unwilling to take any risks.

The meeting that led to the formation of the FWTAO was held in connection with the annual convention of the OEA in 1918. Not surprisingly, the women demonstrated a complete lack of confidence that men could be counted upon to help improve their status. They realized that they must rely entirely on their own united efforts. Their resolution had been greatly reinforced by the active role they had been called on to assume during the war. There was nevertheless a good deal of opposition to the proposed federation. French ascribes this attitude to the dislike many teachers had for trade unions and to the lack of commitment of many of those who had their eye on marriage. During the war many of those who advocated the formation of an organization were accused of being unpatriotic.

The organization meeting was attended by teachers from Toronto, Hamilton, North Bay, Port Arthur, Prescott, Ottawa, Chatham, and Galt. It was chaired by Helen Arbuthnot, a Toronto teacher whom French singles out for particular credit for the achievements of the period. In the first constitution the purpose of the federation was stated as the formation of local associations to promote the professional and financial status of women teachers. There was vigorous opposition to the idea of including a reference to financial objectives, but the wording remained.

The province was divided into four regions for organizational purposes, and a teacher was selected from each to join the executive. A major pursuit during the next few years was the extension of membership which, even in those days of penurious salaries, seemed reasonably modest at $0.10 per member per year. School inspectors showed a commendable amount of co-operation by naming one or two of the best teachers in each area who might be interested in recruiting activities. The salary issue was one of overwhelming importance at this stage. An acceptable minimum of $650 a year was established and local associations were urged to make every effort to attain it. Individual teachers were exhorted to refrain from undercutting one another in the competition for desirable posts. As time went on, the organization blossomed out into other fields. One resolution, for example, asked for much stricter censorship of moving picture and vaudeville performances.

In 1921 the federation was incorporated under *The Ontario Companies Act*, with somewhat elaborated purposes:

To encourage the formation of local Women Teachers' Associations for the promotion of the professional, literary and social interests of teachers:
> to raise the professional and financial status of women teachers;
> to arouse and foster a spirit of professional etiquette;
> to stimulate public interest in the work by press propaganda;
> to direct any united effort of the women teachers;
> to co-operate with other organized bodies of teachers.[3]

At the annual meeting of that year the members voted financial support for the newly formed CTF. Fees were raised to a dollar a year and arrangements were made to put the secretary-treasurer on salary.

Criticism from the Ontario School Trustees' and Ratepayers' Association was taken as evidence that the federation's salary campaign was having some effect. There were fruitful negotiations with this organization, however, over a proposal to have a regular contract, which would continue in force unless terminated at least thirty days before school reopened in the fall. The federation also began to press the Minister of Education to arrange for boards of reference to settle disputes between teachers and school boards. When a substantial surplus of teachers developed, the government was urged to restrict admission to normal schools by more careful screening, to add a second year to normal school training, to abolish the model schools, and to end district or temporary certificates.

A great deal of credit for the progress of the federation between 1924 and 1944 is given to Harriet Carr, who served as secretary throughout the period, for the first two years on a part-time basis and then full time. For a number of years she edited the official publication of the federation, at first called the *Bulletin* and later the *Educational Courier*. Much of her work consisted in defending members who were being treated unjustly by their school boards and in persuading teachers who were guilty of unjustifiable behaviour to make amends. Through her successes she made a continuous contribution to the prestige of the organization.

Activities during the depression of the 1930s
The great problem of the depression of the 1930s was of course that of salary reductions. At the same time pressure was put on those who were employed to contribute to relief funds. Although the federation appealed to the government to improve the situation, there was little it could do in the face of the economic forces that left a large part of the population in penury. It was able, however, to set up an employment exchange service, to help members work out with their boards the total grants payable by the Department of Education, to organize a sick benefit scheme, and to provide a legal service for teachers who were having difficulty over their contracts. Social gatherings and other recreational activities were also promoted.

Leading members of the federation were aware of new and more progressive trends in education developing in other countries. At the annual meeting in 1935 a resolution was passed urging a drastic revision in curriculum. It was suggested that arithmetic that was too difficult for the children be dropped from the course of study, along with most of the formal grammar, that English be taught by the composition method, that stress be removed from final examinations and placed on daily work, activities, and learning, and that textbooks be completely revised. It may be assumed that this expression of views had something to do with the major curriculum reforms of 1937. Unfortunately, however, a large proportion of the FWTAO members were not entirely prepared for such changes.

Participation in the Ontario Teachers' Council

The FWTAO joined the Ontario Public School Men Teachers' Federation (OPSMTF) and the Ontario Secondary School Teachers' Federation (OSSTF) in 1935 to form the Ontario Teachers' Council. Among the factors leading to this development, French stresses the difficulty these three organizations were encountering in raising the annual fee of $1,000 for membership in the CTF. As a single organization, they could make their contributions jointly. The new council, which developed into the OTF, did not significantly reduce the autonomy of its three components. To judge by its lack of success in its efforts to persuade the provincial government to raise the salary minimum to $800 from the level of $500 to which it had sunk, it did not speak with a very powerful voice.

Effect of the Second World War

Women teachers were called upon to undertake a variety of special activities during the Second World War. In the early stages they contributed substantial funds through the Ontario Teachers' Council for Czech, Polish, and British children who arrived in Canada as refugees or to seek safety from the dangers of the war zones. Until the 1942–3 school term, when they were frozen in their positions, many of them abandoned their profession for work in munitions factories or in other occupations that seemed more urgent than school teaching. After this course of action was forbidden, many of them spent their summers picking fruit on farms, mailing ration books, doing volunteer Red Cross work, or working in service men's canteens. Although some of the immediate results of the war were a loss of federation membership and a lowering of standards of instruction because of the necessity of employing emergency replacements for properly qualified teachers, the groundwork was laid for more effective federation action. Teachers gained a broader knowledge of the occupational world, and were less willing to submit to the depressed conditions under which so many of them had hitherto worked. The support of the FWTAO for consolidation of one-room rural schools was considerably strengthened during this period.

The Teaching Profession Act of 1944
Among the federations, none benefited more than the FWTAO from the passage of *The Teaching Profession Act* of 1944 which legislated automatic membership. The FWTAO had never been able to induce as many as half the eligible members to join voluntarily, and much effort had been expended in keeping some of the local associations alive and functioning. There was thus great rejoicing to see Ontario follow the lead of Saskatchewan and Alberta, which had made federation membership compulsory in 1935, and New Brunswick and Manitoba, which had done the same in 1942. The passage of the required legislation by the Conservative government, newly elected in 1943, followed a long and unsuccessful campaign to persuade the previous Liberal government to take such action. The fact that Premier George Drew had a large CCF opposition breathing down his neck was considered to be of some relevance. There appears to be no reason for doubt, however, that he acted from a strong personal conviction that the quality of education would be improved by more effective professional associations.

Attitude toward emergency training programs
The hopeful mood of 1944 was sharply dashed the following year when a five-week summer course was instituted, leading to an interim certificate qualifying high school graduates of the previous June to teach in elementary schools. The federation established an unequivocal policy of objecting to this solution to the teacher shortage. Although leading federation members were no doubt correct in suggesting that the ultimate solution was to improve the status and salaries of teachers, they did not have a convincing alternative that could be applied immediately. Until the late 1950s their protests seemed to have no effect on government policy. Their reasons for dissatisfaction were heightened during the early part of the crisis when teachers trained in shorter and less rigorous programs were awarded the same First Class Certificate that older members of the profession had obtained with more effort.

Early post-war salary campaigns
The high rate of inflation after the war, along with rapid adjustment of wages and salaries in other occupations, naturally meant that the FWTAO would exert great efforts to improve the financial position of its members. By 1947 the minimum annual salary being sought was $1,500. Of great significance also was the demand for a salary scale with regular increments for experience and allowances for extra qualifications. A few of the larger systems accepted this idea in some form, and the others gradually fell into line. The FWTAO resolutely opposed the introduction of merit rating for salary purposes, which was proposed, although not very resolutely, from time to time.

Relations with the OPSMTF
The possibility of amalgamating the FWTAO with the OPSMTF was raised repeatedly. The latter was consistently prepared for a merger but the women remained opposed. In part the matter was one of tradition; while there had been many examples of fruitful co-operation, the women had been forced to rely largely on themselves for the progress they had made. There were many examples of opposition from the men over such issues as superannuation benefits. More important was the realization that, other relevant factors being equal, men were nearly always given the preference when administrative appointments were being made. Although men could not have dominated a combined organization without the acquiescence of a large proportion of the women members, the politically conscious leaders of the FWTAO feared, no doubt validly, that tradition and custom would have produced just such an outcome. With a good deal of justification, they felt that they could best look after the interests of their own sex in a separate organization. Where it was desirable to combine forces to achieve an objective on which both agreed, such as an improvement in salaries, they could readily co-operate on a voluntary basis.

Women teachers were highly gratified over legislation passed by the Ontario government in 1951 which theoretically guaranteed men and women equal pay for equal work. While this arrangement eliminated open differentials in salary scales, it did little to ensure equal opportunity for promotion. Progress during the next twenty years was, to say the least, disappointing for the advocates of true equality.

In 1969 a merger of the men's and women's federations within five years was rather confidently predicted by I.J. Fife, president of the OPSMTF. He saw a rapid rise in pressure for the union of all teachers – male and female, elementary and secondary, and French and English – in a single organization. He minimized the danger that men would dominate such an organization, and pointed to the success of local amalgamations in Windsor, Nepean, Kitchener, Waterloo, Sudbury, and parts of Metropolitan Toronto. He identified the existing duplication of services as costly and unnecessary. Members of the FWTAO, however, continued to be wary.

Policy with respect to married women teachers
The federation long remained unenthusiastic about accepting married women as teachers. This antipathy was most understandable during the depression of the 1930s when a married woman who taught almost certainly deprived a single teacher of a position. It seemed unfair that some families had both the husband's and wife's salaries while unemployed single people had nothing. Even during the teacher shortage of later years, something of the same attitude continued, however illogically, to

persist. Many single teachers asserted that teaching was a full-time calling, and could not be successfully combined with the management of a household. They were not too readily persuaded that a successful marriage contributed anything important to a woman's personal qualities as a teacher. By the early 1960s the official federation line was reversed, partly as the result of a survey which showed that married women teachers in rural schools were eager to improve their academic standing and were taking their responsibilities just as seriously as single teachers.

Support for the single salary schedule

There was an unequivocal and unwavering conviction on the part of federation leaders that qualifications and length of experience should be the only factors considered in determining salary. That is, they were opposed to the idea that teaching small children was relatively easy, and that the task became more difficult as they grew older. The issue had to be fought at the elementary level where differentials once prevailed from grade to grade, and between the elementary and secondary levels. Although the OSSTF successfully resisted any formal acceptance of the single salary schedule, school boards could not be prevented from a *de facto* integration of the two scales.

Relations with school boards

Paralleling the "pink letter" of the OSSTF, the FWTAO developed the "grey letter" to indicate its displeasure with a school board with which its relations were unsatisfactory. For the most part it was sufficient to warn members that they would receive no help from the federation if they got into difficulties with a grey-listed board. Professional cohesion ensured that recalcitrant boards would sooner or later come to terms. The most difficult case was one encountered at Lakefield between 1962 and 1964. Matters reached a point where the sixteen teachers and the principal of the local school resigned and the board proved able to replace them. A settlement acceptable to the federation was finally reached in 1964. There was some friction over the case with the OTF, which opposed the kind of drastic action advocated by the FWTAO and the OPSMTF, and declined to recommend to the Department of Education the cancellation of the certificates of the teachers who had acted against the spirit of the grey letter.

Efforts to improve teacher competence

Despite the doubts of many of its members, the official position of the federation was always favourable to high levels of pre-service preparation. When protests against the so-called emergency programs of the 1950s and early 1960s failed to produce satisfactory results, the organization introduced an in-service training program of its own, as well as offering bursaries to persuade outstanding grade 13 students to attend teachers' colleges. Book lists were prepared as a guide to home reading and speakers were suggested for meetings. A four-day conference on reading was held in 1955, followed by one on social studies in 1956, and one on creative English in 1957. Centrally organized conferences were supplemented by those held at the local level. By 1959, according to French, fifty in-service programs were sponsored by the federation, most of them lasting for one day or a weekend. A Professional Development Committee functioned between 1958 and 1964, when it was disbanded on the grounds that this activity was the responsibility of the whole organization.

The bursary program began in 1954, when five awards of $200 each were made to girls who graduated from grade 13 with a first-class average and were in financial need. By 1959 the number of these bursaries reached thirteen. In the same year the first Helen Keefer Scholarship, amounting at first to $1,000 and later to $2,000, was established for advanced study in special education at Columbia University. A fellowship of $3,000, later raised to $6,000, was established in 1960 for graduate study at the Ontario College of Education. Later in the 1960s $1,000 bursaries were provided to enable Indian and Eskimo girls to attend teachers' college. A fund was also established to assist promising girls to finish high school as a preliminary to teacher training. In 1966 the grade 13 bursaries awarded since 1954 were discontinued in favour of Centennial Scholarships of $1,000 each to help Ontario women teachers obtain the final year of their university degree.

Influence on educational policy
Centralized control over the curriculum and classroom practices was at a peak during the 1920s. Despite some teacher influence on the formulation of the new program of studies introduced in 1937, there was comparatively little sign of relaxation of controls during that decade. At the end of the war, however, the teachers showed an increasing desire for a voice in deciding what should be taught and by what methods. The FWTAO established eight research committees in 1945 to study various aspects of the educational system. Other evidences of growing professional interest included a resolution that elementary teachers be employed to write textbooks and that travelling libraries be made increasingly available in rural areas. Local committees were formed to examine the course in religious education prescribed in 1944. In 1950 the federation appointed Gertrude Bergey to conduct in-service workshops and thus to encourage participation in departmental curriculum planning programs. The response from members was considerably less enthusiastic than leading federation members had hoped it would be.

There is support in French's account for the conclusion that the 1950s and 1960s were mainly notable for what the federations failed to achieve in terms of professional control over the educational process. The attempt to establish local curriculum committees as a vital force weakened rather promptly when W.J. Dunlop succeeded Dana Porter in the education portfolio. The growing proportion of ill-trained, immature teachers in the 1950s made the voice of the organized profession seem less credible than it would otherwise have been. Elementary teachers did not carry a great deal of weight in the committees set up by the Ontario Curriculum Institute, although a good deal of lip service was paid to their importance. Teachers were offered opportunities to participate in various activities of the Ontario Institute for Studies in Education, but there was little scope for them to exert real initiative. While secondary school teachers took a very modest step toward control of admission to their ranks by working out a system of licensing, which did not in any way supersede government control over certification, elementary teachers did not even get that far.

There were nevertheless some hopeful developments. In 1965 a conference on programmed instruction was attended by three hundred teachers. Some research was sponsored and conducted in co-operation with various outside agencies. One project, which involved a study of the relative achievement of pupils in schools of varying sizes, helped to point up the handicaps under which the diminishing number of very small schools still suffered in 1965. A Research Committee, set up during the same year, undertook a long-term study on Elementary School Teaching as a Career for Women. Members of the FWTAO, as the writer's personal involvement at one stage can attest, have demonstrated a realistic awareness of the need for specialized assistance in designing studies. They are also noted for the warmth of their appreciation for outside help.

Efforts to increase awareness of the federation
among new teachers
The realization that many students in teachers' colleges had neutral or negative feelings about the FWTAO led in 1953 to the introduction of an information program designed, not only to remedy this deficiency, but also to make young women entering the profession more generally aware of professional ethics and obligations. Annual student-teacher weekends were organized, involving two girl students from each teachers' college and one each from the Ontario College of Education and the Primary Specialist course in Toronto. These girls were given information on the structure and operations of the federation, as well as on such matters as professional ethics, procedures of hiring and changing jobs, and community roles. An effort was made to acquaint them with procedures for self-improvement through reading, university credit courses, and community contacts. The program involved a commitment on the part of each participant to transmit what she had learned to her fellow students

in scheduled classes. At a later stage the number of students attending the sessions was increased, and ultimately local associations began to conduct programs of a similar type at each college centre.

Miscellaneous welfare programs

The attitude of women teachers toward superannuation benefits, particularly during the years immediately after the establishment of the Superannuation Fund in 1917, was often, to say the least, unenthusiastic. Leading members of the federation, who tended to represent the group with a commitment to teaching as a lifetime career, were more in favour of substantial benefits. There was nevertheless room for a good deal of disagreement with the OPSMTF over proposals such as the one advanced in 1940 to provide for widows' benefits. On the other hand, the FWTAO showed constant concern for the welfare of retired teachers whose financial security had been undermined year by year with the rising cost of living. Efforts to persuade the provincial government to raise the minimum were accompanied by voluntary contributions to aid those in need. In 1938, before group insurance was available, a Sick Benefit Fund was created to assist members facing a combination of illness and inadequate financial resources. Another example of generosity was attributed to Dorothy Martin, whose service as executive secretary began in 1961. During the immediate post-war period she persuaded the executive to establish a fund to assist British exchange teachers whose salaries were inadequate to meet the higher costs of living in Canada.

Briefs to major study committees of the 1960s

The FWTAO was quick to seize the opportunity of presenting a set of views to the major study committees established by the minister during the 1960s. Whether or not the opinions of the membership were canvassed before any particular brief was prepared, the contents could not help but be influenced by those who organized them and gave them verbal expression. Thus the views presented could properly be regarded as a considerable modification of those held by the "average" woman teacher.

The Minister's Committee on the Training of Elementary School Teachers

As already noted, the official position of the FWTAO had for some time favoured a university degree as a basic qualification for all elementary school teachers, despite a lack of enthusiasm for such a goal on the part of many of the members. The brief submitted to the Minister's Committee was thus in harmony with the scheme for consecutive academic and professional training that constituted one of the alternatives recommended by that body. On the basis of a study completed by the Teacher

Education and Certification Committee in 1962, the federation opposed the idea of awarding a degree in education after the completion of a composite of academic and professional courses. It suggested that the basic academic qualification for elementary and secondary school teachers should be the same, with areas of specialization indicated. While specific academic courses should not be too rigidly prescribed, a prospective teacher might be well advised to choose from among such disciplines as philosophy, sociology, mathematics, English, and science. An unequivocal stand was taken against a pass arts course specially designed for teachers.

Specialized training for teachers of kindergarten, primary classes, and groups ranging from the physically handicapped to the gifted would be provided after the award of a permanent certificate and two years of successful teaching. It was thought that the unique needs of unusual groups of children would be best served by teachers who were aware of what might be achieved in the normal classroom. For all teachers there should be preparation in guidance to deal with problems created by increased population mobility and changes in school organization and curricula. A well informed teacher with a university degree would be well fitted to help able pupils set their sights on university at a very impressionable age.

The federation offered suggestions that would combine strong incentives for promotion with protection for existing members of the organization. It seemed reasonable to expect that all teachers entering the profession after 1972 would hold a degree. In any case, the deadline seemed far enough away that it was judged desirable to make recommendations for the improvement of the current one-year course. These recommendations centred particularly on the desirability of improving screening procedures for admission to the teachers' colleges. Interviewing committees, on which the federation would be represented, would have the power to bar candidates on personal, physical, or academic grounds.

The Provincial Committee on Aims and Objectives
The brief presented to the Provincial Committee on Aims and Objectives contained some very enlightened views, some notes of caution about the difficulties of implementing radical changes, and some of the standard educational clichés of the period. The proposed aims were said to be based on change in five particular areas: the expansion of horizons in the world and in outer space, advances in the field of technology, new media of communication, changing patterns of living resulting from increased mobility, and philosophical adjustments required to conform to the evolving welfare state.

Among the points made in the brief were these: that textbooks should receive somewhat less emphasis in favour of current material in the form of paperback books, daily newspapers, magazines, and audio-visual communications; that pupils should be taught to subject information received through these sources to a critical examination; that pupils might benefit from more visits by experts from outside the school; that a greater sensitivity to the needs of others and a willingness to share resources to meet these needs might be produced by de-emphasizing competitive aspects of school programs and evaluation systems and by including a larger proportion of co-operative ventures in the classroom, school, and school system; that parochial tastes should be replaced with a desire to experience the new and the untried; that the individual should have more training in problem solving; that children's curiosity should be stimulated and that they should be made aware of the world through deliberate exposure to the wonders of nature, to the facts of science, and to experiences with natural phenomena in and out of school; that mastery of fundamental facts of mathematics and of skills in communication were needed to enable children to use the technological skills of the day and to plan for the future; that skill in critical thinking was of particular importance; that education must aim to encourage the development of creativity among children, particularly the gifted; that a special effort must be made to acknowledge the individual's need for recognition, security, and a sense of belonging in a society demonstrating increasing trends toward regimentation; that there should be continuous research into the learning process, with effective communication of the findings to teachers; that schools should have teachers well qualified academically, well versed in the learning process, and well trained in instructional technology; that modern instructional equipment should be supplied in adequate quantity; that education should help to ensure that scientific discoveries and technological advances are used for human betterment; that the curriculum, while giving the pupil an appreciation and respect for his heritage, should be under constant revision to meet modern needs; that the particular talents and skills needed for communication by means of television should be cultivated in the school; that the development of listening skills was assuming increasing importance; that public demand for thought-provoking television programs might help to counteract family alienation in a way that programs demanding only a passive response were failing to do; that learning to adapt to a number of people and situations in the school environment might help the pupil to cope with increased population mobility; that preparation for an occupational career, or a sequence of careers, would continue to be a major educational objective; and that there should be adequate opportunities for continuing education after the end of formal schooling.

The brief did not favour an attempt to rush into a completely ungraded system. As a means of preparing teachers and parents for more drastic changes, it suggested that a modified unit system be introduced in kindergarten. A unit plan in the primary division might work up into the junior division. The recommended scheme sounded much like the one that had been introduced in the Hamilton system long before, and later adopted in other systems.

Religious education in the public schools
The FWTAO submission to the Mackay Committee was prepared by a committee set up for the purpose. A questionnaire was constructed to solicit facts and opinions from a random sample of the members. The brief consisted largely of a tabulation of the responses to the questions. The majority of the respondents favoured the retention of religious instruction in some form, although a minority thought the existing course might be doing more harm than good. There were many suggestions for improvement in the program, guides, methods of presentation, and materials. Teachers' doubts about their adequacy to teach the course increased with the seniority of the grades. There were indications of "a spirit of great tolerance" toward children from minority groups and a reluctance to impose beliefs on them. Apparently, however, the teachers did not constitute a major force in the reform movement in this area. The changes recommended in the committee's report, when it finally emerged, were considerably more drastic.

Miscellaneous resolutions
In addition to making detailed cases in briefs such as those mentioned, the FWTAO passed numerous resolutions designed to further various worthy causes. Improved opportunities for in-service upgrading were urged in 1963 in a resolution requesting that the OTF ask for concentrated university extension courses in science. The following year it was resolved that the minister be requested to institute a fifth standard for those whose qualifications went beyond the BA degree. In 1965 the federation asked for more Department of Education courses in the teaching of English. A year later a more elaborate resolution on the same topic proposed that such courses lead to a specialist's certificate, that only very carefully chosen people be appointed to teach them, and that they deal primarily with the appreciation of English literature rather than with teaching methods. Another resolution carried at the same annual meeting resulted in a survey of the number of women teachers in Ontario who were pursuing doctoral studies or who had recently completed them. This information was sought as a basis for improving the FWTAO financial award scheme. In 1967 the OTF was asked to approach the minister with the request that in-service training courses which the sponsors regarded as compulsory be given in normal school hours.

Concern for improving the conditions under which teachers served led in 1965 to the formation of a committee to study optimum conditions for quality teaching and to prepare a report on the topic. It was also resolved that school boards be asked to relieve teachers of legal responsibility and supervisory duties during the lunch hour. A resolution in 1966 proposed that the OTF be asked to support the discontinuance of playground supervision by teachers. A more specific resolution the next year requested that the OTF suggest to the minister that supervisory duties prior to fifteen minutes before instruction began, during the noon recess, and later than fifteen minutes after the conclusion of instruction for the day be assumed by the school board through the employment of non-teaching personnel.

The attempt to achieve equality of opportunity for women led to the following motion.

Be it resolved that a directive should be sent out to all boards, principals and inspectorates – that where a vacancy exists, women must be given an equal opportunity of application. That, where women of required qualifications [are] already on staff, [they] must be given first opportunity to fill the vacancy, before advertising, and that women must be given an equal opportunity to teach in all grades in all divisions, according to their qualifications.

Subsequent discussion indicated general agreement with the spirit of the motion, but the wording was considered too strong, and the matter was referred to the executive.

Evaluation of federation services by members
In 1964 fees were raised to 0.75 per cent of each member's annual salary, with a ceiling of $50 established a year later. Part of this levy of course went to the OTF and the CTF. The size of the contribution which was demanded heightened the desire of federation officials to determine the reaction of members to the services offered. An attitude survey conducted in 1965–6 by the Public Relations Council uncovered a certain amount of apathy, particularly among younger teachers. Those who taught in the most remote areas were most poorly informed about federation activities and the least critical. Although a high percentage attended local meetings, comparatively few had ever been at an annual meeting in Toronto. Most maintained contact with the central organization by reading its publications. Not surprisingly, an overwhelming proportion thought the federation benefited the profession. The greatest personal benefits were seen in the provision of legal protection, followed by the salary program, the opportunity for professional association, and conferences and seminars. About half those approached favoured amalgamation with the OPSMTF. About two-thirds felt that a university degree should be the minimum qualification for teaching.

Attitude toward the OTF
The FWTAO showed its interest in examining the role of the OTF by submitting a brief to the OTF Commission on August 7, 1968. While gen-

erally approving of past OTF policies and activities, the FWTAO executive saw room for improvement. They thought it advisable, however, that whatever changes might be made should leave *The Teaching Profession Act* as it was.

In the area of professional development it was suggested that the OTF should launch a well-planned, overall program to co-ordinate the work done by itself and its affiliates in various subject areas from kindergarten to grade 13. Four affiliates would thus have a chance to co-operate in the elementary field and three, instead of one, in the secondary field. The brief recommended a study of the wisdom of integrating the school system from kindergarten to grade 13, both from the point of view of the students and from that of the teachers. The OTF might also conduct investigations into such educational developments as team teaching, ungraded schools, the unit system, pre-school preparation, and the use of computers.

The brief proposed that the *OTF Reporter* be published monthly and enlarged to include professional articles as well as announcements from the minister and the Department of Education and accounts of OTF business. It was also suggested that the OTF produce, publish, and distribute papers, pamphlets, and books at cost in the manner of the National Education Association in the United States. Other methods of communication might also be employed to bring the membership into closer touch with federation matters. These might include radio and TV clips and motion pictures.

A feeling of partnership between the OTF and the Department of Education was said to be desirable. Such a partnership would involve consultation when changes were being considered so that teachers would have an equal share in shaping the system. Appropriate matters for consultation would include teacher education, community colleges, and administration. The OTF was urged to prepare an annual brief for presentation to the minister commenting on existing practices and indicating desired changes. Protests would be in order if the minister acted in areas of vital concern to teachers without prior consultation.

Reflecting the customary determination of organizations to preserve their identity, the FWTAO saw areas of activity that were more significant for some groups of teachers than for others. This diversity of interests seemed to justify the continued existence of all five affiliates. It was suggested that some friction between the OTF and the affiliates and among the affiliates themselves might be avoided if a clearcut division of accountabilities were determined, stated, and followed. The FWTAO found the existing division of responsibility in relations and discipline cases reasonably satisfactory, although it appeared possible that more disputes might be settled by conciliation if they were referred to the affiliates before drastic action was taken.

THE ONTARIO PUBLIC SCHOOL MEN TEACHERS' FEDERATION

Like the FWTAO, the OPSMTF is fortunate in having a history of its origin and development in permanent form. Those who seek detailed information about the role and contribution of this association will find it in *The Long March* by R.A. Hopkins.[4] Published in 1969, this work covers approximately the first fifty years of the federation's existence, as well as supplying a good deal of background information about the earlier period.

Early history
Hopkins refers to the OEA as the incubator of the OPSMTF.[5] As indicated in the section of the present volume dealing with the OEA, that organization was instrumental in organizing the Ontario Teachers' Alliance in 1908. Its activities restricted to the major urban centres and adjacent areas, that organization claimed some success in improving salaries and in protecting teachers against boards that engaged in the practice of dismissing experienced teachers and replacing them with new staff members willing to accept lower salaries. The alliance also had a good deal to do with the passage of the Teachers' and Inspectors' Superannuation Act in 1917. During that year, however, it gave up its independent existence, leaving the OEA with the responsibility of carrying on its activities. Such an arangement could not prevent a kind of vacuum from developing, and three major federations soon appeared to fill it.

While Hopkins acknowledges that a number of places claim to be the birthplace of the OPSMTF, the evidence he presents indicates that the original initiative was taken at Peterborough, although other opinions suggest that the drive for a provincial organization appeared more or less simultaneously at a number of centres. In November 1918, at a meeting held by a group of male public school teachers, a motion was carried to form a local association, and R.F. Downey and K.S. Wightman were elected as president and secretary respectively. A constitution was approved in February 1919, and a letter and circular were sent to representative male teachers in the cities and larger towns of the province. A provincial organizational meeting was held at the OEA Convention during the same year, with encouraging results. Despite initial opposition from some teachers, who objected to paying a fee, and from trustees involved in the OEA, the federation took form in 1920.

The federation was incorporated by letters patent in 1921. What might be called a statement of the purpose of the organization was worded as follows: "To organize into one group the Public School Men Teachers of Ontario, and to co-ordinate and give expression to their aspirations and interests." Incorporation occurred during the presidency of M.M. Kerr, the first to hold the office.

Such early leaders as Charles G. Fraser, who was secretary of the Public School Section of the OEA during the critical organizational period, hoped for a single federation of Ontario teachers operating in close association with the OEA. Since the newly established FWTAO and OSSTF were cool to the idea, however, the OPSMTF was forced to go it own way. The province was divided into ten districts for organizational purposes, each with a representative discharging local responsibilities. A slow growth of membership in the initial stages was attributed to the high fee, which was raised to $5.00 from the initial sum of $1.00. Improvement followed reduction of this amount to $3.00 in 1923.

As was true of the other federations, a great deal of the energy of the leading members of the OPSMTF was spent in recruiting. In view of the lack of funds, the work was done largely on a voluntary basis. Many of those who joined were prepared to let their membership lapse unless they were constantly prodded. Substantial danger accompanied federation membership in many communities, since many trustees and inspectors disapproved and had the means to make their displeasure felt. Hopkins points out that the terms "rebel," "trouble-maker," and "rabble-rouser" were freely used to describe active recruiters. The greatest progress was made in the major urban centres where there were larger numbers of teachers, where boards were more reluctant to take a position of open opposition, and where the trustees were more inclined to be sympathetic.

During the 1920s the federation supported many progressive proposals, some of which were implemented during the period and others not until years later. Among the most important were the appointment of inspectors from among the ranks of properly qualified teachers, more liberal superannuation benefits, the formation of township, county, or district boards of education, the abolition of the Third Class Certificate, and the establishment of a two-year normal school course. During the decade there was a modest but fairly regular increase in salaries for male teachers.

Hopkins speaks of the depression years of the 1930s as the "entrenchment years." The full effect of the disaster did not strike the teaching profession until 1932–3. The growing surplus of teachers after that time made it particularly difficult for male members of the profession who, with family responsibilities, were often unable to engage in competition with those who were prepared to accept positions at almost any salary. Those who were employed had to think carefully before agreeing to pay the meagre federation fee. There were real doubts that the organization could or would survive. Rising interest in the possibility of compulsory federation membership characterized much of the decade, although success was not achieved until 1944. The OPSMTF was strongly behind the formation of the Ontario Teachers' Council as a means of unifying the efforts of the profession.

Implications of The Teaching Profession Act, *1944*
The passing of *The Teaching Profession Act* in 1944 had very important implications for the OPSMTF, as it did for the other federations. Enough has been said about this act in other sections of this volume, and there is no need to repeat its clauses here. Originally it was hoped that inspectors and university professors would be included under the terms of the act, but trustee opposition was strong enough to have them excluded.[6] Had it not been for this change, the development of the OTF would obviously have followed very different lines.

Structural development
A major post-war landmark was the appointment in 1948 of the first full-time General Secretary, Winston Davies, who filled the office until his death in 1967. At that time there were committees on superannuation, educational finance, professional enlightenment, teachers' qualifications, budget, educational research, policy, honorary life membership, and legislation. Committees to implement procedures were the Nominations Committee, the Publicity and Education Week Committee, and the Resolutions Committee.

Salary policy
The OPSMTF naturally favoured the single salary scale when that issue came to a head in 1951. At the same time it agreed to try to formulate and institute a financial policy identical to that of the FWTAO. As recorded elsewhere, the OSSTF successfully resisted any formal adoption of the single salary scale, although the reality of its victory was questionable. During these years the OPSMTF was concerned about the discrepancy between salaries paid to rural and urban teachers. Strong criticism was directed at what was seen as an archaic system of finance, which was incapable of providing anything approaching real equality of educational opportunity.

The OPSMTF was fairly successful in avoiding the ultimate confrontation in its salary negotiations with school boards. The first board to be "grey-listed" was SS No. 2, Westminster. The action produced the desired results, since the dispute was settled within a week. At a later stage the federation found it more advantageous to use the threat of resignations at the times during the year when these could legally be submitted.

Further structural development
There were important constitutional changes in 1953. The executive was henceforth to consist of the president, the first vice-president, the second vice-president, the past president, and the secretary-treasurer. The assembly was to consist of the executive and representatives of each district on the basis of one for each fifty members or major fraction thereof, with each district having at least one representative.

At the December meeting in 1962 some concern was expressed about the efficiency of the federation. There were questions about such matters as the adequacy of the administrative structure, the communication problem, and the level of fees. By the time the spring meeting was held in 1963, a firm of business consultants had been engaged to make a study. When a report was submitted a few months later, immediate action was taken on one recommendation, and an office manager was hired.

Further constitutional changes were announced in 1966. The Provincial Assembly was henceforth to consist of the Provincial Executive plus district representatives in the proportion of one for each eighty members. Total membership in the assembly was to be a minimum of 125 and a maximum of 160. The general secretary-treasurer was to be excluded from membership on the executive. The chairmen of standing committees were to be appointed by the executive, and were not necessarily to be accredited members of the assembly.

The federation resisted the trend toward lowering standards of professional preparation to meet the serious teacher shortage of the 1950s. As early as 1950 a committee studying teachers' qualifications prepared a brief dealing with this problem. Rather than offering as an explanation for the shortage the small numbers in the age group from which new teachers had to be recruited and the rising school enrolment, the brief drew attention to such factors as the lack of a positive plan to alleviate the shortage, discouragement felt by promising candidates over the ease with which mediocre individuals could gain admission, the low prestige of the profession, the lack of economic security, poor teacher attitudes, and unattractive living and working conditions. The committee recommended that attention be given to personality, aptitudes, and physical factors in the selection of candidates for the profession. Faculties of education in universities were identified as the best place for teacher preparation. Considerable attention was devoted to the kind of program that might be offered under such circumstances. At this particular time the Department of Education was not prepared to give any serious consideration to such a scheme.

There was considerable adverse reaction in 1960 over a regulation that those appointed to principalships in schools with an enrolment of three hundred or more must hold a BA degree. Opposition centred on the fact that the decision had been made without consultation with the federation. There was also some objection on the grounds that a blow had been struck at the security of tenure. Later discussions with the minister met with some sympathy, and a more satisfactory arrangement was made for principals who held positions without the desired qualifications.

Involvement in professional improvement

The OPSMTF introduced its first ten-day summer course in school supervision and administration in 1953. The success of this venture was such that it was continued in succeeding years. A few years later a summer school in classroom practices in grades 7 and 8 was added. This course was short-lived because of the entry of the Department of Education into the same field. The course in supervision and administration, which had been conducted successfully for many years by the OPSMTF, was turned over to the OTF.

Among the three federations, the FWTAO, the OSSTF, and the OPSMTF, the latter has been much the most enthusiastic about a merger. A few basic facts about the issue of amalgamation with the FWTAO have been referred to on page 46 and need not be repeated here. That the OPSMTF has been on the losing side in terms of the drive for unity has not discouraged its leaders, who may well see their cause victorious in the years to come.

THE ONTARIO SECONDARY SCHOOL
TEACHERS' FEDERATION

The OSSTF, founded in 1919, was considered the strongest and in many areas the most active of the affiliates of the OTF. It showed a consistent determination to protect what its members saw as the particular interests of those teaching at the secondary school level. At times its relations with the other affiliated federations were uneasy, and there were even threats of secession from the OTF. More cautious counsels, however, prevailed.

Objectives
According to the constitution in force in 1970, the OSSTF pursued the following objectives:

(a) To promote and advance the cause of education;
(b) To promote a high standard of professional ethics;
(c) To promote and advance the interests of teachers and to secure conditions which will make possible the best professional service.
(d) To secure for the teachers more active participation in formulating educational policies and practices affecting secondary schools;
(e) To work toward control of our professional destiny;
(f) To recognize its status as an affiliated body of the O.T.F.

Membership
The by-laws in force in 1970 defined six categories of membership, which were not mutually exclusive. Active membership included both statutory and voluntary members. A statutory member was 1 / one who was legally qualified to teach in a high school, a collegiate institute, a composite school, or a vocational school, and was under contract to teach in such a school, or 2 / one who was qualified as a secondary school teacher and was under contract to teach in a junior high school. A voluntary member was one who was certificated as a secondary school teacher in Ontario,

was employed in Ontario in an educational capacity, and was accepted for voluntary membership by the Provincial Executive. An associate member was 1 / a teacher-in-training at one of the Ontario colleges of education, or 2 / an unemployed teacher who was formerly an active member and had his membership accepted. A member on leave of absence might be classified as an active member on payment of the prescribed fee; otherwise he was considered to be an associate member. If the leave extended beyond a year, membership was continued only on application. An honorary associate membership could be conferred by the Provincial Executive on a member who had retired from teaching. A provincial life membership might be conferred by the Provincial Executive on a member who had given meritorious and outstanding service to the federation at the provincial level.

Statutory members had all the rights, privileges, and responsibilities of membership. Voluntary members were in a similar position, except that they did not receive support in matters of tenure and salary. Associate members, who paid no fees, might receive routine information and official communications at the discretion of the Provincial Executive, and might be invited to attend meetings which would contribute to their awareness of federation activities. Honorary associate members enjoyed the same status as associate members. Provincial life members had all the rights, privileges, and responsibilities of active members.

Ethics and discipline
Members of the OSSTF were expected to subscribe to a pledge with four clauses:

I solemnly dedicate myself to promote and advance the cause of education.
I will strive to achieve and maintain the highest degree of professional competence and will always uphold the honour, dignity, and ethical standards of my profession.
I pledge my loyalty and support to the Ontario Secondary School Teachers' Federation and will comply with the Constitution, By-laws, policies and established practices which govern its members.
I will not accept any Secondary School position until I personally have sought and received from the Provincial Office the assurance of the Provincial Executive that the position is acceptable.

Obviously only the last two of these clauses, and particularly the last, were sufficiently concrete to be considered in any real sense enforceable.

Associated with the pledge was a statement of ethics.

A teacher should present a practical illustration of scholarship and self-discipline, and should maintain the utmost respect for the rights and dignity of the individual.

He should endeavour to foster a regard for law, an appreciation of freedom, and the ideal of public service.
His professional conduct should be characterized by courtesy and good faith, and should imply the obligation to refrain from public criticism of his colleagues.

As of the late 1960s there were several grounds for expulsion from the federation: 1 / deliberate violation of the pledge, 2 / refusal without adequate cause or excuse, when requested in writing, to appear before the executive of the federation, or 3 / acceptance of employment with a school board which had adopted and was maintaining a single salary schedule applicable to both public and secondary school teachers, or with one which offered salaries that were considered unsatisfactory by the Provincial Executive. Any teacher who became eligible for membership by accepting employment might be refused on any of these grounds. If a member was accused in writing of acting in such a way as to merit expulsion, the executive might notify him to appear before the Annual Assembly. Expulsion required a vote of two-thirds of those present and voting. The federation never took advantage of its legal privilege of recommending the cancellation of a teacher's certificate, finding less drastic disciplinary devices sufficiently effective.

In the early days of contact between the federation and certain school boards, enough federation action was taken against arbitrary and unreasonable treatment of its members that many trustees got the impression that they would have to fight to dismiss any incompetent teacher. Federation officials insisted repeatedly that this was not so. They were able to make their point fairly convincingly after 1954 when the two-year probationary contract was introduced. As general secretary, S.G.B. Robinson used to commiserate with boards that found themselves saddled with a teacher of rather doubtful competence after the two-year deadline had passed, and point out that they would have had no difficulty had they declined to renew the probationary contract. While a dismissal could still be sustained after that, a convincing case would have to be made to avoid federation opposition.

The Board of Regents, established in 1955, was assigned as its main duties the maintenance and improvement of standards of professional competence, the improvement of the status of teachers, and the protection of the profession against unqualified or incompetent teachers. Its chief means of performing these functions was through the Document of Approval, which it could issue, renew, suspend, or revoke through established procedures. A member who felt that he had been the victim of an unfair judgment could take advantage of a rather elaborate appeal procedure which, in the mid-1960s, consisted of the following steps. 1 / An Appeal Committee was formed consisting of a representative from each of fifteen districts excluding the one in which the appellant was teaching or had taught. 2 / The members of this committee elected one of their number as chairman. 3 / The Board of Regents presented to the committee a report of the procedures leading to the suspension or revocation of the Document of Approval and the reasons for the decision. 4 / The appellant might choose a fellow member of the OSSTF to assist and counsel him in the presentation of his case. 5 / After considering the statement from the Board of Regents and the presentation of the case by or on behalf of the appellant, the Appeal Committee reported its findings to the Annual Assembly. 6 / Whatever decision was made by the committee was considered to be that of the Assembly, and no further appeal was permitted. According to a report in 1964, the Board of Regents considered 165 cases of alleged incompetence between the time of its establishment and that date. Of those involved, eight had been cleared, fourteen were still being investigated, thirty-five had their certificates suspended or revoked, and the great majority had left teaching. While the machinery was reasonably effective in dealing with the most flagrant cases of incompetence, it obviously did not cut very deeply into the total membership.

The OSSTF was occasionally called upon to assist a principal in a dispute with a board. It never saw fit to give him full backing, taking the view that, whatever the rights and wrongs of the case, he was likely to find his effectiveness destroyed if his relations with the board were not reasonably harmonious. There was some question about a demoted principal's right to insist on a teaching position with the same board. Cases of this kind were settled in such a way as to avoid establishing an absolutely clearcut precedent.

Origin and early development
S.G.B. Robinson, who at the time of writing was compiling the history of the OSSTF, later published under the title *Do Not Erase*,[7] has observed that the appalling salary situation at the end of the First World War was the chief influence that induced the secondary school teachers to organize. He has pointed out that, in the absence of price controls, the consumer price index rose by more than 63 per cent between 1914 and 1919, whereas the average salary for secondary school teachers increased by only 29.2 per cent. At the same time the personal income tax was taking a growing proportion of personal income.

As Robinson reviews the situation, a few of the larger centres had salary schedules. In other places pay was theoretically by merit but actually by caprice. Bargaining, if there was any, was conducted by individual teachers, and mostly in a very unaggressive manner, since the school boards had the upper hand. The only support the federation could offer during the 1920s was the moral backing of fellow members, and the only weapon that could be used was public opinion. There was no means by which the provincial office could give help to local centres in the conduct of salary negotiations. The best that could be done was to formulate provincial salary goals for the guidance of local staffs.

The depression years affected secondary school teachers in a very irregular fashion. In general, their salaries held up fairly well, and the average employed teacher had more purchasing power than he did in the twenties. Yet salary cuts in smaller centres were made erratically and arbitrarily, sometimes even in defiance of contracts, and there was a great deal of insecurity. As the depression deepened, the annual assembly of the federation abandoned the provincial salary schedule as a goal, and did not resume attempts to make progress in that area until after the beginning of the Second World War.

The inter-war period saw the establishment of some important agencies such as the Sick Benefit Fund, which was started in District No. 7 and extended to the other districts in 1934, the Ontario Secondary School Teachers' Fraternal Society, which took final form in 1939, and the Benevolent Fund, set up in the same year. Participation in these, which was voluntary, provided protection that was not at that time available from government sources. Like the other federations, the OSSTF also worked consistently for the improvement of superannuation benefits. The passing of legislation in 1938 making provision for boards of reference was regarded as a major triumph, although the OSSTF struggled for some time to have more teeth put into the measure.

Toward the end of 1941 intensive committee deliberation and debate in open convention ended in a decision to establish a reserve fund. The federation was thereafter able to give more than moral support to members who got into difficulty near the end of the year, and might not have a board of reference decision until it was too late to find a good job. The federation also put itself in a position to ask its members to resign in cases where a board refused to agree to a settlement on satisfactory terms. Such members could be supported until a favourable agreement had been reached.

The year 1941 also saw approval given for the establishment of a hospitalization fund, which came into operation the following year. According to current standards, both contributions and benefits were very modest. Annual fees were $7.50 for men and $13.50 for women and members' wives. The fund paid up to $4 per day to a maximum of $280 for hospitalization or nursing and varying amounts for operations and injuries.

In 1941 the Salary Committee unanimously adopted a resolution that the federation insist on the minimum figures of the salary schedule approved in 1938. This meant that members appointed to new positions would not serve for less than amounts ranging from $1,400 to $1,800, depending on the number of teachers under the board's jurisdiction. Members might, however, continue to teach for less as long as they remained in their existing positions. The recommendation was approved at the annual meeting.

The activities of the Educational Research Committee illustrate the broad professional interests of the OSSTF during the war years. In 1943 this committee reported the results of studies of three problems: 1 / the overburdening of teachers, 2 / the need for a course for a High School Principal's Certificate, and 3 / difficulties in conducting vocational guidance programs. With respect to the first, it recommended that principals attempt to distribute responsibilities equitably among members of the staff and that each teacher's timetable, when submitted to the inspector, be accompanied by a statement of his involvement in extra-curricular activities. At that time no province in Canada required a course for a principal's certificate, but the committee felt that the matter was worthy of further consideration.

Legislation passed in 1943 gave teachers important new protection in providing for a uniform contract for employment with school boards and in requiring a school board to give a written reason when dismissing a teacher. At the same time *The Board of Reference Act* was strengthened by the provision that its findings be mandatory. Some of these measures were strongly opposed by school boards, which mounted a campaign to have them revoked. The federation had to be very vigilant in seeing that the provisions were implemented. In the field of legislation the matter of major interest at this time was *The Teaching Profession Act*, passed in 1944.

Under the new arrangements OSSTF interest in matters of educational policy continued to increase. By 1945 there were reports and recommendations from a School Building Committee, a Curriculum Committee, an Adult Education Committee, a Health Committee, a Committee on Guidance, a Committee on Educational Finance, and a Committee on Inspection and Supervision. Contributions to the educational policies program were also being made by the Teacher Selection and Training Committee and the Teaching of Democratic Citizenship Committee. A director of publicity undertook to make the findings of these committees known among the members and in the wider educational community.

Salaries
New salary schedules were adopted in 1948 as a goal toward which the federation would work. The figures were obtained as a result of a canvass of the membership through a questionnaire sent to teachers in 424 secondary schools throughout the province. The results were considered to be a reasonable representation of what the majority of the five thousand members considered to be fair and reasonable. The establishment of a maximum salary was felt to be a significant forward step.

Salary negotiations were made much more effective from the teachers' point of view by the development of the so-called pink letter, which stated that it was not unprofessional to accept a position with a particular board, but that a federation member who did so would receive no assistance in salary matters from the federation. The rare black letter, issued by the OTF in accordance with the provisions of *The Teaching Profession Act*, stated that it was unprofessional to accept a position with the board in question. The pink letter owed its success to internal cohesion within the profession, which was reinforced by the threat of informal sanctions against a member who did not co-operate.

Arbitration, for which there has never been a statutory provision, was used informally in 1951 when the school board and the secondary school teachers of Brantford could not reach a mutually satisfactory agreement. The OSSTF agreed to arbitration despite its lack of enthusiasm for such a procedure on that occasion. The teachers were awarded the full amount of their original request. No board made a similar request thereafter.

The secondary school teachers' opposition to the single salary schedule was fought out in a dispute with the Toronto Board of Education in 1952. The OSSTF maintained its separate bargaining rights after issuing a pink letter, which was respected by the members throughout the province. With this precedent the issue was regarded as settled more or less permanently.

The following excerpts from OSSTF salary policy were published in the *Bulletin*, January 31, 1964.

A. Ontario Teachers' Federation Policy on Salary Scales
1. Each local negotiating unit shall have the right to establish its own salary schedule with the employing school board.
2. Salary scales should be based on qualifications, experience and responsibility.
3. A salary schedule should be adopted by every School Board, and every teacher employed by the board should be paid in accordance with that salary schedule.

B. The Ontario Secondary School Teachers' Federation Approved Salary Schedule
4. (a) The minimum salary for basic certification (Type B certificate or equivalent) should be a figure which will attract superior candidates to the teaching profession ...
(c) The minimum salary of teachers holding better than basic cerification should be up to 33% above the minimum stated in (a) ...
(e) Teachers should proceed from minimum to maximum by regular increments. The increment need not be uniform throughout the schedule, but in order to strengthen its retentive power, an increased rate of increment or a larger increment should be provided at certain key years ...
(h) The O.S.S.T.F. approves the creation of additional steps in teaching

and administrative positions as an incentive to teachers. A teacher assuming such additional responsibilities should receive an additional amount above group position on the schedule commensurate with responsibility assumed. The amount is a matter for local negotiation ...

c. Minimum Salary and Starting Salary

6. Since the minimum salary is the foundation upon which the salary schedule is built, any change in the minimum salary must result in an equivalent change in the salaries of all teachers in that group, including those at the maximum salary.

7. The starting salary of an experienced teacher is a matter of negotiation between the teacher and the employing board. However, allowances granted for experience, special qualification, etc., should not place the starting teacher at a higher level on the schedule than these factors would have earned for him had all his experience been with the employing board.

8. (a) If the board grants a starting teacher an allowance for experience, special qualifications, etc., a greater than the maximum allowance provided for in its schedule, the local bargaining unit should approach the board within a year to improve the schedule by an equal amount ...

9. (a) Where a teacher holding less [than] basic qualifications is employed, the starting salary of the unqualified teacher should in no circumstances be lower than one annual increment below that of a teacher with basic qualifications and the granting of increments to such a teacher shall be at the discretion of the board on satisfactory evidence of progress towards obtaining basic qualifications.

(b) At such time as the teacher qualifies, he should be placed on schedule (minimum plus years of experience).

10. The Federation approves the following types of experience.

Type 1. Teaching experience
(a) Secondary Schools
(b) Elementary Schools
Colleges and Universities
Technical Institutes
Professional Schools
Trade Schools

Allowance for teaching experience should be at the rate of the annual increment.

Type 2. Experience other than teaching
(a) Business and Industry
Other Professions
War Experience
(b) Vocational Trade
Experience above the basic eight years

Allowance for this type of experience shall be a matter for local negotiation.[8]

Certification

As early as 1952 there were discussions about the possibility of licensing members of the OSSTF as a means of indicating that they met the professional standards of the organization. This procedure was not intended to replace or infringe upon the right of the Department of Education to issue or withdraw teaching certificates. Since the main outlines of the plan are presented in volume III, chapter 12, there is no need to repeat the details here.

Professional development

During the 1940s and 1950s the Education Committee maintained an active and varied program. At the thirty-sixth annual assembly, held in December 1955, the following activities were reported for the previous calendar year. 1 / Refresher courses in chemistry and physics were held at a Toronto collegiate during the summer. The OSSTF selected the participants, who attended free of charge. 2 / A conference was held at Forest Hill Collegiate Institute for principals, who discussed the role of the principal in in-service training for teachers. 3 / All district education committees met in a conference to study different phases of conference planning. 4 / Resource personnel and material were provided for conferences at centres in different parts of the province. 5 / Typical examination papers were prepared for academic subjects in grades 9 to 12. 6 / Articles were supplied for publication in the *Bulletin*. 7 / Answers were given to teachers submitting questions on various academic areas. 8 / Assistance was provided for district in-service training conferences held for new teachers.[9]

During the late 1950s summer courses were offered in the teaching of various subjects in grade 13. Although originally intended as preparatory courses, these came to be treated in part as refresher courses for experienced teachers. An account of them has been given in volume V, chapter 9.

The year 1964–5 was a particularly notable one for initiatives designed to improve the professional status and competence of members. One of the most significant resolutions of the Annual Assembly in December was that a system of subject councils be established to provide support for the practising teacher. These councils, as originally proposed, would perform four chief functions: 1 / assist the classroom teacher in such areas as course content, teaching methods, and teaching aids and resource material; 2 / disseminate information designed to improve teaching in different subject areas; 3 / advise the Provincial Professional Development Committee, the Refresher Course Committee, and the Provincial Executive on matters of course content and methodology; and 4 / provide a pool of outstanding teachers to serve as subject consultants for district and local workshops and for other agencies at the discretion of the Provincial Executive.

Each subject council was expected to produce and publish a handbook for teachers including such items as a statement of the aims and objectives for teaching the subject and its relation to other subjects in various branches and programs; an analysis of the current Department of Education courses of study, with a suggested time allotment; an indication of the trends in the development of the courses of study and an evaluation of courses of study used in other countries; a description of various methods developed for the teaching of the subject, the areas of application of different methods, a typical lesson plan for each method, and an evaluation of the different methods; lists of commonly used reference books, films, filmstrips, records, and charts, with a statement of their source, cost, and usefulness; an indication of the use that might be made of audio-visual aids in teaching the subject; lists of available periodicals and suggestions with respect to their use in teaching the subject; an evaluation of textbooks approved by the department for the subject; an assessment of the value of notebooks and note-taking; homework assignments and methods of checking and evaluation; evaluation of the results of teaching; a bibliography of the most useful books on teaching methods; and a statement of the hallmarks of good teaching.

Some of the enthusiasts for the subject councils obviously had an exaggerated idea of what a teachers' organization could do in an area where even the financial resources of the provincial government and the school boards were not great enough to provide a program on the required scale. The transformation of provincial inspectors into program consultants a short time later, and the increasing tendency for the larger systems to employ their own consultants, soon began to make the need seem less urgent.

A second important initiative of 1964–5 was the establishment of the Ontario Secondary Education Commission. Its five members, appointed by the Provincial Executive, were expected to "initiate, stimulate, direct and co-ordinate" federation activity in the field of educational studies. Some verbal gymnastics were performad to try to define the difference between educational studies and educational research. In an article in the *Bulletin* J.D. McNabb gave an indication of the kind of activity the commission would encourage.

... teacher research will try to observe what effects a new technique has upon the standard relationships of the classroom and upon the kind and quality of pupil thinking. Attention must be directed towards understanding the central, essential principle of a new procedure and to discovering the conditions in a classroom under which this principle can be applied.[10]

One observer commented that this process bore more resemblance to the standard definition of development than to that of research.

The commission was immediately called upon to help establish the subject councils by defining their terms of reference and the areas in which they might operate and by selecting members as well as a Director of Subject Councils. In April 1965 a preliminary meeting was held with the members selected, and in July a working session was convened at the Toronto Education Centre to produce the resource booklets which had been promised. Although there were irritating delays in getting these booklets edited and printed, they were regarded as a very valuable contribution to secondary education in the province. Another promising development was the support afforded by the Ontario School Trustees' Council for the request that school boards release the subject councillors in their employ during Friday afternoons so that they could answer letters from teachers, attend subject seminars in the region, and make themselves available to teachers seeking assistance.

The commission set up committees to study three topics: the Advanced and General Level of Grade 13, the Accreditation of High Schools, and the Aims of Secondary Education in Ontario. In November a second Educational Studies Conference, to which one delegate from each district was invited, provided opportunities for discussion of the place of educational studies at the branch and district level, the priorities among studies to be pursued, and the techniques to be employed in carrying them out. The role of the district educational officer was further clarified.

In December 1965 the commission convened a conference on the problem of updating secondary school teachers. It was attended by representatives of the Department of Education, the OTF, the Ontario School Trustees' Council, seventeen universities, the colleges of education, the Association of Secondary School Superintendents, and other groups. A committee of the delegates was formed to give further consideration to the problem and to report later. The Annual Assembly passed a series of resolutions bearing on the matter: that the Ontario Secondary Education Commission assume the responsibility for updating; that the federation seek financial support for the program from the Department of Education and the school boards; that the Department of Education assume the entire financial responsibility for courses not prepared in consultation with the OSSTF; that updating courses not be held during weekends but rather in concentrated periods of intensive training, along with periodic conferences throughout the year; that the provincial government provide bursaries for all secondary school teachers who were updating themselves in their subject areas; and that the Department of Education ensure that new courses were introduced in accordance with the pace at which teachers could be retrained to teach them, and that none be introduced before adequate teaching materials had been made available for teachers and students.

The commission had been asked to ensure that it avoided duplicating the efforts of outside agencies and of various organs of the OSSTF. In the

Bulletin, October 1966, reference was made to studies and related professional activities by a number of OSSTF committees during the previous year.[11] The Teacher Training and Supply Committee had studied the staffing of the colleges of applied arts and technology, recommended provincial bursaries for teacher updating, and surveyed the reasons why teachers dropped out of the profession. The Professional Development Committee contributed to the formulation of terms of reference for the subject councils, submitted to the Provincial Executive a report reviewing the induction ceremony for new teachers, organized the annual summer workshop for district chairmen, studied the effective uses of the subject councillors at the branch and district levels, and promoted educational conferences. The Conditions of Work for Quality Teaching Committee investigated and prepared reports on pupil-teacher ratios, the effects of the Reorganized Program on work loads, and the professional obligations of department heads. The Scholarship Committee awarded about $10,000 to encourage teachers undertaking graduate studies and other projects. The Text Book Committee formed a joint committee with the Department of Education to explore avenues for improving the system of granting free textbooks. The Certification Committee suggested means of removing inequities in the certification chart, recognized new technological courses for credit for vocational teachers, reprinted the Certification Booklet and printed the certification policy in *Who's Where,* discussed with the Department of Education and the Ontario College of Education the feasibility of making appropriate upgrading courses available to occupations teachers, and asked the Provincial Executive to study the advisability of setting up an independent commission to evaluate courses required for non-academic teachers. Besides investigating the proposed general and advanced levels of study in grade 13, the Ontario Secondary School Headmasters' Council convened educational conferences, submitted comprehensive recommendations to the Department of Education outlining improvements in the format and content of curriculum bulletin HS1, and set up a study committee to investigate the administrative problems of principals in bilingual schools.

Service funds

The service funds maintained by the federation were of particular value before the establishment of the Ontario Hospital Services Insurance Plan and the Ontario Medical Services Insurance Plan, although they continued to play a useful role in the early 1970s. The Benevolent Fund was managed by a Provincial Benefit Fund Committee of five members elected at the Annual Assembly; the Fraternal Society was managed by a Board of Directors elected at the Annual Meeting of the Society; and the Sick Benefit Fund was operated by a sub-committee of the Service Funds Committee, which was governed by a constitution and regulations.

The Benevolent Fund Committee was authorized to make two kinds of awards under appropriate circumstances. A member of the OSSTF or his dependents might receive a grant of up to $500 at a time of prolonged illness, accident, or extreme emergency. In very exceptional circumstances he might receive an additional grant during the same year. A case of extreme emergency might also constitute justification for a loan. Members were warned that an emergency was a sudden development that could not have been readily foreseen or a situation over which they had little or no control, but did not include summer courses, pregnancies, moving expenses, or purchases of automobiles or household goods.

A federation member wanting protection had to apply for inclusion in the Sick Benefit Fund and pay the prescribed fees. He was eligible provided that he was an active, but not an associate or affiliate, member, and had not passed his thirty-fifth birthday, unless he was in his first year of teaching in an Ontario secondary school, in which case he was eligible up to age fifty. If he was between thirty and thirty-five, he had to submit a medical history unless, again, he was beginning teaching service. A teacher over thirty-five who was admissible also had to submit such a sheet. The conditions for re-entry after a membership lapsed were rather carefully restricted to ensure that no one took unfair advantage of the plan. There were two sections of the fund, one for men and one for women, with separate assets, contributions, and benefits. Annual contributions were made on the basis of $0.30 on each $100 of salary for men and $0.50 on each $100 for women. Benefits began on the first teaching day after the twenty days' statutory sickness allowance, and continued to a maximum of 180 days, consecutive or otherwise, in any period of 365 days, or for any one illness, within a three-year period. The amount paid was 1/300 of the yearly salary on which the contribution was made, or approximately two-thirds of one day's pay, for each teaching day the recipient was absent because of illness or accident. No benefits could be paid because of absence resulting from pregnancy or (an intriguing note) illness arising from the marital state. A period of two years had to elapse after a teacher joined the fund before he could claim benefits because of psychological illness or illness contracted in an earlier period.

Membership in the Fraternal Society was open to a federation member who made the appropriate application, paid the required contribution, and was accepted by the directors. He had to complete a medical history sheet, and might be asked to submit to a medical examination at his own expense by a medical referee appointed by the directors. As long as he did not allow his membership to lapse, he was not required to give evidence of insurability or undergo further examination. An applicant might be accepted between the ages of twenty-one and fifty, and membership lapsed at sixty-five. A member might be insured for $1,000 or any multiple of that amount up to $10,000. Payments were based on a sliding scale increasing by a specified amount for each of five age categories up to sixty-five. Under certain conditions payments might be made to members who became totally and permanently disabled from teaching, either from physical incapacity or mental disability.

Brief to the OTF Commission

In its brief to the OTF Commission the OSSTF made it clear that it expected no diminution in its own role. It claimed the unique characteristic among the affiliates of being organized according to "function," a term for which "level" might have been more appropriate, rather than on the basis of sex, language, or religion, and indicated that any reorganization in the affiliate structure might well follow functional lines. The clarity of this distinction was blurred with the establishment of high schools and classes for students whose mother tongue was French. Before this development occurred, teachers in schools where both languages were used for instruction were members of l'Association des enseignants franco-ontariens. Since these schools were elementary, there was no problem of jurisdiction with the OSSTF. With the opening of French and bilingual secondary schools, an agreement was reached on the basis that teachers in such schools who taught only French-speaking students would be members of l'Association des enseignants franco-ontariens, those who taught only English-speaking students would be members of the OSSTF, and those who taught students in both language groups might take their choice between the two federations.

The brief acknowledged a considerable amount of overlapping between the OTF and the affiliates, and called for a sharper delineation of their respective roles. It was suggested that something like the following be added to the statement of OTF policy.

Matters pertaining to the welfare and responsibilities of the teaching profession as a whole are the function of OTF. In areas wherein an official body must make representations to the Department of Education or other government body (such as proposed changes in legislation, superannuation, suspension or cancellation of certificates, and the broad structure of educational finance) OTF is responsible. Matters pertaining to the welfare and responsibilities of individual members or groups of members within an affiliate are the responsibility of the affiliates, since it is the affiliate which has immediate contact with the group or individual concerned. Matters such as teacher training, qualifications, salaries, and working conditions, should be policy matters of OTF in only the most general terms; specific policy and regulations are the responsibility of the affiliates.[12]

The OSSTF chafed at the necessity of having to take certain actions through the OTF which it considered relevant only to the needs of its own members. One of the recommendations contained in the brief was that, where an affiliate wished to make a representation to the Department of Education on such a matter, and provided that the nature of the representation was not contrary to OTF policy, the OTF need only be notified, and the formal approval of its executive need not be required.

Appraisal

During his final year of service as general secretary of the federation, I.M. Robb appraised certain trends in the organization which disturbed him. His comments were published in the *Bulletin*, February 1968.[13] He remarked first on certain effects of the rapid growth of the organization. One of these was that policy and practice were increasingly being determined on political rather than on professional grounds. Many of those who contributed to decisions had an inadequate knowledge of the professional goals of the organization and of the basis on which they had been formulated. He had been disturbed at the suggestion, made frequently during previous months, that policies be decided by referendum of the membership. He was also concerned at the inordinate amount of time being wasted at district annual meetings by eager young debaters who had little or no understanding of the issue under discussion. He thought that consideration should be given to a requirement that a member should hold at least a permanent Ontario certificate before being allowed to vote or hold office in any legislative body of the organization, whether at the district or at the provincial level.

Robb's second major concern also arose out of the rapid growth of the organization. According to a pattern of development characteristic of expanding bureaucracies, there was a tendency to reduce policy and procedures to precise and concise formulas. An attempt to apply such formulas impartially in all cases was commendable, but to apply them impersonally was not. The deficiencies of this approach were being shown particularly in the certification office and in the operation of the service funds. In Robb's words, "it is paradoxical that an organization that has developed its strength on the basis of the loyalty of individual members would now be showing signs of allowing that source of strength to erode because of the pressures to be more 'efficient' and, therefore, less personal in dealings with the membership."[14]

In the *Bulletin*, January 1969, J.M. Paton aired some incisive criticisms of the teaching profession, with particular reference to the OSSTF.[15] The main point of his article was to offer some proposals which he thought the federation, possibly the most homogeneous and the strongest association of teachers in North America, had the money, the power, and the leadership potential to adopt and implement during the next five years. He was not so sure that it had the will to take the necessary action.

Of the three responsibilities of a recognized profession to which Paton referred, the first was the obligation to serve the public good, when necessary placing the welfare of one's clients (i.e., pupils) before personal convenience and gain. In recognition of this responsibility, teachers should hesitate and think carefully before supporting resolutions about mass resignation and the closing of schools. Although extreme positions might sometimes be justified, there should be a willingness to engage in the difficult and slow process of working out institutional and procedural arrangements which would eventually make it unnecessary to take such positions.

The second responsibility of a professional was to master the specialized knowledge and intellectual skills that enabled him to make important decisions affecting the lives of his clients. While these decisions might be influenced by clinical consultation, he took personal responsibility for them. As Paton saw it, Ontario teachers were still failing to live up to the implications of this principle in terms of curriculum control. They continued to show a preference for courses of study and textbooks prescribed by the provincial authority. The federation had not adopted any curriculum policy to the effect that the principals and staffs of particular schools should have the power to decide what would be taught, and not just how it would be taught. In this sense the Hall-Dennis Committee had gone far beyond anything the federation had advocated by way of independence for teachers. Paton might have added that Ontario teachers were still in some measure prisoners of the system that enlightened members of the system were trying to get rid of.

The third responsibility of a genuine professional was to ensure that his association had the power to license and discipline its members. The association should play a major role in setting standards which would exclude those with inadequate skill and education. Paton felt that the granting of statutory membership powers, a feature which made Canadian teachers' organizations unique in the educational world, was intended to lead to the development of professional maturity. Yet a considerable group within the OSSTF was rather scornful of efforts being made by organized teachers elsewhere in Canada to play an effective and responsible part in determining the content and standards of programs of teacher education up to and including the award of a permanent certificate. OSSTF members who held these views did not look forward to the day when a united profession concerned with all levels of schooling would share power equally with other groups with a responsibility for the nature and quality of the work done in the schools, such as the Department of Education and the universities. They did not seem to share the growing conviction among other teachers' organizations that it was feasible to have a board of teacher education and certification in each province which would determine standards of admission to programs of teacher preparation and, subject to university autonomy, the content of the program. Nor were they throwing their support behind the proposal that each provincial association should eventually take over complete responsibility for awarding the permanent certificate.

THE ONTARIO ENGLISH CATHOLIC TEACHERS' ASSOCIATION

Objectives
The Ontario English Catholic Teachers' Association (OECTA) was incorporated on September 8, 1944, with the following objectives:

(a) to promote the principles of Catholic education by the study of educational problems,

(b) to work for the advancement of understanding among parents, teachers and students,

(c) to work for the moral, intellectual, religious and professional perfection of all the members,

(d) to improve the status of the teaching profession in Ontario,

(e) to secure for teachers a large voice in educational affairs.[16]

Membership
Membership was open at the time of writing to teachers in elementary schools, high schools, and colleges and universities. Statutory members included all teachers in Roman Catholic separate schools, in public elementary schools allowed by the Department of Education to operate as Catholic schools, and in dominion government schools, who were not statutory members of any other teachers' organization affiliated with the OTF. Voluntary members included certificated Catholic teachers in private schools, certificated religious community supervisors of teachers in separate schools or Catholic private schools who were not statutory members, certificated Ontario Catholic teachers on leave of absence for study, certificated teachers on the staffs of teacher training colleges, and municipal separate school superintendents, assistant superintendents, inspectors, and program consultants. There were fee-paying and non-fee-paying associate members. The first group included Ontario teachers in private schools who were not eligible for statutory or voluntary membership, Catholic teachers who were statutory members of other affiliates of the OTF, retired Catholic teachers drawing superannuation benefits, provided they were not members of school boards, certificated Ontario Catholic teachers who were temporarily unemployed, subject to the approval of the provincial executive, and Catholic teachers on leave of absence not approved by the Ontario Superannuation Commission. Associate members not subject to fees included Catholic teachers-in-training attending teachers' colleges and Catholic teachers on exchange. Associate members

could attend association meetings, conferences, and conventions, receive the *OECTA Review* and other communications, and obtain advice from the Counselling and Relations Committee. They might not, however, hold office or vote on questions affecting the finances of the association or on salary matters affecting statutory members. There was also provision for life membership and for honorary membership.

Structure

The affairs of the federation were in the hands of the Provincial Board of Directors, which consisted of 1 / the elected members of the provincial executive, 2 / the district presidents and the first, second, and third vice-presidents of the Metropolitan Toronto district, and 3 / the chairmen of standing committees, the executive director, and the deputy executive director, who did not vote. The Provincial Executive consisted of a president, an immediate past president, a first vice-president, a second vice-president, a third vice-president, a treasurer, two executive counsellors, an executive director, and a deputy executive director. Most of these officials were elected for one-year terms at the provincial annual meeting. The executive director and deputy executive director served for terms defined by their conditions of employment.

The Board of Directors was responsible for creating districts and for changing district boundaries with the concurrence of the majority of the members of the district in question. There were district executives consisting largely of elected officials and with responsibilities corresponding to those of the Provincial Executive. Among their functions they were to report to the Provincial Executive cases of alleged unprofessional conduct, of alleged unfairness of any school board within the district, or of any professional difficulties among members of a staff, and, if necessary, to work with the provincial Counselling and Relations Committee to secure settlement. At a third level was the unit, which also had an executive, and was supposed to hold at least three meetings a year.

There were twelve provincial standing committees: Awards, Counselling and Relations, Economic Policy, Finance, Legislation, Nominations, Professional Development, Resolutions, Secondary School, Secretariat, Salary Review, Superannuation, and Teacher Education. The executive might appoint special committees as necessary. Chairmen of standing committees were also members of the corresponding committees of the OTF.

Origin and early development

Considerable thought was given to the possibility of organizing the Catholic teachers of Ontario before the OECTA was actually formed. A major motive was the feeling that the contribution of such teachers was not properly appreciated, to judge by the low salaries they received. In 1917 the lay separate school teachers in Toronto organized and succeeded in obtaining pay increases of approximately 100 per cent. Another local organization of separate school teachers was established in Ottawa in 1930. The leader of that movement, Inspector F.J. McDonald, advocated the formation of a broader provincial organization. Support for the idea was secured from the church hierarchy and from inspectors of separate schools. This preliminary work provided valuable background for the organizational steps taken in 1944.

Consideration was given to the possibility of having a single organization for all Roman Catholic teachers in the province. However, there was obviously strong sentiment among English Catholic teachers for a separate federation. Majority opinion in l'Association de l'enseignement français de l'Ontario also favoured retaining the identity of the group of bilingual teachers.

The original organizational work was done largely by part-time voluntary workers. In 1949 it became feasible to appoint a full-time secretary, and other members were gradually added to the secretariat. Between 1950 and 1960 the provincial office was located in Federation House on Prince Arthur Avenue in Toronto, after which it occupied quarters in the new Federation House on Bay Street.

Professional development
For illustrative purposes, brief reference may be made to professional development activities in the mid-1960s. The report of the Professional Development Committee in 1964 indicated that there had been 10,868 participants in professional development programs during the previous year. Some of the programs were half-day or full-day Saturday sessions, ranging up to a total of ten successive sessions. The most popular subject area explored was that of the new approach to mathematics. Workshops were also held in science, reading, social studies, art, music, physical education, guidance, and testing. One district sponsored a series of lectures on communism by four eminent authorities. A weekend conference was held in Toronto to enable principals to review their leadership role. The federation produced a handbook called *Principles for Principals* to facilitate this kind of study.

A Practice Teachers' Seminar was held in 1963, with the co-operation of Department of Education officials and teachers' college staff members. A feature of the session was the teaching of lessons by student teachers, which the practice teachers present had an opportunity to appraise. Discussions involved inspectors, teachers' college masters, and principals, as well as student teachers and practice teachers.

Causes promoted
The federation has devoted itself to the strengthening of the peculiarly Roman Catholic atmosphere of the separate schools. It worked for

equality of opportunity for separate school pupils by supporting the case for more generous financial provisions, a cause that was largely won by the end of the 1960s, although some discrepancies between the public and separate school systems still remained. The federation joined with other organizations promoting the extension of the Roman Catholic separate school system to the end of grade 13. It supported the formation of larger units of administration in 1969 as a means of providing a comprehensive range of programs, with classes to meet the needs of pupils with special talents or handicaps. Its brief to the Hall-Dennis Committee stressed the need for improved teacher preparation and for better stocked libraries.

The OECTA brief to the OTF Commission advocated the continued existence of independent federations.

While we recognize that in the union of all members of the Ontario Teachers' Federation there is strength, we stress that in diversity there is a greater allowance for individuality. The strength of OTF comes from the unity not only within itself, but from that which exists among its five affiliates, each fulfilling its own purposes and serving its own members, but all striving for a common goal. However, we insist that our affiliate while co-operating whole-heartedly with the other affiliates, must retain its identity in order to fulfil the very purpose of its existence – to preserve our Catholic philosophy of education and to further the cause of Catholic education.[17]

L'ASSOCIATION DES ENSEIGNANTS FRANCO-ONTARIENS

Origin and early development

The formation of l'Association des enseignants franco-ontariens (AEFO) arose out of a meeting of the teachers' section of the Société Saint-Jean-Baptiste of Ottawa in 1936. What was at first called l'Association de l'enseignement français was founded in 1939. The aims of the association, as ultimately formulated, were to improve education for French-speaking Ontarians by upgrading the academic and professional preparation of its members, by studying the problems of education, by taking action conducive to the solution of these problems, by inculcating respect for professional obligations, and by co-operating with other affiliates of the OTF. Listed as secondary objectives were the improvement of the financial status and working conditions of the members.

Structure

In 1969 the members, numbering approximately five thousand, were located in twenty-six regions, some of which were divided into local associations. Final authority was vested in the annual assembly consisting of ninety-three delegates plus ten committee members. The Board of

Directors, which met four times a year, had forty-nine members. There were six standing committees and fourteen special committees.

Membership
Membership regulations in force in the 1960s recognized regular, associate, and voluntary members. There were two categories of regular members: 1 / any French-speaking Catholic teacher holding a teaching certificate valid in Ontario and teaching in a public or separate bilingual elementary school in Ontario; 2 / any French-Canadian Catholic teacher of secondary school courses holding a teaching certificate valid in Ontario who was not a member of the OSSTF and who was in the employ of a school board. Associate membership was open to any French-Canadian Catholic teacher who taught in an independent school at the elementary or secondary level, or who taught secondary school courses and belonged to the OSSTF, and to any inspector of bilingual elementary schools and any instructor in the University of Ottawa Teachers' College. Inspectors and teachers' college instructors were ineligible for offices except that of adviser to the executive committee. Honorary membership could be conferred by the executive provided that the decision was ratified by the general assembly. The Discipline Committee could deprive anyone of the rights and privileges of membership on the grounds of contravening the rules of the association or of working against the association's objectives. Associate members lost their membership status if they failed to pay their dues.

Relationship to other associations
The AEFO had a close association with l'Association canadienne-française d'éducation d'Ontario, which became l'Association canadienne-française de l'Ontario. It was also affiliated with l'Association canadienne des éducateurs de langue française. Its right to name ten members of the Board of Governors of the OTF did not lead to a very close relationship with other affiliates of that organization. In a report to the AEFO in December 1968, Reverend Maurice Lapointe criticized the parent organization for failing to give full recognition to the French fact. He felt that certain publications issued by the OTF should be in both French and English, and suggested that the time must come when members could use French at OTF meetings.

THE ONTARIO TEACHERS' FEDERATION

Origin and early development
Mention was made in connection with the history of the older teachers' federations in Ontario of some of the conditions prevailing in the teaching profession prior to and during the early 1940s. In 1942 only the OSSTF, with over 90 per cent of the eligible membership in its ranks, could make

a credible claim to speak for its constituency. The corresponding percentage for the OPSMTF was somewhat over 65; for the FWTAO, about 45; and for AEFO, about 35.[18] Not only did these unsatisfactory figures weaken the voice of the respective organizations in protective and professional matters, but they also indicated that the time, effort, and money spent on annual membership drives were producing something less than the desired results. The fact that membership was voluntary meant that the organized profession had no effective means of ensuring that teachers observed professional and ethical standards, to say nothing of guarding against undercutting desired minimum salaries during times of teacher surplus.

The Ontario Teachers' Council, on which the FWTAO, the OPSMTF, and the OSSTF had representation, provided for only a limited degree of co-operation. It dealt with salaries, tenure, superannuation, and teaching conditions; it maintained some contact with the Department of Education, although departmental officials did not hesitate to ignore it when they saw fit to do so; it co-operated with the Ontario Federation of Home and School Associations in sponsoring Education Week. It did not, however, represent the separate school teachers; it lacked legal status; and it had limited financial resources. It nevertheless provided a very useful basis on which to build a stronger and more comprehensive organization.

The Ontario Teachers' Council was beginning to make some headway with the Department of Education during the Hepburn regime, when it provided assistance in drawing up a draft act for circulation among the members of the three federations. By the time overwhelming approval had been registered and the council had decided to proceed, George Drew had become Premier and Minister of Education. Among Drew's conditions for support of the desired legislation was that all teachers be brought into the professional organization. As a result, council members approached some leading separate school teachers with the suggestion that they form an association. Opinion, as indicated earlier, favoured two federations of separate school teachers, one for each of the language groups. According to the report of the OTF Commission, little consideration was given at that time to the possibility of forming a single comprehensive teachers' organization.[19]

According to *The Teaching Profession Act* of 1944, the objects of the OTF were as follows:

(a) to promote and advance the cause of education;
(b) to raise the status of the teaching profession;
(c) to promote and advance the interests of teachers and to secure conditions which will make possible the best professional service;
(d) to arouse and increase public interest in educational affairs; and
(e) to co-operate with other teachers' organizations throughout the world having the same or like objects.[20]

Every teacher was to be a member of the federation, although one who was in active service when the act was passed could withdraw within six months by giving written notice to the minister.

The act provided that the federation would have a Board of Governors of not more than forty members. There was to be an executive consisting of the immediate past president, the president, the first vice-president, the second vice-president, and the secretary and treasurer. The second, third, and fourth officials in this list were to be elected annually by the Board of Governors from among its own members. The secretary and treasurer could be similarly elected or appointed from the membership of the Board of Governors or otherwise. Subject to the approval of the Lieutenant-Governor-in-Council, the board could make regulations on the following matters:

(a) prescribing a code of ethics for teachers;
(b) prescribing the fees to be paid by members of the Federation;
(c) providing for the suspension and expulsion of members from the Federation and other disciplinary measures;
(d) prescribing the manner in which the members of the Board of Governors shall be elected;
(e) providing for the holding of meetings of the Board of Governors and of the executive and prescribing the manner of calling and the notice to be given in respect of such meetings;
(f) prescribing the procedure to be followed at meetings of the Board of Governors and of the executive;
(g) providing for the payment of necessary expenses to the members of the Board of Governors and the executive;
(h) conferring powers upon or extending or restricting the powers of and prescribing the duties of the Board of Governors and of the executive;
(i) providing for the appointment of standing and special committees; and
(j) providing for the establishment of branches of the Federation or of the recognition by the Federation of local bodies, groups or associations of teachers which shall be affiliated with the Federation.[21]

The act went through the Ontario Legislature with almost no discussion and with absolutely no opposition. In very short order the five affiliated federations selected their governors, and met at the invitation of the minister under the chairmanship of J.G. Althouse, the Chief Director of Education. The next three days were spent in organizing the new federation, the structure of which remained substantially the same in succeeding years. The first president was Norman McLeod, and the first, and to the date of writing, the only, secretary-treasurer was Nora Hodgins.

In the very first year of its existence two members of the federation were appointed to serve on the Royal Commission on Education. Attention was given immediately to such matters as teachers' qualifications, salary scales, discipline, contracts, and superannuation. In its second year the organization made recommendations on adult education, curriculum, textbooks, school buildings and equipment, educational research, and radio programs. Pressure was successfully exerted to bring about the passage of legislation relating to teachers' boards of reference. Although occupancy was long delayed, the federation showed its initiative in purchasing the property at 34 Prince Arthur Avenue, Toronto, for the first Federation House.

During the early years there were various manifestations of interest in community issues. In 1948, acting through the CTF, the OTF requested that the income tax exemption for single people be raised to a minimum of $1,200 and for married people to a minimum of $2,000. Support was given the next year to federal legislation to prohibit the distribution of crime comics. In 1955 the federation registered its approval of the efforts of the Parents' Action League to induce the provincial government to compile information about the incidence of sex offences against children and about the number of persons serving sentences after conviction for such offences. The government was also being urged to establish psychiatric clinics in Toronto to serve the area.

Relations and discipline
Considerable attention was given during the organization's first year to the problem of maintaining professional ethics. Procedures also had to be devised to ensure that appropriate measures were taken against teachers or principals who were not giving satisfactory service. It was decided that consultation and advice should be provided by supervisory personnel to give offenders adequate opportunity to improve. A record was to be kept of all cases of professional difficulty brought to the attention of the OTF. The minister was asked in 1946 to grant the federation the right to be consulted in cases where complaints were made to the Department of Education before any certificate was cancelled. Although a procedure of this type was agreed to in 1947, there was dissatisfaction during the next few years over the methods used by the department in dealing with some members.

In 1959 the Board of Governors discussed the action of the department in cancelling some certificates, and expressed the view that early notice of unsatisfactory performance, along with assistance, should be given by inspectors. Reference was made to the cancellation of one certificate after the teacher had given thirty-seven and a half years of service, and to others where the period of service was over thirty years. For a time during the mid-sixties the department notified the teacher whose work was unsatisfactory, but then discontinued the practice.

Some of the most difficult cases referred to the OTF involved sexual offences against children. When an accusation was proven, cancellation of the certificate invariably followed. The federation explored the possibility of rehabilitating deviates in 1955, but no specific action was taken.

The charge that a school board refused to meet representatives of the OTF or one of its affiliates was regarded as a very serious one. In 1951 it was decided that the appropriate procedure in such a case was to declare the board not in good standing. Since the processes of conciliation were used to good effect, it was hardly ever necessary to resort to this step.

Protective concerns

Superannuation
The OTF exerted great efforts from the time of its formation to secure improved superannuation benefits for its members. The nature of the changes is discussed at some length in volume III, chapter 13, and need not be repeated here. Among the changes for which the federation claimed the most credit were improvements in the provisions for dependents, increases in minimum and maximum pensions, a reduction in the number of years used for the calculation of the pensions, and an integration with the Canada Pension Plan without loss of benefits. Assistance was given to superannuated teachers in organizing to press for more generous treatment as more favourable conditions were introduced after their retirement and as inflation reduced the value of their allowances.

Salary policy
There was a serious crisis in 1952 when the OPSMTF introduced a motion that the single salary scale be accepted as OTF policy. When the OSSTF registered solid opposition, the OTF seemed about to disintegrate. The crisis was ultimately settled when the OTF decided to abandon salary matters to the affiliates. The OSSTF won and maintained a technical victory on the issue in that it continued to insist on separate negotiations. It had no means, however, of preventing school boards from paying salaries on the basis of qualifications, experience, and responsibility, without regard to level, and thus in effect maintaining a single scale.

The OTF salary policy, as summarized in early 1969, was as follows. 1 / Under *The Teaching Profession Act* the OTF had the right to negotiate collectively for its members. This right was delegated to the affiliates and to the affiliates' members employed by a school board. Groups might combine in local councils, or in any other way they saw fit, for negotiating purposes. 2 / Each affiliate had the right to establish its own salary scale with a board. Where the members of more than one affiliate employed by one administrative body had reached an accord in salary policies, they might agree to take joint action. Salary scales should be based on qualifications, experience, and responsibility. 3 / The OTF was opposed to compulsory salary arbitration legislation, but not to voluntary conciliation or to a voluntary arbitration agreement between the parties concerned. 4 / Any conciliation in the event of salary disputes between trustees and teachers was to be in the hands of the affiliate or affiliates concerned, and in any dispute between an affiliate and a board of trustees, the OTF would take action only on the request of the provincial executive of the affiliate involved, and with the approval of all affiliates. 5 / The OTF favoured equal opportunity and equal pay for men and women with equal qualifications and responsibilities in the schools of Ontario. 6 / The OTF was opposed to provincial, regional, or zone salary scales. 7 / The OTF was opposed to any amendment to *The Municipality of Metropolitan Toronto Act* to put teachers' salaries under the jurisdiction of the Metropolitan Toronto School Board. 8 / The OTF was opposed to any system of payment of teachers according to merit rating. 9 / The OTF regarded refusal of teachers to carry out the duties defined by the regulations or *The Schools Administration Act* during the term of their contracts as strike action, and considered such action to be a breach of contract and contrary to the obligations of a teacher.

Concern with supervisory issues
Concern with supervisory matters at various stages involved the role of the inspector, his relationship with the teacher, and the form and effect of his report. A summary of opinion in 1945 indicated that teachers thought the inspector's work should be more consultative, with emphasis on constructive suggestions. Written reports were favoured, with the teacher receiving a copy. For a long time little progress was made in the attempt to achieve federation objectives. By 1965, however, it was officially agreed that inspectors in secondary schools would automatically inform teachers in writing of their rating if they fell into one of the three lowest categories, and that others would be given their ratings on request. At the same time a new rating scale was provided for elementary school teachers, and arrangements were made to notify those in the two lowest categories, with reasons for their placement there. Further changes were made a year later. As far as the Department of Education was concerned, the whole matter became rather academic when provincial inspection ceased at the end of 1968. In this way a source of considerable friction with the OTF was ended.

Legal liability of teachers relating to supervision
Certain issues of legal liability were involved in the McGonegal case shortly after the Second World War. A damage suit was brought against a teacher and a school board on behalf of a pupil who was injured in school when a gas stove exploded. The initial assessment of damages against the teacher was reversed by the Supreme Court of Canada after

a long defence undertaken by the FWTAO. The incident led the OTF to seek means to protect teachers in the performance of their duties. An issue of major concern involved the legal liability of teachers transporting pupils in connection with curricular and extra-curricular activities.

Positions taken on issues involving education

Administrative developments
The issue of class size has always been of keen concern to the organized teaching profession. An OTF motion was made in December 1944 to urge the Department of Education to limit by regulation the number of pupils in a class to a maximum of thirty-five. A similar resolution in 1950 attempted to fix the limit at thirty, and later the same year an objective of twenty-five was agreed on for grade 1. Because of the extreme teacher shortage of the 1950s, it was difficult to make much progress on the issue. There were discussions with Department of Education officials over differences in methods of calculating pupil/teacher ratios. Teachers felt that the official method did not help to protect individual teachers against excessive loads. The issue of class size entered into relations cases with certain school boards. The situation showed a continuous improvement during most of the decade of the 1960s.

Teacher recruitment and supply
Interest in the issue of teacher supply prompted the OTF executive to request an opportunity to discuss entrance to normal schools with the Chief Director of Education in 1945. This request was rebuffed with an assurance that appropriate steps were being taken to deal with the matter, but that the department's plans were not open for publication. Uneasiness over the possibility of a return to the teacher surplus of the 1930s no doubt prompted the federation to seek assurances from the minister in 1946 that the teacher training institutions would be prevented from accepting more applicants than appeared to be required. There was an expression of consternation the following year when the chief director announced that requirements for admission to normal schools would be kept at their wartime level because of a shortage of candidates. The OTF asked that school boards be prevented from hiring "permit" teachers before August 15 of any given year. In 1948 it requested that the number of permits issued be held to a minimum, and that the grant system be used to discourage the practice of seeking permits. Concern over the shortage led to support for a recruitment program in 1952. The federation encouraged teachers to assist teachers' college masters when they began to visit secondary schools in order to encourage promising candidates to enter teaching. Co-operation with the Ontario School Trustees' Council involved a study of the need for teachers and the publication of *The*

Teacher Supply in Ontario in 1957. In 1963 London was the scene of the first of a series of workshops held to improve liaison between the teachers' colleges and the teachers associated with them. Continued appeals were made to the department to increase the remuneration provided for practice teachers in elementary schools.

University involvement in teacher education
OTF relationships with the universities in connection with teacher education have involved both pre-service and in-service programs. Concern over the inadequacy of preparation in health education led to an unsuccessful request to the University of Toronto in 1954 to offer courses in the subject. The Department of Education was asked in 1958 to establish post-graduate colleges of education in other Ontario universities modeled on the Ontario College of Education. At that time the minister felt that the costs of such a step would be excessive. When a residence requirement of a minimum period of one year was established for the Doctor of Education degree in the University of Toronto in 1959, the federation appealed for a reversal of the decision on the grounds that some candidates could not obtain relief from their duties for that period of time. Again the appeal failed. A request was also made that graduate degrees in education be offered in other universities. An effort was made in the early 1960s to have the University of Toronto offer extension courses at Orillia as else turn over the responsibility to another university. Waterloo Lutheran proposed to open Simcoe College at that location, but lack of an assured source of funds continued to delay action. It was consistent OTF policy to have pre-service preparation of teachers incorporated into the universities. Unsuccessful efforts were made in the late sixties to speed the implementation of the MacLeod report. Steps were taken in 1969 to have a Teacher Education Advisory Committee set up in each district of Ontario where a university was prepared to discuss problems associated with teacher education.

Units of local administration
A further matter of continuous concern to the OTF has been the provision of units of local administration large enough to maintain schools of reasonable size. In 1945 a request was made to the department to adopt a policy of compulsory amalgamation of rural school sections. The federation did not, however, pursue the matter far enough to be able to identify the advantages to pupils or teachers. There was great interest in the same question when the government eliminated school sections in favour of the township area as of January 1, 1965. An Optimum Size Committee investigated problems associated with this development. For the most part the federation attitude continued to be favourable. A considerable amount of effort went into the preparation of a brief to the Goldenberg

Royal Commission with respect to the reorganization of Metropolitan Toronto. A consistent theme was that local interest and autonomy should be maintained and the disadvantages of excessive size avoided. The OTF position on the creation of divisional boards of education throughout the province is explored in volume II, chapter 5.

Teachers' aides
Toward the end of the 1960s there was increasing evidence that elementary school teachers felt that playground and lunchroom supervision should be handled by non-teaching personnel. A survey revealed that very little clerical help was provided in most schools. A committee recommended that paraprofessionals, to be called "educational resource technicians," be employed for noon and after-school supervision and for clerical and technical duties. A request was made to the Department of Education to assist school boards through the grant structure to employ these technicians. Proposals were made for a liaison committee to work with the Department of Education and the colleges of applied arts and technology on the preparation of suitable courses.

Integration of the elementary and secondary school levels
Because of the varying interests of its affiliates, the OTF was forced to maintain a cautious policy with respect to the integration of the elementary and secondary school levels. When North York established a three-level system in 1956, dissatisfaction was expressed, not over the educational consequences of such a move, but over the lack of prior consultation with teachers. Cautious support for some measure of integration might be read into the establishment of a committee in 1962 to study existing guidance practices and to make recommendations relating to the co-ordination of efforts between elementary and secondary schools. An Integration Committee of the OTF was established in 1967, but little progress was made.

The status of women
While occasionally taking a position in favour of equal treatment for men and women, the OTF avoided militant stands on the issue. It did not, for example, make a presentation to the Royal Commission on the Status of Women in Canada. On the other hand, it attempted to persuade the Department of National Defence to drop certain discriminatory policies in schools under its control: for example, women over forty years of age were ineligible for appointment in these schools, while men might serve up to the age of sixty; also, a married woman could be appointed only if her husband was a teacher, while there was no such restriction on a male teacher. Protests to the Minister of National Defence, approved by the Board of Governors in 1966 and 1967, were unsuccessful.

School buildings

As early as 1949 the OTF set up a School Buildings Committee as an expression of concern that many new schools were being constructed with undesirable architectural features. While this committee considered good and bad aspects of design, Department of Education requirements, design of buildings for community use, teacher participation in planning schools, and the development of OTF policy on school design, activities did not get beyond the discussion stage. A School Architecture Committee, later called the OTF School Planning and Building Research Committee, was established in 1961. It concentrated on specific problems, appealing to the Department of Education in 1965, for example, to provide grants for adequate lunch facilities in schools where large numbers of pupils remained at school during lunch hour. OTF representatives participated in the conference on school design called by the minister in 1963. The federation maintained liaison with the Division of School Planning and Building Research established as a result of this conference, and continued to express its concern over various aspects of the learning environment.

Grade 13

By 1964 dissatisfaction with the grade 13 departmental examination system led to the establishment of a departmental Grade 13 Study Committee. In the same year the OTF set up a similar committee for comparable purposes. One of its recommendations was that the school year should be lengthened by restoring examinations to the latter part of June. Another was that more markers be hired in order to get the results ready in time for consideration by the universities. The department was asked to restore the August supplemental examinations to provide an additional opportunity for students who had failed up to two subjects or who needed to improve their standing to gain admission to university. It cannot be said that these recommendations showed a very keen perception of the problems then being faced by the department.

As a means of counteracting the rigidity of the grade 13 program, the OTF advocated a wider choice of questions on the examinations and an opportunity for students to spend 25 per cent of their time on independent work. Approval was given to the proposal of the departmental committee to offer subjects at the general and advanced levels. The OTF pointed out, however, that the scheme would involve difficulties in staffing in small high schools and in upgrading teachers' qualifications so that they could handle the advanced work. Briefs to the relevant departmental committees urged that 25 per cent of the final mark for the year be based on teachers' appraisals of the year's work.

Indian and Eskimo education

As early as 1960 the Board of Governors set up a study committee to consider the educational problems of Indian and Eskimo children. In 1967 pressure was brought to bear through the CTF for special preparation for teachers of Indians, Métis, and Eskimos. The OTF recommended pre-school programs to offset language and other handicaps, as well as a curriculum designed to support valuable aspects of the aboriginal cultures and to assist the children to integrate more effectively into the society of the majority of Canadians. It was also recommended that Indians, Métis, and Eskimos be more deeply involved in decisions about the education of their children.

Educational television
Suggestions and recommendations on the subject of educational television were particularly numerous before 1965, when the Department of Education began to involve itself on a large scale. In 1964 the appropriate organs of the OTF suggested that plans might be made for the next five years with respect to budget and the number of programs. It seemed reasonable that the production of programs of good quality might be undertaken by the following year. The view was expressed that programs should correlate with the course of study and bring to the classroom an enriched experience beyond what the teacher could provide. Teachers wanted a high standard adopted and enforced so that they could rely on the quality of programs.[22]

Some suggestions were of a general and rather platitudinous type, while others were quite specific. There were examples of both in a list emanating from the Committee on Teacher Training, presented here in abbreviated form. 1 / Senior officials must be enthusiastic about the use of educational television and must demonstrate their interest when visiting classrooms. 2 / The principal must show the same attitude and must co-operate by timetabling to ensure the use of the medium. 3 / Each school should have an enthusiastic teacher to look after the equipment and ensure the availability of sets when required for classroom use. 4 / There should be enough sets to enable all pupils at a particular grade level to view a program at the same time. 5 / Programs must meet a need felt in the classroom. 6 / The teachers' manual should be issued early enough to enable the principal to timetable the broadcasts and to permit the teacher to plan for their use. 7 / A larger, more meaningful, and more colourful teachers' manual should be produced. 8 / Participation of teachers should be encouraged by full OTF support. 9 / More in-service training workshops should be held to arouse teachers' interest and increase their confidence.[23]

As the Department of Education flung itself vigorously into the production of programs and attempted to develop better means for their dissemination, OTF interest continued. A desire for strong teacher influence on the proposed Ontario Educational Communications Authority was indicated in 1968–9 when the Board of Governors and the Educational Media Committee expressed concern about receiving so little information about the agency. The board asked that the OTF be represented on the planning body, and that at least one-third of the governing body of the authority be from their membership.

Participation in curriculum development
and related activities
OTF interest in the development of curriculum, textbooks, materials, and resources fluctuated over the years. The work was done on a part-time basis, mostly by teachers with full-time duties putting in extra time during weekends. They were handicapped by a lack of resources, and had limited opportunities to develop and experiment with new materials and methods. They nevertheless managed to exert considerable influence.

Committees were particularly active during the period when the Royal Commission on Education was preparing its report. In 1948 the OTF received the Greer Memorial Fund award for its research work in the area of curriculum. Reports on several subject areas were prepared and presented to the Department of Education. Because some of these reports advocated more detailed course prescriptions, specific textbooks, handbooks, and teaching aids, they were regarded by departmental officials as disappointing and reactionary. In 1950 an effort was made to evaluate products on the market and to prepare reference lists for teachers. Educational films were screened for suitability and listed. Recommendations were made to the Department of Education with respect to textbooks, and appeals were made for library books and for better school libraries. The OTF co-operated with the Ontario Library Association in the 1960s in preparing a set of standards for school libraries and in publishing them. A research project on programmed learning materials was undertaken in conjunction with the Scarborough Board of Education.

Because of its composition the OTF had to avoid involvement in issues relating to religious education. It did not make any presentations to the Committee on Religious Education in the Public Schools of the Province of Ontario (the Mackay Committee), although some of the affiliated federations did so. Positions on the moral implications of certain instructional materials were sometimes taken.

The OTF set up a Committee on Mathematics and Science which, in early 1957, expressed serious concern over the shortage of teachers in these two fields, the inadequacies of teacher preparation, and the lack of satisfactory textbooks. As a result the executive arranged in 1959 for the establishment of the Ontario Mathematics Commission, which included representatives from elementary and secondary schools, the universities, the Department of Education, and the Ontario College of Education, and budgeted $10,000 for its support. The commission became an independent body in 1960, but continued to receive a substantial part of its financial support, as well as office space during its early years, from the federation. Materials were produced, first for the secondary schools and then for the elementary level. Summer courses were offered to acquaint teachers with the new mathematics, and information was disseminated beginning in 1962 through the *Ontario Mathematics Gazette*.

A science committee set up in 1960 found that there were serious inadequacies in this field in philosophy, content, presentation, and preparation of teachers. The committee offered a one-week seminar in August 1961 in an effort to develop a better arrangement of topics from grade 1 to grade 13, and to provide for the development of science concepts based on scientific principles. A natural science seminar in the summer of 1963 offered guidance to teachers in making use of the out-of-doors in science teaching. This event was the forerunner of several weekend seminars offered annually for teachers. The curriculum guide, *Science Units K-6*, published in 1966, encouraged the use of the discovery method.

Similar activities were carried out in a variety of other fields, including English, reading, health and physical education, and French. These had varying amounts of influence on departmental policy. The importance of federation initiatives was greatest at times when the department was relatively quiescent.

Involvement with other organizations

Educational research organizations
The OTF consistently demonstrated interest in and support for educational research at the national and provincial levels. While the need for a national body was recognized at an early stage, the OTF Board of Governors felt that it was beyond the capacity of the teachers' organizations to maintain it on their own. Support was given through the CTF to the National Advisory Committee on Educational Research during the 1950s, and to the establishment of the Canadian Council for Research in Education in 1961. At the provincial level the OTF was the prime mover in the establishment of the Ontario Educational Research Council in 1958. This action followed rejection of the proposal that the federation itself should appoint a research director. The OTF continued throughout the 1960s as the main financial supporter of the Ontario Educational Research Council. Some prominent OTF members felt that the federation itself should have been engaging more actively in research activities.

The Canadian College of Teachers
The OTF considered a preliminary proposal for the establishment of the Canadian College of Teachers in 1955. When the concept was formally endorsed in 1957, the hope was expressed that control of the college would remain in the hands of professional teachers. After the college was

formally established in 1958, numbers of Ontario teachers became members. The organization was closely linked with the CTF until 1965, when it became a separate body.

The Canadian and Ontario Conferences on Education
Through the CTF the OTF gave active support to the proposal to hold the first Canadian Conference on Education in 1958. Federation delegates attended and participated in the discussions. At the conclusion of the conference the OTF gave general approval to the thirty-one resolutions that were passed without, however, adopting them as policy. It opposed the idea of making the conference a continuing organization which would involve itself in matters of provincial concern, and took a firm stand against the establishment of provincial chapters or education councils of the Canadian Conference on Education. The second conference, held in 1962, again had active federation support.

The Ontario Conference on Education, held in Windsor in 1961, represented a kind of preliminary to the Canadian Conference a short time later, as well as being a very significant event in its own right. It was a co-operative venture on the part of the Ontario Association for Curriculum Development and the OTF designed to explore the purposes and problems of Ontario education and to improve communication among the groups and individuals in and responsible for education in the province. Of approximately one thousand participants, about half were teachers sponsored by the OTF or one of its affiliates. Topics explored by representatives of the whole educational community and the public ranged from the provision of different curricula for different types of learners at various levels, through teacher preparation and responsibility, to means of organizing and financing education.

Briefs to committees and commissions

The Select Committee on Youth
An OTF brief to the Select Committee on Youth of the Ontario Legislature recommended 1 / the provision of more facilities for further education beyond the four-year program of the Robarts Plan (a need that was soon met by the colleges of applied arts and technology), 2 / greater flexibility in school programs, 3 / the extension of special education programs for slow learners, deaf children, emotionally disturbed children, and others, to all parts of the province, 4 / the extension of guidance services to include social and personal counselling as well as guidance in academic matters, 5 / the introduction of work-study programs, 6 / improved liaison between the schools and the family and juvenile courts, and 7 / better co-ordination of social agencies involved in the treatment of delinquents and their return to school.[24]

The Provincial Committee on Aims and Objectives
When the Provincial Committee on Aims and Objectives was being set up, the OTF submitted the names of five of its members to the minister for possible appointment. Curriculum committees submitted five briefs and made presentations to the committee on three different occasions. Emphasis was placed on the need for education to develop the personal potential of each pupil, to develop ethical, moral, and social values, to foster adaptability in a rapidly changing world, and to produce intellectual commitment to responsible citizenship.

The Ontario Teachers' Federation Centennial Library
The Ontario Teachers' Federation Centennial Library, established as an OTF centennial project, began with the purchase of an original collection of 3,500 books from H. Douglass, a secondary school art teacher in Guelph. Additions were made in the form of school texts, reference books, pamphlets, magazines, and school artifacts from the early days of public education in Ontario. Appeals were made for donations of materials that were in danger of being destroyed as older school buildings were replaced by new structures. The collection included documents of value to reseachers as well as items that might be read purely for enjoyment.

Relations with successive Ministers of Education
Relations with successive ministers varied from cordial co-operation to open atagonism. The OTF of course owed its existence to *The Teaching Profession Act*, passed through action taken by George Drew. As a result Drew was always regarded as a friend of the teachers. Liaison with his successor, Dana Porter, was good, but there was dissatisfaction over the fact that he did not consult the federation before announcing the curriculum changes embodied in the Porter Plan. The Dunlop regime represented a low point in department-federation relations, and conflict became public through press releases issued by both sides. The federation objected to being excluded from the process of planning the two-year program for the training of elementary school teachers, and took exception to the minister's optimistic statements about the teacher shortage and about the effect of emergency courses on the quality of education being provided in the schools. At one stage Dunlop agreed to set up committees with the OTF to explore the teacher shortage, but later reversed his decision. The federation unsuccessfully took issue with the decision to build a new Toronto Teachers' College on the old site rather than in proximity to the University of Toronto campus.

A new era began with the appointment of J.P. Robarts in 1959. However, although Robarts established amicable relations, he did not consult the OTF to any great extent. There was considerable dissatisfaction when the Reorganized Program was introduced without discussion in advance. The development of what might be called a close working relationship awaited the appointment of William G. Davis in 1962. In accordance with the provision of *The Teaching Profession Act*, Davis began to make a practice of attending some meetings of the Board of Governors and taking part in its discussions. He engaged in regular consultation with OTF representatives on matters such as superannuation, boards of reference, the role of school inspectors, and many others. In 1963 it was agreed that the Department of Education would give the OTF prior notice of contemplated changes in the regulations affecting teachers. The OTF would have a role in the selection of members to serve on curriculum committees, and would participate in special ministers' committees. Consultations involving the minister, his officials, and the OTF executive took place about ten times a year. Agenda items were submitted by each side in advance, and discussion was frank and thorough.

Appraisals of the OTF

Comments of the Provincial Committee
on Aims and Objectives
The Hall-Dennis Committee thought that the existing pattern of teachers' organizations was inadequate to meet the demands of an up-to-date unified system of education.

While the central organization has had many achievements, the special interests of the various affiliates have often remained paramount, and these groups have not submerged their individual loyalties for the common good of education. The one reason that the separate groups have been able to act as effectively as they have is that the educational system itself was stratified, with the various affiliates representing the teachers of different divisions. The Committees advocates a unified system of education from K to 12. In the face of this, it is hoped that the Federation and its affiliates will re-evaluate their present organization. It is difficult to visualize the complete and successful integration of the present elementary and secondary levels by teachers whose loyalty is to a specific division or level. A unified federation will be essential if the professional organization is to assume a position of leadership in the new curriculum.

The OTF Commission
An OTF Commission was established in response to a resolution passed by the Board of Governors at the Annual Meeting in 1965. The resolution indicated that it should consist of five members, one from each affiliate, with the power to select their own chairman and co-opt other members. The commission was asked to make recommendations on the

structure of the OTF, its functions, its relationship with its affiliates, and the co-ordination of internal operations. The last of these four objectives reflected claims, heard repeatedly over a period of years, that there was duplication of services resulting in excessive costs.

The OTF Commission observed that the particular affiliate structure in existence at the time of its investigation was inconsistent with other policies accepted by the federation. It was in conflict with the trend toward integration of the curriculum from grade 1 to grade 12 or 13. It was also said to be inconsistent with the policy that there should be no discrimination on the basis of grade taught or on the basis of sex. Since there was no discussion of the affiliate structure recorded in the minutes, it appeared that the matter was either of no interest or considered too dangerous to tackle.

The argument against curtailing or eliminating the autonomy of the affiliates was also presented effectively in the report of the commission.

... there is an underlying theme that the Federation must present an image of power, unity and harmony. Again, it seems that this image of harmony is related to the feeling that it is the main source of strength for the Federation today, as it was in 1944. However, the implication of 80,000 members in agreement is that there must be latent conflict. Further, when harmony takes on the character of being the main goal, innovations and new ideas are often discouraged. It is very likely, in fact, that this is a factor contributing to membership apathy. At least one Governor, in commenting upon the lack of free discussion in the Board of Governors' meetings, complained of the tendency of the members to come to the meetings "with a closed mind and a directed vote". If this is the case at the Board of Governors level, the chances are great that the membership is also discouraged from expressing its opinions.[25]

Those in leadership roles in the existing affiliates felt for the most part that the system had worked well in the past, and were reasonably satisfied with the status quo, although they thought the federation should be strengthened. On the other hand, a survey of teacher opinion indicated that the majority of teachers favoured a single organization in preference to the affiliate structure. Further, many people who were not directly associated with the OTF believed that teachers should be represented through one organization.

In its examination of the possibility of integrating and improving the efficiency of internal services, the commission did not make any very promising discoveries. With respect to telephone services, for example, the affiliates had different types of installations, and felt that their needs differed. Each affiliate preferred to retain control of its own mailing facilities because of the necessity for direct and speedy contact with large sections of the membership. There was fear that the effectiveness of communication would suffer in a combined operation. Much the same attitude was discovered with reference to data processing. The commission concluded that for the time being there was no point in making further efforts to co-ordinate and combine internal services.

The commission commented on a number of important educational issues which had elicited little evidence of OTF interest over the years. The federation, it said, tended to avoid co-operation with external agencies such as the CTF. It had offered no more realistic solution to the shortage of teachers than that of eliminating "undesirable" students. There was little sign of concern over the French-English problem, and no record of an effort to have French introduced into the elementary grades. There had been no discussion of the fact that a relatively small percentage of young people had been able to go to university. Except for studies made by the FWTAO, there had been little attention to the problems of rural areas. The minutes did not indicate any special efforts to accommodate the large number of immigrants during the 1950s, although concern had been expressed about allowing those who had lived under totalitarian regimes to teach in Ontario. There had been no discussion of the role industry did and could play in education. Since the utilitarian aspects of education had been considered less respectable than the study of arts and letters, vocational and commercial courses had been regarded as inferior and, by association, those who taught such courses, or studied them, had also been looked upon in the same light. Many of the forces of change leading to a more democratic educational system had been generated by urbanization and industrialization rather than by the federation. The fact that the staffs of the colleges of applied arts and technology expressed no interest in joining the federation could be partly explained by the fact that the federation had done nothing to encourage their development.

The commission researcher found that the principle of confidentiality appeared to be an important aspect of the proceedings of the Board of Governors. While this approach might produce the illusion of a united front, it was even more likely to discourage free discussion among the governors and apathy among the members. Since it concealed sources of disunity within the profession, it was likely to result in a deterioration in the situation. A failure to deal openly with controversial issues was said to be inconsistent with OTF criticism of the CTF and the Department of Education for failing to provide for adequate communication and for the expression of OTF opinion.

The commission recommended an increase in the powers of the OTF in relation to the affiliates, involving the retention of more money and the establishment of a presence at all levels. This change would be brought about in part by defining more clearly the areas of responsibility in the central office and by relating them more closely to the various interests and activities of the OTF and its committees. Four areas of activity or departments were proposed: Professional Development, Membership Services, Information, and Administration. Under the general supervision of the secretary-treasurer, these departments would be the responsibility of three associate secretaries and an associate treasurer. Five assistant secretaries might be needed in the Professional Development Department to work with teacher committees and perform other services in the following respective areas: 1 / working conditions, organization of schools, educational facilities, community use of educational facilities, and related matters; 2 / teacher education and certification; 3 / research; 4 / such aspects of curriculum as development, planning, and co-ordination; and 5 / other aspects of curriculum, such as materials, resources, and methods. Three assistant secretaries in the Membership Services Department might deal respectively with 1 / salaries, educational finance, and superannuation; 2 / legislation and related matters; and 3 / counselling and relations, contracts and tenure, and a transfer review board, should one be established. The Information Department might have an associate secretary in charge of public relations and an editor in charge of publications. In the Administration Department the associate treasurer should be responsible for investment, finance, and budget control. One assistant might deal with office management, personnel, mailing procedures, records, facilities, and maintenance, while a second might handle fee collections and computer operations.[26]

The policy of permitting the president of the OTF to be released from his teaching duties and, if necessary, to move his residence to Toronto seemed to the commission to be a good one. This arrangement allowed him to take advantage of the *ex officio* relationship he had to all committees and, even more important, to represent and speak for the federation to the members at large at educational functions and through the news media.

The commission had reached the conclusion that the standing committees as delineated by *The Teaching Profession Act* were inadequate to meet current needs. The setting up of special committees, often on the spur of the moment, did not seem to offer a satisfactory solution. A reorganized system was therefore recommended. In the area of professional development there would be an Educational Innovations Committee, a Working Conditions Committee, a Continuing Education of Teachers Committee, a Teacher Recruitment, Preparation and Certification Committee, and a Bilingualism and Biculturalism Committee. In the area of membership services, there would be a Legislation Committee, a Superannuation Committee, an Educational Finance Committee, a Relations and Discipline Committee, a Status of Women Committee, and a Salary Policy Committee. The committees corresponding to the other two central departments would be an Information and Publicity Committee and a Budget and Investment Committee. Fairly detailed terms of reference were formulated for each of these committees. The commission regarded service on committees as the best single means of ensuring the participation of members in and knowledge of the OTF's activities and policy making within the organization.

As a means of bringing the federation closer to its members, the commission proposed that there be five regional offices, which might differ in their operations according to local needs. Each region might have a regional secretary in charge, with status comparable to that of a provincial associate secretary, and an appropriate office staff. Each region would decide what committees to set up in the light of local interests and problems. It would be important to keep the regional offices informed of the progress and work of provincial committees.

THE CANADIAN TEACHERS' FEDERATION

Purposes
According to a constitutional statement valid in the 1960s, the CTF pursued the following goals:

To obtain co-operation and co-ordination of all provincial teachers' organizations upon policies and activities of common interest, and in particular, but without restricting the generality of the foregoing:
(1) to provide means for the ready exchange of information of mutual interest to those engaged in the teaching profession;
(2) to improve the social and economic well-being of those engaged in the teaching profession;
(3) to encourage the exchange of teachers and students in Canada and between Canada and other countries;
(4) to stimulate interest in and seek to give leadership in matters which tend to foster a national outlook;
(5) to foster good will and mutual understanding between those engaged in the teaching profession in Canada and other countries;
(6) to co-operate with governments and to co-operate or affiliate with public organizations, societies, institutions and others in furtherance of the purposes set forth above;
(7) to accept and receive gifts, bequests, donations and endowments, designed to further the purposes set forth above.[27]

Origin and early development
The formation of the CTF in 1920 followed on the heels of the establishment of the FWTAO, the OSSTF, and the OPSMTF in Ontario.[28] It would appear that the creation of a national organization at this time owed a good deal to the altruistic impulses of its potential members, since there was little of evident value to be gained in the struggle for better salaries

and working conditions and for security of tenure, all of which had to be won through provincial action. In fact the idea of establishing a Canada-wide organization seems to have been almost an after-thought, since the original meeting, held in 1919, was intended to involve only the federations in the four western provinces.

Credit for initiating the original meeting has been given to H. Charlesworth of British Columbia, with major assistance from J. Barnett of Alberta. The presence of two delegates from eastern Canada apparently had a good deal to do with diverting the original plan toward the formation of a national rather than a regional organization. In the beginning each provincial association paid a flat fee of $100 a year, with the three Ontario federations counted as one for this purpose. In 1922 a per capita fee was substituted, and in 1924 a compromise arrangement was made by which each affiliate paid $0.50 per member for the first 1,500 members and $0.25 per member for the next 1,000 members, up to a maximum of $1,000.

The organization of the CTF took definite form with the adoption of a constitution in 1927. This document provided for an annual assembly of delegates appointed by the affiliated provincial organizations. Each province, regardless of its number of members, had the same number of delegates and the same voting power. The constitution provided for four elected officers and an executive committee consisting of the officers and a representative of each province. The executive was empowered to take action between annual meetings, although there was no great number of major matters requiring hasty decisions.

At the very first meeting those present placed themselves on record with respect to a number of issues. They favoured having teacher representatives acting as advisers to school boards, the introduction of superannuation plans for teachers, cumulative sick leave with pay, the establishment of arbitration boards, and the formulation and enforcement of provincial codes of ethics. They were opposed to short teacher training courses and the issuing of letters of permission to unqualified teachers. They agreed that the CTF should give the strongest possible support to provincial campaigns for the improvement of salaries.[29]

During the twenties the tendency for the teacher shortage to turn into a surplus kept the attention of the CTF, as well as that of the provincial organizations, focused on protective measures. The general lack of security of tenure enabled many boards to dismiss experienced and qualified teachers in favour of those who had little to commend them except that they were willing to teach for less. Aside from whatever moral force the CTF could generate, however, effective action by the national association was severely limited in view of the completeness of provincial and local control over schools. The CTF did manage to slow the importation of teachers from other provinces to some of the western provinces where boards were determined to undercut the minimum salaries that the teachers' organizations were trying to maintain. This objective was mainly achieved by appeals to conscience and professional solidarity and by improved communication.

Early CTF attempts to mobilize the full strength of the teaching forces in various provinces behind local groups fighting for worthy causes had rather spotty results. A resolution passed in 1921 constituted a kind of assurance that certain groups in British Columbia and Alberta would be reimbursed for losses sustained through conflicts with their school boards. The executive was, however, left to devise a method of raising the necessary money. After some dispute it was decided that a fund would be created for the purpose by voluntary contributions from the affiliates. Eventually a modest amount of assistance was provided to the groups that had been promised relief. This type of activity never proved to be a very strong feature of the CTF program.

Somewhat more successful were efforts to deal with school boards considered guilty of engaging in unfair practices. At the annual meeting in 1922, for example, a resolution was passed censuring the school board in Brandon for dismissing all its teachers with a month's notice and offering new contracts at reduced salaries. When the board refused to submit the matter to an independent arbitration board, the teachers withheld their services. The CTF helped to prevent its members in Manitoba and other provinces from accepting positions with the censured board, and also assisted the teachers to obtain positions elsewhere. The result was considered highly favourable from the teachers' point of view. A similar situation developed a short time later in Alberta, and received the same kind of support from the CTF.[30]

During the early years of CTF activity provincial affiliates were relied upon to act in certain respects as committees of the national organization. In this capacity the Saskatchewan Teachers' Alliance produced a model agreement between teachers and school boards, and later drafted sample legislation that would ensure security of tenure for teachers. Affiliates in a number of other provinces found these contributions helpful in dealing with their own problems. The British Columbia Teachers' Federation performed services of similar value in the field of pensions. The meetings held under CTF auspices ensured that the results of provincial efforts would be communicated to teachers across the country.

During the late twenties and early thirties the federation settled into a passive role with respect to protective activities. These consisted of emergency assistance to affiliates, direct approaches to the federal government on behalf of one or more affiliates, the compilation of relevant information, and the passing of hortatory resolutions at annual meetings. The resolutions were judged to have been relatively ineffective in strengthening the affiliates. Attention came to be concentrated mainly on non-protective matters, which the federation was in a much better position to promote.[31]

Standards of training and certification received a good deal of attention during the 1920s. A resolution was passed in 1921 favouring four years of high school and two years of professional training as a minimum for admission to teaching. An abortive attempt was made to have a committee study the question of certification for school principals. There were sporadic efforts to have the CTF exert influence in favour of national certification, but such an idea never won the support of a majority in the organization. The possibility of having interprovincial recognition of teaching certificates had more appeal, although the cause was not pursued vigorously or successfully.

The CTF demonstrated an interest in teacher exchange that proved to be of long standing. It helped to persuade the Overseas Education League to arrange for interprovincial exchanges to supplement those among various countries of the British Empire. Another evidence of interest in non-protective activities was demonstrated by contacts with the National Union of Teachers of England and Wales and by the establishment of affiliation with the World Federation of Education Associations. The latter body met in Toronto in 1927, when the CTF was persuaded to conduct a world survey of teacher tenure, training, certification, and exchange.

Resolutions passed up to the end of the 1930s indicated federation support for a number of worthy causes in the areas of curriculum and school services. For example, the development of Canadian literature, art, and music were supported and their use in Canadian schools was recommended. Approval was expressed for French instruction, medical-dental clinics, nursing for school children, free education up to the normal school level, larger school administrative units, national scholarships, and teacher exchange with the United States. These resolutions remained for the most part indications of constructive professional attitudes rather than providing the basis for positive action. More definite results followed a display of interest in audio-visual developments when the CTF established a committee to work with the CBC to determine the best types of radio programs for school children. In the general areas of public relations a contribution was made in the form of support for the Canadian Education Week movement. This event was first celebrated in Canada in 1936.[32]

During the thirties a good deal of interest was shown in surveys and analyses in such areas as salary schedules, teacher training, and educational finance. Provincial affiliates were urged to undertake certain research tasks, and to make the findings available generally. A recommendation was made by the British Columbia Teachers' Federation in 1934 that an educational research and statistical bureau be set up. For the next three years a voluntary, part-time bureau was maintained in British Columbia, whereupon it was moved to Ottawa to facilitate co-operation with the Dominion Bureau of Statistics.

During its early years the CTF consistently advocated a larger role for the federal government in supporting education. It repeatedly urged the establishment of a federal office of education. In a brief to the Royal

Commission on Dominion-Provincial Relations in 1938, it recommended an extension of the work of the Education Division of the Dominion Bureau of Statistics and a federal subsidy to help produce a better balance of resources for the support of education throughout the country. Although no permanent success in obtaining federal subsidies was achieved, the federation was instrumental in persuading the federal government to provide special assistance to Saskatchewan, which was especially hard hit by the depression, aggravated by years of drought. Credit for this achievement was given largely to A.C. Lewis, president in 1937, and to the secretary-treasurer, C.N. Crutchfield.[33]

In many ways the story of the CTF during the Second World War was similar to that of its affiliates. It naturally encouraged teachers to play whatever part they could in the war effort. It was unable to prevent the development of a serious shortage of teachers or to do much to help raise salaries from the extremely low levels to which they had fallen during the depression. The great increase in the powers of the federal government at this time tended to enhance the importance of the federation as a national body which could make some claim to speak for teachers throughout the country. During this period some of the main areas of CTF concern were finance, research and statistical services, audio-visual media, and public relations. While international activities were naturally restricted, the important decision was made to support the formation of the World Organization of the Teaching Profession.

The CTF had begun with affiliates in five provinces. In subsequent years other organizations were added until, in the immediate post-war period, only the French-speaking teachers of Quebec and the rudimentary associations in the territories remained outside. Largely because of a lack of clearcut definitions of their respective roles, there was increasing conflict between the CTF and certain affiliates. Officials in the affiliates, where almost the entire responsibility for protective measures had come to rest, tended to regard the national organization as excessively pretentious, particularly after it became incorporated in 1946 and acquired a full-time staff.

The Croskery era

A CTF office was officially opened in January 1948 in the Ottawa Normal School. The new secretary-treasurer, George Croskery, initiated a period of vigorous activity, and one with a considerable element of controversy. One of the major developments of this era was the establishment of a Research Division, with the appointment of a research director becoming effective in 1953. Funds were sufficiently abundant to make possible the addition of an executive assistant in 1955. Croskery supplied a great deal of the initiative and energy that resulted in a successful first Canadian Conference on Education in 1958, which he directed on a part-time basis. Activities connected with this event led to further additions to the regular staff. One of the major innovations of the period of Croskery's service was the introduction of the CTF practice of paying the expenses of its own committees, and thus of relying less on the affiliates. Committees were formed to deal with matters such as federal aid, pensions, films, audio-visual media and radio and television broadcasting, publications, international relations, and research.[34]

The OTF played a particularly active role in enlarging the research interest of the national organization. This type of activity was seen as more appropriate than protective measures, which the provincial federations had well in hand. As a means of determining the most suitable approach, the CTF and the CEA jointly studied the possibility of establishing a new council for educational research. In 1952 the committee recommended that each organization continue its own research program, but that all co-operate by setting up a National Advisory Committee on Educational Research. The new committee was established in 1952, with most of its secretarial work being done by the CTF.

Under successive research directors, J.D. Ayers and F.G. Robinson, a wide-ranging program was undertaken. Despite interest in the conduct of pure research repeatedly expressed by members of the board of directors, most of the projects were of a practical nature. Among matters that received early attention were school broadcasting, educational finance, and teacher influence on the curriculum.

Production of the *C.T.F. News Letter* began while C.N. Crutchfield was secretary-treasurer. At first it concentrated on providing information about federation activities, but Croskery preferred to stress ideas and comment on educational issues. An attempt to develop the publication into a full-blown educational journal and to mail it directly to members was beaten back by the affiliates, some of which feared that they would be weakened if they were bypassed in this way. The news letter was therefore distributed in bulk to the affiliates for transmittal to their members. This procedure did not prove to be very satisfactory and, as production costs increased, the number of copies printed was drastically reduced.

One of Croskery's initiatives resulted in the establishment of the Canadian College of Teachers in 1957. This body was intended to be a learned society operating within the teaching profession. The first council of the college was appointed by the CTF in 1958 and subsequently, except for three federation appointees, the members were elected. Annual meetings of the Canadian College of Teachers were held in conjunction with those of the CTF for economy and convenience. The college has hardly had the kind of impact on Canadian education that its founders apparently hoped.

Activities in the 1960s

In material prepared for the second Canadian Conference on Education in 1962, the CTF was reported to be engaged in eleven chief functions.

1 / It acted as a clearinghouse, collecting and disseminating information about the activities of its eleven affiliated provincial organizations and about national and international organizations concerned with education. 2 / Its Information Service answered an average of one hundred inquiries a month. 3 / Its Research Division, consisting at that time of a director, a research assistant, and two clerk stenographers, conducted research, provided encouragement and assistance to those in the affiliates undertaking research, and maintained liaison with other bodies involved in this type of activity both inside and outside Canada. 4 / Its consultative service helped the affiliates to prepare briefs and to study salaries, pensions, working conditions, curriculum, finance, and other such matters. 5 / It conducted seminars, workshops, and conferences to facilitate the exchange of ideas among provinces and among different educational levels. 6 / It published reports, bulletins, and studies based on material from its Research Division and General Office, contributed articles to provincial teachers' magazines, and circulated a newsletter four times a year. 7 / It represented Canadian teachers in dealings with other national agencies. For example, it participated in the CBC National Advisory Council on School Broadcasting and Television, the CEA–NFB Advisory Committee on Educational Films and Filmstrips, the Canadian Council for Research in Education, the United Nations Association of Canada, the Canadian National Commission for UNESCO, the External Aid Office Advisory Committee on Teacher Training and Supply, the Council of the Health League of Canada, the Canadian Citizenship Council, the Canadian Association for Adult Education, and several committees of the Canadian Conference on Education. 8 / It dealt with the federal government on its own behalf and as a representative of the affiliates over such matters as assistance to education, UNESCO affairs, Canadian assistance to Commonwealth and other countries, international conferences and seminars, studies of professional manpower, surveys of salaries and working conditions, monographs and films on teaching in Canada, vocational training, the education of new Canadians, teachers in Indian schools, teachers in the Yukon and Northwest Territories, taxation problems, and the affairs of Canadian teachers in Department of National Defence schools in Canada and overseas. 9 / It represented Canadian teachers in international matters, participating actively in the World Confederation of Associations of the Teaching Profession, and maintaining contacts with the International Labour Office, the International Bureau of Education, and UNESCO. 10 / It promoted good public relations for education through contacts with national press bureaus, the Canadian Weekly Newspapers' Association, the CBC, and other radio and television outlets. 11 / It advised provincial teachers' organizations on request on problems in the protective area, especially those that were common to a number of provinces.[35]

The range and nature of CTF activities in the mid-sixties may be illustrated by reference to actions taken by the Board of Directors at its meeting in May 1965. 1 / The CTF representative on the Council of the Canadian College of Teachers was reappointed for 1965–8. 2 / CTF opposition to the inclusion of teachers under the *Unemployment Insurance Act* was reaffirmed, and the Minister of Labour was to be so notified. 3 / An "Information Sheet for Teachers in DND [Department of National Defence] Schools Overseas" prepared by the CTF was to be circulated among the affiliates. 4 / Certain proposals by the British Columbia Teachers' Federation with respect to the reception of delegates of the World Council of the Teaching Profession (WCOTP) and Centennial Projects in 1967 were approved. 5 / The National Film Board was to be asked to produce a film on the development of education in Canada as a centennial project. 6 / The president of the Jamaica Teachers' Association was to be invited to the CTF Annual General Meeting at the expense of the federation. 7 / A motion was referred to the secretary-treasurer for report to the Pre-Annual General Meeting Board of Directors' Meeting that the board clarify the terms of reference for the establishment of the CTF Library and the procedure to be followed in related expenditures. 8 / The anual $5,000 centennial allotment was to be placed in the reserve fund when it was established. 9 / The CTF fiscal year was to be changed from June 30 to June 15, subject to the advice of the auditors and the approval of the Annual General Meeting. 10 / The executive was to consider a request that the Board of Directors produce long-term projections of its needs and plans to enable the Finance Committee to begin to study the financial requirements involved. 11 / Approval in principle was given to the establishment of a CTF Trust Fund. 12 / The CTF was to urge the WCOTP, on occasions when it sponsored conferences in the Americas, to make these multilingual by providing adequate translation and to open them to attendance by representatives of all teachers in the Americas. 13 / The three CTF appointees on the 1965 WCOTP delegation were to investigate the possibility of holding specialized seminars at the secondary school level. 14 / The CTF research program was to include the following activities in order of priority: communication and dissemination of research knowledge, status surveys, implementation and demonstration projects, evaluative research, design studies, and developmental and theoretical studies. 15 / The research director was to answer to the Board of Directors through the secretary-treasurer. 16 / Various provisions were made for the membership and functions of the CTF Advisory Research Committee. 17 / Arrangements were made for the appointment of a new research director and his duties were defined. 18 / Certain financial provisions were made for research activities. 19 / The publication *Books about Canada* was to be updated by a committee or, should that be impossible, it was to be reprinted. 20 / The Finance Committee was to give high priority to a proposed Subject Matter Newsletter. 21 / The secretary-treasurer was to investigate interprovincial teacher exchange with the CEA and report to the Pre-

Annual General Meeting Board of Directors' meeting. 22 / The Board of Directors was to advise the Annual General Meeting to hold a national conference of teacher organizations on educational finance in the fall of 1965, and to make certain suggestions about how such a conference might be conducted. 23 / The Advisory Committee on Audio-Visual Education was to be reconstituted and its functions broadened. 24 / Consideration was to be given to the holding of a seminar to consider courses that might be offered in in-service training programs in audi-visual education organized by the affiliates. 25 / The president and the secretary-treasurer were to continue to represent the CTF on the CEA Board of Directors. 26 / The board endorsed in principle the establishment of an association of science teachers along certain specified lines. 27 / The CTF was to consider providing comparable services to the Canadian Association for the Social Studies. 28 / A representative was named to attend the eighteenth conference of l'Association canadienne des éducateurs de langue française. 29 / The CTF was to award two prizes of $100 each, one in physics and one in chemistry, at future science fairs. Most of the other actions taken at the same meeting had to do with routine business.

One of the most significant of the national conferences of teachers' organizations was organized by the Committee on Educational Finance in 1965. The discussions revealed that there was no real consensus among the affiliates on the question of the form and extent of federal aid to education. Agreement was, however, registered on five points: 1 / that educational finance should be an area of greater CTF effort, involving greater support by the affiliates; 2 / that the CTF should secure information from the affiliates regarding existing financial practices and policies; 3 / that the CTF should institute a study of provincial grant systems to see what type of controls were associated with them and what effects these controls had on decision making; 4 / that the CTF should prepare material for submission to the affiliates for study and debate at the Annual General Meeting; and 5 / that steps should be taken to initiate the establishment of some central form of planning agency to give direction and leadership to Canadian education.

In 1967 there was further elaboration of policy with respect to subject matter associations which might be recognized as being associated with the CTF. 1 / The approval of the Annual General Meeting had to be obtained before any such association was founded. 2 / Direct membership would not be open to individuals, but only to such organizations within the provinces or territories as were approved by CTF affiliates. 3 / The Board of Directors would have the power to approve the offer of any or all the following services to the associations: consultative service, secretarial assistance, convening and accommodating organizational meetings, planning and making administrative arrangements for conferences, and publicity through CTF channels. 4 / The CTF would be responsible only for the expenses directly involved in providing these services, and not for any expenses of members or delegates at any meeting or conference of the association. 5 / The constitution of each association would require that the president hold a valid teaching certificate and be a member in good standing, or a member of the staff, of a CTF affiliate, that a CTF representative or observer be authorized to attend all meetings of the executive of the association, and that the association be bound to make representations to educational authorities only through the machinery of the provincial, territorial, and national teachers' organizations.

The CTF opposed the establishment of the Service for Admission to College and University. A major reason offered to justify this position was that such a system would have an undesirable effect on the secondary schools, forcing a degree of conformity on them that was not consistent with current curricular emphasis on discovery, enquiry, experimentation, creativity, and divergent thinking. Another factor of major importance was that the CTF was not invited to participate in the formation of the agency nor offered the membership status to which it considered itself entitled.

In accordance with a resolution approved in 1969, CTF officials approached the Minister of Manpower and Immigration to seek support for the education of adults in non-vocational fields in addition to the adult retraining program then in operation. The minister gave an unequivocally negative answer. Federal assistance for occupational training for adults was regarded as a contribution to the national economy, and not to education, which was a provincial responsibility.

As a result of the passing of resolutions at successive Annual General Meetings, the CTF accumulated a substantial list of policy statements. Some of these were idealistic generalities, with whatever inspirational value such formulations usually have. Others were specific enough to offer a basis for definite action. A few references to the minutes of the Annual General Meeting of 1970 will provide sufficient illustration. The first statement under the heading "General Quality of Education" asserted that it was the "inalienable right of all Canadians to have equal access to that form and level of education to which they are suited by their natural endowments." This right implied the services of carefully selected and adequately trained teachers. Another right of Canadians of all races, creeds, and colours was that of participating in educational policy making. Aims of education, it was said, should include the inculcation of an appreciation and understanding of the obligations, privileges, and responsibilities of citizenship, the promotion of interprovincial co-operation and national unity, and the development of sympathetic world understanding.

An outline of Canadian goals referred to rights and obligations of individual teachers, parents, and the CTF. These goals were said to include equality of status for all Canadians, the right of parents to have their children educated in the official language of their choice, the recognition of the special needs of the native people of Canada, and national unity. Policies with respect to educational finance referred to the duties of all levels of government to expend funds in such a way as to promote equality of educational opportunity. Although provincial responsibility for the administration and control of education was recognized, the federal government was held responsible for making funds available for the support of all levels of education in regions where there was a clear deficiency in tax-paying ability relative to the rest of the country, and for stimulating educational improvement in order to realize national goals. Local financial responsibility was advocated to the point of permitting flexible planing and the exercise of local initiate in improving services.

Policies with respect to the teaching profession tended to be quite specific. Among the rights, privileges, and responsibilities advocated for teachers were eligibility to hold public office and to give active support to candidates for public office without prejudice to their continued employment. It was claimed that the organized teaching profession should have a major role in the control of teacher education and certification, and official representation on all official bodies directly concerned with educational policies in their provinces or territories. The CTF was identified as the organization through which teachers should have representation on all bodies established by the Council of Ministers of Education. A university degree, or an accepted equivalent, was advocated as the minimum desirable qualification for teaching.

With respect to the general welfare of teachers, CTF policies referred to objectives that Ontario teachers had attained. These included 1 / security of tenure, involving immunity from dismissal except for stated cause or reason, with the right of appeal before an impartial tribunal; 2 / the right to negotiate salaries and conditions of employment with employing authorities through collective bargaining; 3 / pay according to a schedule providing salaries high enough to attract and retain the services of well qualified professional teachers; 4 / eligibility for participation in pension plans providing for adequate retirement allowances for teachers who retire on grounds of age, service, or disability, as well as adequate allowances for surviving dependents; and 5 / cumulative sick leave. It is perhaps not amiss for an organization to keep pointing out that rights and privileges may be eroded if they are not guarded vigilantly.

One of the policy statements regarding the CTF itself indicated that the organization accepted a responsibility to work for the implementation of policies designed to alleviate economic and social inequalities, in so far as they were related to education. At the Annual General Assembly, motions were in fact passed dealing with a wide range of issues related to education in a rather tenuous and indirect way. One of those carried in 1970 was worded as follows:

BE IT RESOLVED that the Canadian Teachers' Federation make representation to the federal government urging it to reduce the proposed tax increase on the middle income taxpayers by retaining the progressive nature of personal income tax to a level of at least 65%.

Another motion in the same category read thus:

BE IT RESOLVED that the Canadian Teachers' Federation urge the federal government to increase the exemption for income tax purposes of wholly dependent children to $500 per child.

THREE

Other associations
of educators
for professional
and fraternal purposes

The small group of associations placed in the category of other associations of educators for professional and fraternal purposes may be distinguished from the teachers' federations in that they were not particularly concerned with protective matters. Moreover their membership was either exclusively or heavily drawn from the university level. The Canadian Association of Professors of Education and the Canadian Educational Researchers' Association might legitimately be grouped with other associations concerned with scholarship. They differed from these in that they were concerned with education itself as an area of study.

THE CANADIAN ASSOCIATION OF PROFESSORS
OF EDUCATION

The organization that became the Canadian Association of Professors of Education originated in a meeting of fourteen representatives of twenty Canadian university institutions and the Canadian Education Association at the Ontario College of Education in 1955. This conference, a direct outgrowth of the CEA–Kellogg Project in Educational Leadership, was called the Canadian Conference of Deans and Professors of Educational Administration and Supervision. The purposes of the first conference were stated thus:

(1) To provide an opportunity for furthering informal working relationships among members from the various institutions represented.
(2) To provide an opportunity for exchange of information and co-operative study of the role of Canadian universities in pre-service and in-service education for educational administration and supervision.[1]

At the second conference, held the following year in conjunction with the Learned Societies, the name of the organization was changed to The Canadian Conference of Deans and Professors of Education, with implications for broader membership. It was resolved that all Canadian degree-granting institutions offering programs in education would be invited to participate, and that activities would be closely related to degree work. Rather than depending on funds from the CEA–Kellogg Project, the association was thereafter to be self-sustaining.

A further change of name, this time to The Canadian Association of Professors of Education, preceded by a year the adoption of a constitution in 1959. The objects, as listed in the amended version of this constitution in 1963, showed a shift in interest:

a. To encourage scholarly study and research in education;
b. To provide for the membership a national forum for the presentation and discussion of significant studies in education;
c. To encourage the publication of scholarly writing;
d. To associate in a suitable way with other national and international organizations having similar purposes;
e. To engage in such other activities as are appropriate to a learned society.

Full membership was open to assistant, associate, and full professors in education in any Canadian institution granting education degrees or in any institution that was legally affiliated with such a degree-granting institution and was approved by the association. A category of associate membership was defined to cover 1 / retired professors of education from institutions acceptable for full membership, 2 / members who had taken up service in education in other countries, and 3 / individuals employed in the federal government or in national organizations and agencies with interests closely related to the purposes of the association, who were sponsored by at least two members of the association and accepted by the executive.

The association made only one significant effort to engage directly in research. At the first conference in 1955 the Planning Committee was empowered to arrange for a detailed examination and analysis of programs and offerings in colleges and faculties of education in Canadian universities, with particular reference to work in educationl administration. It was hoped that the study would encourage and facilitate an exchange of credits among universities and provide a sounder basis for comparison of BEd programs. A grant of $1,000 from the CEA–Kellogg Management Committee made possible the employment of two graduate students, one of whom surveyed English-speaking institutions and the other French-speaking institutions. While the enterprise was regarded as successful, research was not continued because of lack of funds and because it was thought better to leave such activity to agencies that were better equipped for it.

An idealistic description of the association was offered in material prepared for the second Canadian Conference on Education in 1962, when a stable pattern of activities, largely centring on the annual meeting, had been established.

It is a body that concerns itself primarily with the educational problems in the training of teachers and with the provision of graduate work for future educators in Canada. Its outlook is essentially adventurous, pioneering, experimental. Its contribution to society is to advance new ideas, fresh approaches, and to foster and make known the results of experimental research. It is a body that has been in the forefront of educational thinking and practice for Canada. It is a body that should keep Canadian education up-to-date, forward looking and of high quality. It is free of provincialism, political consideration and sectional interest. It is an entirely impartial body of scholars and experts to whom all teachers in Canada should look for help, guidance and leadership, on matters connected with theory and practice of education in schools.[2]

During its early years, the association was heavily weighted toward western interests for two main reasons: 1 / the western provinces were the first to incorporate all pre-service teacher preparation in the universities, and thus had a much higher number of potential members in relation to their population than did the central and Atlantic provinces, and 2 / individual faculty members in western universities demonstrated a relatively active interest in research. For a number of years Ontario had hardly more than a token representation among active members. Perhaps nothing was more symptomatic of the isolationism that characterized certain aspects of education in Ontario at the time. By the late 1960s the situation had, of course, changed greatly.

THE CANADIAN EDUCATIONAL RESEARCHERS'
ASSOCIATION
Discussion about the possibility of forming an organization of educational research workers began as early as 1964, when a conference on educational research was held at Ste-Anne-de-Bellevue under the auspices of the Canadian Council for Research in Education. It was not until 1967, however, that the Canadian Educational Researchers' Association was actually formed. Its objectives were to initiate, promote, support, and improve educational research and development. It was "to serve as a single official voice for individual educational researchers on the acquisition and distribution of essential resources."[3] The publication of a newsletter called *Communiqué* was begun in October 1967. The compilation of a directory of research personnel and resources was promptly undertaken.

One of the major activities of the association was to assist in the planning of the annual conference which had been sponsored by the Canadian Council for Research in Education. These conferences consisted of the presentation of papers, symposium sessions, and seminars or colloquium sessions. The symposia for the 1969 conference dealt with school research; student unrest, power, etc.; the Alberta Human Resources Council; organizational structures and the facilitation of educational research; priorities for research and development in education, and individualizing instruction. Papers covered every imaginable topic.

PHI DELTA KAPPA, GAMMA NU CHAPTER

Discussion of Phi Delta Kappa will be confined in the present context to the activities of Gamma Nu Chapter, associated with the College of Education at the University of Toronto. This chapter was formed in 1955 on the particular initiative of A.C. Lewis, who was at that time dean of the college. The staff of the institution already included a number of members of the American organization, whose association with institutions of higher education in the United States had led them to join. These people formed the nucleus of the new chapter. Invitations to the first general meeting were sent to all male members of the college staff and all male graduate students attending summer school. At a further meeting in October sixty applicants were accepted as members. An initiation team consisting of Paul Cook, J. Roy Leevy, and R.S. Merkel attended from the United States.

The activities of the organization revolved around an examination of topics of current interest to educators. The organization proved quite successful in attracting speakers of a high level of competence from inside and outside the province. Because of the close association of many of the members in the normal course of their duties in the provincial educational system as well as within the fraternity, discussions typically elicited an unusual degree of frankness. The members could not legitimately be accused of meeting merely to reinforce one another's prejudices.

An example of an effort to produce lively controversy was a meeting held in February 1969, to which students from junior high schools, secondary schools, teachers' colleges, colleges of education, universities, and other institutions were invited. Members of the organization made an effort to find especially bright and articulate young people from among their acquaintances. Members and students ate and talked together, moving around in an informal manner. According to reports of some of the conversations, at least a few straightforward opinions were expressed.

The chapter initiated a *News Letter*, distributed in mimeographed form to active members. A typical issue contained reports of past and future events, names of new members, articles on various educational topics, and other matters of fraternal interest. It was left to the headquarters of the fraternity in the United States to undertake major ventures in the publication field.

FOUR

Associations providing general support for education

The associations providing general support for education were characterized by the fact that their interests ranged over many areas of study, groups, and levels. They did not have direct authority over the operation of any part of the educational system. They represented three sources of support: researchers, parents, and financial interests. The last in the group, the Industrial Foundation on Education, disappeared in the early 1960s, and no comparable body arose to take its place.

THE ONTARIO EDUCATIONAL RESEARCH COUNCIL

The forerunner of the Ontario Educational Research Council (OERC) was the Research Section of the Ontario Educational Association, which was founded following the submission of a report by a formative committee set up in 1952. This section attracted only a very small group, and failed to provide the leadership or promote the interest in educational research that was so clearly required. There was persistent discussion at the meetings of the Ontario Association for Curriculum Development in 1956 and 1957 of the need for a more broadly based organization. Despite the protestations of certain members that the association was not a resolution-making body, the following resolution was passed in 1957:

WHEREAS:
There is strong evidence of increased interest in research as a means of improving education in Ontario;
WE RECOMMEND:
That the Executive of the Ontario Association for Curriculum Development request the Ontario Teachers' Federation to convene a meeting of interested educational organizations and agencies in Ontario for the purpose of:
(a) discussing present needs in educational research;
(b) recommending appropriate steps that might be taken to meet these needs, including the possible establishment of a Research Council sponsored by organizations and agencies interested in education.

The OTF called the requested meeting in May 1958, and subsequent discussions resulted in the formation of the council.

Eight objectives of the association were defined in the constitution:

1. The advancement of educational research in the province by:
   (a) Providing a liaison between the research efforts of all interested educational organizations.
   (b) Collection of information about research being done in the province.
   (c) Publicizing research findings through various publications.
   (d) Making available to all members the findings of selected research studies deposited with the Council.
   (e) Sponsoring of meetings and conferences.
   (f) Exchange of information between members and between similar associations.
   (g) Conduct of such research projects as are within the capacity of the Council in terms of financial resources and staff.
   (h) And such other methods as the Board of Directors may deem necessary.
2. Provide liaison with other organizations on a national or provincial level.

Three classes of membership were defined: corporate, sustaining, and individual. Corporate members were named in the constitution, and changed somewhat over the years. In 1965 they included l'Association canadienne des éducateurs de langue française – Ontario Branch, the Association of Ontario Secondary School Superintendents, the Federation of Catholic Parent-Teacher Associations of Ontario, the Metropolitan Toronto Educational Research Council, the Ontario Association for Curriculum Development, the Ontario Association of School Business Officials, the Ontario College of Education, the Ontario Curriculum Institute, the Ontario Department of Education, the Ontario Educational Association, the Ontario Federation of Chapters – Council for Exceptional Children, the Ontario Federation of Home and School Associations, the Ontario School Inspectors' Association, the Ontario School Trustees' Council, the Ontario Teachers' College Association, the Ontario Teachers' Federation, the universities of Ontario, and school board educational research departments not included in the Metropolitan Toronto Educational Research Council operated by school boards that were sustaining members. Sustaining members were other groups, organizations, business firms, or school boards wishing to support the work of the council by making an annual financial contribution. Individual members were individuals wishing to participate in the work of the council. Most of the corporate members were represented on the board of directors. Sustaining members and individual members received notice of all open meetings and conferences of the council, copies of special publications, and, for a time, a subscription to the *Ontario Journal of Educational Research*, a publication which was abolished by the Ontario Institute for Studies in Education.

The council did not begin with the intention of conducting educational research studies. The founders realized that the contributions of members would not be sufficient to maintain a staff with the necessary skills or to defray the expenses of other aspects of a research program. The possibility that the organization might eventually evolve into a research-conducting agency was not, however, ruled out. The one important departure from recognized policy was a commissioned study undertaken by C.J. Wilkins in 1964 to describe and evaluate the research departments established by school boards. The contents of this study are reviewed at some length in volume VI, chapter 9.

The annual conferences, held in early December, became much the most important contribution of the council. At an early stage the two-day program was divided into two sessions: a "technical" session at which papers of interest to professional researchers were presented, and a general session, concentrating on reports and studies of interest to classroom teachers, administrators, and other practitioners. For the first few years presentations centred on selected themes such as programmed instruction, the Cuisenaire method of teaching arithmetic, measurement techniques, the teaching of French, the New Castle method of teaching reading, and studies of student potential. After the formation of the Ontario Institute for Studies in Education, the program concentrated for a time on the interests of the non-professional group, although some specialized papers continued to be presented by professional researchers. In 1967 the technical session was restored, and attracted a considerable number of professional researchers who presented specialized papers. The frequent references in volume VI of ONTARIO'S EDUCATIVE SOCIETY to reports on developments in different parts of the province indicate the range and value of the OERC conference programs. Although many of the papers did not deal with research by any recognized definition of the term, they constituted a record of some of the most important initiatives in the provincial system.

Beginning in the mid-sixties, a number of workshops were held on specific topics. The attendance at these was normally a restricted number of participants, mostly sent as delegates of teachers and other groups. The workshops were for the most part regarded as quite successful in disseminating information and in producing a better understanding of research.

An early service provided by the council was the production of a series of newsletters designed to focus attention on certain important issues and to indicate the contribution of research to an understanding of them. They dealt with topics such as programmed instruction, educational television, the use of test results, the role of research, and promotion practices. Some newsletters were written by officials of the council and some by authorities in the field on the request of the council, while some were reprints of articles written for other purposes.

A number of other projects had varying degrees of success. 1 / Of substantial value were several surveys of educational research being conducted in Ontario. Within a few years the responses to questionnaires indicated a shift from studies that should properly have been called educational operations to those that had a reasonable number of the characteristics of genuine research. 2 / The declared willingness of the OERC to assist groups and organizations interested in hearing about the contribution and potentialities of educational research to find suitable speakers on these topics failed to elicit much response. The intended beneficiaries of this service apparently preferred to find their own speakers. 3 / There was a somewhat better response to the offer to locate expert advisers for those wishing to undertake research projects, but acknowledging a lack of expertise. 4 / The development of a registry of educational research in Ontario was regarded as a reasonable success. A card file was maintained on studies of provincial and local interest, and information was supplied on demand at token cost.

To a very limited extent the council found it possible to render financial assistance to individuals undertaking research projects. Small grants, often amounting to no more than $50 to $100, went mainly to classroom teachers and others. Such sums may have helped defray the costs of administering a questionnaire or of having some agency analyse data, but the chief effect was probably to provide encouragement to those interested in research on an amateur basis.

The establishment of the Ontario Institute for Studies in Education posed something of a dilemma for the OERC. It seemed probable that the institute would undertake to perform many of the functions for which the council had assumed some responsibility, and there was some doubt about whether the council should continue to exist. H.O. Barrett, secretary of the council, was a leading spokesman for the view that the institute would have primarily academic interests, and that classroom teachers and other practitioners would continue to need a forum to express their own points of view. Despite the proliferation of specialized meetings, seminars, workshops, and conferences, the annual meeting did in fact continue to be very popular and to attract a large number of participants. However, in many other areas where its contribution might have grown, the council was completely overshadowed by the institute.

THE CANADIAN COUNCIL FOR RESEARCH IN EDUCATION

The roots of the Canadian Council for Research in Education (CCRE) may be traced back at least to an initiative of the CEA, then the Canada and Newfoundland Education Association (CNEA), in 1939, which led to the establishment of the rather short-lived Canadian Council for Educational Research (CCER). That organization had seven members representing five provinces and provincial groupings (the prairie provinces and the maritimes) as well as the chairman of the CTF Research Committee and the chief of the Education Branch of the Dominion Bureau of Statistics. An initial program was made possible by a grant from the Carnegie Corporation. Local branches or committees were established in nearly all the provinces, but did not prove to be very productive. Wartime concerns have been offered as the reason why the council did not get off to a very good start. Studies for which grants-in-aid were made were constantly being interrupted or abandoned as seemingly more important activities called for attention. Friction developed with the CNEA executive, to which the CCER was responsible, in part because the former supported separate research activities. Discussions in 1945 led to the disbanding of the CCER and the formation of a CNEA Research Council as an alternative.

Subsequent years were marked by the creation or expansion of the research divisions of national organizations, the formation of provincial and regional research councils, and the establishment of journals to publish or summarize research activities. It was increasingly evident that there was a need for co-ordination if wasteful duplication of effort was to be avoided and maximum advantage realized from efforts being made in different parts of the country. Sources of funds for the support of educational research that were not accessible to provincial or local organizations were not being tapped.

A significant step forward was taken in 1952 with the formation of the National Advisory Committee on Educational Research, sponsored at first by the CEA and the CTF, later joined by l'Association canadienne des éducateurs de langue française, the Canadian Association of Professors of Education, the Canadian Association of School Superintendents and Inspectors, the Canadian School Trustees' Association, and the Education Division of the Dominion Bureau of Statistics. This committee was expected to promote research, in particular by recommending to its members areas in which research was needed. Among the weaknesses preventing it from fully meeting the obvious needs were the lack of a secretariat and the absence of facilities for publication. The establishment of the CCRE represented an effort to overcome these and other deficiencies.

The council, as originally organized, was sponsored by the same organizations that were involved with the National Advisory Committee on Educational Research, except for the Canadian School Trustees' Association, which became a sustaining member. The sponsors ranged from the moderately well financed to the impecunious. Later additions were the National Conference of Canadian Universities and Colleges and the Canadian Home and School and Parent-Teacher Federation.

The sponsoring organizations, which were treated as corporate members, each had three representatives on the council. Fees for these members were determined by the council at its annual meeting, and varied according to the resources that each had at its disposal. Associate members were national, interprovincial, or provincial organizations or bodies elected by the voting representatives on the council. They were entitled to one representative on the council with the right to participate in discussions but not to vote. Fees of members in this category were also determined by the council. Sustaining members consisted of institutions, organizations, and individuals approved by the council. They were entitled to receive the annual report and other designated publications, but not to attend meetings.

The objectives listed in the constitution were as follows:

(a) To initiate, encourage and develop research in education in Canada.
(b) To identify worthy research projects and to promote and assist such projects under the sponsorship of corporate members of the Council or other bodies having objects similar to the objects of the Council.
(c) To prepare and maintain an index of educational research materials available in Canada.
(d) To publish a national journal of educational research and such other bulletins and reports as may be deemed advisable.
(e) To collect and disseminate on a national scale information about educational research activities.
(f) To sponsor meetings and conferences of research workers for the exchange of information about research studies and research methods related to education.
(g) To solicit, receive and disburse funds for financial assistance for educational research activities and for the conduct of the business of the Council.
(h) To provide liaison among the various provincial or inter-provincial research councils and national agencies in the field of educational research.
(i) To provide liaison with disciplines having an interest in educational research.
(j) To promote public appreciation of the nature of and need for educational research.

During the three regular meetings of the council in 1961, 1962, and 1963, the organizations represented surveyed and discussed the field of educational research in Canada. An active program, however, awaited the assumption of duties by a full-time director in the person of F.G. Robinson in 1963. By this time the council had been able to obtain funds amounting to $35,000 per annum from the provinces, $5,000 from the teachers' associations, and $3,000 from membership fees and donations. A thorough survey was undertaken to identify the research facilities, activities, and personnel in Canada. The compilation of a research index was also initiated, with the assistance of research librarians in various parts of the country. The council assumed the responsibility for sponsoring the invitational research conferences which had been introduced under other auspices. Assumption of responsibility for the identification of worthy projects and for the promotion and assistance of such projects led to the preparation of reports, two of the earliest of which dealt respectively with the use of the initial teaching alphabet in teaching reading and the Cuisenaire method of teaching arithmetic.

As expected, other agencies began to make requests for assistance in the conduct of their own projects. Among these were the CBC, which sought advice on a study of the value of national school broadcasts; the Canadian Association of School Superintendents and Inspectors, which requested review and criticism of a study of school drop-outs; and the federal Department of Labour, which asked for guidance in trying out programmed learning techniques for training adult workers. The council adopted the policy of referring to a member organization any request that came within its sphere of operations. A decision was also made to assemble a panel of experts to contribute advice to the council or the director and to handle inquiries. Much of the consultative work was done by the director himself.

During the organizational period one of the leading figures in the council, G.M. Dunlop of the Faculty of Education of the University of Alberta, prepared a plan for the publication of a Canadian journal of educational research. In order to produce four issues a year the council would need an editor and an executive secretary or business manager. An advisory committee would meet semi-annually to advise and consult with the editor and executive assistant. Despite the stress placed on the importance of producing the journal, the plans were not realized. A newsletter, later called a bulletin, was soon launched.

The council soon began to encounter certain difficulties in carrying out its mandate. These were reviewed by the director in his report for 1964–5.

With provincial power and educational expansion on the upswing, the idea that there are legitimate or necessary "national" functions in educational research tended to be discredited in some provinces. Certainly the validity of the concept of national research studies has been challenged – except when such studies are conducted by a federal department which is also the sponsor of a joint program with the provinces (e.g., the Department of Labour). The role of many of the national education organizations has been cast in doubt; some would have it that the third parties – i.e., those standing between the federal and provincial power centers – have no crucial role to play which cannot be met by the provinces individually, or collectively through interprovincial cooperation.

While those of us who work at the national level do not subscribe to the proposition that province means everything and nation nothing, the reality of CCRE's predicament was nevertheless thrust vigorously upon us. It is now perfectly clear that some of the CCRE objectives did not work, and simply cannot work, under its present Constitution. Moreover, it has recently become clear that the prospects for continued financial support from the provinces are meagre unless some basic alteration is made in the way of representation and Constitution; in fact, at various times during a flurry of activity in April and May, it looked as though CCRE was in danger of ultimately losing all its provincial government support in favour of an expanded CEA Information and Research Division.[1]

When an increase in funds for the CCRE program became an urgent necessity, and in view of the federal government's continued policy of declining to make contributions, the provinces were asked to provide additional funds. The question of provincial government representation was thereupon raised. The ministers of education, in agreeing that CCRE was providing certain services that could not be rendered by any single provincial organization, expressed the opinion that departments of education and research workers must be included among the membership. It was agreed that two-fifths of the members should be from the existing sponsors, two-fifths from departments of education, and one-fifth from among professional research workers. Those in the last group would be nominated by regional organizations such as the Ontario Institute for Studies in Education and the provincial research councils.

The Council of Ministers offered to provide an annual sum of between $45,000 and $50,000 for a five-year period on condition that the money would be used to further four objectives, and that projects not meeting such objectives would have to be financed from other sources. The four categories were 1 / to sponsor meetings and conferences for the exchange of information about research methods related to education; 2 / to provide liaison among the various provincial, inter-provincial, and national agencies in the field of research in education; 3 / to provide liaison with disciplines having an interest in research related to education – the Learned Societies, psychologists, sociologists, etc.; and 4 / to collect and disseminate on a national scale information about research in education and educational research activities, to publish bulletins and reports as might be deemed advisable, to serve as a co-ordinating body in the preparation of an index of educational research materials available in Canada, and eventually to publish a national Journal of Research in Education.

A further significant development occurred at the annual meeting in 1968. At that time a decision was made to include faculties of education, school boards, corporations and business firms producing educational products, and other such organizations. The reasoning behind this decision was that, since the CCRE must be involved with the whole spectrum of research and development and with producers and consumers, each of these interests should have a voice in determining policy. It can hardly be said, however, that this change resulted in any obvious increase in the productivity or influence of the council. The departure of Robinson from the directorship at the beginning of 1966 constituted an irreparable loss.

THE ONTARIO FEDERATION OF HOME AND SCHOOL ASSOCIATIONS

Purposes
The constitution and by-laws of the Ontario Federation of Home and School Associations, as amended in 1967, outlined purposes and objects as follows:

1. TO LINK together all groups organized to promote co-operation between the Home and School.
2. TO ENCOURAGE the study of child problems and in every way possible to create the best conditions for the training of boys and girls to become good Canadian citizens.
3. TO SUPPORT Boards of School Trustees and the Department of Education in progressive measures and to help to make public opinion favourable to reform and advancement.
4. TO ENCOURAGE the formation of a Home and School Association in every school in the Province of Ontario.
5. TO UNITE with similar federations in other Canadian provinces in educational undertakings of national concern.
6. TO CO-OPERATE with the forces that are stimulating the international understanding and work for the peace of the world.

There were some differences in the objects of the Canadian Home and School and Parent-Teacher Federation, which were accepted by the Ontario Federation in 1950. There was more reference, for example, to the educational interests of the individual child. The eight points read thus:

(1) To promote the welfare of children and youth.
(2) To raise the standards of home life.
(3) To promote and secure adequate legislation for the care and protection of children and youth.
(4) To foster co-operation between parents and teachers in the training and guidance of children and youth, both during and after the school period.
(5) To obtain the best for each child according to his physical, mental, social and spiritual needs.
(6) To give parents an understanding of the school and its work, and to assist in interpreting the school in all its aspects to the public.

(7) To confer and co-operate with organizations other than schools which concern themselves with the care and training of children and youth in the home, school and community; and with the education of adults to meet these responsibilities.

(8) To foster high ideals of citizenship and patriotism; and to promote through educational means, international good-will and peace.

Origin and structure

The first Home and School council was formed in Toronto in 1916 as a result of efforts by Mrs A.C. Courtice. During that period associations were organized as independent units, with little effort devoted to co-ordination. Although a loosely structured federation was formed in 1919, it was not until 1933 that a legally constituted structure appeared. Affairs of the federation were managed by a board of directors which grew from 9 members to 115 within a few years.

The entire province was divided for administrative purposes into eleven geographical areas, which in some cases were further subdivided into districts. Local associations, of which there were approximately 1,600 in 1962, mostly linked with elementary schools in urban areas of the province, might join in groups of five or more to form councils. These councils, numbering about fifty in 1962, constituted a useful, if not essential, part of the structure. Later by-laws stated that all associations "shall be grouped together in conference bodies known as Councils." The duties of the councils were to co-ordinate the activities of the constituent associations and to offer them practical advice and assistance, to ensure the exchange of ideas, to develop leadership, to interpret the Home and School movement to the larger community, including civic, educational, and other community organizations, to interpret the associations to the provincial federation and vice versa, and to promote the federation program as it applied to the associations.

The federation defined a series of policies to be followed in the pursuit of its objectives. Membership was open to all those with an interest in the welfare of children and youth. Neither the federation nor its component units was authorized to interfere in the administration of any individual school, although representations might be made to appropriate educational authorities through the proper Home and School channels. While co-operation with other organizations and agencies was encouraged, the federation and its components were barred from membership in these bodies. There might be no partisan political or commercial activity.

In defining the duties of certain committees and sub-committees, the constitution and by-laws give some insight into the way in which the federation attempted to carry out its program. For example, the Children's Reading and Library Services Committee was expected to recommend books for children's reading; to promote interest in the value and enjoyment of good reading habits for both adults and children; to encourage students to understand and use the library facilities available in the schools and community; and to work for the extension of existing libraries and library services and the provision of additional services. The functions of the Child Study Committee were to promote the better understanding by parents and teachers of the mental, physical, and social development of the child; to prepare and promote study courses for parents and teachers; and to suggest books, pamphlets, and other material for study by groups seeking an increased knowledge of children and young people and a better understanding of their role as parents and teachers. The Citizenship Committee was supposed to try to promote an understanding of the history, geography, governments, institutions, and people of Canada; to promote good citizenship through an understanding of the rights, privileges, and responsibilities of the people of Canada; to study the influences affecting the health and welfare of children and young people; to work for an understanding of cultural differences with a view to ensuring equal rights for all; and to provide leadership in planning programs on citizenship education. The duties of the Communications Committee were to inform the membership and the general public of the activities of the federation; to promote both inside and outside the federation a better understanding of the purposes of the Home and School movement and of the reasons for its continued existence; to assist the area boards and councils, and through them the individual associations, with public relations and publicity campaigns; and to foster, through all available media, a continuing and increasing awareness of the benefits of Home and School programs. The School Education Committee undertook to study "the educational philosophy and programme" at all levels; to produce a better public understanding of the close relationship among parents, teachers, and school trustees and of the responsibility of each for the provision of education for children and young people; to advise the associations of the findings of educational research relating to their interests and to help them promote the discussion and understanding of new and progressive techniques; and to maintain liaison with agencies working for the improvement of educational methods and facilities. Additional committees functioning in the late 1960s were the Constitution and By-Laws Committee, the Convention Committee, the Finance Committee, the Leadership Training Committee, the Membership Committee, the National Projects Committee, the "Ontario Home and School" Editorial Committee, the Programme Development Committee, and the Resolutions Committee. There were also sub-committees as follows: the Safety Sub-Committee, the Juvenile Protection Sub-Committee, the Radio and T.V. Sub-Committee, the Awards Sub-Committee, the Audio-Visual Programming Sub-Committee, the Fine Arts Sub-Committee, the Elementary Education Sub-Committee, the Secondary Education Sub-Committee, the Intermediate Education

Sub-Committee, and the Rural Education Sub-Committee. It hardly seems surprising that these many groups found some difficulty in keeping their responsibilities from overlapping.

Submissions on educational policy
Submissions were prepared and presented to various committees studying educational issues and problems in Ontario. In view of the complexity of the organization, it is sometimes difficult to define the exact group whose opinions were reflected in particular resolutions. The views offered to the Minister's Committee on the Training of Elementary School Teachers in 1964 were said to have been expressed through resolutions at the annual meetings of the Ontario Federation, through recommendations from the Board of Directors of the Ontario Federation acting on behalf of the members, and from suggestions received by the School Education Committee from various councils acting on behalf of their constituent associations.

The federation's brief to the Minister's Committee advocated the recognition of personal qualities and character as equal in importance to academic qualifications. Wider discretionary powers in granting or refusing admission for reasons other than academic qualifications were recommended for selection committees in teachers' colleges. It was suggested that greater efforts be made to recruit the most promising young people into teaching by providing opportunities for practice teaching in elementary schools before they completed high school and by offering adequate scholarships, bursaries, and loans. By meeting university admission requirements, candidates for teachers' college would ensure that there was no adverse reflection on their prestige. The federation joined the many other agencies calling for a four-year degree program for teacher education.

An invitation to offer advice and counsel to the Select Committee on Youth of the Ontario Legislature led to the preparation of a brief of substantial proportions. The contents of this brief deserve some attention, since they indicate many of the major concerns of the Home and School movement during a period of several years. As matters of major importance for the education of youth, this brief pointed to the grade 13 problem, the demand for educational opportunities beyond the secondary school level, and the importance of providing wider and more competent guidance counselling. With respect to the first of these three areas, the brief urged the Department of Education to investigate the feasibility of providing a twelve-year curriculum leading to senior matriculation. It was suggested that a greater amount of subject matter and more depth of study be incorporated in the earlier grades of both elementary and secondary school. In the area of post-secondary education, the federation was apprehensive lest facilities prove inadequate by the end of the decade to meet the needs of the increasing school population, and urged that appropriate measures be taken to deal with the developing crisis. Suggestions were advanced with respect to student awards of various kinds. In the third area, that of guidance counselling, the brief indicated that the Robarts Plan could not be made fully effective without a greater effort to disseminate information about the new opportunities that were being offered. The federation was providing a small bursary to assist a student at the Department of Education summer course in guidance. Suggestions were made about the kind of qualities and educational preparation a good guidance teacher should have.

In the same brief the Ontario Federation supported the Canadian Federation in its demand for the establishment of a federal office of education. The main functions of such an office would be to represent Canadian education in the international spheres, to co-ordinate and disseminate information, to stimulate, support, and conduct educational research, and to co-ordinate expenditure. The federation also expressed approval of the case made by the CTF and the OTF for federal financial assistance to counteract some of the variations in the quality of education in different parts of the country.

Returning to the provincial level, the federation mentioned its continuing desire to see the formation of an Advisory Council on Education. It also hoped for a greatly increased emphasis on educational research in such areas as the classroom, the school system, the university, and teachers' colleges. The fact that the Ontario Curriculum Institute had to seek a large grant from an American foundation seemed a kind of reproach to the province. The federation asserted that generous support should come from industries and foundations within provincial boundaries. Attention was also called to the need for improved teacher education. At that time the list of annual scholarships and bursaries offered by the organization included a Home and School Ryerson Scholarship of $100 for a student in the Home Economics course at Ryerson Polytechnical Institute, a $100 bursary available at each of the twelve teachers' colleges in the province, the Katharine Sherk Memorial Bursary of $500 for a student attending the Ontario College of Education, the Ontario Home and School Bursary of $500 for a student attending a session at the Ontario Library School who planned to be a children's librarian or a school librarian, an Ontario Home and School Bursary of $150 for a student in the Department of Education summer course in guidance who would use this training in his work, and an Ontario Home and School Bursary of $150 for a student in the Department of Education summer course in auxiliary education, with similar restrictions. In addition to the federation program, many councils and individual associations were said to be carrying out scholarship and bursary plans of their own.

Views were offered on a number of aspects of the curriculum. Among recent initiatives, the federation had urged the Department of Education to promote the teaching of conversational French beginning in the primary grades, to examine the need for teaching French grammar and composition at the elementary and intermediate levels, and to ensure that earlier programs were co-ordinated with those of grade 9. Support had been offered for the introduction of an improved program in home economics. Delegates at the annual meeting of 1964 had requested a review of the controversial course in religious education. Though not advocating complete curricular uniformity, the federation deplored differences in curricula among provinces, between rural and urban areas, and from one municipality to another. Because of increasing population mobility, children were said to be suffering a considerable amount of inconvenience as a result of existing variations.

Mention was made of the interest members of Home and School associations had in the buildings and equipment available in their community. Parent education was said to be needed to determine what constituted frills and to distinguish between these and certain desirable kinds of equipment. Home and School representatives had appreciated the opportunity to send representatives to the Minister's Conference on School Design, and recommended that a similar conference be repeated at intervals.

The federation pointed to the substantial efforts it had made to encourage the provision of appropriate library services for all children and to control the distribution of horror books, crime comics, and salacious literature. An extensive survey of public and school library services had been conducted across Canada in 1961 and 1962. This project had revealed a pressing need for a Supervisor of Elementary School Libraries for Ontario and for basic standards for central and classroom libraries. Library facilities and services in many parts of the province had been shown to be far from adequate.

The Ontario Federation was reported to have made an extremely important contribution in the field of parent education. A discussion course entitled Meet Your School-Age Child had been prepared in co-operation with the Canadian Mental Health Association and the Community Programs Branch of the Department of Education, and thousands of copies had been distributed. Also, several Parenthood in a Free Nation courses had been conducted.

Reference was made in the brief to contributions made by Home and School associations in the field of recreation. A common type of project involved the founding and supervision of playgrounds and skating rinks in co-operation with school boards. An appeal was made for more complete utilization of recreational facilities in school buildings, where the community had a large capital investment. While some school boards made these facilities fully available, others declined to co-operate.

Home and School interest in the physical and mental health of young people had been shown in a variety of ways. In 1964 the Department of Health had been asked to review visual acuity testing in the schools. Requests had been made for a ban on the use of foot x-ray machines for shoe fitting, except in the hands of qualified radiologists, and for regulations on the handling and labelling of chemicals and other substances of a poisonous or harmful nature. The Department of Education was commended for bringing to the attention of teen-agers the problems of alcoholism and cigarette smoking through the use of films, booklets, and classroom instruction. The federation favoured severe penalties for trafficking in drugs and more effective detention and psychiatric treatment for dangerous sex offenders. A case was made for full income tax exemption for medical expenses, including treatment for emotional disturbances and mental illness of youth and for the treatment and care of eyes and teeth. Pensions were advocated for those over sixteen with permanent physical and mental disabilities. Most large school boards had been persuaded to make accident insurance available to school pupils, and pressure was being maintained to have the practice adopted throughout the province.

A submission to the Provincial Committee on Aims and Objectives in 1965 contained references to certain broad educational causes such as the need to improve the social and economic system, to impart a regard for democratic government, and to create skills and knowledge. Mention was made of the importance of equal educational opportunity for all, which might be furthered through the extension of economic assistance. The brief urged the expansion of library facilities, more provision for special education, the relaxation of the graded system, improved guidance services, efforts to raise the status of non-academic programs, the continued enlargement of facilities in universities and other institutions of post-secondary education, research into the learning process, careful training and selection of teachers at all levels, cultural enrichment at the kindergarten and pre-kindergarten stages, the compulsory establishment of kindergartens, the continuance of student exchange projects, a study of the concept of education for leisure, improved health services for school children, the establishment of a federal office of education, and provision for easier transfer of students from one province to another.

In a submission to the Board of Broadcast Governors in October 1966, the federation added its voice to those urging maximum provision for educational television. Priority was urged for the needs of education in the re-allocation of very high frequency channels and in the establishment of ultra high frequency channels. A satellite communications system was seen as a promising means of facilitating the distribution of programs. It was regarded as desirable to require that all receivers sold in Canada be capable of UHF reception. These and other recommendations led up to the assertion that the development of a co-ordinated, comprehensive system of ETV for in-school programming was a basic requirement for a technologically oriented society.

Similar matters were pursued in a submission to the House of Commons Committee on Broadcasting, Films, and Assistance to the Arts in 1967. Educational television was said to have demonstrated its value over and over again in second-language instruction, the new mathematics program, and science presentations, as well as in pre-service and in-service teacher preparation. The federation urged that the federal government make educational television accessible to all Canadians regardless of geographical location. A further plea was made that the necessary facilities be given the highest priority. It was said that the benefits and advantages accruing from educational television must not be confined to schools, colleges, and universities, but must also be available to adults in their homes. It would help parents to understand the school, the tasks it sought to accomplish, and the means it proposed to employ if they could view school broadcasts. By contributing to the educational development of adults themselves, ETV would promote the economic, intellectual, and cultural welfare of the country. In order to ensure the availability of ETV programs, the federation advocated that existing stations be required, with reasonable remuneration, to carry these programs during school hours.

An example of a campaign for quite specific objectives was offered by the Toronto Home and School Council in 1967–8 when it undertook to persuade the responsible authorities to provide lunchtime supervision by responsible lay assistants and to convince the Department of Parks and Recreation to institute a supervised active free play program in school yards after school hours. Claims were made that the cost of the first of these two services would be very low. If the relevant acts and regulations were amended, it was said that individual school boards might be left to decide whether the expenditure was worthwhile.

In 1967 the federation welcomed the opportunity to present a brief to the Mackay Committee on Religious Education in the Public Schools. The establishment of this committee was in line with a resolution adopted at the annual meeting in 1964 urging that a group of professional educators investigate and evaluate the effectiveness of the existing course and consider appropriate methods of imparting moral and ethical values to all students regardless of their religious heritage. The brief contained the results of a questionnaire designed to ascertain parents' opinions with respect to the importance of the aims of the existing course, the inclusion of such a course in a public school system, the primary responsibility for the religious education of children, the advisability of including a course in comparative religious thought at the secondary school level, and alternative methods of establishing ideals, building attitudes, and influencing behaviour. The questionnaire was submitted to all presidents of Home and School associations, of whom 313 responded. Some members-at-large also accepted an invitation to present their general views without the limitations of the questionnaire. Replies indicated that 75 per cent of the presidents thought the course should serve one or both of two purposes: 1 / setting up ideals, building attitudes, and influencing behaviour, and 2 / teaching scriptural fact and biblical text. The majority of this group thought that the main emphasis should be placed on the first of the two objectives. The remaining 25 per cent felt that neither of the two aims should be pursued in the public school system. A majority of the individual respondents favoured the retention of religious instruction in the curriculum. The prime responsibility for religious training was placed on parents, with the church designated as the second most responsible group. About 86 per cent of the responses indicated support for a course at the secondary school level dealing with comparative religious thought and stressing similarities and differences among the major world religions. Of those answering the relevant question, about 75 per cent thought such a course should be optional, and the others that it should be compulsory.

Other activities
The national organization took a leading part in arousing in the public an awareness of the need for better educational opportunities for the Indian population of Canada. The so-called Tillicum Project, a study of the Canadian Indian, was undertaken as a means of celebrating the centennial in 1967. Its basic purpose was to foster a general climate of friendship and neighbourly help. Member groups were urged to engage in a series of activities such as the following: to hold meetings devoted to the Canadian Indians; to show such films as "No Longer Vanishing" and "The Transition," and to follow them up with discussions; to urge parents of any Indian children enrolled in the local school to attend Home and School meetings; to participate in the work of a local friendship centre, or organize one where none already existed, and to have a member attend the next Friendship Centre Training course at the University of Saskatchewan; to co-operate with the local Indian Affairs Branch or the Indian-Eskimo Association in encouraging cultural or economic projects on an Indian reserve, such as helping to organize a library, a series of film nights, a community centre for adult education classes and leisure-time activities, or a co-operative for producing and marketing Indian handicrafts; to ensure that Indians living in the community were not deprived of services and conveniences through discrimination; to persuade the local municipal council to take constructive measures; and to send recommendations to the provincial and national federations for transmission to the provincial and federal governments.

Evaluation
The Home and School movement acquired some unfavourable images over the years. Some local associations appeared to be unduly preoccupied with bake sales and raffles to raise money for some item of school equipment. Efforts to establish fruitful contacts between parents and teachers often seemed to produce rather inconsequential results. Rather than regarding the association as a useful vehicle for promoting fruitful co-operation, many teachers considered it a nuisance or, even worse, a potential source of interference in their work. There were complaints

that local members had shown too little imagination in devising ways of helping the school improve the performance of its functions. As a result of widespread dissatisfaction membership fell drastically during the 1960s. Some local groups gave up their provincial affiliation and continued operations on an independent basis.

As far back as 1962, the Ontario federation secured an evaluation of its organizational structure by the firm of Peat, Marwick, and Mitchell. This firm uncovered a number of what were labelled problem situations: 1 / a poor definition of duties and responsibiliites, 2 / a lack of clear understanding and acceptance of the objectives of the federation, 3 / a poorly established pattern of reporting relationships, 4 / a low level of delegation of responsibility and authority, 5 / an over-extended span of control, precluding effective direction, and 6 / a poor flow of communication between organizational levels.

The firm recommended an extensive re-organization to overcome these problems. The most important of the changes would give the local associations greater influence at the higher administrative levels. Further, the existing Board of Directors, with its 115 members, would be replaced by a 54-member executive, the position of the councils would be strengthened, and nine areas would be established under the control of area boards. It was suggested that the *Ontario Home and School* bulletin could be made a more effective means of communication between the federation and the members. This step would do something to counteract the pronounced lack of awareness of the existence of the federation which the investigators found among the ordinary membership.

The evaluation had some influence on the evolution of the federation, although the evidence would suggest that some basic causes for concern were not eliminated. The familiar criticisms continued to be voiced throughout the 1960s. A perusal of the constitution and by-laws suggests a preoccupation with legalistic detail that could prove a handicap to effective adaptation to changing conditions. There appears to be a perpetual temptation for associations to devote so much attention to the way things are done that the inconsequential nature of the activities themselves is overlooked.

THE FEDERATION OF CATHOLIC PARENT-TEACHER ASSOCIATIONS OF ONTARIO

In 1949 a move to consolidate local school associations led to the formation of the Federation of Catholic Parent-Teacher Associations of Ontario. The prime mover behind this development was the Most Reverend J.C. Cody, Archbishop of London, whose efforts were supported by the Ontario English Catholic Teachers' Association. Further promotional contributions were made by the Roman Catholic hierarchy and certain school inspectors, particularly those in Ottawa, Windsor, Kitchener, and Peterborough. Credit for drawing up the first constitution is given to

Reverend B.W. Harrigan, who was appointed by the bishops of Ontario as the federation's first spiritual adviser.

The federation's aims were defined as follows:

To promote the interests and objectives of education in the Catholic Elementary Schools, Secondary Schools and Colleges of Ontario.

To facilitate the harmonious and effective co-operation of the home, the school, the Church, the State and the child in the field of education in such schools.

To encourage the maintenance of, or the restoration of, the highest ideals of family life and to obviate or mitigate the evils arising from parental and child delinquency.

To promote the other recognized objectives of Catholic Parent-Teacher Associations of Ontario.

To engage with other agencies interested in the welfare of education.

To co-ordinate the work of Catholic Parent-Teacher Associations of the Province.

To assist Diocesan Councils, Regional Councils, and school Units of Catholic Parent-Teacher Associations in their formation and function.

Diocesan councils were established in 1950, with the approval of the bishops, in Ottawa, Toronto, Hamilton, Kingston, London, and Peterborough. In subsequent years most other dioceses followed suit and, in areas of heavy population, regional councils worked with the diocesan office. In 1951 the federation was incorporated under provincial charter.

One of the earliest significant actions of the federation was the passing by the assembly in 1949 of a resolution of protest against objectionable comic books. A letter was sent to the Minister of Justice and to the Attorney-General of the province asking that the admission and sale of such materials be discontinued. Among other early activities, a Counselling Committee assembled a travelling library and exhibits of literature. A Good Reading Committee was responsible for the preparation of a brief to the Senate designed to draw the attention of government leaders to the needs of young readers. Interest in federal education led to the submission of a brief on that topic to the Massey Commission. The provincial organization did a good deal during the same period to ensure that the question was thoroughly studied by local units.

An interest in adult or continuing education led to the early introduction of leadership training programs. Christopher Leadership courses, consisting of ten sessions for federation and other parish leaders, were first introduced at Windsor, and spread from there to other Ontario centres. An outgrowth of this program was a course in conducting effective meetings. The provincial association assisted local units with talks, panel discussions, and encyclical studies. Audio-visual workshops were held and a film library was created to provide supplements to other program material.

A major step was taken in 1959 when an anonymous donor supplied sufficient funds to open a provincial office in Toronto. This development gave the central organization a much stronger sense of purpose and enabled it to perform a greatly increased range of services. Another notable structural development was the addition of an Advisory Committee in 1960. The recognition of new areas of interest was signalled by the formation of a Safety Committee and a Citizenship Committee. Efforts were made to reach the mass media through a press information program, and a press clipping bureau was established to keep the federation office informed about what was happening in various areas of education.

The federation made a practice of holding its annual meetings in conjunction with those of the Ontario English Catholic Education Association during the Easter week each year. It established co-operative relationships with a considerable number of additional organizations as well. Delegates were sent to Christian curriculum conferences, to meetings of the Ontario Educational Research Council, the Ontario Association for Curriculum Development, and the Ontario Safety League, to Education Week gatherings, and to Social Life Conferences.

A manual for Catholic Parent-Teacher Associations which was in use in 1963 presented a list of achievements credited to local associations. They had 1 / through meetings of parents and teachers made possible an exchange of views and the development of mutual sympathy and understanding; 2 / given teachers an opportunity to present and explain the work done by children and to discuss their strengths and weaknesses with parents, thus giving the latter a better idea of their part in the supervision of the child's work at home; 3 / made it possible for teachers to encourage parents in the active practice of their religion, and to bring instruction to non-Catholic parents who had children in the school; 4 / enabled teachers and parents to hear especially qualified speakers discuss topics of interest to both groups; 5 / improved the home atmosphere through the correlation of the interests of parents and children; 6 / encouraged parents to attend daily mass, to receive the sacraments frequently, and to influence their children to do the same; 7 / helped to give teachers and parents a greater appreciation of Catholic education and of the work of those who contributed toward it; 8 / guided parents with respect to the role that movies, radio, and television should play in their children's use of leisure time; 9 / created a friendly spirit among members of the parish; 10 / developed a better understanding of the nature of children; 11 / assisted with the operation of religious vacation schools; 12 / offered monthly mass for members, children, pastor, and teachers; and 13 / sponsored the erection of outdoor Christmas cribs.

Various units across the province had performed quite specific services in the pursuit of their more general objectives. These had included purchasing First Communion outfits for needy children, serving First Friday breakfast to school children, providing milk and wholesome food for underprivileged children, providing clothing for needy children, arranging transportation and supervision for class excursions and field trips, sponsoring outings for teachers, members of religious orders, lay people, and pupils, acting as hostesses for nuns attending meetings and conventions, financing special teachers for public speaking, dramatics, and art, conducting hobby fairs, science shows, and art exhibits, maintaining school bulletin boards with listings of approved movies and radio programs, securing the showing of approved pictures at neighbourhood theatres, and conducting good visual education programs.

In 1962 the federation had a paid membership of 39,659 in 427 units in various parts of the province. By 1967–8, despite the large increase in enrolment in separate schools, there were only 30,783 members. This decline in membership meant a reduction in revenues, and thus necessitated some decrease in services. A loss of interest seemed particularly deplorable to the leaders of the movement at a time when the range of potential contributions seemed greater than ever.

THE INDUSTRIAL FOUNDATION ON EDUCATION

The Industrial Foundation on Education was founded as a result of deliberations and resolutions made at the landmark conference of educators, business executives, and others held at St Andrews-By-the-Sea in New Brunswick in 1956. At that time a crescendo of apprehension had developed in the face of recent evidences of Soviet progress in science and technology. It was feared that the free world might succumb to superior force and technique. Industrial leaders demonstrated a resolution, unprecedented and unsustained thereafter, to strengthen certain aspects of the nation's educational effort by voluntary means.

The purposes of the foundation were listed as follows in a statement prepared for the second Canadian Conference on Education:

(a) To promote moral and financial support of education, and especially higher education, by business and industry.
(b) To undertake such research and investigation of matters related to education as will assist the Foundation in furthering its prime purpose.
(c) By the dissemination of its findings and its public relations activities to promote a climate of opinion favourable to the support of education, to the effective motivation of students, and to development of their full educational potential by a greater percentage of those who are intellectually qualified.[2]

The foundation undertook studies in such areas as corporate aid to education, the availability and adequacy of student aid, the retention and motivation of students, the needs of society for trained personnel, the characteristics of institutions of higher education, and the status of education in other countries. During the several years of its existence, it published reports and newsletters relating to its investigations, and carried on a program of public relations and public information through addresses, radio programs, and participation in conferences, councils, committees, and discussions. A counselling service was maintained for the industries which held membership in the foundation in order to assist them to establish giving policies and programs. A record of all forms of student aid was maintained to provide information to schools, colleges, business and other organizations, and individuals. At the time this record was first assembled, it was the only one of its kind in Canada.

One of the forms of corporate giving which the foundation encouraged was that of matching gifts. A fairly standard program was worked out by which the company matched dollar for dollar the donations made by its employees to educational institutions. In order to be eligible, the employees' contributions usually had to be made either directly to the recipient institution or to an alumni or other fund, foundation, or association which transmitted them to such an institution, or else used them entirely for its benefit.

The foundation claimed a large share of the credit for a seven-fold increase in corporate giving between 1958 and 1962. There was, of course, no way of establishing the validity of this claim. If it had been generally acknowledged, one might assume that the foundation would not have disappeared within a very short time. Perhaps the most fundamental reason for the relative decline in corporate effort after that time was that the educational enterprise was rapidly growing so large that voluntary contributions seemed less and less likely to make a fundamental difference. As the provincial government tried to keep up with the responsibility, it found other agencies increasingly ready to leave it in possession of the field. There was also some disillusionment with the foundation itself. There were a great many initial hopes that it would prove a source of funds for all kinds of worthy purposes. As time went on, it was realized that the chief executive officer was not sitting on the top of limitless money bags which he might be persuaded to distribute among those who were fortunate enough or assiduous enough to win his favour.

FIVE

Associations for the promotion of specific causes relating to formal education

Most of the associations in this group concentrated on a single subject area or aspect of the educational program. They might be national or provincial, and, if the latter, might operate as part of the OEA or independently. Some were concerned only with school education, while others were interested in all levels, including the post-secondary.

THE INTERNATIONAL READING ASSOCIATION

The International Reading Association (IRA) was an outstanding example of a large organization devoted to one particular aspect of education. Apart from the restriction implied in its title, the scope of its operations was very comprehensive. It was open to lay and professional members in a number of countries whose interest in reading ranged from the pre-school to the adult level.

As stated in the by-laws according to a revision made in 1968, the purposes of the IRA were as follows:

A. To improve the quality of reading instruction at all levels by:
  1. encouraging the study of the reading process and its attendant problems;
  2. stimulating and promoting research dealing with all aspects of reading;
  3. publishing the results of pertinent and significant investigations and practices in reading;
  4. acting as a clearing house for information relating to reading;
  5. encouraging the development of high quality teacher education programs, both preservice and in-service.
B. To develop an awareness of the impact of reading upon our citizenry, and consequently to:
  1. encourage the development of worthwhile reading interests;
  2. promote the formation of lifetime reading habits;
  3. develop an appreciation of the values of reading in a democratic society.
C. To sponsor conferences and meetings planned to implement the purposes of the Association.
D. To promote the development among all peoples of a level of reading proficiency that is commensurate with each individual's unique capacity.

The organization, which was for a time the National Council for the Improvement of Reading Instruction, and later the International Council for the Improvement of Reading Instruction (ICIRI), originated through the interest of a group of students in a summer course on Foundations of Reading Instruction at Temple University in 1947. These students were aroused to action on learning about the seriousness of the problem of reading retardation in American schools. E.A. Betts provided the leadership for the formation of the organization which from the beginning welcomed all those who were interested in any phase of reading. The international dimension was added almost immediately when membership was requested by Janet M. Doxsey and Mrs G.H. Heslam of Montreal, Margaret Gerrard of Toronto, and Grace Hayes of Saint John, NB, and the word "international" was adopted in the title.

The objectives of the organization were stated more briefly in the early days than they were in 1968, and gave less indication of an interest in public promotional activities.

1. To stimulate and encourage research in:
   a. developmental, corrective, and remedial instruction in reading
   b. the diagnosis of disabilities in reading
   c. readability
   d. the improvement of textbook construction and publication from the point of view of the reading problems therein and of their effect on reading instruction.
2. To publish results of pertinent, significant investigation and experimentation to the end that general practices in reading instruction be improved.[1]

Early plans for action to attain these objectives included the publication of a bulletin, the first issue of which was mimeographed and circulated in November 1948. Arrangements were made for meetings to be held in conjunction with nationally known conventions. Steps were taken to assist in the creation of local groups and to supply members with materials needed for their own activities. In order to help overcome the financial burden many groups encountered in obtaining effective speakers, Betts and other board members undertook a heavy schedule of engagements in the United States and Canada.

Although the organization had members from outside North America before 1958, it was only then that the IRA, as it was now called after its merger with the National Association for Remedial Teachers in 1955, began the active promotion of international relationships. Affiliation was successfully sought with the World Confederation of Organizations of the Teaching Profession. One of the members whose regular duties would require his presence in Europe for a two-year period undertook to help organize councils there. The international interests of the IRA were demonstrated during the next few years in a number of different ways: by the inclusion of articles in the *Reading Teacher* by writers from outside the

United States and Canada, by the sponsorship of international meetings of leaders in the reading field, by the sponsorship of an international directory of individuals who were interested in improving reading instruction, by the expansion of an Overseas Committee to strengthen the expression of views from other countries, and by increasing contacts with foreign students and educators.

The Canadian response to the founding of the organization was enthusiastic at the beginning. Three delegates from the Toronto school system were sent to a reading institute at Temple University in February 1949, and, on their return, urged Toronto teachers to form a reading council. In October 1950 over seven hundred people became associate (i.e., local) members, of whom 106 were international or active members, meaning that they were eligible to receive copies of the bulletins. Margaret Robinson, who was appointed Canadian representative by the International Executive Board, undertook to promote the cause throughout the country by sending out copies of addresses of ICIRI speakers, quotations from ICIRI bulletins, articles on reading from the publishers, and other suitable material. These efforts had disappointing results, and for a few years most of the Canadian activity was centred in the Toronto and District Council for the Improvement of Reading Instruction (IRI), the Niagara Council for IRI, and the Kingston Council for IRI.

The Toronto council organized its conferences around specific themes. In 1950–1, for example, the topic was Developing Comprehension, and the program consisted of a lecture on A Developmental Reading Programme with Special Emphasis on Teaching the Reading Skills, classroom demonstrations on Developing Comprehension in grades 7 to 10, a lecture on How to Make More Effective Use of Instructional Materials with Emphasis on the Encyclopedia, a lecture on Prevention is Better than Cure, and reports of delegates to the Annual Institute on Reading at the Temple University Annual Meeting. A series of distinguished speakers, many of them from the United States, assisted with the programs at these meetings.

In 1957 M.K. MacDonald, Inspector of Public Schools in Toronto, wrote of the activities of the Toronto Council in the 13th Yearbook of the Ontario School Inspectors' Association.[2] He referred with approval to the demands for more information and greater teacher participation which had grown out of general meetings at which prominent authorities had outlined current philosophies and methods of teaching reading. Members of the council had conducted demonstrations in many classrooms throughout the city, which teachers from neighbouring schools had attended. MacDonald identified some of the beneficial results of this activity: "In this way, teachers acquired more confidence in their own abilities and consequently assumed leadership in grade and division committees. Much professional growth was evident and participation on the part of teachers became more widespread."

MacDonald referred to the growth in demand for workshops at which teachers could exchange views and discuss problems. In his view these had not been very successful because teachers were not ready for them. The turning point came when more attention was given to the proper procedures and when the services of competent resource people had been acquired. The development of leadership in the field had been particularly notable. At the time he wrote, three workshops were held each year on Fridays and Saturdays with an attendance of about 150 teachers.

MacDonald concluded with a tribute to the council, and attempted to identify the nature of some of its achievements.

The success of the reading council has been due to the fact that it is a voluntary organization of teachers who have a desire to improve professionally. Its growth has been rapid because its members are able to participate in activities which will increas their classroom efficiency. At this time administrators and teachers tend to be more and more professional in their outlook, and we like to feel that the council has contributed to this growth. Certainly, it has encouraged its members to take a critical view of their methods. There is considerably more interest and experimentation in the teaching of reading than ever before. Finally, there is a sincere attempt on the part of all to implement programmes which will take into account the individual differences among children.[3]

The report of the Board of Education for North York in 1960 referred to official encouragement for the formation of the North York Council, which had been set up in 1956. Since that time membership had grown to more than five hundred. The activities of the council included lectures, workshops, and courses for its members, as well as participation in the in-service training program for staff members. A handbook had been prepared for all teachers of grade 4 to assist in the teaching of reading skills, including phonics. Members were also working on a booklet explaining the primary reading program in North York for the benefit of grade 1 children.

The Oshawa and District Council of the IRA, another of many active branches, was given a charter from international headquarters in 1957 after drawing up a constitution the previous year. The council made a practice of devoting one meeting each year to the primary level, one to the junior level, and one to the intermediate level. Workshop themes were also rotated among grade levels.

In 1968 the first president of the council, L.T. Savery, gave his appraisal in an informal context.

The Oshawa and District Council of the International Reading Association has been in existence for some twelve or thirteen years. As one of the charter members, now retired from active teaching, I look back upon my association with it as a great source of help and inspiration to me in my work.

It provided me with the opportunity of hearing many outstanding speakers, not only in the Reading area, but also in the fields of Language and Mathematics as well. The discussions which have always followed the addresses were most helpful to me, as I am sure they were to everyone in attendance. Moreover, I feel that it has been a means of enabling the teachers of the area to become better acquainted with one another, both socially and professionally. In short, it has grown from a very small beginning, to become a very important factor in the training and development of the teachers of the district.

In 1968–9 the eighteen local councils which had existed in Ontario the previous year were reduced to thirteen, apparently because the formation of larger school boards was accompanied by the amalgamation of some of the smaller organizations. In North York the IRA Council became a Language Arts Council affiliated with the National Council of Teachers of English. Remaining councils were those in Oshawa and District, Hamilton and District, Etobicoke, Norfolk, London, Toronto, Ottawa, Greater Niagara, Windsor, Halton County, the Borough of York, Brantford, and East York. There were 371 active Ontario members in 1968, a number which the Co-ordinator for Ontario estimated to be no more than 10 per cent of the total of the local membership.

A leaflet issued in 1968 listed several benefits from active membership, such as contact with others among the estimated fifty thousand active participants, receipt of membership journals, the privilege of purchasing at reduced prices certain IRA publications reporting in-depth studies on many subjects in the field of reading, and the opportunity to submit articles to IRA journals and to present papers at conventions. Membership included a subscription to one of three periodicals: the *Reading Teacher*, primarily concerned with elementary education, *Journal of Reading*, concerned with secondary school, college, and adult reading, and *Reading Research Quarterly*, a scholarly journal devoted to research in reading.

Annual conventions, ordinarily held in the United States, but sometimes in Canada, were of five days' duration, and attracted approximately ten thousand members. A world congress was also held every two years. The one in Copenhagen in 1968 was attended by about 1,500 people from two dozen countries. Other activities of the same nature included regional conferences, seminars, and meetings held in co-operation with other organizations.

THE CANADIAN COUNCIL OF TEACHERS OF ENGLISH

Until comparatively recently there was no national professional organization to serve the needs of Canadian teachers of English at all levels, and no meeting ground where teachers and scholars from all parts of the country could exchange ideas. In order to keep up with professional developments, about two thousand Canadian teachers of English were reported to have become members of the National Council of Teachers of English (NCTE) in the United States in the early 1960s. That organization was unable, however, to become involved in issues that were distinctly Canadian. Accordingly, at a Conference for Canadian Teachers held during the annual convention of the NCTE at Cleveland in 1964, twenty-six teachers of English from several Canadian provinces elected a committee to investigate the state of professional English associations in Canada and to explore the possibility of forming a Canadian council. While the committee, reporting at the convention held the following year in Boston, recommended the formation of such a council, definite action was rather slow. In the first stage provincial representatives met in Banff and at the convention of the NCTE in 1966 to make initial plans. In the next stage, reached in 1967, they took action to establish the council.

The objectives of the Canadian Council of Teachers of English (CCTE) were to improve the quality of instruction in English at all levels, to encourage research and experimentation in the teaching of English, to facilitate professional co-operation among the members, to hold public discussions, to sponsor the publication of appropriate articles and reports, and to integrate the efforts of all those concerned with the improvement of instruction in English. Membership was open to all those engaged in the teaching and supervision of the teaching of English at any school level and to all others interested in the improvement of such teaching. By the second year of its existence the council had nearly eight hundred members. At the same time seven provincial associations of teachers of English, as well as the Association of Canadian University Teachers of English, had become affiliates of the council.

Early conferences of the council attracted registrants from all over the country, and were regarded as highly successful. The first issue of the *CCTE Newsletter* appeared in 1968, and the first issue of the official periodical, the *English Quarterly*, a short time later. The council planned to make the latter publication a true quarterly by 1971. After conferences and publications were established on a firm basis, research, development, data collection, and education in English were expected to receive more emphasis.

THE ONTARIO COUNCIL OF TEACHERS OF ENGLISH
The Ontario Council of Teachers of English was created by the initiative of the English Section of the OEA in response to directions to all sections in 1966 to explore the possibility of vertical integration to overcome the limitations of identification with only one of the three traditional levels of education. The section had hitherto consisted of teachers of English in secondary schools. Another major influence was the formation of an action committee in 1965 to establish a Canadian Council of Teachers of

English. Each province was expected to set up a body wide enough in organization and membership to contribute appropriately to the national organization. Within the section there had been a growing realization that the crucial issues relating to the teaching of English had to be tackled on a broader front.

After the initial decision was made, there was considerable committee activity to outline a central and regional structure. A *pro tem* executive, which served until the annual meeting in September, set up subcommittees to deal with immediate problems of finance, aims and objectives, and programs. An early decision was made to continue affiliation with the OEA. A full conference was scheduled for the fall to enable delegates from fifteen university-centred regions of the province and from all levels of the educational system to investigate the possibility of forming local associations. It was hoped that strong lines of communication would be formed with the central organization.

THE SCIENCE TEACHERS' ASSOCIATION
OF ONTARIO

The Science Teachers' Association of Ontario (STAO) is fortunate in having a record of its history in half a dozen concise pages written by D.C. Moyer. The association was formed in 1890 against a background of complaints about the lack of proper teachers, learning by rote, unsatisfactory courses of study, inappropriate examinations, and the opposition of unprogressive examiners. While science was introduced into the grammar schools at least as early as the 1850s, there were for a time almost no teachers. Although this deficiency was gradually remedied, the subject was for some time taught only as a collection of facts, with no attempt to give students an understanding of scientific methods. About the time the association was formed, attention was shifting from chemistry to physics, laboratories were being built in some of the better schools, and students were beginning to be allowed to perform experiments themselves.

The first president of the association, F.W. Merchant, headed a long list of distinguished science teachers who served in the same capacity in subsequent years. Annual meetings were held in close association with those of other sections of the OEA, and speakers on science subjects customarily addressed the entire group in attendance. Since there were very few secondary schools, the OEA members tended to concentrate on issues relating to elementary school education. Between 1910 and 1940 science teachers met primarily to hear ideas expounded by university professors. The association repeatedly expressed concern over the fact that high school courses were rigidly controlled by the Department of Education and the universities, leaving little scope for teacher initiative.

A change of meeting places in the 1950s from the laboratories of the University of Toronto to Bloor Collegiate Institute accompanied the assumption of a larger role on the part of secondary school teachers.

There was an increased interest in developing courses that would better meet the needs of students who were not bound for university. The introduction of the Reorganized Program in the 1960s greatly expanded the opportunities for curriculum development. The ample quarters provided at Bloor Collegiate Institute contributed to another facet of the activities of the association by making it possible for many suppliers to display their scientific apparatus. During the same period increased interest in professional activity among science teachers led to the formation of a local association in Metropolitan Toronto, loosely affiliated with the STAO, which met four times a year. The provincial association at the same time established international connections by affiliating with the National Science Teachers' Association in the United States.

Affiliation with the American association and visits by many Ontario teachers to conventions in various parts of the United States speeded changes in Ontario courses of study. Impressed by the earlier introduction of serious science courses in American elementary schools, leading members of the STAO became convinced that their province should follow suit. As a means of exerting more influence at this level, they arranged for the inclusion of elementary science teachers on their executive.

THE CANADIAN ASSOCIATION FOR
THE SOCIAL STUDIES

A small group of members of the Faculty of Education at the University of Alberta took the initiative in 1963 to establish the Canadian Association for the Social Studies as a means of furthering the improvement of instruction in the social studies, promoting research, and encouraging communication and co-operation among agencies concerned with instruction in this area. The new agency was seen as a counterpart to the National Council for the Social Studies in the United States. It appeared at a time when many educators, particularly in Ontario, had been advocating separate treatment of social science disciplines at various levels of the school system. The association used the term "social studies" to include history, geography, economics, sociology, political science, anthropology, and any modification or combination of such subjects.

Membership was open to all those with an interest in social studies at any level of education, as well as to such bodies as provincial social studies organizations. Annual conventions were held in various locations in Canada beginning with the first one in Montreal in 1964, when a constitution was adopted. A research director was appointed the following year, and immediately began to prepare an inventory of research being conducted in the teaching of social studies subjects in Canada. This work was regarded as preliminary to the task of publishing a journal.

One of the main concerns of the association was the problem of Canadian unity. It was felt that teachers of social studies were in a particularly good position to promote understanding between the two main cultural groups. The programs at the successive annual conventions reflected the unity theme.

THE CANADIAN SOCIETY FOR EDUCATION THROUGH ART

The Canadian Society for Education Through Art (CSEA) developed out of a special concern for art education among a number of members of the CEA. For a time the CEA encouraged the group by providing for art education on its agenda. In December 1953 a Founding Committee drafted a constitution and a set of rules which were accepted by the members at the first general assembly held in Quebec in 1955. An executive had been elected at the CEA convention at Edmonton the previous year.

The constitution and rules were changed and updated as the society developed. According to a 1968 version, the purpose was simply "the encouragement and advancement of education through art in Canada." This purpose was to be achieved through the regular publication of a newsletter for the exchange of general information; the publication of an annual report; the organization of exhibitions of original art, reproductions, and illustrations of methods of art education; the organization of conferences, meetings, and study groups; and the encouragement and co-ordination of research concerned with art education. A meeting of the society was to be held at least once every two years, although in practice such meetings were held annually. The basic membership categories were active and associate, the first category consisting of provincial and national members, and the second of student, patron, and educational members.

At the first conference of the CSEA the president, C.D. Gaitskill, articulated some of the feelings that inspired the original members.

As artists and educationists, we must believe that art is one of man's highest forms of expression and communication. Again, we must hold that creative activity in art is a basic need common to all people. As teachers, whether of kindergarten children or of university students, we must maintain that education through art is a natural means of learning at all periods of the development of the individual, and that such an education fosters values and disciplines essential for full intellectual, emotional and social development of human beings in a community. As members both of this Society and of the teaching profession, we must feel strongly that association in Canada of those concerned with education through art is necessary in order that we may share experiences, improve practices, and strengthen the position of art in relation to all education. Finally, since education has no 'water-tight compartments' we must hold that co-operation with those in Canada concerned with other disciplines of study and domains of education would be of mutual advantage in securing closer co-ordination of activities directed to solving problems in common.[4]

The address of the president in 1957 indicated some of the things the society had done to further its objectives, and suggested others that it might consider. The annual meeting had made a contribution by bringing together Canadians from widely scattered areas in Canada to discuss artistic and educational matters. A research project was currently being conducted across the country to identify opportunities for art education in Canada. The society had become linked with a network of national and international cultural organizations, including the Canadian Arts Council, the International Society for Education Through Art, and, through the latter, UNESCO. The president hoped that the society would from time to time be able to produce reports based on careful research and that it would be able to bring speakers of international repute before audiences composed of both general and art educationists.

By 1960 the activities of the society had expanded considerably. Newsletters had begun to appear in 1958, followed by annual reports, membership lists, a Who's Who in Canadian art education, and statements of policy about the organization. Other activities had included the distribution of scholarship funds, the organization and distribution of didactic exhibitions of children's art, the establishment of commissions to study the problems of art education in Canada, and the conduct of certain other research projects. Advice had been offered for the improvement of art conferences sponsored by commercial interests and art teaching as it was found in certain religious organizations such as Sunday schools. The society had worked closely with the Junior Red Cross Society in providing travelling art exhibitions. Closer liaison had been established with the National Gallery of Canada.

An example of the society's involvement in the scholarship field is provided by its administration of the Hallmark Art Scholarships provided by William E. Coutts Co, Ltd, publishers of Hallmark cards. In 1969 there were five scholarships worth $500 each designed to assist high school seniors who displayed outstanding artistic ability through drawings and paintings submitted to the CSEA to undertake studies in art or art education in centres of higher education of their choice. These centres might be colleges, universities, teacher training institutions, or accredited art schools. Other things being equal, the candidate who was unable to continue his studies without financial assistance was to be given preference.

The society did not regard art competitions as a desirable way to encourage the development of artistic talent among children. In a policy statement in which such competitions were strongly opposed the following points were made. 1 / Competition is contrary to the purposes and procedures of art education in our schools. 2 / Competition is contrary to an artistic tradition which influences art education in our schools. 3 / Competition depends upon the whims of the judges. 4 / Competition does not improve the standard of children's art, but often degrades it. 5 / Co-operation, not competition, should be fostered through art education in our schools. Policy statements were also issued on such matters as the conditions under which the correlation of art with other subjects was desirable and the harm done by the use of non-creative commercially prepared devices that interfered with the artistic development of school children.

THE ONTARIO SOCIETY FOR EDUCATION THROUGH ART

The Ontario Society for Education Through Art (OSEA) was established as an affiliate of the CSEA in 1955. At that time the Ontario Society of Teachers of Art joined the new organization. The most important part of the program was the annual meeting held in conjunction with the OEA convention. The program at this meeting might consist, in addition to the inevitable addresses, of discussions on such topics as art courses offered at various grade levels in the schools, community art programs, the purposes of art education, and other such matters. There might also be demonstrations of techniques and tours of artists' workshops. A display at the Toronto Education Centre in 1963 included child art from around the world collected by the Red Cross, art assignment books, books on the history and techniques of art, asbestos modelling, tin can sculpture, puppetry, wood carving, crayon techniques, graphic creation, and three-dimensional works by senior public school students.

Four categories of members were defined. 1 / Ordinary members were members of the OEA who made the OSEA their section choice. 2 / Subscription members were ordinary members who belonged to an OEA section other than the OSEA, but who wished to attend meetings of the OSEA and to receive its publications. 3 / Special subscription members were those whose sole interest was in OSEA matters. 4 / Group subscription memberships were open to regionally established art education groups. Both ordinary and subscription members were entitled to attend all general meetings of the society, to vote on matters brought before such meetings, to hold office, and to receive copies of all the society's publications. Special subscription members could not vote or hold office. A group subscription member could send one member to the Advisory Council, with voting privileges at general meetings.

A list of projects under study by the OSEA in 1965 was provided in the Annual Report of the CSEA: 1 / a revision of the constitution to enable regional groups of art teachers to become active affiliates of the OSEA; 2 / certification of graduates of the Ontario College of Art who were teaching in the elementary schools; 3 / education and training of elementary school teachers with particular reference to art education; 4 / curriculum at the elementary level, with emphasis on art education from kindergarten through grade 13; 5 / tentative plans for the annual meeting in 1966 to include the establishment of commissions to study the problems at the elementary, secondary, post-secondary, and supervisory levels; 6 / an increase in the number of issues of the journal of the society to three; and 7 / membership matters.

The society exerted major efforts to bring about an improvement in the quality of art teaching in academic secondary schools. A statement issued in 1964 declared that the ideal art teacher was creative, technically accomplished, and educated in the liberal arts tradition, as well as having certain qualities of character and temperament. Up to that time only a university degree, not necessarily related to art, had been required of teachers in this area. The society thought it would be desirable to establish university fine art courses. The statement suggested that such courses should aim primarily at the production of original artists, with some attention also to technical training in the craft sense, to free expression, to art history or archaeology, and to criticism. A pattern of courses was proposed for a university art program, with a brief outline of the content of certain courses.

THE ONTARIO EDUCATIONAL TELEVISION
ASSOCIATION
The Ontario Educational Television Association (OETA) was a short-lived organization which demonstrated the interest of leading members of a number of key groups and individuals in the potentialities of television as an educational medium. Its lack of success in achieving the majority of its objectives also demonstrated the frustrations experienced by many would-be innovators in the late 1950s and early 1960s. Fortunately a reinvigorated Department of Education eventually acted in a manner and on a scale far beyond the capacity of any voluntary association, no matter how well financed.

The inspiration for what was later organized as a council came from the OTF and the Ontario School Trustees' Council. In 1959 and 1960 a joint committee consisting of representatives of these two organizations, and later enlarged by representation from a small number of other groups, undertook certain activities, including a survey of viewers' reactions to CBC educational broadcasts. The scope of the intended program was outlined in a statement of aims and objectives in a brief to the Board of Broadcast Governors in 1960.

1. To keep in close contact with all educational television programmes that are now or will be placed into effect, whether they are experimental or established programmes and to learn all that is possible from the experience of others.

2. To evaluate the results of this continuing study in the light of our own peculiar circumstances and determine the most feasible research projects that could be profitably undertaken in Canada.

3. To support and promote such research projects in such ways as we are able.

4. To aid in increasing public understanding of this powerful means of communication in its application to educational purposes.

5. To finally gain as clear an understanding as possible of the most practical and advantageous manner in which television may be employed in education in Ontario on a permanent basis.

6. To promote and support the action needed to establish educational television in our system of education on a permanent basis, in such ways as we are able.[5]

In this particular brief, which constituted one of the major achievements of the committee, it was suggested that the provision of network facilities for nationally or provincially sponsored educational television should be primarily the responsibility of the CBC, while the provision of local facilities should be the responsibility of the local community station. Where a city had only one television station, and that an affiliate of the CBC, it should carry both types of telecasts. While the committee was not prepared to suggest a specific number of hours per week to be devoted to educational television, it indicated that the Board of Broadcast Governors should insist, in general terms, that stations allocate adequate time for this purpose, having regard to the requests made by the education authorities and the resources of the station. The brief contained several forward-looking recommendations, including a suggestion that, in granting licences and formulating broadcasting regulations, the board take into consideration the possibility of the extensive use of television for educational purposes in the future, and that enough UHF channels be reserved for eventual educational use in all parts of Ontario.

When a decision was made in late 1960 to put the organization on a more permanent basis, the sustaining members were listed as follows: the Ontario School Trustees' Council, l'Association des commissaires des écoles bilingues d'Ontario, the Ontario Headmasters' Association, l'Association des parents et d'instituteurs de langue française d'Ontario, the Canadian Broadcasting Corporation, the Ontario Federation of Home and School Associations, the Industrial Foundation on Education, the Ontario Association of School Business Officials, the OTF, the Ontario Department of Education, the Associated High School Boards of the Province of Ontario, and the Provincial Council of Women of Ontario. Most of these organizations had a single representative, although the Ontario School Trustees' Council and the OTF each sent two or three. There was also an associate member from each of the following: the CBC, the Ontario School Trustees' Council, the Research Department of the Toronto Board of Education, the Teaching Aids Centre of the Toronto Board of Education, and the Ontario College of Education.

The objectives of the association were more comprehensive and ambitious than those of the predecessor committee, as the following extracts from the constitution indicate.

1. To undertake such work and investigation as are deemed necessary to keep the members of the Association and others fully informed of the developments, experiments, regular programmes, evaluation of experiments and regular programmes and any other relative aspect of educational television and other teaching aids.
2. To evaluate such information and data as is developed from the above work and investigation in its possible application to educational television in Ontario.
3. To determine gaps that may exist in our knowledge and understanding of educational television and promote or participate in the research and investigation necessary to close these gaps.
4. To determine the future possibilities and potential of using television as a medium of education in Ontario and encourage research to determine the subject areas in which television can be employed effectively as a teaching aid.
5. To suggest the most feasible and practical ways and means of introducing educational television programmes of the highest standard into our schools in subject areas where they are proven to be of value.
6. To place the resources of the Association at the disposal of school boards, communities and television stations within the province to further their efforts in the introduction and maintenance of a high standard of educational television.
7. To take such action as deemed necessary to ensure that adequate provision is made in government regulations to satisfy such future needs of educational television as they are envisioned.
8. To promote and otherwise participate in the provision of adequate equipment and other facilities including trained technical and teaching staff to satisfy the needs of educational television insofar as its application is considered desirable and effective by the Association.
9. To foster a widespread interest in educational television and to sponsor a programme designed to keep the public well informed of the progress being made.
10. Endeavour to ensure that educational television be available to all areas, including rural areas, in the province as soon as facilities permit.

Although there were supposed to be annual meetings and additional ones called by the chairman after adequate written notice, nothing was heard from the chairman, S.H. Deeks, until October 1962, when he sent a letter to the writer, then an associate member of the council, explaining that his responsibilities had increased so extensively during the previous year that he had been unable to devote any effort to the work of the council. He made alternative suggestions: that the council amalgamate with the Metropolitan Educational Television Association (META) or that, if other members wished to continue the council, a new chairman be chosen. Action was taken to explore the first of these two proposals, although it seemed rather doubtful that a way could be found to enable a weak and relatively impecunious provincial body to amalgamate with a flourishing and comparatively well financed local one. The joint committee, chaired on behalf of OETA by the writer, worked out proposals for a more effective provincial body that might achieve some of the objectives outlined in the OETA constitution, and which META might support. There was a recommendation that a secretary be employed to help prepare for a conference to which all interested and concerned bodies in Ontario would be invited, and which would make long-term decisions about the existence, role, composition, and financing of a province-wide ETV body. The cost of such a conference, including the secretary's salary, was estimated at $5,000 dollars.

The OETA-META meetings produced agreement on seven points.

1. There is sufficient interest in the possibility of improving education in Ontario by means of educational television to justify a serious organized attack on the problems involved.
2. Optimum development of the medium requires both central organization and enthusiastic participation at the local level. The pioneering activities of M.E.T.A. could serve as a useful example for other Ontario communities. Ultimately a considerable proportion of educational television programmes used might be produced locally provided that the necessary funds could be obtained.
3. A strong provincial organization should perform the following functions:
   (a) It should ensure the necessary integration of television activities at all levels of education, including pre-school, elementary, secondary, university, and adult education. Working toward agreement on the apportionment of limited broadcasting facilities would be a most important part of this function.
   (b) It should assemble and circulate up-to-date information on the uses of educational television in Ontario and elsewhere.
   (c) It should encourage evaluation of educational television programmes, and itself conduct studies where possible.
   (d) It should present the case for educational television as a competitor with other interests for the use of television facilities in general.
   (e) It should encourage the establishment of local chapters on the M.E.T.A. model where local interest indicates the practicability of such a step.
   (f) It should gather and distribute funds among local chapters for worthy projects.

(g) It should co-ordinate activities among chapters and ensure maximum interchange of advisory services, films, etc.

4. One possible form of the central organization might involve the expansion of the membership of O.E.T.A. to include representatives of all major provincial educational organizations, representatives of local chapters as these developed, and individuals with specialized knowledge of educational television. The full membership would assemble periodically to discuss major issues and make policy decisions. In addition, a central office with a full-time executive secretary, clerical assistance, and certain facilities would have to be provided to perform many of the functions of the organization.

5. If the prospects of establishing such an organization seemed favourable, its activities might begin with an invitational conference of interested educators from all parts of the province. Such a conference might clarify the functions of an expanded O.E.T.A. and approve a constitution.

6. Since a substantial guaranteed annual budget would have to be assured, the question of further progress would have to await assurance of the availability of funds from public or private sources.

7. The usefulness of any provincial organization would be entirely dependent on the approval of the Department of Education. It was, therefore, considered essential to ascertain the attitude of the Chief Director of Education before any definite action was taken.

In accordance with the implications of point 7, the chairman of the OETA group was asked to approach the Chief Director of Education for an indication of his attitude. F.S. Rivers, who occupied the position, was not sympathetic. He declared that the department was actively exploring the problem, but had not yet decided on the most effective kind of provincial organization. An advisory committee to the minister might well perform many of the functions suggested for OETA, and would give the organizations represented on OETA an opportunity to express their views. This verdict spelled the effective end of OETA.

THE EDUCATIONAL MEDIA ASSOCIATION
OF CANADA

The Educational Media Association of Canada was established as recently as 1968, and held its first annual meeting in 1969. It had roots in the National Education Association Department of Audio-Visual Instruction extending back over a period of many years. A small group of Canadians involved in audio-visual education established the practice of holding a breakfast at the annual convention of the American group as a Canadian Audio-Visual Association. In 1965 a number of companies distributing materials and manufacturing equipment obtained the support of this group for the publication of the *Canadian Audio-Visual Review*.

The next year the organization began holding business meetings, and in 1968 organized a seminar in conjunction with Canadian Education Showplace. At the next meeting in the United States a constitution was adopted along with the new name The Educational Media Association of Canada. The organization remained associated with the National Education Association Department of Audio-Visual Instruction.

THE CANADIAN COUNCIL FOR PROGRAMMED LEARNING

An organization which reflected the peak of interest in programmed learning, but which lasted only from 1963 to 1964, was the Canadian Council for Programmed Learning. Had this council been able to overcome its organizational problems and find an adequate source of funds, it might have made an important contribution in an area of high promise. As things turned out, it was unable to continue after a grant of $15,000 from the Ford Foundation was exhausted.

Much of the initiative for establishing the council came from outside the educational establishment. The founders consisted of a group who saw a need for communication and co-ordination of effort. They felt that there should be some means by which the writers of programs could become aware of one another's efforts. It also seemed very desirable to avoid duplication of field trials.

The honorary president, president, and national director of the association were Samuel Beatty, Arthur V. Pigott, and D. Toppin. During the year of activity the council held regular meetings, symposiums, short courses, and workshops for educators and industrialists. One of these was a four-day meeting in Toronto in December 1963; another of similar length in April 1964 featured an appearance by B.F. Skinner. During the year the council published two issues of a *News Bulletin* and a glossary of terms called *Programmed Learning in Canada*. The lack of durability of the organization was attributed by some to its adoption of an excessively promotional approach and by others to its formation and operation outside formal educational agencies. Although these factors may indeed have been of considerable significance, it is doubtful that an agency devoted to a single instructional approach could have maintained for long the scale of operations which it undertook at the beginning with only voluntary financial contributions to sustain it.

THE ASSOCIATION OF EDUCATIONAL DATA SYSTEMS

The Association of Educational Data Systems (AEDS) was founded in the United States in 1962 to advance education through the development of a greater understanding of the impact of educational technology. It undertook to disseminate information about ideas, techniques, materials, and applications in the data systems field. A major aspect of its program was a large convention held in a variety of locations in different parts of the United States where addresses were given by various authorities and papers were presented by theorists and practitioners in the field.

Between conventions the association developed a program of activities extending throughout the year that expanded rapidly, particularly after the appointment of an executive secretary in 1965. Local chapters held workshops in which certain topics were discussed in small groups; attendance varied from 25 to 175. Typical workshop groups examined the practical problems involved in automating certain procedures in large city school systems, studied developing information systems in colleges and universities, inquired into instructional programs in data processing in secondary technical schools and colleges, or took a criitcal look at educational data processing. Another AEDS activity of a similar type involved the sponsorship of invitational conferences of deans of colleges of education to discuss the role of colleges in training teachers in educational data processing. The association undertook to encourage secondary school students by sponsoring a competition in programming. Publication activities included the production of the *Monitor* and the *Journal of Educational Data Processing.*

From the beginning a number of Canadians attended AEDS conventions. As early as 1965 there was some discussion of the possibility of establishing a chapter of the association in Ontario, with F.W. Minkler, Director of Education in North York, taking the lead in pressing for action. Positive steps were taken toward this end early in 1969, when representatives of the Department of Education, school boards, colleges of applied arts and technology, colleges of education, and industries involved with education met under the chairmanship of C.H. Westcott, Executive Assistant to the Minister of Education. Plans were made to draw up a constitution and to elect officers. There was a prospect that the annual convention of the association for 1971 might be held in Toronto.

THE ETHICAL EDUCATION ASSOCIATION

The Ethical Education Association was formed in 1959 as a non-political, inter-religious group with the declared purpose of promoting certain causes in the public schools. It asserted its support of religious and racial understanding, the improved teaching of moral and ethical values, the abolition of instruction in any particular religious doctrine, and the improved teaching of all subjects so that students might be better prepared for citizenship in a world community. The particular concern of the association was the provision for religious instruction in Ontario public schools introduced in 1944, which its members regarded as thoroughly undesirable. They attempted to arouse public opinion against the pertinent regulations, and to bring pressure to bear on political and educational leaders to have them rescinded.

The essence of the case was presented in A Report on Religious

Education in Ontario Public Schools, an informal mimeographed document issued in March 1960. The document noted that, when elementary education was made free and compulsory in Ontario in the 1870s, neither religious instruction nor religious observance had been part of the school day. There had, however, been persistent and often successful efforts made on the part of the clergy and laity of the larger Protestant denominations to introduce compulsory religious instruction into the public schools. For nearly six decades after 1884, when Bible reading without comment was included in the opening exercises and clergymen were given permission to teach in the schools after hours, no significant concessions had been made by the Department of Education. However the Inter-Church Committee for Weekday Religious Instruction, formed in 1936, had succeeded in inducing many school boards to adopt its syllabus for use by teachers from 9:00 to 9:30 each morning.

The report recalled the heated debate in the Ontario Legislature when the newly elected Conservative government introduced the program of religious instruction to be given for one hour each week.[6] Opponents of the scheme urged as an alternative that moral and ethical values be taught by precept and example. They could, however, muster only 43 per cent of the members present to vote against the government measure. A public opinion poll taken at the time was said to have indicated that 49 per cent of the people were in favour and 44 percent opposed. It was thus by a slim majority that Ontario became the only political entity in Canada, the United States, or England to have a compulsory (with provisions for exemption) course in religion in what purported to be a public school system.

A section of the report dealing with the curriculum identified what members of the association regarded as a number of objectionable features of the course. 1 / The regulations stated that issues of a controversial or sectarian nature were to be avoided. Members of the association felt, however, that it was impossible for instruction in a particular religion to be non-sectarian. The Teacher's Guides to Religious Education for Grades 1 to 6 seemed to demonstrate that there was no real intention of adhering to such an injunction. One section, for example, stated frankly that the ultimate aim of instruction was the acceptance of the historic Christian faith. 2 / The stories presented in the course contained statements and encouraged concepts that were not acceptable to some Christian groups. Teachers were enjoined, for instance, to give biblical references to support worship on Sunday, a teaching that flatly contradicted a fundamental belief of the Seventh Day Adventists. Further, various stories associated mental and other forms of illness, lameness, and blindness with sin, an idea that few Christians or non-Christians thought suitable to introduce to young children. 3 / The guide books contained many statements deprecating the Jews and their religion. They were described as being given to "treachery and violent hatred," and their leaders were said to be "hypocrites" and "bent on murder." In the course for grade 6 the teacher was asked to emphasize the difference between the attitude of Jesus toward people in distress and that of "the ordinary Rabbi, who with face turned aside and robe gathered up would pass as far distant as possible." 4 / The course outlined in the guide books inhibited the development of a sympathetic understanding of other races and religions by its frequent assertions of their inferiority to Christianity. A particularly objectionable example read thus: "Children are made much of (in the East) as they are in the West, though character training is not taken as seriously, for in the East the customs and traditions require different moral standards. No insistance on truth or personal integrity is made ..." Throughout the course, great emphasis was placed on small Christian groups in other countries, but no mention was made of other religious faiths and their humanitarian principles.

In an effort to determine how a representative number of parents who objected to the existing regulations were handling the problem, and how the program was being conducted in the schools, the association carried out a survey in sixteen widely scattered communities in Ontario, including several of the larger cities. 1 / Among the respondents, 25 per cent revealed that there was no religious instruction in the schools attended by their children, and another 25 per cent indicated that less than one hour a week was devoted to the subject. On the other hand, 6 per cent of the schools used more than the required time, the allotment ranging up to two and one-half hours. Thus in a majority of the schools there appeared to be a contravention of the law. 2 / Sixty per cent of the parents responding claimed that there was a conflict between what the children were taught at school and what they were taught in the home. In some cases, children of the Jewish or other faiths were made to feel guilty or inferior, those holding Christian beliefs not in accordance with those taught in the course were perplexed, and those who could not report that they regularly attended Sunday school were singled out for expressions of opprobrium. 3 / Provisions of the regulations for parents to exempt their children, for the teacher to exempt himself, and for the school board to request exemption for all the schools under its control were not being effectively implemented. Among the reasons were that parents were not being given adequate information about the course, that a request for exemption might be the source of acute embarrassment for the child, and that suitable alternative accommodation and activities were not being provided for those for whom exemption was requested. The association's verdict was that exemption, rather than being a guarantee of the rights of the individual in matters of conscience, was a penalty the child had to pay because his parents' beliefs differed from those of the majority.

The Hamilton brief gave seven reasons for regarding the existing practice of "religious indoctrination" as a tragic mistake. 1 / It departed violently from the Ontario tradition of public schools where children of all religions received equal treatment. 2 / The majority violated democratic principles when it imposed its faith on the children of minorities in a public institution. 3 / The use of public funds to promote any particular religious creed violated the taxpayer's freedom to support only those religions and spiritual groups which he favoured. 4 / The schools had been partially diverted from their role as educational institutions in that they had assumed a responsibility for indoctrination. 5 / Exemption from religious instruction in a public school constituted a penalty rather than a privilege. 6 / It was unfair that little children should have to choose between indoctrination in an alien faith and isolation from their classmates. 7 / Separation of children according to religious belief negated, or at least discouraged, the development of tolerance and understanding.

It would, of course, be impossible to estimate the extent of the influence of the Ethical Education Association in the 1960s. There is no doubt, however, that public opinion moved strongly in the directions which it favoured. By the time the Mackay Committee issued its report in early 1969 it appeared that only formal action remained to nullify the 1944 regulations. The fact that such action had not been taken in 1970 appeared to indicate only a minor delay, although evidence of a certain amount of opposition to the committee's report undoubtedly played a part.

The Ethical Education Association presented one of the strongest briefs to the Mackay Committee. Its members could take considerable satisfaction in the fact that the committee's recommendations seemed to reflect most of their major views. Ironically, some of the most acute criticism of these recommendations was based on the accusation that they would give the schools an undesirable responsibility for indoctrinating children in a particular set of ethical and moral values. The Ethical Education Association had been quite unequivocal in some of its assertions that the school should not be concerned in any way with indoctrination, although it had apparently referred to indoctrination in a restricted sense.

THE ONTARIO ALLIANCE OF CHRISTIAN SCHOOLS
The Ontario Alliance of Christian Schools was formed in 1957 to support a group of private schools organized and maintained by Protestants holding fundamentalist Christian beliefs, although not restricted to any single church group. The alliance declared its intention of aiding schools and school societies to further the larger cause of Christian education. As stated in its constitution, its objectives were as follows:

1. To encourage, promote, extend and assist Christian education;
2. To foster and promote uniformity and high standards of Christian education;
3. To foster and promote high standards of teacher training;
4. To attract desirable and efficient personnel to the teaching profession;

5. To secure, where possible and when necessary, Provincial legislation establishing and/or recognizing for parents the right and the freedom to establish free, parent-controlled Christian schools in which these objectives may be achieved.[7]

Like other private schools in the province, the Christian schools had to meet academic standards established by the Department of Education. For this purpose a full-time inspector was maintained by the alliance. As was also true of other private schools, the parents or other benevolent agencies supporting such schools had to meet the entire cost, nor were supporters thereby relieved of the obligation to pay taxes to support the public school system. This issue was a paramount one with members of the alliance, who contended that those who supported their schools had every justification for being treated in the same way as the supporters of the separate schools. In terms of logic or justice it seemed difficult to refute their case. The only distinction that could be demonstrated between the two groups was that the status of the separate schools was grounded in long historical tradition.

These concerns were reflected in the recommendations which completed a brief to the Provincial Committee on Aims and Objectives of Education in the Schools of Ontario. These recommendations would have had the government of Ontario

1. declare that the formulation of aims and objectives of education reflect the religious commitment and belief of those who define such statements.
2. declare that it is unrealistic to expect that one type of public school will be satisfactory to all in the diversified society of our present age.
3. declare that the freedom of religion acknowledged in the Canadian Bill of Rights, must be honoured in a freedom of education opportunities.
4. declare that no discrimination will be tolerated against schools which provide basic elementary education reflecting the religious commitment of the organizing body.
5. acknowledge the Christian schools represented by the Alliance of Christian Schools in the Province of Ontario as schools which are entitled to the same privileges as the public schools and/or the separate schools.[8]

In its brief the alliance identified some of the fundamental differences between the objectives pursued in its schools and those identified for the public schools in literature issued by the Department of Education. The department seemed to make adaptation to society, rather than to the will of God, the chief aim. A statement from the *Programme of Studies for Grades 1 to 6 of the Public and Separate Schools* asserted, for example, that the school "must seek to lead the child to choose and accept as his own those ideals of conduct and endeavour that a Christian and a democratic society approves." The use of the word "Christian" did not, evidently, add to the palatability of the statement.

In another context Reverend Jacob B. Vos gave a further explanation of the reasons why parents who sent their children to the Christian schools were not satisfied with the education offered by the public schools. It was not that they thought the academic standards of these schools inadequate, or that the teachers lacked the ability and dedication necessary for effective teaching.

In what sense, then, is the public school "not good enough"? In that it does not provide the kind of education that, in our view, the Christian child should receive. The public school cannot do so. The public school is a comprehensive institution. Its population represents the widest diversity of religious commitment in Canada. Already for this reason it cannot give a truly Christian education. Furthermore, as a comprehensive public institution it expresses the predominant current of the culture which it represents. And Canadian culture, when judged by Biblical standards, is not a Christian culture, even though many Christian influences have helped shape it; it is overwhelmingly man-centred. This public school cannot properly educate the *Christian* child.[9]

The alliance's brief did not have much visible impact on the Provincial Committee on Aims and Objectives, to judge by the nature of the latter's recommendations. Encouraging the child to conduct his own self-initiated search for truth conflicts with the alliance's position that the school must not hesitate to lead the child unequivocally along a clearly defined path. Nor did the committee see fit to recommend tax relief for the supporters of private schools.

A brief from the alliance to the provincial cabinet of Ontario in September 1968 included an appendix which suggested a legal framework under which a system making adequate financial provision for independent schools might operate. The scheme was designed to create conditions that would ensure both the highest standards of educational excellence and maximum autonomy for all school systems. Proposals were made for matters of provincial responsibility such as the handling of curriculum, methods of instruction, textbooks, length of school year, attendance requirements, and teacher training and qualifications.

The brief approved compulsory instruction in basic subjects such as history, English, and mathematics, with sufficient options to suit the abilities and preferences of individual students. While financial support from the government would depend on the adoption of a curriculum meeting basic educational requirements, each system would be free to handle the program in the light of the educational philosophy held by its supporters, provided that such a philosophy was in harmony with the maintenance of a democratic and pluralistic society. It was suggested that there was enough latitude in instructional methods under existing conditions, with even more encouraged by the Provincial Committee on Aims and Objectives, to satisfy all systems. Textbooks might be required to meet basic standards, but beyond that there could be considerable variation, as in curriculum. The Department of Education would determine the length of the school year and attendance requirements for all systems. While the department would specify educational requirements for teachers, it would accept the qualifications of graduates of teachers' colleges or universities established by or affiliated with any system.

With reference to local responsibility, it was suggested that the divisional boards of education might exercise regulatory jurisdiction over all systems, including the Independent Christian Public System, without having the right to infringe on the freedom of such a system to educate children according to the philosophy of education endorsed by its supporters. The divisional board might be composed of members representing all systems that complied with provincial legislation and were prepared to submit to the board's authority, including the separate school system as well as the Independent Christian system. The board would have the complete responsibility for transporting students, maintaining school facilities, and determining the size of classes. In other areas, such as hiring teachers and approving textbooks and curriculum, there would be provision for each system to make its own decisions. Such a system would have its own board, elected by its supporters, to handle these matters. Thus the Independent Christian schools could ensure that they had teachers who were sympathetic to their particular aims provided that they met the training requirements applying to all systems.

There seemed to be little likelihood that a scheme of this type would be adopted by the Robarts government, nor did the open espousal by the Liberal and New Democratic parties of the proposal to extend the Roman Catholic separate school system through grade 13 include any demonstration of willingness to extend public financial support to any group of independent schools. Yet there was a development in 1970–1 that seemed to demonstrate the possibility of going much further to meet parents' wishes in a large school system than had been the practice up to that time. The Board of Education for North York undertook an experiment to permit parents to choose between schools run along the lines suggested in the Hall-Dennis report and those adhering to more traditional approaches. One might well ask if it would not be equally permissible to provide a variety of schools operated according to different religious orientations, and to allow parents to choose the one they thought best for their children. Such an arrangement would not, of course, give the Ontario Alliance of Christian Schools all it has asked for, but it might possibly be regarded as a reasonable compromise.

SIX

Associations for
the promotion
of special education

Most of the associations in this group dealt with a single area of physical, mental, or emotional handicap. They made outstanding contributions to the welfare of children with special needs, in many cases supporting educational programs until public authorities were prepared to assume the responsibility. In recent years their tendency to isolate children with particular disabilities has to some extent run counter to the trend to integrate handicapped children of all kinds with regular classes.

THE ONTARIO SOCIETY FOR CRIPPLED CHILDREN

The Ontario Society for Crippled Children was formed on the initiative of a small group of service clubs in 1922, and incorporated by the provincial government in 1930. Its purposes were to provide a comprehensive treatment and training program for retarded children and to encourage research into crippling disorders in children. The program consisted of diagnostic services, surgical and medical treatment, physical restoration, the promotion of social and psychological adjustment, education, vocational training, and job placement. Funds to support these activities were raised through Easter Seal campaigns. Participating service clubs, called Easter Seal service clubs, maintained crippled children's committees, which co-operated in the care and treatment of children in the community, and Easter Seal committees, which assisted the society in the annual fund-raising campaign. Half the proceeds of these activities were used to meet the needs of the local community and the remainder for provincial projects and services.

According to a recent statement, children eligible for assistance came under this definition: "A physically handicapped child is one under the age of nineteen years whose restriction of activity by reason of neurological, musculo-skeletal, or other non-acute organic defect produces a physical handcap." Unless they have a physical handicap, emotionally disturbed and mentally retarded children are not included. A somewhat more specific classification scheme employs the following categories: 1 / birth deformities such as bands, cleft lip, cleft palate, club feet and hands, congenital amputation or arrest of limbs, congenital defects of appendages, dislocated hip, scars, scoliosis, spina bifida, web fingers, and wry neck; 2 / common disability-producing diseases such as cerebral palsy, cystic fibrosis, Legg-Perthes disease, muscular dystrophy, polio-myelitis, rheumatoid arthritis, rickets, and tuberculosis of the bone; 3 / accident-produced disabilities such as burns, fractures, juvenile amputa-tions, and soft tissue injuries; and 4 / other conditions.

At the end of the 1960s the society was managed by a board of directors consisting of members elected annually from different parts of the province. Execution of policy was the responsibility of an executive director. A medical director and the Medical Advisory Committee, con-sisting of consultants in a variety of specialties, took the lead in developing a medical program, medical policy, and research projects.

A major enterprise of the society was the Ontario Crippled Child-ren's Centre, established in Toronto in 1962. This centre was designed to make handicapped children self-sufficient and able to face life in the home, school, and community. The program co-ordinated medical treat-ment with education adapted to each child's potentialities. The length of time a particular child remained in the centre depended on the nature and extent of his disability and his response to treatment. The centre did not offer indefinite care of an institutional nature for those who ceased to progress. The major financial support came from the Ontario Hospital Services Commission, with lesser contributions from the Department of Education for the educational aspects of the program. In addition to programs for children, lectures and demonstrations were offered for medical, nursing, therapy, and other paramedical students. The facilities of the centre also provided excellent opportunities for basic and clinical research.

In its report for 1968 the board of education for the school at the centre claimed that what it was trying to do in the educational field was perhaps unique on the continent. The total enrolment of 180 covered the program between nursery school and grade 13 and included the broadest intellectual spectrum and all areas of exceptionality. Because of the dearth of authoritative information, there were few criteria against which the school's activities could be judged. One prominent feature of the program was the heavy emphasis on audio-visual equipment to help handicapped children learn through their remaining sensory abilities. The North York Board of Education assisted with staff training in the most advantageous use of such equipment. Another special characteristic was the flexible assignment of children to classes where they could make the most prog-ress, regardless of age. Teachers were provided with funds for visits to comparable institutions as a means of keeping up with the latest develop-ments.

Variety Village, a residential vocational school in Toronto completed in 1949, was built by the Variety Club of Ontario, financed jointly by the Variety Club and the Department of Education, and operated by the Ontario Society for Crippled Children. It catered to the needs of orthopaedically handicapped boys between sixteen and eighteen years of age who were unable to secure training elsewhere. Programs offered in 1968 were Special Commercial, a Watch and Clock Repair course, and a General Shop course. Formal studies were supplemented by dramatics, music appreciation, physical training, and recreation. The hobby program involved evening instruction in copper-tooling, etching, plastic-craft, photography, oil-painting, philately, and model building.

Among the activities of the society with a less direct bearing on education was the public health nursing program. The nurses provided consulting services to provincial groups, co-operated with members of the medical profession, public health units, hospital clinics, other welfare organizations, and service clubs, assisted in organizing surveys and special clinics, supervised medically prescribed treatment in the home and interpreted the work of the society to the general public. Assistance was provided for the organization of diagnostic and consultant clinics. Several camps enabled crippled children to enjoy a two- or three-week holiday while continuing an active program of physical and emotional rehabilitation.

THE ONTARIO ASSOCIATION
FOR THE MENTALLY RETARDED

Before 1947 there was no Canadian organization devoted to the needs of the mentally retarded. In that year parents, service clubs, the Community Chest, and the Department of Education united their efforts to establish a school for retarded children in Kirkland Lake. A movement to work for the provision of better training opportunities developed in 1949 with the formation of a Parents' Council for Retarded Children in Toronto. This organization was operating two schools in the area by 1952. Representatives of a number of local community associations took the first steps to establish the Ontario Association for Retarded Children at a meeting in Hamilton in 1953. In 1965 the adoption of the name Ontario Association for the Mentally Retarded signified that the association was concerned with the welfare of the mentally retarded of all ages.

According to the constitution of the association incorporating amendments up to 1968, the aims were as follows:

1. To encourage scientific research and study into the reasons for mental retardation, with a view to preventing it; and to seek the co-operation of all the authorities toward that end.
2. To promote the education, training, development and welfare of all mentally retarded persons at home, in residences and institutions, in public and private schools; and to co-operate with public and private agencies, the various departments of government, and other groups and organizations having a similar purpose.

3. To assist such persons in realizing their individual potential contribution to the community.
4. To develop a better understanding of the problem of mental retardation by the general public.
5. To further the training and education of personnel in the field of mental retardation.
6. To co-operate with other provincial, national and international organizations promoting the education and welfare of the mentally retarded.
7. To encourage the formation of a local association for the mentally retarded in every centre in the Province where the needs of such persons require special consideration.
8. To link together all such local associations in the Province of Ontario.
9. To unite the efforts of all parents and friends interested in any one residential or institutional centre.
10. To solicit and receive funds for the accomplishment of the above purposes.

During the 1950s the local association operating under the mantle of the provincial association established and maintained their own schools, in most ways carrying out the functions of school boards. They secured government assistance for the construction of schools and for their operation. One of the conditions for the receipt of government grants was that the local school inspector be a member of the education committee of the local association. As costs increased and as the public conscience was stirred, the burden was shifted to provincial and local government agencies during the 1960s, as explained in volume III, chapter 10.

The provincial association campaigned persistently for better government provision for retarded children. A brief submitted to the Department of Education in 1959 asked for the mandatory establishment of auxiliary classes, permissive legislation with respect to the operation of Ontario Association for Retarded Children schools by local school boards, a widening of the conditions under which exceptional children were permitted to attend these schools, and an increase in grants for the schools.

The home care committees of the provincial and local associations co-operated in offering assistance to parents, particularly to those who had to keep their retarded children at home. These committees co-operated with public health nurses and other community agencies in attempting to locate parents needing assistance. A major undertaking of the same committees was the development of pre-school nursery programs. There were seventy of these in 1967, operating from half a day to five days a week.

The history of the association includes the provision of a number of services to children in addition to the operation of schools. A six-week summer camp was maintained with three-week camping periods for boys and girls respectively. With the help of such groups as the Loyal Order of

Moose and the Kiwanis clubs, similar facilities, at first for one and then for two weeks, were provided for young adults. Additional projects reported in 1961 included a three-day workshop for parents of mentally retarded children living in areas not serviced by local associations, a one-day research conference attended by medical and lay people, and a $17,000 study of mongolism.

The extent to which the association concerned itself with the adult retarded was demonstrated by the fact that there were sixty specially designed programs for this group in 1968. These programs were stimulated and guided by the provincial Adult Services Committee in cooperation with counterparts at the local level. Originally established to contribute to the continuing welfare of day school graduates, such programs expanded to include former opportunity class students, adults without formal education, and school drop-outs who sought vocational training for simple jobs. In some places there were three levels of training: one for the severely retarded, sheltered employment for the trainable retarded, and training for competitive employment on the labour market for the mildly retarded. In 1968 it was estimated that 1,400 retarded young adults were being served in these programs.

By 1968 the number of affiliated associations of the Ontario Association for the Mentally Retarded had grown to more than 110. These had been responsible for the establishment of an equal number of schools, more than sixty training centres for young adults, nearly seventy preschool nursery programs, nine regional residential camps, and a variety of other programs. A very substantial part of the work was carried out by volunteer workers. It would be difficult to find a more impressive mobilization of community resources for the benefit of the less fortunate.

THE CANADIAN AND ONTARIO ASSOCIATIONS
FOR CHILDREN WITH LEARNING DISABILITIES

The Canadian Association for Children with Learning Disabilities pursued four stated aims: 1 / to educate professionals, parents, and the public with respect to minimal brain dysfunction in children, 2 / to encourage various levels of government to establish diagnostic, treatment, and educational services for this group, 3 / to provide referral services, and 4 / to gather data. At the outset the association was mainly concerned with activities at the local and provincial levels, but requests for information from clinics, school boards, professionals, and parents across the country soon established a national outlook. It was most appropriate for a national organization to work with the federal Departments of Labour and Health and Welfare, as well as with other national organizations concerned with problems of mental health and certain kinds of disabilities.

The association became involved in a large number of specific activities. It compiled a comprehensive directory of films, slides, tapes, and records; produced a directory of day and country camps in North America and distributed copies to all the associations on the continent concerned with minimal brain dysfunction in children; collected files on teaching aids and diagnostic services throughout North America; obtained information about research and about school facilities; conducted a study of public and private secondary school programs; distributed a large number of pamphlets, some of interest to professionals and others to parents; maintained an audio-visual library and a library of books on minimal brain dysfunction and other disorders; and distributed a monthly journal entitled the *Perceptual Post*.

The Ontario Association for Children with Learning Disabilities, which became an extremely active chapter of the national organization, was formed in 1963 by a small group of parents of perceptually handicapped children. Within a few years there were sixteen branches in the province with more than five thousand members. Until June 1, 1967, the work of the association was carried on by volunteers; at that time a grant from the Atkinson Charitable Foundation made it possible to open an office with a full-time staff.

As did the other provincial chapters, the Ontario organization held regular meetings, seminars, and workshops for professional workers, parents, or both. A grant from the Department of Education helped to bring in speakers, many of whom came to Metropolitan Toronto. On some occasions the program was designed for members of specific professions such as pediatricians, psychologists, and others. The Department of Education also contributed financially to an annual workshop in August, which was attended by professional workers from various parts of the country as well as by a number of parents. The causes of education and communication were further served by field visits to local universities, clinics, and school facilities.

Branches in various provinces provided limited direct services such as nursery schools, physiotherapy and occupational therapy groups, tutorial clinics, recreation groups, and parent education groups. These were on much too small a scale to meet the full needs of the community. It was considered much more advisable to concentrate efforts on persuading provincial governments and agencies to develop a satisfactory program. Briefs were presented to various departments and committees, and regular communication was maintained with a number of agencies. The Ontario association called continuously for better facilities for the preparation of teachers of children with various exceptional needs. It was gratified to observe a rapid increase in the number of classes for children with perceptual handicaps, itinerant teaching programs, gross screening tests for kindergarten children, post-kindergarten readiness programs, and perceptual enrichment and motor activities for grade 1 pupils. The Department of Education supported a campaign to permit brain-damaged young people with normal intelligence to remain in the five-year program at the secondary school level, while the minister expressed an interest in having a college of applied arts and technology offer a course for young people with minimal brain damage. Other developments, actual or proposed, in which the association was interested or involved, included the establishment of diagnostic and treatment centres, the development of courses at York University for teachers of children with learning disabilities, the organization of a learning centre in the Department of Psychology at the University of Guelph, the operation of a research and graduate study program at the Ontario Institute for Studies in Education, and the introduction of diagnostic and treatment programs at many hospitals in Ontario.

THE ONTARIO ASSOCIATION
FOR EMOTIONALLY DISTURBED CHILDREN

The Ontario Association for Emotionally Disturbed Children was incorporated under provincial legislation in 1957. It was originally made up largely of parents of children with emotional problems, but later expanded to include professional workers such as psychiatrists, social workers, and teachers, as well as members of the general public with an interest in the field. As stated in a brochure issued in 1968, its aims were as follows:

1. To work for the education, training, development and welfare of all emotionally disturbed children.
2. To encourage scientific study and research into the reasons for and the reduction of emotional disturbance among children.
3. To aid and organize local groups and unite all persons with an interest in emotionally disturbed children into an active group.
4. To give fellowship and comfort to parents of emotionally disturbed children and to seek to provide some of the answers to their immediate difficulties.
5. To publicize, in the community, the needs of the emotionally disturbed child, in order to get greater understanding of the problem.

A large part of the work of the association consisted in the dissemination of information. Materials were distributed free of charge to students in institutes of technology and colleges of applied arts and technology, to child-care workers in training and in practice, to undergraduate and graduate university students, to teachers and teachers in training, to public health nurses and students in nurses' training courses, to librarians in a variety of training and research institutions, to government departments, to hospitals involved in the training of nurses, and to individuals and agencies in other provinces and in the United States. A journal entitled *EDC. Emotionally Disturbed Children* contains a valuable selection of information, ideas, and inspirational material.

Among the causes consistently promoted by the association were better education for teachers in training in the understanding of children with emotional disturbances or other handicaps, maximum integration of the troubled child into the normal group, special classes leading to such integration, and the use of volunteers and lay assistants, particularly in special classes. Among the major recommendations made to the Provincial Committee on Aims and Objectives were that the Department of Education attempt to discover the number of emotionally disturbed children in Ontario; that teachers be taught to recognize emotional disturbances in children; that extra staff be provided, where possible, to supervise emotionally disturbed children during periods of recreation; that residential neighbourhood centres be established to educate emotionally disturbed children lacking the capacity to profit from attendance at regular schools; that provision for special education, where needed, be made compulsory; that the Department of Education provide more assistance for special education programs; and that the curriculum be adapted to take account of specific deficiencies in perception or development. When the report of the committee appeared, members felt that the recommendations on special education closely paralleled those contained in their own submission.

The association opened the Woburn Day Nursery School in Scarborough as an autonomous project. Up to 20 per cent of the total number enrolled were disturbed children who were to be integrated into the normal group. Only lack of money prevented a substantial extension of this service to cover the opening of similar schools in other areas.

THE COMMISSION ON EMOTIONAL
AND LEARNING DISORDERS IN CHILDREN

Concern about the large numbers of children in Canada with certain types of problems led in 1966 to the formation of the Commission on Emotional and Learning Disorders. According to the executive secretary of this commission, Margery R. King, one of the basic premises of the body was that the magnitude and range of the problem were so great that the existing methods of providing service and deploying staff were completely inadequate. There appeared to be a need for new, imaginative, and radical approaches if there were to be any hope of dealing effectively with the problems faced by emotionally disturbed children and their families.[1]

The commission was sponsored initially by a number of Canadian organizations with an interest in the field: the Canadian Association for Retarded Children, the Canadian Council on Children and Youth, the Canadian Education Association, the Canadian Mental Health Association, the Canadian Rehabilitation Council for the Disabled, and the Canadian Welfare Council. Dr Barnardo's (formerly Dr Barnardo's Homes) of London, England, acted as an international sponsor and provided a link with similar projects being undertaken in Great Britain and elsewhere.

The commission undertook to establish liaison with professional organizations and other associations concerned with the same problems.

Through a study of between three and five years' duration, the commission undertook to achieve the following objectives:

- To study existing systems for providing services to children with emotional and learning disorders and their families.
- To search for new principles and more effective patterns of practice and organization through which the needs of such children, and their families, may be more fully met.
- To report upon and recommend ways and means of improving current efforts in dealing with these problems, including those of prevention.
- To stimulate collaboration and support from all levels of the public and private sectors of the Canadian community, and from all parts of the nation, in the study and implementation of the Commission's recommendations.[2]

The organization of the commission consisted of a Board of Management from the sponsoring organizations, an Expert Committee consisting of professionals from the relevant disciplines, and a secretariat. Initial operating procedures included visits to various communities to examine existing services and to observe the way in which those who organized and provided the services perceived the extent and nature of the problems. Interviews were conducted with government officials, with leaders in voluntary organizations, business, industry, and labour, with workers in the fields of health, education, welfare, and justice, and with the recipients of service. Attention was directed toward current methods of meeting the needs of children with emotional disorders and learning disabilities, different patterns of service, the organization of services in urban and rural areas, and the provision of special education and clinical services.

Efforts were directed toward the preparation of a series of background papers designed to explore and clarify the issues identified in the field studies. One background paper undertook to define the nature and scope of emotional and learning disorders, to place these in the context of normal child development, and to examine some of the causal factors. A second paper explored the research and survey evidence of the magnitude of the problem. A third compared the professional resources that were currently available, or likely to be in the near future, with the number that would be required to meet the need. The second and third of these studies were supported financially by the Department of National Health and Welfare.

Certain issues were given more complete attention at a later stage. The first of these was communication, which the visits had shown to be a source of serious problems. There was concern about a lack of understanding among the different professions, leading to a dissipation of efforts, about lack of liaison among services, often preventing a child from receiving help, and about the absence of support for parents and teachers. Close communication appeared to be the essential factor in referral. The second issue was training and the use of manpower, involving an examination of the relationship between the traditional patterns of training and inter-professional relationships, conjoint training for different professions, and deployment of human resources to make the best use of a wide variety of talents, including those of semi-professionals, indigenous non-professionals, and volunteers. The third issue had to do with the way in which services developed – whether as a result of social planning or as a response to a crisis. Among important aspects of this issue were the consequences of professional rivalries and the effect of voluntary associations. A fourth issue was the impact of the environment, which included the influence of such factors as poverty, social dependency, cultural deprivation, and the way in which schools were operated.

The report of the commission, a very comprehensive document, appeared in 1970. Successive chapters or sections covered the following topics: the developing child, names and numbers (terminology and statistics), the child as student, the child as patient, the child as ward, the child as offender, the child in residential care, proposals for change, new ideas and programs, those providing care, the professions and society, the citizen's role, and recommendations. Among the principles in treating emotional and learning disorders in children that received particular stress were that all efforts must be made to ensure that children have the maximum of normal childhood experiences in the family, the school, and the community; that the child could no longer be divided into water-tight compartments as student, patient, ward, or offender, but must be treated as a whole individual; that there must be comprehensiveness of service to guarantee continuity of care rather than a constant shifting of responsibility; that help must be provided at the earliest possible moment of need. The report called for a new spirit of partnership and respect among the various professions in the field and an end to the fragmentation of services that were found to be so prevalent.

The recommendations were grouped under three headings: organization of services, personnel, and research. Those in the first group were further subdivided according to whether they dealt with local services, regional services, or federal and provincial organizational roles. Aspects of local services given consideration were policy and planning, co-ordination of services, services in a local community, operation of services for all children, and co-ordination of support and personnel. Recommendations with respect to federal and provincial roles included separate and combined activities involving the two levels, standards and funding, and juvenile court operations. Personnel matters covered policy and planning, pre-service and in-service training, professional roles and responsibilities, and the roles of citizens and voluntary associations. The report as a whole constituted not only a sober warning of the consequences of failing to improve the inadequate services being provided, but also a comprehensive blueprint for constructive action.

THE COUNCIL FOR EXCEPTIONAL CHILDREN

The International Council for Exceptional Children, established in the United States in 1923, had Canadian participants from the beginning. The first meeting was attended by S.B. Sinclair, Inspector of Auxiliary Classes in the Ontario Department of Education, and Edith L. Groves, an official of the Toronto Board of Education. The annual conventions were held in Canada on a number of occasions, and attracted members from the Special Education Section of the OEA and from the special education associations in various parts of the province.[3]

In 1955, the year in which the word "international" was dropped from the title, initiatives taken by a committee under the leadership of Helen Delaporte led to the organization of the nine chapters in Ontario in a provincial federation. Special-class teacher associations gradually merged with existing chapters or with new ones formed at later stages. An understanding was reached with the Special Education Section of the Ontario Educational Association on the respective spheres of interest of the two organizations. The separate identity of the organizations depended to a considerable extent on the different traditions they had already built up. Many of the leading figures in special education were active members or leaders of both.

According to an early version of the constitution of the Ontario Provincial Federation of Chapters, the purposes of the association were as follows:

Section I The primary purpose of this organization shall be to promote the education and general welfare of exceptional children resident in the Province of Ontario.
Section II It shall also be the purpose of this organization to promote the education and welfare of all youth through the support of the purposes and programme of the Special Section of the Ontario Educational Association, The Canadian Education Association and the National Education Association of the U.S.A.

The council arranged to co-operate with the Special Education Section of the OEA in the production of the periodical *Special Education in Canada*. The purpose of this journal was said to be to serve the interests of progressive education in general, as well as those of special education. Its particular value to special education teachers in isolated rural districts or small communities was to serve as a source of new ideas and to provide a standard of comparison and evaluation among those doing similar work. For those in larger communities it offered an incentive for co-operation. In 1960 it shared the Greer Memorial Award with J. Bascom St John for outstanding service in the field of education.

A major cause of the council was the advocacy of better opportunities for the preparation of teachers of special education. A resolution formulated in 1965 by the appropriate committee read thus: "Resolved that the Executive of the Ontario Federation of Chapters, Council for Exceptional Children, be requested to search for ways and means of promoting the establishment of University Courses and Degrees in Special Education at the post-graduate level, either by or through a University in Ontario, and assist groups who may already be working to this end."[4] The council was gratified that such a program was established in the Department of Educational Theory of the University of Toronto after the formation of the Ontario Institute for Studies in Education. Concern about teacher education was also expressed in a brief to the Minister's Committee on the Training of Elementary School Teachers. The council supported the general proposition that all elementary school teachers should have university degrees. While acknowledging that the educational psychology course offered in teachers' colleges included topics dealing with individual differences, it expressed the view that these topics could not be developed sufficiently in a one-year course. A plea was made that specialized training beyond the teachers' college level obtained outside Ontario be recognized by the Department of Education for certificate purposes. It is reasonable to assume that these views had some influence on later events.

In a somewhat similar category were efforts to have the Department of Education facilitate the development of courses for educational psychologists under auspices other than those of university departments of psychology. The council felt that, although graduates of honours university courses had high standards, it was desirable that psychologists dealing with children have a greater knowledge of classroom procedures and teaching techniques. Again, the program introduced at the Ontario Institute for Studies in Education might be considered to have been a reasonable response to this desire.

SEVEN

Organizations of school trustees

There have been numerous associations of school trustees in Ontario, organized at various times to give voice to particular interests. Running through their activities have been certain common threads which have given their development a good deal of similarity. They have, for example, held meetings, usually at least once a year, at the provincial level to discuss common problems. Naturally, in view of the nature of trustees' responsibilities, they have tended to concentrate on financial problems, legal provisions, the supply of teachers, teachers' salaries, bargaining procedures, teachers' benefits, school building, transportation, and the like. They have made it a practice to formulate numerous resolutions for submission to the Minister of Education, or perhaps to the Prime Minister. Provincial conferences have had their regional counterparts where similar activities have been engaged in. Efforts have been made, often in co-operation with the teachers' federations, to study certain crucial issues or questions. The results of these efforts have sometimes been agreement on a common trustee-teacher front. The trustees' organizations have attempted to standardize employment practices and salary scales. While they have consistently attempted to strengthen the boards' bargaining position, they have often taken a positive stand on the need to improve teachers' salaries, particularly in poorer parts of the province.

In view of the similarities of the different organizations, no attempt has been made in the following pages to give a full account of the development of each one. Further, there has been no effort to trace resolutions passed over an extended period of time, since these are really commentaries on issues of the day, most of which are dealt with at length in some part of ONTARIO'S EDUCATIVE SOCIETY.

THE ONTARIO SCHOOL TRUSTEES' AND MUNICIPAL COUNCILLORS' ASSOCIATION

The first meeting of what was known as the Public and High School Trustees' Association of Ontario was held at Whitby in 1887. This organization united with the OTA in 1892 to form the OEA. A constitution was drafted in 1921 and the name Ontario School Trustees' and Ratepayers' Association (OSTRA) was adopted; in 1968 it became the Ontario School Trustees' and Municipal Councillors' Association. In 1922 the

Trustees' Department was divided into School Attendance, Rural, and Urban Elementary and Secondary sections. The department was later divided into four sections: the County and Municipal Councils Section, the Rural and Township School Area Section, the Separate School Trustees' Section, and the Urban (Elementary and Secondary) School Trustees' section. Each section operated according to its own procedure, elected its own officers, and had its own representative on the Board of Directors of the OEA. Constitutional provision was also made for the organization and operation of regional and county branches.

The objects of the association were outlined briefly in 1887:

1. To consider all matters having a practical bearing on Education and the School System.
2. To provide a medium of communicating to the Minister of Education the views of the people of this Province on Educational questions and pressing the same on his attention.[1]

It was hoped that each school board in the province would send a delegate to the Easter convention. School ratepayers were also urged to take advantage of their local annual meetings to discuss educational topics and to forward them to the county or provincial association where they would be given further consideration and, if passed, presented to the Department of Education. Trustees and ratepayers were also given an opportunity to receive information at county meetings, which were attended by local public school inspectors.

The major concerns of the association during the first thirty years of its existence were indicated in the *Ontario School Board Journal* in 1922: pupils' fees in high schools and collegiate institutes; improved methods of financial support of public and high schools; assessment for public and separate school purposes; holidays in rural public schools; the method of payment of public school grants; how to give the high school curriculum more of an industrial character without making it less useful for purposes of general culture; provincial Third Class Public School Certificates; the amalgamation of high and public school boards in cities and towns; the election of public school trustees by ballot; the contract between teachers and boards; the public school leaving course; county model schools; physical education in high schools; agriculture in public schools; the school building and equipment, the school fair and its place in the educational system; the hygiene of the subnormal child; *The Adolescent School Attendance Act*; the consolidation of rural schools; and the necessity of health supervision.[2]

A statement in the *Canadian School Journal* in 1933 indicated the range of subjects covered at county meetings and appraised some of the benefits resulting from the discussions.

Many subjects are discussed at the County meetings such as Grants, Examination Fees, Medical Inspection, Costs of Education, Salaries, Certificates, Qualifications, and the engaging of teachers, Second Year Normal course, Courses of Study, the teaching of Manual Training, Household Science, Agriculture, Music and many other topics. Through the discussion of these subjects many points are brought out by the trustees and ratepayers from the administrative point of view, and by the teachers and inspectors from the point of view of the Department, and the teacher. By coming together in this way many differences are overcome, many rough places smoothed out, better feelings are maintained, and many improvements are made.[3]

The association published the *Ontario School Board Journal*, beginning in 1921,

1. To co-operate with Trustees and Ratepayers to secure the best interests of Ontario Schools and Scholars.
2. To keep the readers of the Journal informed upon subjects connected with the welfare of the School and the Scholar, considered particularly from the viewpoint of Trustees and Ratepayers.[4]

The name *Canadian School Journal* was adopted in 1923. This periodical contained reports of county conventions, articles on educational issues of current interest, letters from subscribers, information about changes in legislation, and other such matters. Copies were sent to school boards throughout the province as well as to individual members.

One of the services performed for rural school boards during the 1930s was the provision of graded lists of books considered suitable for school libraries, which helped to remedy the inability of many trustees to make an appropriate choice. Books on the list were recommended by the Department of Education or by an inspector. The total value of all items on each year's list was $10, the minimum amount that entitled the board to a departmental grant. The association took the view that an expenditure of $10 a year was sufficient to keep the library up to date.

The 1950s constituted a period of marked growth for the OSTRA. In 1949 it had approximately three hundred members and in 1959 approximately nine hundred, representing every kind of board in the province. Among its principal activities during that period were regional and district conferences with in-service training for trustees. Advice and guidance in setting up salary schedules were made available to members, and representatives assisted boards in negotiations with the affiliates of the OTF.

One of the major projects of the OSTRA during the mid-fifties was a campaign to alleviate the teacher shortage by persuading British teachers to immigrate to Canada. The secretary, Jean M. Watson, reported in 1954 that the British press, the *Canadian School Journal*, and the mails had been utilized in this cause, and that hundreds of letters from potential immigrants had been answered. The Canadian Department of Citizenship and Immigration was requested to extend arrangements for assisted passage. Eventually the Department of Education assumed responsibility for the scheme, which it conducted in co-operation with the OSTRA and the OTF.[5]

A recurrent theme in OSTRA discussions was that of merit rating of teachers for salary purposes, a concept which many members of the association tended to favour. A Joint Committee, consisting of members of the various teachers' federations, Nora Hodgins of the OTF, and representatives of the trustees' associations, studied the matter and reported in 1957. There was a sharp division of opinion about relating a merit plan to teachers' salaries, the teachers being generally opposed to the idea. The committee was, however, able to agree on certain principles of rating not related to salaries.

The association was incorporated in 1958 under the provisions of *The Companies Act*, with a more detailed statement of objectives than that formulated in 1887:

(a) TO take an active interest in every phase of education;
(b) TO co-operate with any other association or organization with the same or similar aims and objects;
(c) TO make representations concerning education to any association or organization or any department of government;
(d) TO promote an interest in and the study of education;
(e) For the purposes of effecting these objects, to carry on printing and publishing and to sell and distribute literature;
(f) TO accept gifts, donations, legacies, devises and bequests; and
(g) TO invest the moneys of the Corporation not immediately required for the purposes of the Corporation in any securities in which, under *The Trustee Act* or any other Act, trustees may invest trust funds ...

In a resolution passed by the OSTRA in 1968, the desirability of forming larger areas of school administration was recognized, and the soundness of the government's general policy in forming divisional boards was acknowledged. The association supported the view that each area should be large enough to provide "complete, proper and adequate education," but recognized a limit in size beyond which community needs would not be adequately served. Generally speaking, the county was regarded as the most satisfactory administrative unit. It was felt, however, that there were exceptions, and that recognition must be given to situations where existing county boundaries did not provide satisfactory boundaries for a school area unit if educational and community interests were to be protected. The association accordingly requested that the proposed legislation provide for situations where only part of a county, or parts of more than one county, would constitute the most satisfactory unit. It also requested the opportunity to present to the minister, or to the appropriate commitee of the Legislature, information on situations that required special consideration, without restricting the right of individual boards to make representations on their own behalf. It favoured adequate provision in the legislation for expeditious changes in area boundaries, with the minister's approval. As noted in volume II, chapter 5, the association failed to persuade the minister that these changes were desirable.

THE ONTARIO URBAN AND RURAL
SCHOOL TRUSTEES' ASSOCIATION
Founded in 1920, the Urban School Trustees' Association had as its main centre of interest the development of education in large urban systems. Its members felt that there was not sufficient concentration of attention on this area in the OSTRA. Some of them also saw advantages in working outside the structure of the OEA. They felt that the OSTRA was too loosely organized, and that a more tightly structured association might be more effective.

As stated in the constitution drawn up in 1920, the objects of the association were

(1) To consider matters of general interest to Public and High Schools or Boards of Education, and to procure the enactment of such legislation as may be of advantage to education in the province of Ontario.
(2) To take united action in all matters where the rights of Boards may be effected [sic] and generally to promote their interests.

Each urban board could send as many representatives as it wanted to the annual meetings, but there could be no more than two with votes from boards in municipalities with a population below fifty thousand, and no more than three from those in larger municipalities.

The particular concerns of the association during the early 1940s may be illustrated with reference to a series of resolutions passed in 1943:

1. Ask the Dept. of Education to declare a school holiday on May 24th, King's Birthday and Armistice Day;
2. That the Department forward to all school Boards copies of circulars, announcements, etc., which may from time to time be issued by the Department;
3. That summer courses be re-established in order to provide a more adequate number of teachers qualified to instruct in Auxiliary Classes, Home Economics, Physical Education, Art, General Shop, etc.;
4. That schools similar to those formerly in Bowmanville and Galt be re-opened as soon as possible;
5. That for the duration of the war and one year thereafter, supperannuated teachers who have been granted a pension, not on the ground of disability,

be allowed to teach six months in any one year without the loss of pension
for such teaching period;

6. That Vocational Guidance be included in the regular course of study
during teaching hours;

7. That the Dominion Government be asked to consider some form of
higher rating for material allocation in supplies and equipment for
schools;

8. That the grant for inspectors engaged by boards be increased from $6.00
per room to $10.00;

9. That the Federal Government be asked to help provide replacement of
machinery and equipment that gets extra wear and tear because of being
used in Vocational schools;

10. That the Assessment and Public and High School Acts be so amended
that a non-resident owner of property may not have his children educated
free in addition to those of the tenant.

11. That deferment of teachers called by the selective service be to the end of
the school term;

12. That the standing obtained in the Commercial and Technical Departments of Secondary schools should have the equivalent of Academic
standing in determining admission requirements to schools of nursing;

13. That the Provincial Government be urged to give immediate consideration to plans whereby at least 50% of the gross cost of education be borne
by forms of taxation other than real estate;

14. That liberal representation be given School Boards and teacher groups
on Provincial Rehabilitation and Post-war committees;

15. That School Inspectors be permitted and encouraged to familiarize themselves at first hand with other national and provincial systems and practices in Education;

16. That a Transfer Form to be used when pupils moved from one school to
another be suppied by the department for uniform use in all schools,
Rural and Urban, in the province;

17. That greater opportunities be provided for returned soldiers who may not
have completed their Public School course for securing Technical or
Vocational training.[6]

The association operated more at the administrative level than did
the OSTRA, and in some ways was the strongest of the associations. In 1951
it became the Ontario Urban and Rural School Trustees' Association.
Although it brought in one or two small rural boards, its essentially urban
character was not changed.

THE ASSOCIATED HIGH SCHOOL BOARDS
OF THE PROVINCE OF ONTARIO
The Associated High School Boards of the Province of Ontario held their
first annual meeting in 1932 as the result of initiatives taken by an associa-

tion of York County school boards. This group had organized as a means of opposing the York County Council which, in an attempt to curtail the costs of secondary education, had appointed a special committee to prepare a private bill for presentation to the Legislature giving it wide and drastic powers of financial control. Realizing that many of its problems were of provincial scope, the York association sent out a questionnaire to other boards and, on the basis of a very gratifying response, made arrangements for a convention in Toronto. About sixty boards were represented at this convention.

At the first convention consideration was given to the fact that there were already two other organizations of school trustees: the Ontario School Trustees' and Ratepayers' Association and the Urban School Trustees' Association. The decision to form a third association was based at least partly on the claim that the other two did not give sufficient attention to the financial problems of high school boards. The first statement of objectives read as follows.

OBJECT – The object of this association shall be the furtherance of Secondary Education in the Province of Ontario.
1. Through closer contact with – (a) The Minister of Education and the Department of Education. (b) The County and Municipal Councils.
2. To advise and assist individual School Boards in any of their difficulties where such help is requested.
3. To study the cost of Secondary Education especially from the point of view of the ratepayer.[7]

Membership was open to any board of education, collegiate institute board, or high school board in the province. Each board, regardless of size, was given one vote at annual meetings. The original annual fee was $5 per year.

In the October 1932 issue of the *Canadian School Journal* an unnamed urban trustee questioned the need for a third organization.

During the present year there have been held three Conventions all dealing with problems of Secondary Education. First there was the Urban Trustee Section of the Ontario Educational Association which met in Toronto in April; the Urban Trustees' Association which met in Fort William in June; and the Associated High School Boards which met to organize in Toronto in June. The question one naturally asks is, "Why are three Conventions necessary?" Is it because there are problems of Secondary Education peculiar to certain classes of schools in districts? In one sense it may be quite true that each district town or city has its peculiar local problems but where such exist, they may well be left to local Boards to solve, with the assistance of officers of the Department of Education. Speaking generally, however, the problems of Education, such as concern our High Schools, are practically the same throughout the Province. This is plain I think, from resolutions discussed and passed by the three Conventions. There is scarcely a resolution dealing with Secondary Education, passed at one Convention which could not have been passed by all three. In point of fact one such resolution dealing with Examination fees was passed by all three, ... In reviewing the reports of the various Conventions I find that some of the papers read cover much the same ground, again proving that much the same problems are discussed at all three centres. When one considers the expense involved in holding three Conventions – grants from the Department of Education, expense of sending delegates, one is compelled to ask – are three Conventions in Ontario necessary?[8]

The president of the association, H.A. Cruickshank, discussed what he hoped would be a major thrust during the convention in 1935. He felt that the organization of high school boards should parallel the Ontario Secondary School Teachers' Federation, and that the two bodies should co-operate to check the municipal councils in their desire to get control of the school boards. The trustees and the teachers by no means always found their interests to be completely harmonious. The trustees' association could not, for example, bring itself to pass a resolution favouring the adoption of a legal provision for boards of reference.

THE ONTARIO SEPARATE SCHOOL
TRUSTEES' ASSOCIATION
The Ontario Separate School Trustees' Association began operations in 1929 as a co-ordinating body to promote the interests of Catholic education in Ontario. It acquired a provincial office in 1960. Publication of the *Catholic Trustee* was begun in 1961 to disseminate information of interest to the trustees and to explore issues and causes of particular concern to them.

According to a version of the constitution drawn up in 1960 and revised in 1968, six objects were listed:

(a) to encourage the attainment of high standards within the school system;
(b) to increase the zeal and ability of Trustees;
(c) to provide a medium for the exchange of information;
(d) to improve the knowledge and appreciation of the aims and objectives of Catholic Schools;
(e) to engage in educational research and the publication of the results of studies and investigations;
(f) to recommend appropriate improvements in legislation pertaining to the Catholic Separate Schools of this Province.

The constitution defined two kinds of membership: regular membership, open to any board of trustees of an Ontario Catholic separate school; and honorary membership, which might be conferred upon anyone who, in the opinion of the directors, had made a contribution to Catholic education in Ontario of sufficient distinction to merit public recognition.

Much of the effort of the association was spent in expounding the rationale behind the separate school system. A particularly lengthy and carefully prepared brief was submitted to the Hall-Dennis Committee in January 1966. The list of twenty recommendations contained a number pertaining to separate schools, as well as others which indicated the association's position on a variety of issues. They are quoted here (with the paragraph references omitted):

1. That the primary objective of the school system be to assist in every possible way in the fullest possible development of each individual student ...
2. That the school be considered a means by which the general community collaborates with parents in their pre-eminent role as educators ...
3. That the school be diversified according to social commitments of parent and pupils, whether local, religious or cultural ...
4. That at all times the "Public" and "Catholic" schools be recognized as equally authentic forms of public education in Ontario ...
5. That the present efforts be intensified to make known the various services available through the schools of the province and to enhance their value in the eyes of parents and pupils ...
6. That spot checks on schools be made by the Committee to ascertain the quality of the education being dispensed, with particular attention to skill in communications ...
7. That more extensive referral services be made available by school boards to children of school age to enable them to continue their education to the extent of their willingness and ability ...
8. That courses be developed in the critical use of the mass media and specialized personnel be trained for the purpose to circulate from school to school for consultation and demonstration ...
9. A close liaison between parents and schools should be cultivated, especially in larger centres, by associations, news letters and other media, without interfering with professional autonomy or trustee prerogatives ...
10. That consideration be given to a more greatly diversified programme of courses in the non-academic field ...
11. That audio-visual equipment and material be developed in order to supplement in a more realistic way the teaching of Canadian geography and history.
12. That Canadian history be taught with a more commonly accepted content and with greater emphasis on peaceful pursuits and future greatness ...
13. That bilingualism between French and English cultures be promoted through courses in conversation and through accelerated research, particularly in the field of psychology ...

14. That a committee be appointed to prepare for the responsibility of Indian education ...
15. That periods for religious instruction be made available in the regular public school programme, daily, on an optional basis, with credit standing, as desired by substantial groups of parents ...
16. That the religious contribution to Canada's growth be better emphasized in the study of history ...
17. That the particular problem of providing equality of opportunity, for pupils whose mother tongue is French, be given most urgent priority ...
18. That the possibility of a course in the rights of man be explored along the lines of "Pacem in Terris" and "Mater et Magistra" ...
19. That periods for religious instruction be available in technical-vocational schools as described in recommendation number 15 ...
20. That in smaller centres some form of collaboration be worked out for joint establishments of a technical-vocational nature ...[9]

Particular efforts were made toward the end of the 1960s and at the beginning of the 1970s to further the campaign for the extension of the separate school system to the end of secondary school. The Ontario Separate School Trustees' Association could probably claim a considerable part of the credit for winning the support of the Liberal and New Democratic parties on this issue.

L'ASSOCIATION DES COMMISSIONS DES
ECOLES BILINGUES D'ONTARIO

During the period between 1927 and the early 1940s l'Association canadienne-française d'éducation d'Ontario was making efforts to secure the appointment of French-speaking school inspectors, and ratepayers were encouraged to elect more Franco-Ontarian representatives on school boards. By 1944 the considerable number of school trustees in the organization recommended the formation of their own association. A constitution was drawn up during the same year.

According to the constitution, with amendments up to 1959, the objectives of the association were as follows: 1 / to safeguard the academic, religious, and linguistic interests of the bilingual schools of Ontario, 2 / to ensure closer co-operation among trustees of the bilingual schools, and 3 / to co-operate in matters of common interest with associations of school trustees and others. Membership consisted of all the boards of the bilingual schools of Ontario which paid their annual dues, the administrative staff of bilingual school boards which had paid their annual dues, and trustees and members of the administrative staffs of bilingual school boards not forming part of the association who belonged on a personal basis and paid dues according to the current scale (*membres isolés*).

The association consisted of regional sections, one for each of the bilingual inspectoral districts of the province. These sections were grouped in five large divisions, defined in the constitution as follows: 1 / Ottawa Nos. 1, 3, and 5, and Plantagenet; 2 / East – the inspectoral districts of Hawkesbury, Alexandria, and Cornwall; 3 / West – the inspectoral districts of North Bay, Sturgeon Falls, and Sudbury Nos. 1, 2, and 3; 4 / North – the inspectoral districts of Haileybury, Timmins, Kapuskasing, and Hearst; 5 / South – the inspectoral districts of Toronto, Windsor, and Chatham. Each regional section was supposed to hold at least two meetings a year.

Membership in the association increased from 142 in 1945 to 1,200 trustees representing four hundred school boards in 1968. After the school board reorganization which became effective in 1969, the number of boards was reduced drastically. In 1969–70 the membership consisted of thirty-one Roman Catholic separate school boards and sixteen boards of education, represented by 246 French-speaking trustees and administrators and sixty members of French Language Advisory Committees. The member boards operated 335 bilingual separate schools with an enrolment of 87,858, and eleven bilingual public schools with an enrolment of 2,336 pupils.

After its formation the association engaged in a variety of activities designed to promote the welfare of bilingual schools. An important feature of its work was the submission of briefs to the Department of Education, other government agencies, and a number of organizations with an interest in education. As a service to parents and trustees who were not familiar with them, provision was made at an early stage for translating the school acts into French. The practice was adopted in 1950 of making available to secretary-treasurers and trustees information relating to the efficient operation of school systems. Pressure was exerted on the government to provide services for French-speaking pupils equivalent to those offered to English-speaking pupils. As indicated in volume II, chapter 8, there were regular requests that a larger share of corporation taxes, or the equivalent in provincial grants, be made available to the Roman Catholic separate schools. A one-week summer course was offered for the first time in 1950 for school trustees and secretaries. Between 1950 and 1968 enrolment grew from 30 to 160 and then, after the reorganization of 1969, dropped to 71. Topics dealt with included communications, public relations, human relations, and decision making.

THE PUBLIC SCHOOL TRUSTEES' ASSOCIATION
OF ONTARIO

On the invitation of the Toronto Board of Education, about two hundred school trustees representing fifty-seven school boards met on November 23, 1939, to take action "against new and renewed demands to undermine and weaken the great common school system of Ontario." There was a clear implication from the beginning that the association intended to fight the extension of further privileges to the Roman Catholic separate schools. Reverend J.V. Mills, who served as executive secretary of the association for many years, devoted himself wholeheartedly to this cause.

An issue that aroused strong feelings at the time arose out of a challenge by the Windsor Board of Education to the Ford Motor Company's practice of paying part of its taxes to the separate school board. The Board of Education won the legal battle with a court decision that the company could not legally pay a larger proportion of its taxes to the separate school board than the proportion of its shares held by separate school supporters. Since there was no practical way of determining this proportion, the whole amount had to go to the Board of Education. The issue, although determined in accordance with their wishes, caused a good deal of apprehension among public school boards.

In explaining why the founders felt that a new association was needed, Leslie H. Saunders pointed out that the separate schools had for many years had a section in the OEA (through the OSTRA), but that there was no similar section for the public schools. He felt that the general trustees' section was indifferent to the public school cause. There was concern that the repeated campaigns of the Catholic Taxpayers' Association were making headway.[10]

Provision was made for three classes of membership. 1 / Active members were those members of boards of school trustees who had jurisdiction over any public schools in Ontario. 2 / Associate members were those who had been associated with or interested in the work of the public school system, including ex-trustees, teachers, school officials, and representatives from other organizations interested in the promotion of public schools. These members did not have voting privileges at special or general meetings. 3 / All past presidents, and others whom the association might elect, were honorary life members.

Some discussions were held in the earlier years with a view to amalgamating the association with the Ontario School Trustees' and Ratepayers' Association. One reason why this merger proved impossible was that the latter included the Separate School and the County Council Sections, to which the Public School Trustees' Association was opposed. There was also a difference of opinion as to whether or not ratepayers should be permitted to be members.

As a result of the presentation of the famous brief of the Roman Catholic Bishops of Ontario of 1962, the Public School Trustees' Association of Ontario summarized its position in the following statements:

1. No tax-supported Roman Catholic separate high schools under any conditions or in any guise
2. No tax-supported Roman Catholic separate teachers' colleges under any conditions
3. No control by the Roman Catholic Church of the curriculum of any tax-supported schools, elementary or secondary

4. No selection by the Roman Catholic Church of textbooks used in any tax-supported schools, elementary or secondary
5. No federal or provincial funds for the building or operation of Roman Catholic separate technical schools and colleges.[11]

The association in fact suggested that the Minister of Education consider withdrawing such extensions of privileges as had been granted to the separate schools since Confederation.

In 1965 the association listed twelve services which it provided for members. 1 / It maintained an office in Toronto with a full-time executive secretary who was a trained business administrator and who acted as editor of the *Argus*. 2 / It sponsored Church and School week annually during the third week in September. 3 / It presented a copy of the Bible at the opening of all new or rebuilt public schools in Ontario on the request of the board concerned. 4 / It kept careful watch over any changes or contemplated changes in the assessment regulations which would affect the public school rate. 5 / It provided liaison between the member boards and the Department of Education. 6 / On invitation, it assisted member boards with local assessment revision plans. 7 / It assisted member boards with legal advice when necessary and on the decision of the Board of Directors. 8 / It maintained regional salary negotiation teams of experienced trustees. 9 / It held regional trustee gatherings throughout the province under the general directorship of the chairman of zone representatives. 10 / It held an annual four-day convention for public school trustees. 11 / It maintained membership in the CEA, the Canadian School Trustees' Association, the National Education Association, the Ontario School Trustees' Council, the Association of Assessing Officers of Ontario, and the Association of School Business Officials of the United States and Canada. 12 / It published the *Argus*.[12]

THE NORTHERN ONTARIO PUBLIC AND
SECONDARY SCHOOL TRUSTEES' ASSOCIATION[13]

During the period immediately after the Second World War there were many urgent problems facing school trustees in northern Ontario. In particular, the lack of construction during the war and the prospect of increased enrolment raised the spectre of a serious shortage of accommodation. For a time building materials were in short supply, and the necessary construction program was delayed. Potential advantages and immediate problems stemmed from new ideas which inexperienced architects and contractors had difficulty in implementing. There were problems peculiar to the north relating to frost depth, snow load, extra heating equipment, double glazing, insulation, shipping costs, and seasonal construction.

Membership in trustees' associations based in the southern part of the province and heavily weighted with members from that area did not seem to be providing adequately for the needs of northern boards. The few trustees who could travel the long distances to attend meetings in the south felt that they were submerged and ineffective. Many of the issues that were dealt with held little interest for them. In 1946 and 1947 trustees from northern boards accordingly met in Sault Ste Marie and Sudbury to discuss common problems and visit new schools. At a meeting at North Bay in 1948 a decision was made to form an organization. This plan was implemented at Sudbury the following year with the adoption of a constitution. Two months later the deputy minister extended departmental recognition.

From that time on, the association met annually in one of the eight largest cities in northern Ontario. The most important matters receiving attention were increasing enrolment exerting continuous pressure for expanded accommodation, the demand for updating curriculum and equipment, the teacher shortage, caretaking arrangements, increased operating costs, and equipment shortages. The association took some of the first steps to collect information on teachers' salary schedules, thus providing the trustees of the area with a basis for appropriate action. It played an important part in forming the Ontario School Trustees' Council, which thereupon assumed the chief responsibility for gathering and disseminating this type of information. The association continued to press for teacher-training facilities in the north, for special building grants to compensate for higher northern construction costs, for the election of all trustees, for an increase in the responsibilities of trustees, for special consideration for northern Ontario teachers in terms of salary allowances, for institutes of technology and later for colleges of applied arts and technology in the north, for universities in the north, for student travel allowances, for the provision of secondary education in outlying areas, for courses of study to meet the needs of the north, for student boarding allowances, and for reconsideration of mining grants. The association operated at minimum cost by avoiding duplication wherever possible, by reducing travel to a minimum, and by making effective use of the Ontario School Trustees' Council.

The constitution, as amended in 1968, defined the objects of the association thus: 1 / to discuss matters of educational policy and administration, 2 / to act as a medium for exchanging ideas and information concerning school matters, 3 / to take united action in promoting the interests of school boards and education generally in northern Ontario, and 4 / to refer to the Ontario School Trustees' Council or to the provincial government matters which should be considered for legislative action. These points were broadly enough stated to cover the activities of the association since its foundation.

Membership was open to all public and secondary school boards in the province located in and north of the territorial districts of Nipissing and Parry Sound and, by resolution of the association, to other boards requesting membership. Elected and appointed board members and board officials, provided that they were duly appointed delegates, could participate in discussions and deliberations. Only trustee delegates, however, were authorized to vote. Annual fees were paid according to a schedule which might be revised by the executive when necessary, provided that approval was secured at the following annual meeting.

THE ONTARIO SCHOOL TRUSTEES' COUNCIL

Steps were taken at a meeting in June 1945 to form a "School Trustees Association or Council" for the province of Ontario. In attendance were representatives of the Ontario School Trustees' and Ratepayers' Association, the Urban School Trustees' Association, the Association of Ontario Public School Trustees and Ratepayers, the Associated High School Boards of the Province of Ontario, and l'Association des commissions des écoles bilingues d'Ontario. The result was the approval of the following resolution:

That an advisory council of two representatives from each trustees' organization in Ontario, shall be formed which shall discuss matters of common interest to the school boards of Ontario; shall meet with the Department of Education to discuss matters of common interest and to represent as far as possible the view of their constituent association – it being understood that the council shall act in an advisory capacity only and shall have no power to bind the various trustees' organizations.[14]

Although delegates began to meet, there remained considerable difference of opinion as to whether a single organization should be formed or whether it would be better to have a federation in which each association would retain its identity. The Urban School Trustees' Association passed a resolution favouring the unitary body, while the others favoured a federation. In 1946 the Urban School Trustees' Association withdrew from the council. This action put an end to the meetings that had been held with representatives of the teachers' federations and officials of the Department of Education.

A meeting was held on December 2, 1949, which had more substantial consequences. The initiative was taken by the Associated High School Boards of the Province of Ontario, represented by H.E. Dickinson. The minutes of that meeting contain an explanation of the reasons why some form of co-ordination seemed increasingly desirable.

At that convention an informal discussion of representatives of trustee groups in attendance, more or less agreed that some form of trustee group should be organized where information could be had, decisions made, etc., rather than have to go through the long drawn out procedure of contacting each individual group. It was pointed out that the individual groups held meetings only three or four times a year, so that it was more or less impossible to secure an early

decision or necessary information under the present set up, and while it was
recognized this meeting could not adopt resolutions which would be binding
on the various Associations, recommendations could be made, and it was the
sincere wish and thought of the Associated High School Boards that from this
meeting, something would develop eventually leading to the forming of a
trustee council or whatever name would be chosen, and which would be a
central clearing house for all trustee groups.[15]

Speaking for the Department of Education, L.S. Beattie expressed approval of the idea of forming a council.

In 1950 a constitution was adopted and officers were elected. All six
of the existing trustees' organizations were represented in the new Ontario
School Trustees' Council (OSTC), which was to pursue the following
objects:

1. To consider all matters having a practical bearing on both Elementary and
   Secondary Education.

   BUT

   (a) As each of the individual Trustee Organizations in this Province
       has been formed for a specific purpose and has its own particular
       problems, each organization must, of necessity, retain its autonomy.
   (b) That only matters of mutual concern shall be considered by this
       Trustee Council, and only by unanimous consent of the participating
       Trustee organizations.

   The foregoing being agreeable we then become an agency to:

2. Provide a medium of communicating to the Department of Education
   and the Ontario Teachers' Federation the considered views of the Trustee
   Organizations of this Province on Educational and Administrative matters
   within our jurisdiction as School Trustees.
3. To study the School Acts and Regulations and suggest amendments
   thereto.[16]

This statement was soon revised, but the substance remained much the
same.

The Northern Ontario Public and Secondary School Trustees' Association soon joined the council as a seventh member. In its early stages
the council established a Legislative Committee to study the legal provisions for education as a basis for recommendations to the proper
authorities. Another committee considered salaries and salary schedules
and held discussions on the subject with the OTF. The intention was to
evolve a practical plan that would constitute a guide to all school boards.
Still another committee studied the question of arbitration of disputes,
again in co-operation with the OTF.

There were lengthy discussions with the OTF during the early 1950s
on the question of arbitration to settle salary disputes. There was not
sufficient agreement on the desirability of having compulsory arbitration

at any stage in negotiations to have provisions for such a procedure instituted. The Department of Education was unequivocally opposed to the principle of arbitration, although the representatives of the teachers' federation tended to feel that it was desirable on a voluntary basis as a last resort.

In 1957 the council began on an experimental basis to distribute bulletins on salary negotiations to affiliated boards. These were designed to ensure that the boards were kept up to date on the latest developments in this area. Information was supplied to smaller boards, which were being pressed to institute salary schedules, indicating the advantages and disadvantages of schedules from a board's point of view.

Considerable interest was shown during the 1950s in the problem of teacher supply. A joint committee was formed involving the OTF, the Home and School and Parent-Teacher Associations, and members of the council. Two sub-committees, one for the elementary and the other for the secondary level, undertook to assemble statistics on the existing supply and to forecast future conditions. A report issued in 1957 proved to be excessively optimistic in predicting the end of the shortage by 1960, and had to be revised.

In 1955 the council, in co-operation with the Department of Education and the teacher training institutions, began the practice of fixing dates for the beginning of interviews with student teachers and for advertising for teachers for September appointment. The policy did not apply to the appointment of principals and vice-principals. As a result, boards were in a position to compete on something like an equal basis for competent teachers, although there was of course no way of equalizing the attractions of teaching in schools in different parts of the province.

An example of the service provided by the council to school boards was a project undertaken in 1964 to determine losses by fire during the period between 1960 and 1964. When the fire loss ratio was revealed to be very favourable, a rate reduction of 15 per cent was granted on approximately 75 per cent of school construction. The report resulting from the study also provided information on various forms of insurance coverage and insurance company facilities that were available in the insurance market.

The member associations retained the privilege of submitting resolutions directly to the Minister of Education, or to the Prime Minister, if they wished. This course of action was the only one open to them if they did not secure council approval for a particular resolution. For the most part, however, they preferred to act through the council. Perhaps the best way to gain an adequate concept of the scope of this activity is to consider the substance of the resolutions offered by the council in a single year. For this purpose, 1965 seems particularly appropriate, since the reform program of the Davis ministry was by this time in high gear. The list, it will be noted, was heavily weighted toward financial problems, particularly those involving provincial grants. Although a considerable number of the recommendations were not accepted, subsequent departmental action was consistent with many others. One gains the impression that the minister and his department treated the council and its components with considerable respect.

In submitting its resolutions, the council commended the minister particularly on these items: 1 / the continuing increase in the proportion of provincial revenue devoted to education, 2 / the consolidation of school sections into township school areas, 3 / the establishment of a system of colleges of applied arts and technology, 4 / the establishment of the Ontario Institute for Studies in Education, 5 / the progress being made toward the development of a system of educational television, 6 / the department's continuing recognition of the value of trustee representation on ministerial committees and study groups, 7 / the granting of authority to elementary school boards to enter into transportation agreements for a period of up to five years in length, 8 / the provision of authority for the boarding of secondary school students in unorganized territories, 9 / the legislation making school trustees eligible to serve on other local boards and commissions, 10 / the granting of authority to include in budget estimates provision for a reserve for working funds, 11 / the granting of authority for public school boards to include in their estimates an amount from current funds for permanent improvements. The inclusion of the first five of these items indicated that the council was firmly behind a number of the most outstanding achievements of the Davis era. Most of the others were related directly to the functions of trustees and school boards.

The recommendations for the same year which would require for implementation the co-operation of ministers of departments other than the Department of Education, and which were therefore directed to the Prime Minister, were as follows: that the Legislature increase the Department of Education grant to 50 per cent of the approved costs for elementary schools and 60 per cent of the corresponding amount for secondary schools; that the grant on capital costs for subsequent school construction be paid on a cash basis in a lump sum at the time of debenture issue; that legislation be enacted to require vehicular traffic to stop when making a frontal approach to a standing school bus with its signal devices operating; that the relevant legislation be amended to enable a member of a board of education or a public, separate, high school, or other board to be eligible for nomination and election to any municipal office, but that he be required to present his resignation from such a board before the official nomination date, his resignation to take effect on December 31 of the same year; that the Departments of Education and Labour give serious consideration to the establishment of a system of credits or partial credits for trade training time in vocational shops in lieu of apprenticeship time.

A second group of resolutions consisted of those approved by the council and submitted to the minister for the first time. The substance of these was that the Department of Education amend the grant regulations to provide for the continuation of grants on debenture payments on school buildings necessarily vacated in the program of centralization, without decreasing the amount approved for grant on new school buildings in the same area; that the department reduce the subsequent estimated enrolment from thirty-five to thirty pupils per classroom; that school boards be permitted to use a five-year instead of a two-year estimate when requesting tentative approval for a building proposal; that the existing grant structure be revised so that grants for general purpose rooms or playrooms would be in direct proportion to the number of classrooms in the school applying for such a grant; that the department make an initial grant for the establishment of new school libraries sufficient to provide the basic books necessary to make a beginning on a reasonably adequate basis; that the list of approved books acceptable for grant for established elementary school libraries be extended to include more reference books and that the list of elementary school reference books eligible for grant be published annually; that grants for textbooks in grades 9 and 10 in elementary and junior high schools be restored to $12; that increased grants be allotted to introduce, equip, and conduct auxiliary classes; that an accredited course be set up for elementary school principals; that a concerted effort be made to increase the level of education of all those without degrees before they were granted a licence to teach; that the department continue its program of expansion in the operation of summer courses by the utilization of all teachers' colleges to the fullest possible extent and by the establishment of additional summer courses in other local areas; that the department offer a summer course as soon as possible in new mathematics in the Lakehead area for the benefit of all teaching staffs in northwestern Ontario, and that all boards encourage and urge their elementary school teachers to attend and support such a course; that the department, as soon as practicable, increase the number of qualified guidance teachers available for service in elementary and secondary schools; that the department investigate the possibility of operating the night schools, Programs 4 and 5, Advanced Technical Evening classes, and other forms of continuing education under the direction of a central administration, and possibly under a director responsible for the whole program, and that consideration be given to allowing full and free use of the educational facilities, and other facilities in general, to obtain the maximum grants available; that the department be asked to prepare curricula leading to certificated courses that could be taught in adult training programs; that there be early study, adoption, and support of new and greatly accelerated programs for the systematic education and retraining of adults even while they were gainfully employed; that the Department of Education request the Fire Marshal to inspect all new school construction and that the marshal's approval of such construction be delivered to the board within the one-year warranty period; that the department conduct a critical examination of the efficiency of reviews of architects' plans by its officials with a view to reducing delays and enabling schools to proceed with construction; that the Minister of Education seek legislation requiring parents to assume liability for the wilful acts of their children when such acts resulted in damage to school property; that legislation requiring honoraria for trustees be amended so that trustees of all rural school boards would be permitted to receive remuneration; that *The Public Schools Act* be amended to delete the provision for judges, members of the Legislative Assembly, members of municipal councils, and clergymen to be school visitors. Two other items on the list, accompanied by lengthy preambles, were too long to be included here.

The presentation of the OSTC contained two further sections, one dealing with a resolution which the department had been unwilling to accept in previous years and which was being resubmitted for further consideration, and the other dealing with resolutions toward which the department had been receptive, but on which it had not yet acted. The rejected resolution proposed that all Ontario scholars be allowed to collect the full $400 award regardless of other scholarships or awards received. The council published its interchange of views with the department on this issue and on those in the fourth section of its brief on which no action had been taken despite expressions of sympathy. The fourth section included resolutions urging that school boards be supplied with new grant regulations at an earlier date each year; that the term "resident" in *The Public Schools Act* be defined in such a way as to eliminate misunderstanding and confusion; that *The Separate Schools Act* be amended to permit separate school trustees to be appointed to local boards and commissions as had recently been provided for public and secondary school trustees; that the provincial government make it mandatory for school trustees to be represented on planning committees with full voting powers; that the grant for elementary school construction be increased to $25,000 per classroom; that the maximum capital grant per classroom for new construction be increased in northern and northwestern Ontario; that the department extend the policy of grants on major repairs to other repairs without applying the existing clause limiting grants on capital expenditures from current funds to elementary school boards in urban municipalities with a population under 2,500 and in rural municipalities having a population under 25,000; that grants policy be broadened to cover the installation of new heating plants when schools aged thirty-five years and over were being renovated; that grants on textbooks for grades 9 and 10 be determined on the basis of total registration of pupils or on average daily attendance plus 5 per cent, rather than on average daily attendance, since boards had to buy books for all students; that expenditures for a book-storage room up to a maximum of $25,000 in new secondary school construction be recognized as an approved cost of education;

that schools employing a staff of four teachers, instead of a minimum of six, might avail themselves of a 16-mm sound projector under the grant system and that schools employing two teachers might acquire a 35-mm strip film projector; that tape recorders and television sets be included among items eligible for grants; that the number of classrooms in a school considered large enough to receive grants for audio-visual aids be reduced or the requirement removed; that secondary school boards be permitted to provide testing and counselling services to the grade 8 pupils attending public elementary schools lying within the secondary school district; that consideration be given to the establishment of a college of education in northern Ontario; that the Department of Education revoke its requirement that schools be closed on November 11 when this day fell on a week day so that school boards could arrange for Remembrance Day services in the schools; that school principals should be divorced from the associations which existed for the protection of teachers; that school boards in organized municipalities or townships be permitted to appoint any auditor appointed by the Department of Municipal Affairs, even if he was not the one chosen by the municipality in which the school board was organized.

The council regarded as one of its main duties the definition of certain desirable practices and standards of behaviour for school trustees. In a list of "do's" trustees were advised to remember that the administration of education was one of the most important functions of government; to remember that their responsibility was not to run the schools, but to see that they were well run; to try to interpret to the school staff the attitudes, wishes, and needs of the people and to the people the needs, problems, and progress of the schools; to give all school officials authority in keeping with their responsibilities; to support and protect school officials in the performance of their duties; to voice opinions frankly in board meetings, but to support board policy once a decision was made; to do everything possible to establish a friendly working relationship with the staff; to remember that the school trustee's responsibility was to the electors and not to the municipal council; to try to establish a harmonious working agreement with the municipal council and to keep its members acquainted with the probable future building needs of the school board; to remember that trustees were permitted under school acts to charge the board reasonable expenses in connection with educational conventions; to read the *Argus*, the *Canadian School Journal*, or other worthwhile trustees' magazines; to support a safety program; to be careful to get the complete story before making a decision involving criticism of the teaching or administrative staff; to support administrators, principals, and teachers whenever possible in order to sustain morale; to co-operate with the local inspector; to co-operate with the Department of Education; to keep buildings and equipment up to date and in a good state of repair; to hire an efficient secretary-treasurer; and to check with the inspector before purchasing new types of equipment and supplies.

Some of the things trustees were admonished *not* to do were to interfere with the day-to-day details of school administration and supervision; to show favouritism to relatives or friends; to make promises or commitments before the questions were fully discussed at board meetings; to join a clique to control board action; to use board membership to obtain business or political advancement for themselves or their friends; to divulge confidential information such as bids submitted by tendering firms for building projects; to assume authority in school matters when the board was not in session; to favour the school near their home or the one in which they had the greatest personal interest; to let personal animosity toward a teacher or another trustee affect their decisions at board meetings; to be niggardly with the staff lest they drive good teachers away; to interfere with the private lives of teachers unless they were certain that their actions adversely affected their work in the school; to discuss teachers outside school board meetings; to hire a teacher without checking his previous record; to visit schools except on invitation.

One of the most significant developments in the area of trustee education was represented by an Advanced Institute for School Trustees and Administrators held in Toronto in April 1964. This institute, lasting for two and one-half days, was sponsored by the OSTC, with the support of the Department of Education, the Ontario Association of School Business Officials, and the Ontario Association of Directors and Superintendents. The purposes were to explore the leadership roles of trustees and their officials, to help each group develop a better understanding of the other's responsibilities, and to formulate procedures whereby school boards and their officials might work more productively together. The response was enthusiastic, and many of the participating boards put into practice some of the concepts expounded by the American guests who acted as leaders.[17] The program of trustee training according to this pattern was continued during the years that followed.

The school board reorganization of 1969 gave the trustees' organizations a smaller and relatively stronger membership. Their power was shown in the spring of 1970 when they maintained a united front against hiring any new teachers until the dispute between the boards and teachers in Metropolitan Toronto was settled, or at least until a temporary *modus vivendi* was worked out. Effective action was attributed in part to a series of provincial salary conferences in which ideas were exchanged and a co-operative mood was developed.

The formation of the Ontario Public School Trustees' Association raised questions about the future role of the OSTC. The new organization was very much larger than any of the other three that remained, and threatened to overshadow them completely. There were suggestions that the Northern Ontario Public and Secondary School Trustees' Association might soon join. Some of the members of the organization felt that they were equipped and prepared to take over many of the major responsibilities of the council, and that it might as well be dissolved. Others pointed out, however, that there was still a need to co-ordinate all associations, large and small, and that they could carry more weight working together than operating individually. For the time being, this view seemed to prevail. The Ontario Public School Trustees' Association was given seven representatives and the others three each. There was no indication at the time of writing that the northern association would give up its separate existence.

THE ONTARIO PUBLIC SCHOOL TRUSTEES' ASSOCIATION

It had become increasingly obvious to many participants and observers that the number of trustees' associations in Ontario was incompatible with the most efficient administration and provision of services. Serious discussions began in March 1967 with a view to amalgamating four organizations concerned with the public elementary and secondary school systems: the Ontario School Trustees' and Ratepayers' Association, the Urban and Rural School Trustees' Association of Ontario, the Public School Trustees' Association of Ontario, and the Associated Secondary School Boards of Ontario. A Committee on Amalgamation of the Four Associations worked on plans for the new association under the chairmanship of John Ronson, with Jean Watson as secretary-treasurer. Strong impetus was given to the development by the Prime Minister's announcement regarding the formation of larger administrative units.

The objects of the new Ontario Public School Trustees' Association (OPSTA) were

1. To promote interest in education throughout the Province of Ontario;
2. To make representations concerning education to any association or organization or any department of government;
3. To promote an interest in and the study of education;
4. To accept gifts, donations, legacies, devises and bequests; and
5. To invest the moneys of the Corporation not immediately required for the purposes of the Corporation in any securities in which, under The Trustee Act or any other Act, trustees may invest trust funds.

One of the early achievements of the Committee on Administrative Practices of the OPSTA was the production of a booklet entitled *School Board Administrative Practices*, designed to further the committee's objective of encouraging the attainment of sound standards of administration among member boards. The suggestions in the booklet were said to be based on new findings and experiences of established boards. It was the association's intention that the material would be the basis for discussion in workshops and seminars. Information was supplied in relation to the streamlining of business operations of school boards, the elimination of duplication of educational services, the elimination of unnecessary departments and internal functions, the updating of time-worn practices, and the introduction of long overdue techniques in quality control.

The committee supported a system of unitary control, with a director of education and an administrative council of senior officials. Trustees were said to form a board only when in formal session, at which time they participated in setting broad policy in the light of community needs. When not acting as a board member, a trustee was entitled to exercise his citizen's right to freedom of speech – on education as well as on other subjects. Although he had a responsibility for explaining the operations of the board, he was not, however, to undermine its effectiveness.

The organization of larger units of administration was seen as a threat to effective communication between parents and trustees. Remedies were to be sought in planning and effort to establish contacts involving the board, the students, the staff, the parents, and the ratepayers. Trustees might gather pertinent information through association with organized groups, in some cases with committees of parents and lay people. Meeting of board-staff relations committees were recommended as a means of exchanging information and building confidence between trustees and teachers. Contacts with students might be developed by means of publications, meetings, and conferences. Trustees were warned to use the proper avenues of approach in order to avoid undermining the position of school officials.

The booklet referred to certain provisions of school legislation with respect to the appointment, powers, and duties of the director of education. It also outlined the role of other elements in the administrative structure. It was said to be desirable for senior officials to be aware of and involved in all aspects of the educational operation, including business as well as academic matters. In this way empire building might be held in check at a time when available economic resources made such activity particularly inappropriate.

EIGHT

Associations of school administrators

The associations in this chapter were largely organizations of school principals and administrators at higher levels in local systems. The members assembled mostly to discuss common problems, to consider the possibility of taking a united stand on certain issues, to get to know one another, and to strengthen their esprit de corps. They were somewhat interested in protective measures, but less so than the teachers' federations.

THE ONTARIO SECONDARY SCHOOL HEADMASTERS' COUNCIL

The Ontario Secondary School Headmasters' Council (OSSHC) had two parent organizations. One of these was the Ontario Secondary School Headmasters' Association, which originated in a section of the OEA. This organization, assuming its final form in the mid-1950s, became the influential voice of the principals, and received strong support from the trustees' associations. The latter generally favoured the idea of dealing with this group independently rather than in combination with the teachers. During the 1940s and 1950s the Ontario Secondary School Teachers' Federation (OSSTF) accepted principals along with teachers as members but made no particular effort to provide the principals with a program appropriate to their special role in education. Although there was no evidence that the principals were particularly unhappy with their status in the federation, or that they were considering withdrawal, leading federation members began to fear an evolution in that direction.

At the annual assembly in 1960 the OSSTF set up a Principals' Standing Committee to give more attention to the particular interests of that group and to prevent a cleavage of forces. The existence of the two overlapping bodies, however, involved a duplication of time, effort, and expense, and threatened to weaken the effectiveness of the principals as educational leaders. In 1964, therefore, members of the Principals' Standing Committee approached the executive of the Ontario Secondary School Headmasters' Association with the suggestion of a joint meeting to discuss matters of common concern. Eventually the two bodies amalgamated in a new organization called the Ontario Secondary School Headmasters' Council (OSSHC). An OSSHC constitution was drawn up and incorporated in that of the OSSTF.

The objectives of the new council included the following:

a) To provide a means whereby the secondary school headmasters of the Province of Ontario shall have an opportunity to consider problems of school organization, administration and curriculum.
b) To enhance the status of the secondary school headmasters and to give clear and vigorous expression of the thoughts and opinions of our principals throughout the Province.
c) To make provision for appropriate liaison and direct communication with the Department of Education, and other educational bodies, in matters affecting the headmaster.[1]

In a set of notes for principals' courses used in 1968 C.W. Perry, the executive secretary of the council, indicated some of the benefits provided for the members. 1 / Conferences and workshops were organized by the regional boards of directors. There were eight OSSTF regions: Bay of Quinte, Central, Eastern, Georgian Bay, Hamilton-Niagara, Northern, Northwestern, and Southwestern. In four of these, vice-principals were invited to participate. An attendance rate of at least 90 per cent was said to indicate a keen interest in the programs, which dealt with topics of current educational interest. 2 / There were at least two provincial conferences each year: the spring annual meeting and the annual summer conference. The spring meeting held in March 1968 dealt with the theme How Effectively is the School Communicating?, while the Niagara Conference of the late summer focused on Education for Enduring Values. 3 / Principals had someone at OSSTF headquarters to whom they could turn for another point of view or a sympathetic hearing when they encountered difficulties. 4 / The *Headmaster* published articles designed to assist the members to provide enlightened leadership. Some of these articles were inspirational, others presented points of view on controversial issues, and still others described actual educational developments in Ontario and in other parts of Canada and abroad.

The council has taken a stand on educational issues of current importance to principals, and in some cases brought pressure to bear on the Department of Education to modify objectionable decisions or policies. For example, there were objections to the announcement during the middle of the 1968–9 school year that the closing date in June would be later than school officials had supposed. While indicating that there was general support for a firm stand on the part of the minister for consolidation of an instructional year of reasonable length, the executive pointed out that the decision had come after schools had made their plans for examinations and promotion meetings, and in many cases had announced them publicly. The minister found it possible to make certain compromises to ease the difficulties caused by the decision. In a matter closely related to the date of school closing, the council secured an agreement on the part of the universities to delay the mailing of early admission letters until May 30. A later request was made for an extension of this date until June 10 so that grade 13 students could be compelled to maintain interest and attendance. A third example of the council's influence had to do with changes in the requirements for the Permanent Secondary School Principal's Certificate, Type A. The council pointed out that the "abrupt" change would have an unfair effect on some candidates who, after securing their Type B Certificate, had postponed attendance at the second course on medical advice or on the grounds that they should give their attention to a school building program. While there was no objection to higher qualifications for Secondary School Principals' Certificates, it was claimed that candidates who had already been approved and had taken part of the existing program should be given ample forewarning of intended changes. An amendment to the announcement in accord with the recommendations of the OSSHC was subsequently made.

THE ONTARIO PRINCIPALS' ASSOCIATION

In the early 1940s a small group of Toronto school principals organized an Urban Principals' Section of the Public School Department of the OEA. It was intended at that time that membership would be limited to principals of large schools, since it was assumed that principals of one-room and two-room schools would find more assistance in meeting their problems in the Rural Teachers' and Elementary Teachers' Sections. It was said that these sections did not want principals of small schools to be accepted by the Urban Principals' Section, and thus reduce their ranks. As the trend toward larger administrative units continued, however, and as the number of very small schools decreased, the Urban Principals' Section grew while the Rural Teachers' Section shrank.

When the departmental organization of the OEA was abandoned in 1966, the Urban Principals' Section of the Elementary School Department became the Ontario Principals' Section, and continued its operations as before. The rural teachers maintained a section for two more years, and then disbanded. Some of the remaining members joined the Ontario Principals' Section while others gravitated to subject-oriented groups. At this time, the Ontario Principals' Section had members who were principals of various types of schools such as K-8 schools, junior schools (K-6), senior schools (7 and 8), junior high schools (7, 8, and 9), separate schools, and private schools.

The major activity of the association or section was the program at the annual convention of the OEA. In addition, there was some distribution of publications throughout the year. District conferences were inaugurated in the fall of 1968, with one held in the fall of that year in each of Barrie, Kitchener, and Oshawa. Locations selected for 1969 were Sudbury, Peterborough, and London.

THE ASSOCIATION OF HEADMISTRESSES OF CANADA

What was called the Canadian Headmistresses' Association was formed at a meeting at Branksome Hall, Toronto, in 1931. The headmistresses of Branksome Hall, Havergal College, and Bishop Strachan School decided to invite their counterparts in leading private schools in Montreal, and possibly in other parts of Canada, to form a national organization. Provincial groups would meet every year and special meetings of the national organization would be held every three years. The new association quickly enrolled thirty-five paid-up members from schools across Canada.

According to the constitution the objectives of the association were to "provide a medium of expression for girls' Private Secondary Schools of Canada, and to be an instrument for action in case of necessity – to afford an opportunity for the Headmistresses to meet for discussing and sharing their educational problems – to keep in touch with what is being done in the educational world." In pursuit of these objectives, the program of one of the earliest meetings dealt with music in the schools, preparation for citizenship, prizes and the marking system, movies, and professions open to women in Canada.

Although most of the members were headmistresses of secondary schools, the whole school program, from nursery school to university entrance, was represented. Some schools had church affiliations, some were incorporated, and a few were privately owned. Some were almost exclusively residential, others had accommodation for some boarders, and still others catered only to day school students. Most of them placed considerable emphasis on religious instruction and on the all-round development of the student.

During the earlier years the association had an Appointments Bureau, affiliated with the Overseas Education League of Canada, which helped to recruit teaching staff. The membership has, however, been too small and funds too scarce to sustain any comprehensive program of activities. It has been impossible to support any administrative or clerical staff, much less conduct research.

ASSOCIATIONS OF EDUCATION OFFICIALS

The development of associations of education officials was a post-war phenomenon of a particularly informal nature. There was an atmosphere of the exclusive club about the organizations, along with an apparent lack of concern for recording their history. When J.R.H. Morgan undertook in 1968 to set down some of the facts about their origin and evolution, he was forced to rely on his own memory and that of some of his colleagues who had participated from the beginning. Thus the following brief account, based mainly on Morgan's reminiscences, is short on dates and specific detail.

Urban school boards were given the authority to appoint their own supervisory officers as early as 1847. The customary title given these officials was chief inspector. Hamilton began to use the term superintendent at the beginning of the 1930s, and other large systems followed suit. The usual pattern at that stage was to have a superintendent who was largely concerned with instruction in the elementary schools, while a business administrator, with parallel authority, looked after business matters. This set-up existed in Toronto after 1932 when C.C. Goldring, the first official to exercise real authority over both levels of a system, was appointed as superintendent of schools.

Hamilton pioneered again in 1944 by appointing the first superintendent of secondary schools, T.W. Oates, and Toronto followed suit in 1945 when C. Robb assumed the same role. A few months later Z.S. Phimister was appointed superintendent of public schools, completing the pattern by which a director of education co-ordinated the work of two superintendents. In 1958 the business administrators were brought under the control of the director.

By 1950 J.R.H. Morgan was superintendent of secondary schools in Toronto and there were officials with similar status in other large systems. The beginning of a feeling of concern over the threatened shortage of secondary school teachers brought about a meeting involving Morgan, F.G. Patten of Ottawa, and T.C. White of Windsor. A short time later these three were joined by G.E. Price of Hamilton. The eventual outcome of this initiative was the establishment of a Teacher Recruitment and Service Council, later called a foundation, which had representatives from the newly formed Association of Directors of Education of Ontario, the Association of Ontario Secondary School Superintendents, the Ontario School Trustees' Council, and the Ontario Secondary School Teachers' Federation. The founders hoped that the business community could be persuaded to co-operate in a significant fashion with education authorities to improve the supply of teachers. Part of the intended program involved raising funds for bursaries and loans to assist young people who would commit themselves in advance to secondary school teaching. The results of the effort were rather disappointing, but the organization did give the new associations of school officials a specific cause.

As the number of secondary school superintendents increased, the initial group set up a more formal organization under the name Association of Ontario Secondary School Superintendents. There was frank discussion over the question of whether directors of education should be invited to join. There were ambivalent feelings because a number of these officials had a background largely restricted to elementary school work, and were not thought to have an adequate understanding of secondary school interests. They were finally extended such a lukewarm invitation that they formed their own Association of Directors of Education of

Ontario. A number of them also participated in the third organization of the trio, the Ontario Association of School Superintendents and Directors, which was formed on the initiative of the superintendents of elementary schools. The Association of Ontario Secondary School Superintendents demonstrated the exclusiveness of its interests in another way by failing to respond to an overture from the Ontario Secondary School Teachers' Federation to form some kind of link.

Members of each of the three associations met regularly to engage in discussions of problems of common concern. The sense of cohesion thus built up no doubt had desirable consequences. It was impossible to take the same kind of protective actions that were open to the teachers' federations, since formal guarantees of job security for administrators are unrealistic. The members of the associations occasionally expressed concern over their inability to exert much influence over school board decisions with respect to their salaries. They could be reasonably sure, however, that they would be given increases to keep them ahead of teachers and principals.

THE ONTARIO ASSOCIATION OF EDUCATION OFFICIALS

The formation of the Ontario Association of Education Officials represented a response to the radically changed administrative structures produced by the formation of the divisional boards of education in January 1969. Even before this development took place, there had been a move toward reorganization along the lines followed in the Department of Education: that is, the sharp division between the elementary and secondary levels was being abandoned and senior officials were being given the responsibility for certain facets of education from kindergarten to grade 13. A few examples of this type of reorganization are presented in volume VI, chapter 6. The basis for the distinctions among the earlier associations of school administrators was seriously undermined by these developments.

The association was officially formed on October 29, 1968. A little over a year later, the members assembled at Niagara Falls to consider and adopt a constitution. The first item in the preamble to this document was a statement that the formation of the association arose "from the need for a coherent and informed voice in educational affairs from the executive officials in the municipal educational systems in the province." Five purposes were defined:

a) To further the cause of education;
b) To support sound ethical practices;
c) To engage in a continuous program of professional development for executive officials of school systems;

d) To advise the Department of Education on matters pertaining to education in Ontario;

e) To liaise with other government agencies, organizations and groups interested in the cause of education.

There was considerable difficulty in defining qualifications for membership. According to the constitution, active members were municipally employed officials of public and separate school systems who held executive positions as directors of education, superintendents or assistant superintendents with responsibility for academic and business matters, or area superintendents with executive responsibility. Associate membership was open to education officials in roles equivalent to those of active members but employed by authorities other than municipal boards; to inspectors meeting certain requirements; and to school business officials serving as department heads and holding a university degree or other professional qualifications, including architects, professional engineers, and chartered accountants. Associate members had all membership rights except that they could not participate in business meetings, vote, or hold office. Honorary membership could be granted by a resolution of the Board of Governors to any active member on retirement or to any other individual who had made an outstanding contribution to education in Ontario. Like associate members, honorary members were barred from voting or holding office.

Although the constitutional provisions left some unsettled questions about eligibility for membership, there were considered to be about six hundred potential members in the fall of 1970, of whom approximately half had joined. Since the effectiveness of the association would depend to a considerable extent on the availability of funds, and since there was no obvious source of such funds other than the members themselves, an early decision was made in favour of a high fee structure. Each member was expected to contribute 0.5 per cent of his annual salary. This requirement no doubt had something to do with the difficulty in increasing the membership.

During the 1969–70 school year the association purchased services from the secretariat of the OEA. At four regional conferences held in early 1970 to discuss future activities, it became clear that the members expected to see their own central office established. I.M. Robb, who had recently retired from the position of General Secretary of the Ontario Secondary School Teachers' Federation, was accordingly recruited to assume his duties as secretary beginning on July 1.

During the summer of 1970, two residential seminars on Educational Management and Planning were held at York University with the assistance of the Department of Educational Administration at the Ontario Institute for Studies in Education. Major attention was given to educational planning and budgeting, student unrest and other kinds of conflict involving the administrator, and social and political issues affecting educational planning. In the association's newsletter, *NEWSCAP*, the results were appraised very favourably.

The enthusiasm and expertise of the staff, the equal enthusiasm and willing involvement of the limited number of participants, the timeliness of the topics, the problem-solving approach used, and the pleasant residential conditions at York all contributed to the very worthwhile experiences enjoyed by those attending.[2]

There were several issues of importance to be dealt with in 1970–1. 1 / Members hoped to be able to work out policies that would enable them to take a uniform stand on matters such as the amount of school time teachers should be granted for conferences, seminars, and other non-teaching activities. 2 / Standards would be more carefully defined for the administrative positions which the members held. Salary levels might be established in terms of experience, qualifications, and performance. 3 / A program of regional conferences might be worked out to cover the whole province. These might cater both to broad, general interests and to those of a more specialized nature.

THE ONTARIO ASSOCIATION OF GOVERNING BODIES
OF INDEPENDENT SCHOOLS
The newly formed Ontario Association of Governing Bodies of Independent Schools adopted a constitution in 1968. According to this document, the objects of the organization were "to promote the association of representatives of Independent Schools in Ontario for the exchange of information of mutual interest, and for the development and implementation of such programmes or projects as may be of interest or benefit to the members." Independent schools were defined as schools in Ontario 1 / not operated under *The Public Schools Act, The Secondary Schools and Boards of Education Act*, or *The Separate Schools Act*, 2 / offering courses at least in grades 9, 10, 11, and 12 in a manner approved by the Ontario Department of Education, 3 / having a minimum total of thirty students in that group of grades, and 4 / not operated for gain. Roman Catholic private schools, which were considered to have different types of problems, were not included in the membership. Provision was made, however, for two representatives of the Ontario membership of the Headmasters' Association and one representative of the Ontario membership of the Headmistresses' Association to receive notice of and attend meetings of the directors.

A major influence contributing to the formation of the association was the increase in financial problems faced by independent schools during a period of rapidly rising educational costs. Those responsible for these schools were reluctant to rely on increases in fees because to do so would lead to a further narrowing of the group from which their students were drawn, and in consequence an increasing isolation from the mainstream of society. There were always hopes that the government might be persuaded to make some contribution, in view of the fact that its counterparts in some other provinces had found it possible to do so. For the time being, at least, the government appeared to have set its course firmly against such a policy.

NINE

Associations of administrators of miscellaneous agencies

The associations dealt with in this chapter have existed to promote the interests of the agencies for which their members have been responsible. They have been concerned with devising educational programs for the public or a specific clientele, with the welfare, training, upgrading, and certification of their employees, or with the status of their work in general. They have tended to keep an eye on legislation which is of direct concern to them.

THE CANADIAN MUSEUMS ASSOCIATION

The Canadian Museums Association was organized in 1947 to promote the interests of Canadian museums and the welfare of those who worked in them. According to its by-law, it was to achieve its purposes by 1 / improving the services of Canadian museums as educational institutions, 2 / acting as a clearinghouse for information of special interest to Canadian museums, 3 / aiding in the establishment of one or more museum training schools for the purpose of training art gallery and museum workers, 4 / assisting Canadian museums in securing expert staffs, 5 / promoting the exchange of exhibition material and the organization of exhibitions in Canada and abroad, and 6 / co-operating with other museum associations of the Commonwealth and the United States and with the International Council of Museums.

Institutional membership was open to institutions that were 1 / not operating for profit, 2 / not existing primarily for the purpose of conducting temporary exhibitions, 3 / exempt from federal and provincial income taxes, 4 / open to the public and administered in the public interest, and 5 / in existence "for the purpose of conserving and preserving, studying, interpreting, assembling and exhibiting to the public for its instruction and enjoyment objects and specimens of educational and cultural value, including artistic, scientific (whether animate or inanimate), historical, and technological material." Such institutions included art galleries, art exhibit centres, botanical gardens, zoological parks, aquaria, planetaria, historical society museums and historic houses, and preservation projects. Individual membership was open to anyone employed by or associated with an approved museum or any student sponsored by the Training Committee. Any *bona fide* reputable business firm dealing in goods or services related to the operation of a museum might be an associate member.

As carried out in the late 1960s, the training program of the association was designed to upgrade the qualifications of those engaged in museum work and thus to help them gain a greater insight into modern museum methods and techniques. There were three preliminary levels of training, leading finally to a reading program, an examination, and a thesis. Letters of attendance were granted on request for participation in any program sponsored by the association, certificates were given to those who successfully completed the various levels of training, and a diploma was awarded for attainment of the highest level of instruction.

Preparatory training at level one was intended primarily for those working in small, often isolated, museums with little or no previous training. It was carried out with the aid of staff members of provincial and large regional museums. Part of the program consisted of a correspondence course employing technical reading material supplied by the association. An examination covered such topics as organization and administration, conservation, exhibition, education, public relations, curatorial procedures, and other such matters. In order to obtain the level one certificate a candidate had not only to complete the correspondence course successfully and pass the examination, but also to attend an approved seminar and complete an assigned paper or, alternatively, to attend at least two recognized and approved regional association workshops and also complete an assigned paper. Level two training was intended mainly for staff members in larger institutions who might be called upon to conduct training on level one within the scope of their specialization. A basic element of the course was a seminar on museum organization and management. Seminars consisted of working sessions with assigned problems, reports by students, practical demonstrations, and lecture periods. In addition to the seminar on museum organization and management, a candidate for the level two certificate had to take two other approved seminars, one dealing with the curatorial field and the other with the field of exhibit and extension. Level three demanded written work at a level worthy of publication. The candidate was expected, with the aid of tutors, to choose an area of specialization. Most of his work was to be done in that area, although he was expected to take two seminars and produce a paper in another area. The diploma program consisted of further work in a specialized area, along with seminars and prescribed reading. Examinations had to be passed within five years of the date of registration.

The association was just getting its training program properly established by 1970. Officials were prepared to try to make up for the complete lack of any other provision for training Canadian museum workers, but hoped that the higher levels of their program would ultimately be taken over by the universities. Participation by such institutions as the Royal Ontario Museum and the National Museums of Canada was also thought desirable.

THE ONTARIO ASSOCIATION OF ART GALLERIES

The formation of the Ontario Association of Art Galleries resulted from a meeting held in August 1968. The roots of the organization, however, go back to 1947, when representatives of the art galleries of London, Hamilton, Windsor, and Hart House met to work out co-operative procedures for organizing exhibitions for circulation among themselves.[1] The informal association thus initiated was called the Southern Ontario Galleries Group. By 1952 it had grown to the point where the need for a broader organization was obvious, and the Art Institute of Ontario was formed. Fifteen years later, when the services of this institute had extended to one hundred Ontario communities, the members approved its amalgamation with the Art Gallery of Ontario, and the Extension Department of the latter took over its program. Left by these developments without a place where they could meet to consider matters of common interest, some of the original members of the institute assembled at the Art Gallery of Hamilton to form the Ontario Association of Art Galleries.

As stated in the first issue of the *Bulletin of the Ontario Association of Art Galleries*, the purposes of the association were as follows:

To encourage the closest possible co-operation among member galleries and museums.
To encourage close co-operation between the Ontario Association of Art Galleries and the Province of Ontario Council for the Arts and other similar agencies.
To assist developing visual art centres in the Province.
To promote high standards of excellence and uniform methods in the care and presentation of works of art.
To serve as an advisory body in matters of professional interest.

The membership consisted of directors and curators of Ontario art centres.

THE SOCIETY OF DIRECTORS OF
MUNICIPAL RECREATION OF ONTARIO

What was later called the Society of Directors of Municipal Recreation of Ontario was established as the Recreation Directors' Federation of Ontario in 1946. The new name was adopted when the organization was incorporated by legislation passed in 1958. An important structural element was a training committee appointed each year to make recommendations to the executive with respect to internal and external training opportunities. Several actions of some importance ensued.

An in-service training course was first conducted at the University of Toronto, and later moved to the University of Western Ontario. This was a three-year in-service course carried out with the university's assistance by correspondence with one week of attendance at the university each year. Successful completion of the course qualified a recreation director for a certificate issued by the Ontario Department of Education. The course was discontinued at the end of 1966 when a resident course was introduced at the University of Guelph leading to the award of a diploma in recreation after two years of study. While the society was not involved in further programs of the same kind, consideration was given to the possibility of assisting those working in the field, some of whom have had no special formal training.

The society was instrumental in bringing about the establishment of the two-year Diploma Course in Recreation at the University of Guelph in 1963. In 1967 this course was transferred to Centennial College, and similar courses were subsequently added at Fanshawe College in London, Mohawk College in Hamilton, Humber College in Etobicoke, Algonquin College in Ottawa, and Confederation College in Thunder Bay. Graduates received a diploma, and were eligible for a B certificate from the Department of Education provided that they were employed in municipal recreation.

Assistance was provided in the establishment of four-year programs leading to degrees in recreation at the University of Ottawa and the University of Waterloo in 1968. These led to an A certificate for those employed in municipal recreation.

Annual training institutes, usually held for two days in November, were conducted for the benefit of members of the society. Experts were brought in to speak and to assist with the workshops and discussions. Different themes were selected each year; among them were public relations, office administration, human relations, and recreational services under school authorities. Those attending were given no formal recognition, but were expected to derive sufficient satisfaction from the opportunity to increase their knowledge and understanding.

THE ASSOCIATION OF CANADIAN COMMERCIAL COLLEGES

The roots of the Association of Canadian Commercial Colleges are to be found in the Business Educators' Association of Canada, which was founded in 1896. One of the main functions of this organization, as it developed through the years, was to produce examination papers in a considerable number of subjects and to mark answer papers of candidates from all parts of Canada at the end of each month. A second major responsibility was to keep the curriculum and teaching of Canadian business colleges in line with modern business and office requirements. This objective was pursued through meetings of the general assembly held in June each year, meetings of the Board of Directors held four times a year, and numerous committee meetings and conferences.

The association was incorporated as a non-profit organization under *The Ontario Companies Act* in 1939. In February 1969 it was amalgamated with the Association of Canadian Commercial Colleges. Also active in the same field was the smaller Canadian Business Schools Association.

In recent years the association has offered examinations in subjects leading to diplomas in the following areas: for women, Secretarial, General Office, Junior Secretarial, Stenography, Cleritype, and Machine Calculation; for men, Business Administration, General Office, Accountancy, and Commercial. Several advantages have been identified in the system of uniform external examinations. For the staff of the business schools it has provided relief from preparing and marking final examination papers, and has ensured that there can be no valid charge of favouritism toward or discrimination against individual candidates. For the candidate evidence of graduation has been a valuable qualification for employment.

The 1960s were a difficult period for private business colleges in Ontario and other parts of Canada. At one time these colleges were considered to be the only place where a person could get satisfactory secretarial or commercial training. By the end of the decade nearly all high schools offered commercial subjects, and many had four-year and five-year Business and Commerce programs. As the colleges of applied arts and technology offered increasing opportunities for more specialized training, students tended to abandon the business colleges with their higher fees. The business colleges could only hope to compete by attempting to offer more efficient, practical courses in minimum time and by making greater efforts to meet the needs of individual students. In order to strengthen their competitive position, the colleges, operating through the Business Educators' Association, made some organizational and curricular changes in 1967. In order to avoid duplication and shorten the time certain students had to spend in school, arrangements were made to recognize credits obtained in high schools and universities. College administrators entertained the hope that universities and colleges would eventually reciprocate by recognizing some of their courses. Beginning in 1968, a more flexible program was introduced combining compulsory subjects with electives. The range of offerings was also extended to include advanced training for medical, legal, and executive secretaries.

TEN

Associations of university officials

This chapter covers a number of associations resembling those dealt with in chapter 9 except that they were concerned with university affairs. Some of those who participated in the activities of the Association of Universities and Colleges of Canada would perhaps not appreciate having it called an organization of officials, but administrative interests predominated. Other agencies in the group were involved in some specific aspect of the work of the university. Administrators met to consider matters of policy, to devise common strategies for achieving their objectives, and in some cases to deal with program development.

THE ASSOCIATION OF UNIVERSITIES AND COLLEGES OF CANADA

The Conference of Canadian Universities was formed in 1911 when a number of universities agreed to hold annual meetings to discuss issues and problems of national concern. As a result of a change of name in 1922, when a formal constitution was adopted, the association was called the National Conference of Canadian Universities. The twenty-eight member institutions at that time included non-degree granting institutions, vocational schools, and universities within federations, as well as large multi-faculty universities.[1] During the first twenty-five years of the existence of the organization only two members were added: St Dunstan's University and le Collège d'Agriculture de Ste Anne de la Pocatière. The latter dropped out after a few years. Between 1949 and 1960 there were seven additions, and during the 1960s the rate of increase accelerated considerably. By 1969 total membership had reached sixty-one.

The Canadian Universities Foundation, consisting of twenty-one members elected from and by the administrative heads of institutions belonging to the conference, was set up in 1958 to act as an executive agency for the larger organization. Among the functions of this foundation were 1 / to negotiate with the Canadian government on behalf of the universities, 2 / to distribute federal grants to institutions in provinces that had not reached a special agreement with the Canadian government, 3 / to provide the secretariat for the Canadian Commonwealth Scholarship and Fellowship Committee, and 4 / to carry out miscellaneous projects of interest to members of the conference. A Research and Information Service was set up in 1958 with the assistance of a grant from the Carnegie Corporation of New York.

In 1965 federal legislation set up the Association of Universities and Colleges of Canada (AUCC) as a successor to the original organization and the Canadian Universities Foundation. Provision was made for associate membership for Canada-wide associations concerned with certain aspects of university activity. Some examples of these are the Canadian Association of Graduate Schools, the Canadian Association of College and University Libraries, the Canadian University Service Overseas, the National Committee of Deans of Engineering and Applied Science, and the Canadian Association of Deans and Directors of University Faculties of Education. A category of honorary associates was established to include the Canada Council, the Defence Research Board, the Medical Research Council, and the National Research Council of Canada.

Recent statements of the objectives of the association include the following: 1 / to provide information to its members, government, and the public about major developments in higher education in Canada, 2 / to provide a forum for the discussion of Canada-wide aspects of higher education, 3 / to sponsor studies of the more complex or intractable problems of higher education, either alone or in co-operation with other national bodies, and 4 / to provide a channel of communication between Canadian universities and colleges on the one hand and certain foreign governments and international organizations on the other with respect to higher education, and to represent member institutions on a number of Canadian agencies concerned with international co-operation in higher education.[2]

As of 1969 the secretariat was headed by an executive director, responsible to the Board of Directors for the management of AUCC affairs.[3] One of the associate directors, who was also secretary of the Canadian Commonwealth Scholarship and Fellowship Committee, was responsible for the International Programmes Division. This division provided administrative and information services for foreign students and faculty interested in Canadian higher education, assisted with programs of student and faculty exchange and recruitment for service abroad, advised the Canadian government and Canadian universities on certain aspects of university education for foreign students, encouraged the growth of international and area studies, and maintained liaison with international bodies concerned with higher education such as the Association of Commonwealth Universities, l'Association des universités partiellement ou entièrement de langue française, the Canadian Service for Overseas Students and Trainees, the Canadian University Service Overseas, and the World University Service of Canada. Some contribution was also made in terms of the interpretation of academic documents for universities, government departments, and other institutions.

Another associate director was responsible for the Domestic Programmes Division, which was concerned with membership matters and liaison with member institutions, associate members, government departments, voluntary associations, and other organizations. It was also involved with standing committees on finance, science, and editorial matters, with special committees, and with the steering committees for special studies. It assisted with the organization of conferences and co-operated with the government on major research projects.

The Research Division was responsible for initiating and conducting or supervising studies on Canadian higher education. Among projects carried out in the 1960s were the Bladen report on university finance, the Duff-Berdahl report on university government (sponsored jointly with the Canadian Association of University Teachers), the Ingraham report on university pensions, the Downs report on university libraries, a study of university costs, a study of accessibility to higher education, a study of university aid to developing countries, and a study of relations between universities and governments, sponsored jointly with other agencies. The division maintained a library on Canadian and comparative higher education, which in 1969 contained over 5,000 books and reports, about 7,000 pamphlets, and copies of more than 150 periodicals. The library issued a quarterly called *Select Bibliography on Higher Education*.

The Awards Division advised on and administered scholarship and fellowship programs, collected reference material on student aid, answered inquiries, and maintained contact with university awards officers. It also participated in the administration of the academic aspects of the Canadian Commonwealth Scholarship and Fellowship Plan.

The Information Division provided information to members of the university community, governments, the news media, and the public. Among its publications was *University Affairs*, published eight times a year along with supplements; two of its regular issues listed vacancies in Canadian universities. An annual publication, *Universities and Colleges of Canada*, summarized some of the key information from Canadian university calendars and listed degree courses and articles on other aspects of higher education. A pamphlet was prepared under the title *Notes for Foreign Students*, to assist the large number who made inquiries about opportunities for study in Canada.

Annual conferences of the association produced some of the most thoughtful observations and stimulating ideas about the role and functions of universities. A number of resolutions adopted in 1967 indicated a desire to improve the quality of undergraduate teaching. Interest in this area was identified as a response to student unrest. One resolution urged members to undertake experimental teaching and curriculum projects to complement traditional undergraduate programs. Another suggested that the association appeal to government and other fund-granting agencies to give financial support to proposals by universities for experimentation and innovation in methods of instruction. Still another advocated that the most highly qualified and experienced members of the faculty teach first- and second-year courses.

One of the highlights of the association's efforts in 1968 was an attempt to counteract the increasing tendency to regard universities as nothing other than elements of provincial educational systems. A brief to a study group sponsored by the Canada Council and the Science Council of Canada suggested that universities should pursue national objectives, which included both provincial and federal objectives as well as obligations to the world of learning. Most of the universities' problems were said to be related to such universal dimensions of education as the explosive growth of knowledge and the multiplication of fields of specialization. The brief called for Canada-wide consultation among representatives of the provinces, the federal government and its agencies, and the university community as a means of ensuring adequate planning and the avoidance of unnecessary duplication, overlapping, and wastage of resources. A number of factors requiring Canada-wide consultation were mentioned: 1 / changes in Canadian society and the Canadian economy, population migrations, and differences in economic levels causing drainage of manpower and resources from one region to another; 2 / international responsibilities such as those for the training of specialists in various underdeveloped regions; 3 / the role of students in university affairs; 4 / the portability of student benefits across provincial boundaries; 5 / matters within provincial jurisdiction but with national implications, such as urban and rural development, health and welfare, and forestry; 6 / problems of economic, social, and cultural development such as productivity and economic growth, natural resources, fisheries, inland waters, oceanography, conservation, pollution problems, communication, climate control, nuclear energy facilities, northern studies, upper atmosphere and space studies, and regional computer centres; and 7 / matters within federal jurisdiction such as defence, external affairs, and inter-cultural affairs in Canadian society such as bilingualism. The association advocated the establishment by the federal government of a single body representing the major federal research-funding agencies and advisory bodies.

On August 1, 1969, the AUCC took over the complete responsibility for the administration of the Commonwealth Scholarship and Fellowship Plan, although the Canadian government continued to provide the funds. This meant that the association looked after the payment of the stipend, special allowances, and travel. The Commonwealth plan was initiated as a result of decisions made at a conference held at Oxford in 1959. Its purpose was to facilitate the exchange of outstanding students so that they could take advantage of the wide range of educational resources available in different parts of the Commonwealth and, in the process, strengthen the common ideals of the participating countries. Of the one thousand university scholarships made available under the plan, the United Kingdom undertook to supply one-half and Canada one-quarter. The program was not one of foreign aid, since it enabled many Canadian students to study in other Commonwealth countries.

The fact that the AUCC has been mainly representative of university and college presidents has sometimes resulted in evidence of lack of harmony with organizations representing other university points of view. A certain amount of conflict developed with the Canadian Association of University Teachers over a policy statement produced by the latter in 1968 on the issue of academic freedom. When the AUCC was asked to give this statement its formal approval, the response was that some aspects of it were unsatisfactory. Although the AUCC agreed that it would state specifically what its objections were, the months went by without any action. In a letter to the Toronto *Globe and Mail* J.P. Smith, executive secretary of the Canadian Association of University Teachers, expressed his disillusionment in these terms: "Given the record ... faculty and students will know well where they must look for the defence of academic freedom: to themselves first, and in the long run to an enlightened public."[4]

THE CANADIAN ASSOCIATION OF GRADUATE SCHOOLS

Informal discussions were held at McMaster University in 1962 on the possibility of forming a committee of deans of graduate schools which could come together at the annual meetings of the National Conference of Canadian Universities and Colleges. The first such meeting was held later in the year under the chairmanship of A.G. McCalla, with twenty deans present, along with representatives of the Canadian Universities Foundation. The resulting association was at first called the Canadian Association of Deans and Directors of Graduate Studies, with membership open to deans, assistant deans, and directors. The objectives of the association were defined as follows:

1. To exchange information, experience and views regarding
   a) the initiation, organization and administration of graduate studies,
   b) the admission, support and supervision of students,
   c) the structure of degree programmes,
   d) the promotion of research,
   e) other matters of concern to directors of graduate studies, and
2. generally to promote the improvement of graduate education in Canadian universities.

Three categories of membership were eventually defined. Category I consisted of universities which offered the master's degree in at least five fields of study or had conferred at least twenty master's degrees within the previous five years. Category II consisted of universities that offered doctoral degree programs in at least ten fields of study and had conferred at least twenty doctoral degrees within the previous five years. Associate members, included universities that offered some graduate work on a regular basis but had not necessarily awarded degrees. Total membership in 1969 comprised thirty-one universities.

One of the earliest actions of the association was to bring the Williams Report of Library Resources for Research in the Humanities and Social Sciences to the attention of the Canadian Universities Foundation. At the meeting in 1963, when the name Canadian Association of Graduate Schools was adopted, some of the topics discussed were National Research Council awards, funds available for graduate studies, levels of graduate support, the appraisal of academic documents, new graduate programs, registration in graduate schools, problems of foreign graduate students, the cost of publishing scientific research papers, a list of awards for graduate students, admission requirements, graduate status, and microfilming. A matter of major concern during the next two years was the preparation of a brief to the Bladen Commission. Discussions in 1965 also centred around membership qualifications for the association, microfilming of theses, the Canada Student Loan Program, university student aid officers, joint MD and PhD programs, and the timing of announcements of graduate awards. The practice of inviting representatives of fund-granting bodies to annual meetings was begun at this time.

The association assumed a responsibility for compiling a statistical summary of information on graduate studies in Canada, including the numbers of students in the various departments of each university, the numbers of degrees awarded, and the financial support given to graduate students. By 1968 this enterprise led to the production of an annual statistical report. Other reports produced by the association dealt with developments in MA and MSc programs in Canadian universities and summer faculty stipend practices. Briefs were presented to the Commission on the Relationship between Universities and Government and to the Senate Committee on Science Policies.

THE CANADIAN ASSOCIATION OF DEANS
AND DIRECTORS OF UNIVERSITY FACULTIES
OF EDUCATION

The Canadian Association of Professors of Education originally gave a good deal of weight to the interests and concerns of deans of education in university faculties across Canada. As time went on, however, the programs became more general, and the deans, now forming a more numerous group, felt the lack of a satisfactory vehicle for the discussion of their own problems. In 1968 Deans N.V. Scarfe and H.T. Coutts of the Universities of British Columbia and Alberta respectively took the initiative by suggesting the creation of a new association that would fill the gap. Deans L.P. Desjarlais and V.S. Ready of the University of Ottawa and

Queen's University respectively were delegated to prepare a program. Definite steps toward the formation of the new association were not taken until late 1969.

THE CANADIAN ASSOCIATION
OF UNIVERSITY SCHOOLS OF MUSIC

A small group of Canadian university musicians met in 1964, with the assistance of a grant from the Canada Council, to consider the possibility of establishing a permanent association to provide liaison among music schools in universities throughout the country. The resulting organization was designed to pursue seven principal objectives: 1 / to provide an opportunity for heads and faculty members of Canadian music schools to exchange views, to discuss common problems, and to render mutual assistance; 2 / to establish minimum standards for music programs at Canadian universities; 3 / to maintain and strengthen the role of music study in Canadian universities; 4 / to act as a consultative and advisory body for all Canadian university music schools without restricting individual initiative and freedom in teaching or administration; 5 / to enlist the cooperation of member departments in concerts and lecture projects conducted in common; 6 / to initiate projects and activities which, in the opinion of members, would be beneficial to the cause of music in Canada; and 7 / to stimulate scholarship and improve instructional methods at Canadian universities, and in the wider field of school music and professional teaching throughout the country, by scholarly papers, symposia, and publications.

The first general meeting of the association was held in Ottawa in 1965 under the auspices of the Centennial Commission. A good deal of time was spent in discussing the recommendations of various university music schools, fourteen of which were passed on to the commission. At the same meeting a draft of the constitution was discussed and officers were elected. The first annual meeting was held later in the year along with those of the other Learned Societies. The delegates decided that the first order of business was to study existing curricula in university schools of music and to formulate satisfactory standards comparable to those of other leading universities throughout the world. Eight different committees were set up to undertake the necessary studies and to draw up reports for discussion at the next annual meeting. It turned out that all these reports were of the "progress" type, and discussion continued at later meetings. A new set of committees was formed in 1968 and further additions were made in 1969. In the latter year reports were approved and arrangements were made to have them published and circulated throughout the country as the official opinion of the Canadian Association of University Schools of Music. They were said to constitute the *philosophical* basis for the accreditation of Canadian university schools of music applying for membership in the association, as well as for the accreditation of new programs proposed by member schools. With this work completed, the delegates agreed that the association should turn its attention more in the direction of stimulating scholarship and the improvement of instruction through scholarly papers. It was also agreed that individual memberships should be provided for, in addition to the institutional memberships recognized from the beginning.

THE CANADIAN ASSOCIATION FOR EDUCATION IN THE SOCIAL SERVICES

The Canadian Association for Education in the Social Services was established in 1967. It was a successor to the National Committee of Canadian Schools of Social Work, the membership of which consisted of the directors of all the schools. It had no representation from faculties and no secretariat. By 1967 it was felt that social work education had progressed far enough to enable the association to support a secretariat and undertake national studies, accreditation, and faculty services. The new organization, an affiliate of the Association of Universities and Colleges of Canada, was formed with the financial assistance of the Laidlaw Foundation and the encouragement of the Department of National Health and Welfare. As of 1969, all sixteen Canadian schools of social work were members. Each school had two voting delegates: one from the administration – usually the director – and one elected by the faculty.

The stated objectives of the association were 1 / to promote education in Canada for practice in the social services, 2 / to formulate criteria for use in assessing educational programs designed to prepare students for practice in the social services, 3 / to assist in the development of educational programs designed to prepare students for practice in the social services, and 4 / to represent the collective interests of the members in relation to other educational, professional, learned, welfare, or public bodies. The possibility of attaining these objectives depended on a solution to the financial problem. When the support of the Laidlaw Foundation ceased in 1970, there seemed little prospect of raising from university sources alone the $40,000 a year needed to sustain a secretariat.

THE CANADIAN ASSOCIATION OF DEPARTMENTS OF EXTENSION AND SUMMER SCHOOLS

Participation by a Canadian in a meeting of the Association of Directors of Summer Schools of the United States in 1950 led to the formation of a comparable organization, at first called the Canadian Association of Directors of Summer Schools. At a meeting at Laval University in 1952 it was decided that the new association would meet every second year, while area conferences would be held on the initiative of the directors concerned. At the 1954 meeting plans were made to re-organize the association to include directors of extension, and the name Canadian Association of Directors of Extension and Summer Schools (CADESS) was adopted. Meetings were held annually thereafter, at first with the Learned Societies, but later in close association with the Association of Universities and Colleges of Canada, of which CADESS became an associate organization.

As stated in the constitution, the objectives of the association were as follows.

a) The Association shall be concerned with the university's responsibility in credit and non-credit extension programs.
b) It shall provide a national and regional forum for the discussion of matters relating to university extension.
c) It shall represent university extension in Canada and internationally.
d) It shall encourage the maintenance and development of diploma and degree programs in extension and adult education in Canadian universities and colleges.
e) It shall promote in-service and graduate training of existing and potential university extension staff.
f) It shall encourage and conduct studies related to university extension activities.
g) It shall maintain active liaison with other groups and associations in Canada and elsewhere which are concerned with adult education.

In addition to holding meetings and conferences the association has worked for the benefit of its members by sponsoring in-service training programs. It has issued a regular newsletter, as well as an annual *Directory of Personnel* and a publication called *Canadian University Correspondence Courses*. In 1967 it produced a report on the results of a survey on status and salaries of extension department staff. Other studies were carried out according to need. A trust fund was established in 1962 to assist adult educators from abroad wishing to travel in Canada to study university extension programs and to assist Canadian adult educators pursuing the same objectives in other countries. The fund was supported by voluntary contributions from university extension departments and divisions belonging to CADESS.

THE CANADIAN ASSOCIATION OF STUDENT AWARDS SERVICES

The Canadian Association of Student Awards Services was formed in 1967 as one of the constituent elements of the Canadian Student Affairs Association. Its members consisted of between thirty and forty people with awards responsibilities in universities, some devoting full time to this function and others combining it with additional duties. The association was given a simple structure, with a president, a secretary, and a past president serving as the executive. The objectives were to distribute information, to engage in discussions, and, where some useful purpose seemed likely to be served, to make representations to governments. The national organization had as its counterpart an association operating in Ontario.

THE CANADIAN ASSOCIATION OF UNIVERSITY ATHLETIC DIRECTORS

The Canadian Association of University Athletic Directors was formed as a result of informal discussions held at Fredericton in 1965. In the constitution, adopted in 1968, the purposes of the association were defined as follows:

2.1.1 To provide all members with a medium for discussion of problems of common interest.

2.1.2 To encourage participation in athletic activities.

2.1.3 To reflect and interpret to the public the highest possible standard of amateur sport and sportsmanship.

2.1.4 To give an official consideration as to the part played in the university community by all phases of athletic participation including research and academic pursuits in physical education.

2.1.5 To give official consideration to the role of the athletic director in the university community and to give him support in improving his lot from the point of view of knowledge, status in the university community, and material well being.

There were thirty-seven members of the association in 1966, with qualifications as specified in the constitution. The number rose to fifty in 1968, but fell again the following year when fees were raised and an initial institutional fee of $100 was exacted. In 1970 the constitution was changed to permit membership of athletic directors of all post-secondary school institutions such as colleges of applied arts and technology. At the 1970 conference some of the topics dealt with included administrative functions, new concepts in swimming pools, innovations in facilities, scholarships, publicity and public relations, and budgets.

THE ASSOCIATION OF CANADIAN MEDICAL COLLEGES

The occasion for the establishment of the Association of Canadian Medical Colleges was a meeting of the deans of the twelve medical schools at Ottawa in 1943 where, at the request of the Minister of Health, they considered accelerated training of physicians to meet wartime needs and discussed a proposed Health Insurance Act. Discovering many other areas of common concern, the deans met again later to establish the association, the purpose of which was to promote the advancement of medical education. Membership was provisional, consisting of medical schools, each represented by a dean, and, later, an elected representative of the faculty. Steps were taken in 1961 to incorporate the organization and to obtain financial support for a secretariat. By-laws adopted the subsequent year listed the following objectives: 1 / the advancement of medical education in Canada, 2 / the provision of medical graduates to meet Canada's immediate and future health requirements, 3 / the development of graduate medical education, 4 / the provision of opportunities for continuing education of medical practitioners, and 5 / the provision of facilities and personnel to further fundamental and clinical research. A simplified statement of objectives was adopted in 1967. The secretariat was established in 1963.

Annual meetings were held regularly after 1943. A few random examples of the topics will help to clarify the nature of the association's interests. In 1945 there were discussions of further training for returning medical officers, release of medical teachers from the armed forces, foreign students, and student health services; the 1950 discussions were on visual aids, Medical Council of Canada examinations, internships, licensing of general practitioners, and policies in medical education, and a symposium was held on the teaching of psychiatry; the 1957 discussions were on postgraduate education, the universities conference, accreditation, the teaching of psychiatry, civil defence, hospital insurance, support for medical research, and medical education statistics, with a symposium on the teaching of clinical medicine; the 1963 discussions were on teaching hospital administrators, the costs of medical education, the Royal College of Physicians and Surgeons, a medical library survey, the Medical Research Council, the Canadian Medical Association, the Medical Council of Canada examinations, accreditation, and the Royal Commission on Health Services; the 1969 discussions were on the Health Resources Fund, the relationship between the association and the Royal College of Physicians and Surgeons, clerkships, internships, northern health care, accreditation, government library resources, medical education research, resident training, curriculum change, and teaching hospitals.

The association co-operated with the Liaison Committee on Medical Education of the Association of American Medical Colleges and the Council on Medical Education of the American Medical Association in the accreditation of Canadian medical schools. Canadians assumed a position of predominance on these committees. A major effort in the sphere of accreditation toward the end of the 1960s involved co-operation with the Canadian Medical Association and the Royal College of Physicians and Surgeons to develop a method of co-ordinating the whole span of medical education, including undergraduate, graduate, and continuing education.

Members of the Executive Committee and the secretariat performed a variety of advisory functions. They dealt with questions of curriculum, course organization, the establishment of departments, the search for faculty, financial support for medical students, government support for medical research, and other such matters.

Information services have included the publication of the *ACMC Newsletter*, containing news of association activities, developments in medical schools, and international events. Answers were supplied to a large number of questions from students in Canada and abroad concerning medical schools, graduate education, and financial support. Many inquiries were also handled from overseas institutions and agencies about Canadian medical education, research, and practice. Co-operation in Operation Retrieval, designed to persuade graduates of Canadian medical schools residing in the United States to return to Canada, involved the issuing of the *ACMC Bulletin* and a list of physicians and biomedical scientists training or working abroad and available for employment in Canada. The latter publication, produced annually, was distributed among faculties of medicine, dentistry, and pharmacy, university and medical libraries, teaching hospitals, federal and provincial government departments, Canadian medical associations, societies and clinics, and Canadian pharmaceutical manufacturers.

A large part of the program of the association involved work with other agencies. In the federal government close co-operation was maintained with the Department of National Health and Welfare. In 1965 the association entered into an agreement with this department to carry out a number of tasks: 1 / to conduct studies on the integration of the work of physicians with that of allied health professions, 2 / to evaluate the performance of graduates of Canadian medical schools, 3 / to develop procedures for accrediting medical schools by a Canadian accreditation body, and 4 / to undertake other studies and activities on the request of the department that were consistent with the aims of the association. The contract by which the department paid the association a consultation fee of $25,000 a year was continued for several years. Co-operation with the Department of Manpower and Immigration was the basis for Operation Retrieval, already mentioned. There were also continuous contacts with the Medical Research Council and the National Science Library of the National Research Council. Medical organizations with which the association maintained close contacts included the Royal College of Physicians and Surgeons, the Canadian Medical Association, the Medical Research Council, the College of Family Physicians of Canada, l'Association de médecins de langue française du Canada, the Canadian Association of Medical Students and Interns, the Medical Council of Canada, the Association of Canadian Teaching Hospitals, and the Federation of Provincial Licensing Authorities of Canada, as well as associations representing particular medical disciplines such as the Canadian Association of Professors of Psychiatry. The Association of Canadian Medical Colleges advised many of these bodies on matters relating to medical education.

The association responded to the initiatives of the Association of Universities and Colleges of Canada by engaging in discussions with bodies representing the university faculties and schools of dentistry, nursing, pharmacy, optometry, rehabilitation, and social work on ways of co-ordinating education in the health-related professions in order to provide economies in education and to ensure full utilization of members of the health team. These discussions were among the factors leading to the Conference on Health Manpower and Educational Planning in October 1969, which was sponsored jointly by the Department of National Health and Welfare and the Association of Universities and Colleges of Canada.

Several research studies of some importance were undertaken during the 1960s. One of these involved the collection of data on Canadian medical school students which, as part of an overall Canadian medical manpower tabulation, contributed to the planning of provisions for the training of physicians. A basis also emerged for a fresh scrutiny of admission standards and policies. Studies of those holding Canadian higher degrees in the biomedical sciences who graduated between 1946 and 1963 and of 140 holders of Canadian PhDs residing in the United States were designed as part of a larger examination of the requirements for and supply of faculty in the health sciences. An attempt was made through an analysis of the data collected to identify some of the factors influencing scholars in the health sciences to emigrate. The findings of a survey of residents in hospitals approved for advanced training in specialties and of a pilot study of the opinions of sixty residents provided a basis for changes in the examinations for specialist certification. A series of investigations dealt with program costs in medical schools, program costs in teaching hospitals, teaching hospital costs, private rates of return on investment in education, and the relationship between intern and residency training programs and the cost of physicians' services.

A number of special studies by the association contributed to medical education. Some of these were conducted for the Royal Commission on Health Services between 1961 and 1964. A survey of studies co-sponsored by medical college librarians led to the establishment of a National Library Resources Centre for the Health Sciences in the National Science Library in Ottawa. Studies of the cost of construction of research facilities in medical schools and teaching hospitals influenced the establishment of the Health Resources Fund by the Department of National Health and Welfare in 1966. Assistance was provided to the Medical Research Council in surveys of manpower resources in medical research.

THE ASSOCIATION OF FACULTIES OF PHARMACY
OF CANADA
The first initiatives that ultimately led to the formation of the Canadian Conference of Pharmaceutical Faculties, later called the Association of Faculties of Pharmacy of Canada, may be traced to provisions in the by-laws of the Canadian Pharmaceutical Association, adopted in 1907, which provided for a Committee on Pharmaceutical Education. Local conferences of pharmaceutical educators were held in the prairie provinces

after the First World War and in Kingston in 1937. The new organization, founded in 1944, represented an attempt to bring together the educators and the provincial associations which held the responsibility for providing pharmaceutical education. It was organized within the framework of the Canadian Pharmaceutical Association, and had its financial support.

As stated in a constitution adopted in 1948, there were four main objectives of the association: 1 / to promote pharmaceutical education and research, 2 / to provide opportunities for the interchange of ideas and a discussion of curricula and teaching methods with a view to their continual improvement, 3 / to encourage the maintenance of high and uniform educational standards in pharmacy throughout Canada, and 4 / to make recommendations to the Council of the Canadian Pharmaceutical Association regarding educational policies and the advancement of the science and practice of pharmacy. When the association adopted The Association of Faculties of Pharmacy of Canada as its name in 1969, the fourth of these objectives was modified to include making recommendations to other appropriate bodies.

At the end of the 1960s there were constituent faculties in eight universities: Dalhousie, Laval, Montreal, Toronto, Manitoba, Saskatchewan, Alberta, and British Columbia. In order to obtain and retain membership, each of these constituent faculties had to offer an academic program approved by the association. The general requirement in 1969 was a four-year course following senior matriculation leading to a degree preferably designated Bachelor of Science in Pharmacy.

The association took action in 1945 to establish the Canadian Foundation for the Advancement of Pharmacy as a means of providing financial assistance for various projects. The association and the foundation are given a considerable part of the credit for a series of developments which occurred during the quarter-century after 1944. 1 / Full-time academic staff in faculties increased from eleven to nearly one hundred. 2 / Research, which hardly existed in the schools of pharmacy in 1944, was supported by funds totalling $1,100,000 in 1969. 3 / Master's and in some cases doctoral programs were offered in all the schools. 4 / Five schools established postgraduate hospital pharmacy residency programs in co-operation with teaching hospitals. 5 / Partly because of higher standards of education and new programs established in the schools, the quality of institutional pharmaceutical service improved substantially. 6 / A federal statute provided for the formation of a Pharmacy Examining Board of Canada to facilitate interprovincial transfer of registration.

Most of the educational contributions of the Association of Faculties of Pharmacy of Canada in Ontario have been made through other agencies such as the Faculty of Pharmacy of the University of Toronto, the Ontario Pharmacists' Association, and the Ontario College of Pharmacy. Some of these contributions are as follows: 1 / the encouragement of a high standard of scientific and professional education for professors of pharmacy, 2 / the development of suitable undergraduate curricula for schools of pharmacy, 3 / the exchange of information and ideas relating to pharmaceutical research, 4 / the development of the four-year program in pharmaceutical education in Canada, 5 / the promotion, in co-operation with other professional organizations, of a program of continuing education for practising pharmacists, 6 / the development of research and academic programs for the education of graduate students in pharmacy, 7 / the organization of hospital residency programs for graduate pharmacists in co-operation with the Canadian Society of Hospital Pharmacists, 8 / the formulation of suitable apprenticeship and internship programs in co-operation with the Ontario College of Pharmacy, and 9 / an improvement in the methods of evaluating the academic credentials of candidates for licences whose education was obtained in foreign countries.

THE ASSOCIATION OF DEANS OF PHARMACY OF CANADA

The Association of Deans of Pharmacy was founded in Calgary in 1965 in response to a recognition of the growing need for an exchange of views among those with a leading role in the rapidly expanding Canadian schools of pharmacy. Objectives of the association were set out in the constitution adopted in 1967:

(1) To provide a forum for discussion and the exchange of information related to the administration of the constituent faculties of the Canadian Conference of Pharmaceutical Faculties and to gather and disseminate such data as may be deemed to be useful to the members.
(2) To develop contacts with the academic administrative heads of the other health disciplines and with other university administrative officials.
(3) To co-operate with the Canadian Conference of Pharmaceutical Faculties and to assist that organization in any matters it may specifically refer to the attention of the Association of Deans of Pharmacy of Canada.
(4) To establish and maintain liaison with other groups and organizations having interests related to the objects of this Association.
(5) To provide a means of coordinating activity, in relation to the above objects, when joint action is considered to be desirable.

Like other similar organizations, the association concerned itself mainly with administrative matters, including communications within and among universities. It devoted attention to the Health Resources Fund and to the funding of research in the Canadian schools of pharmacy. Negotiations that began with a brief to the National Research Council in 1966 and later involved the Medical Research Council were followed by the latter's assumption of responsibility for supporting the desired research.

ELEVEN

Associations of university teachers and students

The two organizations of university teachers dealt with in the present chapter, the Ontario Confederation of University Faculty Associations on the provincial level and the Canadian Association of University Teachers on the national level, corresponded in a general way to the teachers' federations. The exercise of protective functions had, however, to be carried out differently because of the distinctive organization of the universities. Unlike the CTF, the Canadian Association of University Teachers bore the main burden of protecting tenure and freedom of expression on the part of its members. Provincially, university teachers' associations lacked the legal status conferred on the teachers' federations by *The Teaching Profession Act* of 1944.

THE CANADIAN ASSOCIATION OF UNIVERSITY TEACHERS

The Canadian Association of University Teachers (CAUT) was formed in 1950. According to the constitution, as revised in 1970, the objects of the organization were "to promote the interests of teachers and researchers in Canadian universities and colleges, to advance the standards of their profession, and to seek to improve the quality of higher education in Canada." Individuals held ordinary membership by virtue of belonging to a member faculty association of a degree-granting institution of higher education in Canada which was admitted, in accordance with the by-laws, by a two-thirds majority of the votes cast at a meeting of the Council of the Association. The maintenance of ordinary membership depended on the payment of the prescribed fees. Associate membership was open to those who were university teachers on the faculty of a university or college where there was no member faculty association, former university teachers, university teachers in other countries who were members of their national faculty association, and professors visiting from a foreign country. There was also provision for honorary membership for those who had made notable contributions in their fields or in serving the purposes of the association.

A main concern of the association in recent years has been the maintenance of academic freedom and tenure. According to Edward J. Monahan, interest in this area was not very great during the early 1950s.[1] The first appeal over an alleged injustice was made in 1954 and failed to produce any action on the part of the association. A suggestion received by the council in 1956 that the association endorse an American Association of University Professors statement of principles on academic freedom also failed to receive support. Two years later a committee was formed to study a possible role for the CAUT in protecting individuals in matters of academic freedom and tenure.

The situation changed dramatically in the same year when the association took up the case of Professor Harry Crowe, who was dismissed by the Board of Regents of United College in Winnipeg. A report by an investigating team found in favour of Crowe and urged his reinstatement. Although this recommendation was not acted upon, the CAUT became firmly established as a defender of academic freedom and tenure. The report of the committee set up to study the matter reinforced this new orientation. A statement of principles was adopted and the committee was reconstituted as a standing committee with the role of dealing with individual grievances. A considerable number of cases came to the committee during the next few years, but all were settled without recourse to formal investigation.

A Faculty Administration Relations Committee was established in 1962 to deal with matters other than academic freedom and tenure, such as grievances over promotion, teaching assignments, and salary increments. The line of demarcation proved difficult to maintain, however, and the committee was dissolved in 1964 and its functions turned over to the Academic Freedom and Tenure Committee. At this time the terms of reference of the latter were extended to cover the interests of faculty members who did not hold tenure. After this change, which was made at a time when university faculties were expanding rapidly and many young members were being added, the number of grievance cases increased markedly.

During this period there was a shift toward relatively open investigations, with a good deal of publicity. Monahan identifies both good and bad results from this development. On the one hand, discreet publicity helped to inform members of the association and of the broader university community where the CAUT stood on certain issues. On the other hand, when cases were dealt with openly, opposing positions tended to become more rigid and settlement proved more difficult. The disadvantages of open investigations seemed to outweigh the advantages.

The most important weapon of the CAUT was patient persuasion based on objective, dispassionate judgment. The possibility of facing the disapproval of a vital part of the Canadian university community was commonly sufficient to overcome opposition. The ultimate measure, of recent development and intended for use only under the most extreme circumstances, was censure.

Another vital aspect of the CAUT program, and one of major concern from the beginning, is that of university salaries. Salary matters are dealt with in volume I, chapter 6 of ONTARIO'S EDUCATIVE SOCIETY. In general, the role of the CAUT has been to assemble information on salary trends, to develop the case for adequate salaries, and to support member associations in their campaigns to meet salary objectives.

Publication of the *C.A.U.T. Bulletin* enabled the members to keep informed about the activities of the association and the extent to which its objectives were being met. It also helped to keep members aware of their responsibilities as members of the university community. Articles were included on more general university issues.

THE ONTARIO CONFEDERATION
OF UNIVERSITY FACULTY ASSOCIATIONS

What was called at first the Ontario Council of University Faculty Associations and, beginning in 1968, the Ontario Confederation of University Faculty Associations (OCUFA) was established in 1963. The appearance of this organization was a manifestation of the general trend toward the formation and strengthening of particular interest groups. Unlike other university associations previously organized at the provincial and national levels, which represented particular discipline groupings and concerned themselves almost entirely with scholarship, OCUFA attempted to mobilize the strength of the entire academic staff of the universities apart from those whose primary responsibility was administration. Among the developments exerting an immediate influence on its establishment were 1 / the formation and rapidly growing role of the Committee of Presidents; 2 / the assumption of the major financial responsibility for the universities by the provincial government, and of concomitant control over key aspects of their operations, which presented a danger that university objectives and modes of operation might be damaged by unsympathetic or uncomprehending officials; 3 / the rapid growth in the size of student bodies and faculties and the extension of administrative structures, which combined to threaten the identity of the individual faculty member; and 4 / the need for strong collective action to prevent university salaries from declining, as compared with those in other fields, during a generally inflationary period.

From the time of its formation OCUFA was closely associated with the major developments in Ontario university education. Points of view were expressed on the most important of the many policy issues raised during the period. Frequent references are made in volume IV of this series to submissions and statements referring to these issues. While in some cases the effects appear to have been slight, there is no question that the organization became an influence to be reckoned with among the forces that determined the general direction of university development.

According to a constitution adopted in 1964 and amended in 1966, the council consisted of one member chosen annually by and from each

Ontario university faculty association which was a constituent part of the CAUT, along with the executive secretary of the CAUT or his deputy. There was an executive committee consisting at first of four, and later of six, members elected annually by the council. All Ontario university faculty associations soon joined the council. Typically the representatives of these associations were their chairmen or past chairmen. An early practice developed by which the associations sent a second representative as an observer.

According to a new version of the constitution approved in 1968, when the change of name was adopted, the purpose of the confederation was "to promote the welfare of the universities of Ontario and to enable individual university faculty associations to act collectively in furthering their common interests." Provision was made for meetings to be held at least twice a year, at the call of any three delegates, or at the call of the chairman. The executive was now to consist of the chairman, the immediate past chairman, the vice-chairman, the executive vice-chairman, the treasurer, and three other members.

Until 1967, when the council had no secretariat or paid officers, financial obligations were met by a levy of $1 a year on each member of the association. In March of that year a decision was made to ask the constituent associations to raise their fees to $13 a year to maintain a full-time executive vice-chairman. Later a sliding scale was adopted, so that the fee amounted to $1 per thousand of the median salary for each rank. Estimated revenue for 1969–70 was over $72,000. The first executive vice-chairman, appointed for a three-year term in 1968 under the new arrangement, was C.M.T. Hanly.

The first significant action of the organization was the submission in December 1963 of a brief to the Prime Minister of Ontario entitled *University Education in Ontario*, to which a number of references are made in volume IV. This document was intended to complement two reports issued by the Committee of Presidents: *Post-Secondary Education in Ontario* and *The Structure of Post-Secondary Education in Ontario*. Discussions with the Prime Minister and the Minister and Deputy Minister of University Affairs led to the participation of the council, along with the Committee of Presidents, in the preparation of a list of nominations for appointments to the Advisory Committee on University Affairs. The council saw its role in part as one of strengthening the position of the Committee of Presidents in causes of which it approved. Where there seemed to be a prospect of serious disagreement, its preferred course was to resolve the differences beforehand. Where the differences were irreconcilable, it did not hesitate to take an independent stand.

It seems desirable to list some of the matters that concerned OCUFA in its submission of 1963 in order to show the nature of its interests at that time (the reader will, however, find a full account in volume IV). In general, the submission was a response to the prospect of a rapid expansion of the Ontario university system and the need for changes in it. OCUFA pointed to the danger that the reputation of the universities for sound teaching might be endangered if large numbers of students were added without certain precautions being taken. In brief form, specific points were made as follows. 1 / The government was dealing with a university system rather than with a provincial university. 2 / Ontario universities had had their greatest success in offering undergraduate degrees in general courses, in the standard honours programs, and in certain professional fields, but less in research, scholarship, and graduate training. 3 / In no university was research conducted, like teaching, as part of the normal activity of the university community. 4 / The ratio of graduate to undergraduate students in Canadian university institutions generally, and in Ontario universities in particular, was much lower than in leading American universities. 5 / The emphasis on the expansion of general arts to meet the crisis of numbers was questionable; grants did not sufficiently recognize honours courses, medicine, and other courses of a specialized nature. 6 / Evidence had been assembled by one faculty association to show that standards of appointments had fallen between 1957 and 1963. 7 / Salaries at the best American universities were higher than those in their Canadian counterparts by between $3,000 and $10,000. 8 / Expansion should be associated with improvement in graduate training, libraries, and other areas. 9 / It was more appropriate to ask how the universities could be made more effective than to inquire how year-round teaching could be introduced. With reference to this point, there should be studies of length of year, examination timing, size of class, and student aid. 10 / Salaries for university faculty were too low in relation to those of high school teachers. 11 / All students should have an opportunity to spend at least one year living in residence; if this goal were to be realized, nineteen thousand places would have to be provided by 1970. 12 / A study should be made of deficiencies and future requirements in libraries, medical schools, nursing, engineering, and the social sciences. 13 / A public statement was needed on government grant policy; a grant formula should take account of basic per student cost, special per student cost, special costs of expansion, and special aspects such as research. Perhaps the most significant item in the brief was the request that a university grants committee be established to recommend the total grant and to allocate it among individual universities.

A brief was submitted to the Minister of University Affairs in November 1965 under the title "Channels of Communication between the Provincial Government and the Universities."[2] The general theme was the importance of preserving university autonomy and academic freedom when the universities were dependent on a single source of revenue for the major part of their expansion. In pursuit of its declared intention of maintaining these values, the government should be well informed on university matters, especially where there was little experience or precedent to serve as a guide. The brief asserted that existing channels of communication were not working well. One problem was that the Committee of Presidents had not always been effective in formulating or communicating a university opinion. In some cases its inhibitions had been attributable to its reluctance to criticize or press for changes in policy on the part of a body on which its members were directly dependent for funds. In others it was impossible to secure agreement among its members. The other constituted channel of communication was the Advisory Committee on University Affairs, which was regarded as ineffective because of the nature of its mandate and its lack of academic representation. The brief repeated the recommendation of 1963 – that this committee be transformed into a grants commission according to the pattern recommended by the Bladen Commission. Enlarged by more members with a university background, it might deal with university expansion well into the future, with student aid, and with capital grants to universities.

The brief concluded with three recommendations:

(a) that as vacancies occur on the Advisory Committee the positions be filled by persons active in academic work;
(b) that there be a full-time chairman or vice-chairman to give continuity and additional strength to the Committee's work, and that this person have extensive university experience; and
(c) that the relationship between the Advisory Committee and the Department of University Affairs be clarified.

In a general way subsequent developments followed the recommended course.

A considerable number of other briefs and statements were prepared during 1965. The following list gives an indication of the areas of interest, although space does not permit a summary of the contents of all of them: a submission to the Bladen Commission on the Financing of Higher Education, a brief to the Minister of Education on community colleges, a memorandum to the Minister of University Affairs on the Ontario Institute for Studies in Education Bill, a memorandum to the Minister of University Affairs on the York University Bill, a memorandum to the Minister of University Affairs on university faculty salaries, and a memorandum to the Minister of University Affairs on matters arising out of the report of the Bladen Commission.

OCUFA's interest in the introduction of formula financing for current expenditure in 1967 was quite in line with its earlier proposals for a grants committee or commission. In 1969 it presented a brief to the Rowat-Hurtubise Commission on the Relations between Universities and Governments. The main topics were 1 / the history of financing higher education in Ontario, 2 / the uses and abuses of formula financing, 3 / criteria for allocating public funds, and 4 / methods of governance for academic and fiscal decision making. The organization was in a good position to identify many examples of distortions in university programs that could be attributed directly to the application of the formula. In some extremely critical comments on the matter, J.S. Kirkaldy, chairman in 1968–9, commented on some of the features which he considered to be most objectionable. He referred in particular to the hardship imposed on emerging universities by the scheme as first devised. The validity of this point received official recognition, and remedial measures were applied. Kirkaldy also objected to special protection offered for certain institutions.[3]

During negotiations between the Committee of Presidents and the provincial government in 1967–9 regarding the conditions under which facilities for teacher training would be established in the universities, OCUFA formulated a series of principles:

1. A Teachers' College may be incorporated into a University only upon approval of the Senate of the University concerned;
2. The University is autonomous in the establishment of a curriculum, the integration of curriculum into a Bachelors' programme, and the organization of a Faculty of Education;
3. The University is autonomous in the establishment of entrance requirements;
4. The University is autonomous in the matter of faculty appointments, and in particular, in the selection of faculty to be transferred from a College to the University;
5. OCUFA is opposed to faculty transferral on any basis that does not recognize that equally qualified professors should receive equal pay and rank.[4]

As indicated in volume v, the organization had grounds for reasonable satisfaction over the way in which the first three points were eventually dealt with. There was some unhappiness, however, in connection with the last two.

As the role of the Committee on University Affairs increased in importance after the appointment of a permanent chairman, university faculties found themselves facing considerable frustrations in salary negotiations. Negotiations with administrators and boards of governors commonly met the response that provincial grants were inadequate to allow demands to be met. In December 1968 requests were made that the Committee on University Affairs receive an OCUFA salary brief and hear arguments concerning the salary component of the basic income unit. The chairman, D.T. Wright, rejected this request, explaining informally that the committee regarded the Committee of Presidents as the only official voice of the universities. This policy, however, was subsequently changed.

THE CANADIAN UNION OF STUDENTS
The National Federation of Canadian University Students was established in 1926 with a constitution committing it to

promote a better understanding, surpassing both geography and language, among all Canadian university students, and to promote greater co-operation and correlation among student government bodies, in order to watch over the progress of student interests and academic freedom and to serve the cause of peace by creating ties with national unions of students around the globe.

For most of the period up to its demise in 1969, the organization conducted a program that was reasonably in line with these objectives.

A major concern during the 1950s was the extension of educational opportunity at the post-secondary level. The organization was determined that the principle of accessibility of university education to all those who could meet objective standards of ability, regardless of economic circumstances, would be recognized in practice. To this end an effort was made to enhance public awareness of the issue and to persuade governmental agencies to take appropriate measures. Beginning in 1958, annual representations were made to the federal and provincial governments urging them to encourage and assist young people to undertake university studies. A brief in 1961 entitled "The National Bursary Plan" proposed that the federal government provide bursaries up to a maximum of $600 each for ten thousand new students each year. Thousands of copies in English and French were distributed across the country.

The federation tended to avoid dealing with the content of education, while at the same time leaving the door open for activity in this area when and if the occasion demanded. One exception was the repeated recommendation that French be taught at all levels in every part of Canada. This expression of sympathy for the minority national culture did not, however, persuade French-language students in Quebec that their interests lay within the organization. In 1960 they formed the militant Union général des étudiants du Québec, which undertook to achieve certain aims by political action.

In the late 1950s and early 1960s the federation engaged in a number of activities designed to enrich student life. It sponsored national debates and contests in literature, art, and photography. It conducted an exchange program to enable students to spend a year at a university in another part of the country, contributing travel allowances and persuading the host university to waive tuition fees. Various forms of scholarship assistance were provided for students from Africa and Asia. National seminars were held to discuss major issues relating to education and the welfare of society in general. Extracurricular study groups were encouraged to meet regionally and locally to deal with some of the same issues. Local committees conducted tours of high schools to arouse interest in university attendance.

At a meeting at York University in 1964 the organization, now called the Canadian Union of Students (CUS), reaffirmed its original purpose, which was defined as "the advancement of education through the promotion of co-operation and understanding in the student community." A crisis developed during 1964 and 1965 when the English-language universities in Quebec were subjected to strong pressure to abandon the CUS and join the French-speaking organization. Sir George Williams University yielded to persuasion while McGill did not. At the same time a more seriously divisive force was developing within the organization. Leadership fell into the hands of those who believed that they should forge an instrument to exert pressure in favour of certain partisan social and political causes which they considered worthy. Resolutions were passed urging the United States to withdraw from Viet Nam, the Canadian government to recognize the People's Republic of China, the appropriate authorities to abolish capital punishment, and the like.

The approach taken by the leaders inevitably aroused opposition, not only from those among the rank and file who disapproved of the stand taken on these issues, but also from those who resented official positions of any kind being formulated on political issues without their wishes being taken into account. In a sense they were involuntary members of the organization, since their university collected fees to support the student society, and a per student contribution went automatically to the CUS. Yet no attempt was made to determine their views on the questions which constituted the basis for resolutions.

Matters reached the point where eight English-language universities, led by the University of Alberta, withdrew in 1966, claiming that the union had gone beyond its proper role. This development apparently did little to change the radical orientation of the leadership. Some of the most extreme of the new leftists were in fact ready to see the whole organization dissolve if they could not make it serve their purposes.

The annual meeting in September 1969 spelled a defeat for moderate forces and the end of the organization. A group of radicals accused their colleagues of selling out reformist principles and supporting mainstream political structures, including student councils. One of their most vociferous spokesmen was reported to have scorned reform in the universities, and to have declared that nothing would satisfy him short of the destruction of capitalism and imperialism. Although the most extreme radical positions were rejected, the group repeated earlier resolutions favouring self-determination for Quebec and the legalization of marijuana, and supported various other positions that could hardly have been called conservative. The effect of the acrimonious interchanges was to ensure the withdrawal of support by some of the major members such as the University of Toronto, and the organization collapsed.

TWELVE

Associations concerned with scholarship

Many of the associations with a primary interest in some area of scholarship, whether broad or narrow, are classified as learned societies, and meet in a single location somewhere in Canada early in June each year. All those dealt with here promote the interchange of ideas through meetings and publication. Most of them operate on very small budgets, since their main source of funds is their own limited membership. They form a vital link among universities across the country, and in many cases with comparable institutions abroad.

THE ROYAL CANADIAN INSTITUTE

The Royal Canadian Institute is the oldest scientific society in the country. It was founded in 1849 by a group of architects, land surveyors, and civil engineers as a means of assembling interested people to discuss scientific subjects. It received a royal charter in 1851, and a few years later was given custody of the library and museum held by the Athenaeum. With the passage of time its interests spread to fields of knowledge other than science.

In the 1960s the institute sponsored a series of lectures during the winter months at which some of the world's leading scientists addressed audiences of laymen and professionals. The topics chosen covered a wide range of modern concerns. Another major contribution was an annual summer science program held at Lakefield College School, where about three dozen gifted grade 11 and 12 students, chosen from among several thousand candidates from across Canada, spent six weeks working with university teachers and research scientists. The program was designed to develop an understanding of science and mathematics through lectures, field work, laboratory visits, and discussions. Students chose their own subjects for inquiry and made their own discoveries by exploring sources of information and asking questions of the experts with whom they associated.

THE ROYAL SOCIETY OF CANADA

The Royal Society of Canada, the senior learned society in the country, was formed in 1881 on the initiative of the Marquess of Lorne, then Governor-General of Canada. It was conceived as a means of promoting literature and science through the reading, discussion, and publication of papers. In 1883 it was incorporated by act of the dominion Parliament and began to receive an annual government subsidy which, along with membership fees, constituted its main source of income from that time on. It survived its early, crucial years despite comments that its formation was premature. One of the main reasons for its success was that it attracted many of the most distinguished humanists and scientists of the day, including Sir William Osler, Sir Sandford Fleming, Sir William Dawson, naturalist and geologist and principal of McGill University, Sir Daniel Wilson, historian and president of the University of Toronto, and G.M. Grant, principal of Queen's University.[1]

The publication of the *Transactions of the Royal Society of Canada*, which contained a selection of the papers read at the annual meeting, was begun in 1882. Since there were almost no other Canadian professional associations concerned with the various fields of learning, either at that time or for many years afterward, and no Canadian journals in which the results of research might be reported, the *Transactions* assumed a very important place in the world of scholarship. One of the major roles of the society was in fact to encourage the development of other associations with their specialized journals. A good example was the Historic Landmarks Association of Canada, which was founded in 1907 and transformed into the Canadian Historical Association in 1922. As the publication activities of such associations increased, the *Transactions* became less concerned with the results of specialized research, and devoted more attention to questions of broader scope cutting across disciplines.

From the time of its origin the Royal Society promoted, in government circles and among the public, the formation of institutions devoted to the improvement of the cultural life of the country. Some of the most important of these were the National Museum, the Public Archives of Canada, the Historic Sites and Monuments Board, the National Gallery of Canada, the Dominion Astrophysical Laboratory, and the National Library. The society was instrumental in the creation of the National Research Council in 1915, and thereafter maintained close relations with it.[2]

One means by which the society encouraged and recognized outstanding scholarly achievement was through the award of medals, which were not restricted to fellows of the society. Beginning in 1932, a grant from the Carnegie Corporation made possible the annual award of ten fellowships to enable Canadians to study abroad. When the grant lapsed after ten years, enough funds were obtained from provincial sources to make possible the continuation of the program on a reduced scale. During the 1950s the society assumed the responsibility of considering applications and recommending awards under the Canadian Government Overseas Awards program, which at first used blocked currency balances in certain European countries, and was later supported by appropriations from

Parliament. The society's role was similar in relation to Canadian applications for the fellowships and scholarships offered by the North Atlantic Treaty Organization.

The society originally had four sections: one for English literature and allied subjects, one for French literature and allied subjects, one for mathematical, physical, and chemical sciences, and one for geological and biological sciences. A separate section for biological sciences was organized in 1918. After the first members were named by the Governor-General, their successors were elected by vote of their respective sections. Although the original rule which limited the number of fellows in each section to twenty was eliminated, the sections were not permitted to elect more than six new members each year. Total membership in 1970 was 630. There was provision for honorary fellows and for unattached fellows.

There was considerable pressure in the 1960s to split the society into two organizations, one for the humanities and social sciences, and the other for the natural sciences. According to its proponents, this step would have made it easier to represent the wide range of scientific disciplines. There was also waning confidence in the possibility of reconciling the interests of scholars in the humanities with those of scientists. According to a proposal by P.R. Gorham of the National Research Council, the benefits of a split and those of continuing a single organization might both be realized if a Canadian Academy of Arts and Letters and a Canadian Academy of Science and Engineering were formed to pursue their separate interests, but continued to hold joint annual meetings as the Royal Society of Canada. After a committee studied the situation, a decision was made to retain the single existing organization. Reforms actually carried out included a doubling of the number of executive meetings, the addition of twelve applied scientists to the membership over a period of time, and the appointment of an executive secretary.

THE ROYAL CANADIAN ACADEMY OF THE ARTS

The Royal Canadian Academy of the Arts was active after its formation in 1880 in the promotion of the visual arts. To the extent that cultural and educational activities represent different categories of human activity, it operated largely in the former sphere. The following were leading aspects of its program. 1 / It organized an annual exhibition open to all painters, sculptors, architects, and designers across Canada, the ninetieth of which was held at the National Gallery in Ottawa at the end of January 1970. This exhibition was designed to encourage the development of the creative arts in Canada, to promote co-operation among the four groups represented, and to help raise the standards of excellence in the various arts. 2 / As a means of discharging its obligations as a national organization, the academy encouraged contact and understanding among creative people in various parts of the country. Its exhibitions were held in cities in all provinces. 3 / Professional advice was given to governments, institutions, and individuals. In some cases assistance was provided in drawing up agreements between creative artists and clients for the production of murals, major works of sculpture, and other items. To consider a specific example, the academy was asked by a group of four architectural firms working on an extension of the Ontario government offices at Queen's Park to appoint an art consultant committee to assist the architects and commissioned artists to produce thirty or forty decorative panels, murals, and sculpture for the new complex of offices. 4 / The academy acted as the ultimate honour society in Canada, recognizing creative ability in the visual arts. It awarded the Royal Canadian Arts Medal to outstanding figures in a number of fields. 5 / After 1882 the academy deposited representative works by academy members-elect in the National Gallery of Canada, which it was largely instrumental in establishing. By 1970 there were between 150 and 200 of these works.

THE CANADIAN AUTHORS ASSOCIATION

The Canadian Authors Association was founded in 1921 with the general purposes of creating a climate favourable to Canadian writing and of promoting recognition of Canadian writers and their works. More specifically, it claimed seven objectives:

1. To act for the benefit and protection of the interests of Canadian authors and for the maintenance of high ideals and practice in the literary profession.
2. To work for the best possible copyright protection for Canadian writers.
3. To act as the writers' spokesman before Royal Commissions and official inquiries.
4. To support the Canadian Writers' Foundation, a benevolent trust fund for Canadian writers.
5. To sponsor a system of awards, and otherwise encourage work of literary and artistic merit.
6. To publish two quarterly magazines, the *Canadian Author & Bookman* and *Canadian Poetry*.
7. To offer help and encouragement to beginning writers.[3]

Active membership was open to those engaged in writing or creative work of any kind who were judged to have produced an adequate body of work. Those interested in Canadian writing, but who had not met the other conditions, might be associate members.

These objectives could not be considered, in the narrow sense, as educational. On the other hand, the success of the organization in helping to enrich Canada's cultural resources could hardly escape having an indirect effect on the content of Canadian education. Further, activities of local branches might be considered as educational in terms of their influence on the members. Most branches across the country were in the habit of holding craft sessions, offering members an opportunity to criticize one another's work. Meetings commonly provided for study and discussion, with frequent addresses on famous writers and their works. In 1968–9 the Toronto branch offered a ten-minute "craft capsule" consisting of practical suggestions from experienced writers.

A major contribution of the association to education was the publication of the *Canadian Author and Bookman*, recently merged with *Canadian Poetry*. After 1921 it provided vital information for and about writers and writing in Canada. The Toronto branch issued a three-page monthly newsletter containing information about members and their work as well as items of a general cultural nature.

A project with a direct bearing on education undertaken by the Toronto branch in the late 1960s was the preparation of a list of Toronto writers of material for juveniles for the use of city librarians. This list was intended to be helpful when parents met their children's librarians, when writers met children, or when special programs were organized, such as those for Young Canada's Book Week. Librarians would be able to ask listed writers to meet parents or young readers on a formal or informal basis. Another project for the benefit of youth was a lyric poetry contest for grade 10 students in Toronto high schools. Members of the association did the judging, and the winners were presented with prizes of books and a subscription to the *Canadian Author and Bookman*.

THE CLASSICAL ASSOCIATION OF CANADA

The Classical Association of Canada originated in the Ontario Classical Association, which was founded in 1944 and became a branch of the national organization upon its formation three years later. As is true of other learned societies, there was doubt in the early stages that the new association could find the strength and support to succeed. The question of publishing a journal was immediately confronted, since without it there was little prospect that the association would have any great appeal. The first issue of *Phoenix* (at first called *The Phoenix*) appeared in January 1946, supported only by the $3 fee from each of twenty-five members and a benefactor who contributed $100 and guaranteed the enterprise against loss. The contents of the journal emphasized new scholarly developments, literary criticism, and reappraisal of Greek and Roman studies.[4]

As the years passed, the quality of the material in *Phoenix* continued to improve. Supplementary volumes were produced in addition to the quarterly issues. Professor Mary E. White, head of the Graduate Department of Classical Studies at the University of Toronto, and in earlier years editor of the journal, was able to point out in 1970 that it had become one of the best known of classical quarterlies. A further project of the association in the publication field was *Classical News and Views*.

In 1944 the association embarked on a venture that seems rather unusual for an organization of its kind. When Greece was liberated from the German occupation, the association undertook to assist the Greek War Relief Fund in providing supplies for the starving and destitute people of that country. As a means of raising money, it co-operated with the Greek community in Toronto in organizing a festival of Greek music and dancing. This project convinced the association that membership should be open to anyone interested in any aspect of the classics, and such a policy was permanently established.

An educational project of the early years involved the production of sets of slides or pictures for use in schools. Five sets of these were produced with a commentary written by one of the members of the association, and substantial numbers were sold inside and outside the country until the Department of Photographic Service of the University of Toronto was closed. Some years later it was found possible to resume the production of audio-visual material for schools.

The annual conference of the association, held at the same time as the meetings of the other learned societies, usually featured a special visiting scholar, thus bringing distinguished classicists to Canada. In accordance with the bilingual character of the organization, some of the papers were given in French. There was participation by four categories of members: university teachers, high school teachers, students, and lay members. For a number of years the association also sponsored two lecturers, one of whom visited the university centres of western Canada and the other the Atlantic provinces.

THE CANADIAN ASSOCIATION OF GEOGRAPHERS

One of the most active of the learned societies, the Canadian Association of Geographers, was founded in 1951 to encourage the exchange of ideas among geographers, to foster scholarship and research in the field, especially on Canadian topics, and to improve the teaching of geography. According to the constitution, full membership was open to 1 / those with a graduate degree in geography, 2 / those with an undergraduate degree with honours in geography, and employed as geographers, and 3 / those who had made significant contributions in the field of geography. Only full members could hold office and vote in the election of officers. Those with an active interest in the affairs of the association but without full membership qualifications were acceptable as associate members. There has also been provision for student members and "benefactors." Total membership reached 922 in 1968.

The association obtained representation on the Social Science Research Council and sponsored the Canadian Committee of the International Geographical Union. In addition to the meeting held annually in association with the learned societies, there were regional meetings in British Columbia and Ontario. Publications included the *Canadian*

Geographer, issued quarterly, the *Newsletter*, and the *Education Bulletin*. The association made awards to undergraduate and graduate students and to individuals conducting research projects.

THE ONTARIO HISTORICAL SOCIETY

The Pioneer and Historical Association of the Province of Ontario was founded at Toronto in 1888. Ten years later it was renamed the Ontario Historical Society. According to the constitution, which was revised a number of times, the purposes of the association were "to unite the various Pioneer and Historical Societies of the Province in one central head or organization, thereby the better to promote intercourse and cooperation on the part of all such societies, to form new societies and to promote and extend the influence and benefits thereof." The constitution also specified that the society would publish a magazine and other material devoted to the history of the province, that it would hold annual meetings in various cities and towns in the province, and that it would cooperate with the Provincial Archives, the Royal Ontario Museum, and other historical societies and museums in preserving the documents and archaeological artifacts that might contribute to the understanding and interpretation of the history of the province. It might also undertake projects to encourage and develop the study of history.

The official journal of the association was the quarterly *Ontario History*. A recent leaflet soliciting membership indicated that more than fifty volumes of papers and records had been published since 1899. A monthly *Newsletter*, telling of pertinent events and activities in this field, was produced for the benefit of those joining the Museums Section. A special program was conducted in 1967 to mark Canada's Centennial, when local societies were encouraged to publish studies.

The society was supported by a modest membership fee, which was raised to $5 in 1967. At the same time the annual grant from the Department of Education was raised to $8,500. The appointment of an executive assistant and a general reorganization were designed to improve services to the continuously increasing membership. Attempts were made to increase financial resources by appeals to foundations, corporations, and individuals.

THE CANADIAN HISTORICAL ASSOCIATION

The forerunner of the Canadian Historical Association was the Historic Landmarks Association of Canada, founded in 1907 by a committee of the Royal Society of Canada to make arrangements for the celebration of the Quebec Tercentennial and to mark and preserve Canadian historic landmarks. The need for the association in its original form diminished as federal government agencies increasingly took over the second of these functions. An entirely new organization called the Canadian Historical

Association was established in 1922 to serve the growing national interest in all phases of Canadian history. It attempted to promote research in history in general and in Canadian history in particular.[5] By 1970 it had a membership of more than two thousand.

The association made a practice of holding its annual meeting in conjunction with other bodies at the conference of the learned societies. Historians and teachers and students of history assembled at these gatherings to present and hear papers on themes of interest. Many of these papers were printed in the *Historical Papers*. Travel grants were made to some members requiring financial assistance to attend the meetings.

A major educational contribution of the association was in the field of publication. Short monographs provided the general reader, the teacher, and the historical specialist with concise treatment of particular questions in Canadian history. The association sponsored the publication of a historical atlas in 1960, and a reissue in 1966. It also offered its members the opportunity to purchase at a reduced rate subscriptions to the *Canadian Historical Review* and the *Revue d'Histoire de l'Amerique française*. The Archives Section sponsored the publication of the *Canadian Archivist*. Assistance was provided for the annual publication of a *Register of Dissertations* containing information on all graduate theses in history and related topics. It included all dissertations involving historical research in progress at Canadian universities, and all those prepared at non-Canadian universities dealing with Canadian historical topics.

A Local History Section recognized individuals and organizations for outstanding achievements in local history by granting certificates of merit. Each year provincial and local societies made nominations for awards in various categories. Among these was the publication of books and periodicals on local history.

In addition to producing the publication already mentioned, the Archives Section provided an opportunity for archivists to meet once a year to hear a paper or engage in a discussion of some topic of interest. The section co-operated with the Public Archives of Canada and Carleton University in 1959, 1964, and 1968 in offering an archives training course leading to a certificate issued by the university. Considerable efforts were also made to acquaint students of history with the material available in archives in Canada. The *Union List of Manuscripts*, published by the Public Archives of Canada in 1968, attempted to give researchers sufficient information about various items to enable them to decide whether the material was likely to be worth further investigation.

The association held three bilingual centennial seminars of one week's duration in 1966 and five in 1967. At these, distinguished scholars, senior and junior historians, and graduate students heard provocative papers and engaged in discussion. Eminent geographers conducted tours into the hinterlands of the host institutions. The papers offered were subsequently published by the association.

Activities of the association in the late 1960s included a submission to the Senate Committee on Science Policy, a study of research information storage and retrieval, and involvement in the development of new functions for the Social Science Research Council. In 1970 a national survey was conducted on the teaching of history, particularly in the high schools. Another study was conducted on the possibility of future employment for historians.

THE CANADIAN LINGUISTIC ASSOCIATION

The Canadian Linguistic Association, one of the learned societies, was founded in 1954 by a small number of individuals who were concerned with linguistic scholarship. The difficulties of the early years and the increasing stability of the organization reflected the emergence of the discipline from a state of serious neglect to one characterized by considerable attention and interest. This development occurred in Canada much later than in Europe and the United States. At the time the association was formed, the only Canadian universities making any pretence of offering courses in linguistics were Laval University and the University of Montreal, but neither of these institutions had a department. Canadians desiring training in linguistics had to go abroad for graduate studies.

The aim of the association was to promote the study of languages and linguistics in Canada, with particular reference to the languages spoken within the country. This aim was pursued through the publication of *The Journal of the Canadian Linguistic Association / La Revue de l'Association canadienne de Linguistique*. This work was made possible in the beginning by the generosity of the University of Alberta, where the first editor, M.H. Scargill, who was also the first secretary-treasurer, was teaching. Vital support was also obtained from Canadian and American scholars who paid the $2 membership fee as a gesture of encouragement. By 1961 there were 346 private and 111 institutional members, most of them from outside Canada.

At that time officials of the association decided to change the name of the journal to *The Canadian Journal of Linguistics / La Revue canadienne de Linguistique*, to improve its physical quality, and to increase its size. The doubling of the membership fee necessitated by this move resulted in the loss of some of the paid-up private members who had only a marginal interest in linguistics, and the number of such members did not again during the decade reach the 1961 total of 346. It was an advantage to the association that, with the growing interest in linguistics, an increasing proportion of these consisted of linguists who were actively engaged in teaching and research in Canada. Unlike the private membership, the institutional membership rose steadily, reaching a total of about 275 by 1969.

Annual meetings were held at the conference of the learned societies each year after 1954, at first covering a one-day period and in time extending to three. These gatherings provided a forum for the presentation and discussion of papers on linguistics, for panel discussions of problems of common interest, and for other activities designed to disseminate new ideas within the field of linguistics.

Standing and *ad hoc* committees promoted a number of the association's interests. An example of these was the Lexicographical Committee, which encouraged the production of dictionaries of Canadian English, Canadian French, and Canadian Ukrainian. An Amerindian and Eskimo Committee tried to remedy long-standing neglect of the languages of the original inhabitants of Canada. An active role was also played by the Grants and Awards Committee, the Fact-Finding Committee on Linguistics, and the Summer Schools of Linguistics Committee.

The last mentioned of these committees exerted considerable influence on the establishment of summer schools of linguistics. The first of these was operated at the University of Montreal in 1956, and repeated in 1961. The University of Alberta offered one almost every year after 1958. The association assisted by offering advice, by securing teaching staff, and by providing bursaries for promising candidates to attend.

In 1969 the president of the association, W.S. Avis, offered an informal review of the status of the discipline. There were some ten Canadian universities with departments of linguistics offering degree programs, several others with linguistic programs organized on an interdisciplinary basis, and still others offering courses taught by professional linguists. In 1966 the Canada Council recognized the important status the discipline had achieved by establishing a committee to deal with applications for pre-doctoral awards in linguistics.

Plans of the association included the conduct of an inquiry into the state of linguistics studies in Canada. It was considered important to know what universities or other institutions were offering courses in the field, how many such courses there were and in what areas, what the student enrolment was, and what plans there were for expansion. Information was to be sought on the number of linguists, both Canadians and others, in Canada, the number teaching at universities, the number engaging in fieldwork, and the number working on government projects. Members of the association were interested in knowing the extent to which the study of linguistics had penetrated into elementary and secondary schools.

THE CANADIAN PHYSIOLOGICAL SOCIETY

During the early 1930s university teachers of physiology found themselves unduly constrained because the Royal Society of Canada provided their only forum for the reading of scientific papers and the discussion of aims, discoveries, and difficulties. Members of local societies in Montreal and Toronto therefore got together in 1934 to form a larger association that would more truly reflect their own interests. At the first meeting, held in Toronto in 1935, the members agreed that their objective would be "to promote the advancement of physiology and its related branches of science, and to promote a friendly spirit among those Canadians who are engaged in these fields." In the constitution the stated purpose was simply "to promote the advancement of physiology in its widest sense."

Basic membership was open to a "person who has conducted researches, who has published papers in scientific journals, and who is actively engaged in investigation, teaching or other form of scholarship in the fields of physiology, biochemistry, pharmacology, clinical investigation or the experimental aspects of biology, pathology, therapeutics, nutrition or hygiene." There was also provision for associate membership for graduate students and young investigators who had not yet had the time to satisfy the requirements for full membership, as well as for research assistants and teachers in physiological and biological sciences. Other categories were honorary membership and emeritus membership. By 1969 the total membership had grown to more than five hundred.

Payment of a nominal fee entitled members of the society to receive the *Canadian Journal of Physiology and Pharmacology*. They were also eligible to present scientific papers at annual meetings. From 1958 on, the scientific program at the annual meeting held in June was integrated with that of other societies constituting the Canadian Federation of Biological Societies. The society continued, however, to hold annual business meetings at which the reports of committees were presented. In 1969 there were committees dealing with career prospects in physiology, science policy, education in physiology, and animal welfare, while appointed representatives served on national bodies which concerned themselves with various activities of physiologists.

As the first association of its type, the society played a leading part in encouraging the organization of basic scientists in the medical field. Although its activities were limited for many years to the interchange of reports of scientific research, it was later concerned with methods of teaching physiology at the undergraduate level in universities, with the broad problems of research support, and with attempts to shape a science policy in Canada.

THE CANADIAN ASSOCIATION OF PHYSICISTS

The Canadian Association of Physicists was founded in 1945 and incorporated in 1951. Its objectives were to further the advance of the science of physics, to promote the development of physics for the benefit of mankind, to disseminate information about science in and between all sections and regions of Canada, and to encourage co-operation between Canadian physicists on the one hand and universities, research organizations, and industry on the other. In 1968 there were over 1,500 members in five specialized divisions: the Theoretical Physics Division, the Earth Physics Division, the Medical and Biological Physics Division, the Solid State Physics Division, and the Plasma Physics Division. Later additions were a Nuclear Physics Division and an Educational Division.

In 1958 the association established an educational trust fund consisting of donations from corporate members and industry, individual members, and the general funds of the organization. The money was used for educational purposes such as high school prizes, university prizes, conferences, lecture tours, and the publication of brochures on educational subjects. Between 1965 and 1968 expenditures from the fund were in the neighbourhood of $8,500 per year.

There were nine provincial examinations set for senior high school students in 1968, with Prince Edward Island schools combined with those of Nova Scotia. The first prize for performance in these examinations in each case amounted to $250, while other successful contestants received amounts ranging from $150 to $25, depending on the contributions of provincial universities. A nation-wide competition among senior undergraduates studying physics was designed to stimulate individual scholarship. The overall results were thought to reflect the merits of different universities, and it was hoped that the competition would help to improve the quality of teaching. The first, second, and third prizes amounted to $300, $200, and $100 respectively; in addition the winner of the first prize had his expenses paid to the annual congress to receive his award.

Lecture tours supported by the fund involved specialists in particular fields, who gave four or five lectures in geographical areas away from their own. It was intended that they would thus introduce students to aspects of physics with which they might not otherwise come in contact, as well as advertise areas of current research being undertaken in Canadian universities. Opportunities for graduate study and employment in Canada might thus be emphasized. Each year the association tried to engage one or two distinguished lecturers to visit and speak at a number of centres. The cost of this service in 1968 amounted to $1,800.

The program for 1969 included an impressive list of special projects, most of them with educational implications: 1 / a new statistical survey of Canadian physicists, covering the available supply, their distribution in research and in research and development enterprises, their employment characteristics, and other matters; 2 / a study of the evolution of enrolment trends in physics at the graduate, undergraduate, and high school levels; 3 / the presentation of a brief to the Senate Committee on Science Policy in the federal government; 4 / the presentation of a brief to the Science Secretariat Study Group on Solid-Earth Sciences; 5 / a high energy physics conference at the University of Toronto; 6 / the organization of symposia on physics education; 7 / a study of ways and means of establishing a physics-based industry in Canada; 8 / support of the 5th

Undergraduate Physics Conference held at the University of Waterloo; 9 / a study of the sponsorship and level of support for summer schools in physics in Canada; 10 / a summary of the state of physics research in Canada; and 11 / a study of the feasibility and cost of preparing a computerized directory of Canadian physicists.

THE CANADIAN POLITICAL SCIENCE ASSOCIATION

The Canadian Political Science Association originated in 1913 to encourage the investigation of economic, political, and social problems in Canada. No meetings were held during the First World War or for some years afterward, and it was not until 1929 that the association was revived and reorganized. Its two major contributions, like those of other learned societies, were in publication and in the holding of annual meetings. In the early 1930s it published an annual volume of papers and proceedings, and from 1935 to 1967 the quarterly *Canadian Journal of Economics and Political Science*.

An account by V.W. Bladen in the February 1960 issue of this quarterly under the title "A Journal is Born: 1935" provides some interesting insights into the problems faced by young and rather shaky scholarly associations in providing regular outlets for Canadian writers.[6] The task was a forbidding one for an organization with only about five hundred members. Although British and American periodicals were prepared to carry Canadian contributions, it was thought that a Canadian vehicle would stimulate Canadian economists and political scientists to increase their scholarly efforts. This idea occurred to some people at the University of Toronto, who gave serious consideration to the possibility of publishing their own quarterly. This prospect caused apprehension among leaders of the association, who feared that McGill University might feel compelled to produce a competing journal. Since it did not appear that the field could support two periodicals of high quality, considerable pressure was brought to bear at Toronto for an agreement to support a single national journal. Bladen gives Harold Innis major credit, and apparently deserves a good deal of it himself, for the successful outcome of the negotiations. Publication of the new journal, the title of which was agreed upon only after considerable haggling, owed much to the contributions of the University of Toronto Press.

The late 1960s saw a change in the nature of the association with the departure of certain specialized groups. The anthropologists and sociologists withdrew to form their own association in 1966, and the economic section followed suit in 1967. The Canadian Political Science Association continued its scholarly contribution through the *Canadian Journal of Political Science*. Membership had reached 6,000 by 1967 but, as indicated by circulation figures, was down to about 2,600 in 1969. About one-third of the members were from Ontario.

A proposal for parliamentary internships was made jointly in 1969 by the Canadian Political Science Association and Alfred Hales, MP, after two years of consideration by the executive of the association. The substance of the scheme was that each year between six and twelve young Canadian university graduates would be given staff assignments in Parliament lasting from eight to ten months in order to supplement their academic education with a practical working knowledge of the functioning of Parliament and the everyday work of the members. Assignments would help members to carry out their duties more effectively in addition to contributing to the education of the young people. The sponsorship of the Canadian Political Science Association was contingent on there being significant academic consequences from the scheme. Most interns were expected to have a background in political science or in a related field such as law, history, or journalism. Preference would be given to those engaged in graduate study in one of those areas. The possession or acquisition of bilingual competence would be a highly desirable asset.

THE CANADIAN SOCIOLOGY AND ANTHROPOLOGY ASSOCIATION

Until the late 1950s the number of members of the Canadian Political Science Association whose primary interest was in sociology and anthropology was comparatively small. As early as 1959 some consideration was given to the possibility of establishing a separate organization for this group. Since there were too few in the interested group to attempt to maintain a completely autonomous association, the members set up a separate anthropology and sociology chapter within the Canadian Political Science Association. By 1966 they were ready for complete independence, and set about preparing a constitution which was approved the following year.

According to the constitution, the objectives of the association were to encourage research and publication in, and teaching and general development of, sociology and anthropology. Arrangements were made to publish a journal entitled the *Canadian Review of Sociology and Anthropology / La Revue canadienne de Sociologie et d'Anthropologie*, copies of which were to be distributed to the members.

The association appeared at a crucial time during the development of its fields of interest. In June 1969 the preseident, in his annual report, noted the enormous increase in the number of social scientists in the country. He estimated that the total in sociology and anthropology had multiplied by four or five in a period of four years. Completely new associations of social scientists had been and were being formed; the government had been re-evalutating its support of the social sciences; the Social Science Research Council was undergoing a process of revitalization; and the Canada Council had greatly increased its contributions toward training and research in the social sciences.[7]

According to the annual report the membership doubled between 1967 and 1969 as a result of the efforts of the Executive Committee. An attempt was being made to extend participation by graduate students. Increased organizational grants from the Canada Council were needed until the membership reached the point where the association could support itself.

In its efforts to promote its purposes the association established affiliations and contacts with a large number of other national and international organizations. These included the Association internationale de sociologie, the International Union of Anthropological and Ethnological Sciences, the Social Science Research Council of Canada, the Canadian National Commission for UNESCO, the Canadian Archaeological Association, the Council for Canadian Archaeology, the American Anthropological Association, the American Sociological Association, the Western Association of Sociology and Anthropology, and l'Association des anthropologues, sociologues et psychologues sociaux de langue française.

Activities of the association included representations to the Social Science Research Council and the Canada Council urging an increased role in them for the learned societies concerned with the social sciences. Briefs were presented to the Macdonald Study Group of the Science Council and to the Lamontagne Senate Committee on Science Policy. Academic issues were discussed with the Dominion Bureau of Statistics, the Canadian Educational Research Association, and the American Educational Research Association.

The Research Sub-Committee completed a survey of anthropologists and sociologists in Canada in 1967 and arranged for the publication of a *Directory of Anthropologists and Sociologists and Their Current Research* in 1968. During the following year the preparation of a monograph dealing with research needs and resources in anthropology and sociology in Canada involved an extensive review of published research in the field and the sending of questionnaires to librarians of institutions offering graduate programs and to deans of the same institutions for data on thesis titles, staffs, and enrolment.

THE SOCIAL SCIENCE RESEARCH COUNCIL OF CANADA

The Social Science Research Council was formed in 1940, mainly as a result of the efforts of R.H. Coats, Harold Innis, and R.G. Trotter. The founders were seeking to remedy the current lack of financial support in Canada for research in history, economics, politics, psychology, legal and constitutional matters, population problems, and human relationships. An informal paper, "The Social Science Research Council: Some Historical Notes," distributed at the end of the 1960s describes the earlier situation in this way:

Insofar as anything at all was achieved before 1940, it was done by isolated individuals, often lacking the most elementary facilities, without significant encouragement and with little recognition of the importance of what they were trying to do.

Financial support in the initial stages was provided by the Carnegie Corporation and the Rockefeller Foundation. The Carnegie Corporation made a grant of $5,000 for each year from 1941–2 through 1950. The Rockefeller Foundation began by giving $5,000, raised its donation periodically until it reached $57,500 in 1951–2, and made a final grant of $125,000 in 1953, half as an outright gift and the rest over the next five years on a matching basis. In 1957 the Ford Foundation gave $150,000, to be paid in three diminishing installments, which helped to tide the organization over the period when Canada Council procedures were being established. After this period funds were derived from fees for services performed for the Canada Council, from foundation grants for special purposes, and from contributions by universities and interested individuals.

Three classes of membership were recognized: representatives of learned societies, representatives of social science groups in universities, and members chosen from the public service. According to recent constitutional provisions, the first group included members representing history, psychology, law, political science, geography, sociology, anthropology, and economics. The university representatives consisted of one chosen by teachers in social science departments or faculties in each university or college constituting a member of the Association of Universities and Colleges of Canada.

In pursuit of its purposes the council carried on a program which included a study of the geography and resources of the Canadian north in 1942; an interdisciplinary research project centring on the Social Credit movement, particularly in Alberta, in 1943; research into French-English relations in Canada in 1947; a study of problems concerning the Indian in 1949; surveys of the teaching of geography and of psychology in Canadian universities in 1951; publication of studies in Canadian economics in 1952; Canadian studies in history and government; the historical statistics of Canada in 1959; a series of studies of the more significant economic, political, and social developments and problems in contemporary Canada in 1959; *The Canadian Centenary History Series – A History of Canada* in 1955; and an Atlantic provinces study series in 1959. Projects carried out in the 1960s included studies of the state of the social sciences in Canada and a study relating to the establishment of a social science research agency and data bank.

THE HUMANITIES RESEARCH COUNCIL
According to the constitution of the Humanities Research Council, as revised in 1967, the council consisted of twenty-four scholars engaged in

research in the humanities, which were defined as ancient and modern languages and literature, philosophy, and certain aspects of history, the fine arts, musicology, archaeology, and mathematics. Each of the learned societies which had been recognized by the council as representing a branch of the humanities was entitled to a representative on the council. Members were eligible for re-election for a maximum of four successive years.

One of the major factors that led to the formation of the Humanities Research Council was the prospect, during the height of the Second World War, that arts studies in universities might be suspended for the duration of hostilities. A committee of the Royal Society of Canada, under the chairmanship of Watson Kirkconnell, prepared a brief to the Prime Minister opposing this suggestion. Although there was a reprieve for arts instruction, the threat was not entirely dispelled, and the founding of the council thus represented something of a defensive gesture.

It became a major objective of the council to offer financial support for research in the humanities, an activity which was made possible by grants from the Carnegie Corporation and the Rockefeller Foundation. Another early undertaking was a national survey of the state of the humanities in Canada, leading to a report published in 1947.[8] This document was considered of such value that it was revised and updated in 1964. The initial version pointed out that research in the humanities was severely handicapped by such factors as inadequate libraries, heavy teaching assignments, and financial difficulties in completing and publishing manuscripts. The council devoted considerable effort to the alleviation of these conditions.

In 1950 the council initiated the formation of the Humanities Association of Canada, which helped to bring interested members of the community into direct contact with scholars in the humanities. The regional conferences which had inspired the formation of this association were gradually taken over by it. The council continued its assistance to scholars in the form of fellowships and other post-doctoral aid as well as grants for publication.

Two enterprises considered to be of particular importance were undertaken in 1947. One was the so-called Dominions Project, which involved comparative studies of the development of Anglo-Saxon culture, particularly in such Commonwealth countries as Canada and Australia. Associated with this project was the production for the council of a *Check-List of Canadian Literature and Background Materials, 1628–1950* by R.E. Watters.[9] The second enterprise, undertaken under the chairmanship of M. Lebel, was called "The French Cultural Evolution of North America" or "Le fait français."

While the work of the Royal Commission on National Development in the Arts, Letters and Sciences (the Massey Commission) ultimately had a beneficial effect on the causes which the council promoted, its report in 1951 ushered in an era of difficulty. Although the Canada Council did not make its appearance until 1957, its establishment seemed imminent for a number of years. For this reason the federal government and the American foundations were unwilling to commit substantial amounts of funds to the council, or to promise any degree of support for an extended period.

With the formation of the Canada Council humanist scholars had access to new financial resources for research activity. The Humanities Research Council was involved in a number of major projects during the period which followed. 1 / It sponsored the production of a literary history of Canada, a comprehensive reference work which encouraged young and established scholars to engage in literary studies. 2 / It supported an effort to produce a comprehensive bibliography of Australian and New Zealand materials in Canadian university libraries, which was expected to enhance interest in the scholarship of those countries. 3 / It co-operated with the Public Archives of Canada between 1962 and 1968 in the compilation of a *Union List of Manuscripts in Canadian Repositories,*[10] which constituted a basic document for those interested in historical aspects of Canadian life. 4 / It launched a series of publications on letters in French Canada under the title of *Vie des lettres canadiennes* and a volume on the literary history of French Canada under the title *Histoire de la littérature canadienne française.* 5 / Co-operating with the Social Science Research Council, it supported the Canadian Centenary History Series, in which an attempt was made to bring together in sixteen volumes all the findings of historical research during the previous hundred years. 6 / It assisted in the publication of *Scholarly Reporting in the Humanities* by R.M. Wiles. 7 / In conjunction with the Social Science Research Council, it supported the formation of a Committee on African Studies, which undertook to further the work of Canadian specialists in African culture and to strengthen their relationship with African scholars. 8 / With a grant of $85,000 from the Ford Foundation paid over a five-year period ending in 1968, it co-operated with the Science Research Council, which received a similar amount, "to bring Canadian scholars and intellectual resources concerned with international problems into co-operative arrangements with similar institutions abroad."[11]

THIRTEEN

Professional associations

It is often difficult to draw a sharp line between professional associations and those dealt with in the previous chapter, since professional interests often involve scholarly pursuits. Associations classified here as professional were in some cases mainly devoted to fraternal activities and to the promotion of the role of the profession. Many of the provincial bodies were authorized by statute to control the conditions of admission to the profession and certification.

A crucial factor identifying a profession is that it must have a specialized body of knowledge based on theoretical principles and confirmed in practice. During the period covered here the recognized learned professions tended, despite variations in sequence and substance, to follow a common pattern in the evolution of their procedures for preparation and for admission. Except for school teaching, the professional status of which thereby remained open to question, the professions largely acquired the right to determine the fitness of a candidate by means of some form of examination and in terms of satisfactory performance during a prescribed period of practical work under the supervision of one or more practising members of the profession. In earlier years education and training were obtained almost exclusively under articles or under indentureship as an apprentice.

In a "Report to the Councils of the Provincial Institutes of Chartered Accountants in Canada on Educational Plans," made in 1967, W.A. Mackintosh identified six definite trends in the evolution of the professions: 1 / retention of a dominant voice in admissions to professional status, even where governments have assumed the formal power of licensing, either directly or through universities; 2 / successive elevations of the standard of requirements for admission to articles and to professional training; 3 / a shortening of the period of articles, usually associated with the progressive separation of full-time study from full-time practical experience; 4 / a reduction in the responsibility of the practitioner for the training of his articled student; 5 / the transfer of professional education to a training institution or a university; 6 / some reduction in the scope of the examinations set by the profession and acceptance of the certificates of other institutions for parts of the educational program. As factors bringing about these changes, Mackintosh mentioned the increase in the scope and complexity of the body of knowledge considered essential for practitioners, a growing recognition of the need for a sufficiently broad education to enable the practitioner to acquire new knowledge as it develops and to apply it to new situations and problems, the availability of members of the profession qualified to teach, increased affluence, which has raised the general level of education and increased the numbers to whom some measure of higher education is available, and the unevenness of conditions of apprenticeship, with accompanying disparities of training.

The brief treatment of the educational involvement and contributions of some of the professional organizations in this chapter will indicate the distance the professions travelled along the common evolutionary path. The necessarily incomplete account that is possible here will suggest to some extent the range of variations on the same theme. It is perhaps of particular interest to note the differences among the various professional groups in terms of the amount of responsibility they acknowledged and the extent of their efforts in keeping their members up to date with respect to the latest developments in their field through continuing education.

THE ONTARIO LIBRARY ASSOCIATION

Reference is made in volume v, chapter 20, to some of the most significant events in the history of the public library system in Ontario. One of these events was the transfer of the responsibility for supervising the mechanics' institutes, the forerunners of the public libraries, from the Department of the Commissioner of Agriculture to the Department of Education. These institutes thus became an integral part of the educational system. The Free Libraries Act of 1882, which provided for the establishment of public libraries by vote of the ratepayers and for their maintenance by public taxation, was regarded as the most important step in the history of Ontario libraries. As a means of discharging its responsibilities, the Department of Education appointed an inspector of public libraries. By 1900 there were 389 free and association libraries under his supervision, with a stock of 989,050 volumes and a circulation of over 2.5 million.[1]

At this time the library staffs worked in almost complete isolation, with no regular provision for meetings. Thus they had little opportunity to learn of advances in library techniques being made in Great Britain and the United States. Since 1876 the American Library Association had been actively pressing for the establishment of new libraries, promoting library legislation in various states, developing library administrative methods, arousing public interest, and helping to secure public and private financial contributions. The Library Association of the United Kingdom had also been functioning since 1877. Immediate inspiration for the formation of a national organization in Canada came from a meeting of the American Library Association in Montreal in 1900. When a provisional committee set up to explore the issue decided that a dominion association was impracticable, an Ontario Library Association (OLA) was formed instead.

A constitution was drawn up, provisional officers were chosen, and a meeting was arranged for 1901.

As defined in the original constitution, the object of the association was

to promote the welfare of Libraries, by stimulating public interests in founding and improving them, by securing any need of legislation, by furthering such co-operative work as shall improve results or reduce expenses, by exchanging views and making recommendations in convention or otherwise, and by advancing the common interests of Librarians, Trustees and Directors and others engaged in library and allied in [sic] education work.[2]

Membership was open to anyone engaged in library work as trustee, director, or librarian, or in any other capacity on payment of an annual fee. Librarians, who paid a higher fee than others, were entitled to two representatives at the meetings.

In the 1969 version of the constitution, the objects were stated in a somewhat different form, but they had not changed greatly in substance:

(a) To extend and improve all types of libraries and library service in Ontario.
(b) To inform the membership of developments and trends in library service.
(c) To publicize all aspects of library service and development in Ontario.
(d) To co-operate with other library organizations and institutions with similar aims and objectives.
(e) To do all such other acts or things as are incidental or conducive to the attainment of the above objects or any of them.
(f) To receive, acquire and hold gifts, donations, legacies, bequests and devises.

In a paper read at the first annual meeting, E.A. Hardy, secretary of the Lindsay Public Library, outlined a future program for the OLA.[3] A primary function of the association, as he saw it, was to provide assistance to local libraries. It might issue quarterly bulletins giving lists of new books, prices, and publishers, produce pamphlets indicating the books that were, in the judgment of a committee of the association, the best of the year for Canadian libraries, and compile bibliographies on special subjects such as Canadian history, electricity, trade unions, monopolies, and combines. Bulletins might describe modern methods in such matters as loan-charging, book-shelving, magazine files, and binding. An attempt might be made to bring at least one library in each county up to modern standards as an example to librarians and trustees in the area. Efforts might be made to bring some order and system into the classification and cataloguing of books. The association might attempt to improve the performance of librarians by working for the establishment of short courses and visits by librarians to large city libraries to observe the work of those who were relatively expert. The Department of Education was urged to provide courses leading to certification and to establish financial incentives for boards to employ certificated people. Inter-library co-operation might be encouraged through loans and exchanges of duplicate material. Efforts might be made to acquaint librarians with the value of public documents and with classification schemes that would make them accessible to the potential user. Co-operation might be promoted between public libraries and teachers' institutes, farmers' institutes, and county historical societies.

A second function was to provide service to the general public. Efforts might be made to arouse public interest in the establishment of new libraries, the changing of subscription libraries into free libraries, and the securing of buildings for libraries. Donations of books and periodicals could be solicited. Bibliographies of temporary and permanent interest might be prepared and circulated among readers. The work of local historical societies might be promoted and libraries urged to obtain and preserve materials relating to their activities. A third function would involve assistance to schools, and a fourth, assistance to Sunday school libraries. At that time there were estimated to be 2,500 Sunday school libraries in Ontario with possibly 250,000 volumes in their possession.

Hardy's address provided fuel for the OLA for a good many years. Records of the subsequent annual meetings demonstrate that a considerable number of his ideas were carried out. One of the most successful enterprises of the association was the conduct of library institutes, with the assistance of the Department of Education, between 1907 and 1918. A great deal of attention was paid to the promotion of legislation to improve the status of libraries.

A major event of the mid-1960s was the production of the St John Report, discussed at some length in volume v, chapter 20. Discussions at the annual meeting in 1966 produced some sharp criticism as well as a good deal of praise for this report. One speaker excoriated it for ignoring the largest single owner of books, periodicals, and pamphlets in the province – the federal government. There was general appreciation, however, of its success in demonstrating the inadequacy of the financial resources that had hitherto been available for provincial libraries.

The growing investment in school libraries was a matter of considerable interest to the association during this period. A resolution presented at the 1966 annual meeting urged maximum co-operation between school and public libraries. There was particular concern lest students fall into the practice of relying too heavily on the former. The resolution suggested in particular that secondary school libraries be kept open beyond school hours so that their routine reference material would not be unnecessarily duplicated at public libraries, that ordering and inter-loan arrangements be co-ordinated to facilitate the use of the more expensive material in both systems, that school visits to public libraries be continued to familiarize children with library attractions, and that school libraries be made available to parents of pre-school children for the loan of picture books and story books where children's libraries in the public system were inaccessible or inadequate.

A major issue in the late 1960s was the creation of new levels of library service. Earlier shortages of professional manpower showed a prospect of being alleviated by a two-year technician program and possibly also by an undergraduate degree program. Members of the OLA criticized their fellow members for being slow to recognize the potential contribution of the new trainees and for hesitancy in defining their exact role. The association did, however, formulate some recommendations which were sent to the Advisory Committee on Library Technician Courses of the Department of Education. These read as follows:

That no course for library technicians should be started unless a local committee of professional librarians and others, including representatives of employer groups, recommends it, after thorough investigation of local needs and job opportunities.

If such a course is recommended, the following principles should be observed:
The Director should be a full-time professional librarian, and recognized library subjects should be taught by professional librarians.

Proper facilities, i.e., staff offices, lecture room and separate laboratory, should be available. The institution where the course is held should have an adequate, already organized library.

Because there is a lack of text books to support the programme, the Department of Education should insure the provision of proper materials for a basic teaching collection, which may include the writing of essential texts.

Practice work is most important, therefore courses should be held in areas where there are a number of diversified libraries, directed by professional librarians.[4]

Library techniques programs were flourishing in eight colleges during the academic year 1970–1, with a ninth expected to offer the courses within a short time. A spokesman for the Department of Education reported that the graduates were being well received in every type of library, and that they were having no difficulty in finding positions. The main problem remained one of finding suitable teaching staff and of ensuring that they were freed from duties in the college library so that they could plan their programs in advance.

In the July 1970 issue of the *Ontario Library Association News* the president of the organization for 1970–1, Irma McDonough, expressed her views about the kind of program that would be most appropriate for her term of office.

OLA's year-long involvement should concentrate on the outside influences that affect a library's work – the Wright Commission on post-secondary education, public library legislation, the reorganization of CLA, censorship, library education. Then at the annual conference, small-group discussion on specific areas of interest should crystallize OLA responses to these influences. Perhaps a pre- or post-conference workshop like the one on Picture Books and Children would help divisions or action groups to give members a chance to concentrate and participate intensively on an area of vital concern – for example, censorship threats that libraries have had to face this past year. Several action groups for regional meetings have already been given the go-ahead for airing matters of local concern.

THE INSTITUTE OF PROFESSIONAL LIBRARIANS OF ONTARIO

The initiative for the establishment of a professional organization of librarians of Ontario is attributed to the staff of the Windsor Public Library.[5] Two members of this staff were members of the Windsor Municipal Employees' Association, which helped in an informal way to make their case for salary increases with the local library board. When the association decided that it would include unions only, a special committee of the library staff made a study of union and professional organizations in Canada in order to determine the best course of action. It concluded that it would be preferable to have a provincial federation of library employees rather than become associated with the Trades and Labour Congress.

Considerable credit for the move toward the formation of the professional organization has been given by C.D. Kent to a controversy stirred up by Philip McLeod of the London Public Library and Art Museum Staff, who contributed an article to the November 1953 issue of the *Ontario Library Review* under the title "The Library Schools – A Modest Proposal." In this article he implied that librarianship did not deserve to be called a profession.[6] This challenge produced strong rebuttals and, apparently, a desire to demonstrate that McLeod's views were in error.

A representative of the Windsor group approached the OLA with their proposal for a provincial professional association along the lines of the Ontario Secondary School Teachers' Federation. Four benefits were seen from such a development. 1 / There would be a gain in prestige if librarians were placed on a par with other professional groups such as doctors, engineers, and teachers. 2 / It would be easier to exert influence in such matters as pension schemes and legislation for the improvement of libraries. 3 / Support would be provided for the many small libraries, which, if they turned to unions, would not be able to maintain locals of their own, and would have to join miscellaneous labour groups. 4 / By forming their own federation, librarians would not be forced to break either with labour or with management. The antipathy of many librarians to membership in unions would be avoided, as would the political and ideological pressures of unions.

Discussion about the form and functions of the proposed organization were held at the annual conference of the OLA, which assembled in Kitchener in 1954. While there was no question about the desirability of having holders of A, B, and C certificates as members, considerable doubt was expressed about holders of D certificates and clerical workers. Discussion also centred on the appropriateness of including public librarians, special librarians, school librarians, and university librarians. There was hope that membership might be made compulsory. It was felt that the new organization should at first be part of the OLA, but might later be independent.

A committee was formed to carry action further. During the conference held the next year, this committee drew attention to a number of conditions which called for an organization of the type contemplated. These included the need for job classification and for assurance of the best use of professional personnel, the interest of labour unions in attracting professional employees, the need for closer co-operation between library boards and professional librarians to counteract the fast-developing shortage of librarians, the desirability of having professional librarians promote graduate training and the establishment of refresher courses, the scarcity of serious professional literature in Canada, the prevalence of salaries below the standards of the Canadian Library Association, and the lack of negotiating machinery on salaries, terms of appointment, and fringe benefits.

Matters moved very slowly, with a great deal of discussion but an absence of firm decisions. In May 1957 the committee, after some changes in membership, reached the point of presenting a constitution for a professional section of the OLA. Further delays were caused by differences of opinion over proposals for membership. Having developed a sense of futiilty over the lack of progress, the committee disbanded. Later in the year a new committee of the OLA was formed, and a draft constitution was circulated among potential members. It was proposed that the new section be devoted to maintaining and raising standards of library service and professional competence and to advancing the interests of professional librarians. Membership would be open to university graduates with a BLS or MLS degree from an accredited library school or with equivalent training and to librarians without full normal training who had been employed in a professional position in a library giving service of recognized standard for a period of possibly five years. By February 1958 a petition was ready for the OLA asking that an Institute of Professional Librarians be formed. A motion to this effect was carried.

At an early stage three committees were formed: the Union Study Committee, the Library Information Committee, and the Publicity and Public Relations Committee. The task of the first of these was to collect information on all aspects of trade unions as they existed in Canada and particularly in Ontario; the Publicity and Public Relations Committee would publicize the role of the professional librarians; and the Library Information Committee would publicize the work of the Institute of Professional Librarians. The necessity of distributing a regular newsletter was recognized.

It was not long before members of the institute realized that their organization would have no legal status unless it was incorporated. Without incorporation it would not be in a position to take firm action to protect members who were, in its view, dismissed without adequate justification. The process of incorporation which was then undertaken necessarily meant withdrawal from the OLA. The key step was taken when letters patent were granted by the Provincial Secretary in 1960 to the Institute of Professional Librarians of Ontario (IPLO). When all the necessary legal arrangements had been completed, the new institute functioned under a Board of Directors consisting of eleven members.

During the 1960s the institute recognized a responsibility for sponsoring and encouraging informal educational programs for the professional development of its members. It attempted to achieve this objective by sponsoring, either by itself or in co-operation with agencies such as graduate schools of library science, a variety of seminars, workshops, lectures, and conferences. According to a Special Supplement to the February 1970 issue of the *IPLO Quarterly*, there was a difference of opinion among the members as to whether continuing education was a legitimate goal for the institute.[7] Some were said to feel that this activity had developed to the point where it excluded other concerns. It was observed that, although meetings held in various parts of the province had been quite successful, they had not resulted in an increase in membership. The majority, however, seemed to be in favour of the program.

The development of the institute was a disappointment to a good many librarians during the 1960s. It did not evolve into a licensing body with control over admission into the profession. The benefits provided for individual librarians were not great enough or obvious enough to give membership the appearance of a moral imperative, and a decreasing proportion of those who were eligible joined the organization. According to the minutes of the fifty-sixth meeting of the Board of Directors, held in February 1969, only 19 graduates of the University of Toronto School of Library Science in 1967–8, out of a possible 151 who were employed in Ontario, had joined the organization.

Writing in the July-August issue of *Canadian Library* in 1969, J.P. Wilkinson asked rhetorically what had gone wrong with a fifteen-year-old dream.[8] He felt that the institute seemed to have instituted too little and that, as an institute of professional librarians, it had hedged on professionalism. There was still a lack of agreement on the nature of the distinction between professionalism and unionism. There appeared to be a prevalent notion that a professional group constituted an end in itself. Those who advocated control over admission to the librarians' ranks through licensing were not able to show that such a development was necessary to protect the public interest. In Wilkinson's opinion,

... an "effective" concern on the part of the I.P.L.O. with reinforcing professional status through self-governing Institute action must involve a demonstration of a public need for protection as well as of a membership desire for self-improvement through professional self-government. The difficulties implicit in attempting such a demonstration are obvious in a calling which lacks a sense of real and present urgency and of strong member homogeneity.

The IPLO did not play a very important part in new developments in the field of librarians' training. It had no significant involvement in the establishment of a library school at the University of Western Ontario. It did somewhat better when the Department of Education introduced a program in the colleges of applied arts and technology for the training of library technicians in that it was given representation on the Provincial Consultative Committee on Library Technician Training. The purposes of this committee were to advise on the establishment, location, and effectiveness of existing courses and to maintain liaison with the local advisory committees appointed to ensure that standards, teaching facilities, and qualifications were maintained at each institution where library technician training was offered.

At the beginning of the 1970s there was a prospect that some Ontario universities might offer an undergraduate library science program. The position of the institute was one of unequivocal opposition to such a development. It was felt that the subject discipline requirements for librarians should not be reduced, as they would be in such a program. Further, the institute was unwilling to support a proliferation of kinds of librarians, particularly at a time when the role of library technicians had not yet been completely defined. There was special antipathy to the idea of a BLS degree awarded at the completion of an undergraduate program.

THE ASSOCIATION OF PROFESSIONAL ENGINEERS OF THE PROVINCE OF ONTARIO

The engineering profession in Ontario, organized under the title The Association of Professional Engineers of the Province of Ontario (APEO), was identified by statute for the first time in 1922. The legislation passed in that year remained in force, although amendments were made from time to time, until the new act replaced it in 1969. The legislation was not at first very satisfactory to those who wanted to see a strong association, since membership was not made compulsory. Several abortive attempts were made during the 1930s to include the desired regulatory provisions.

Finally in 1937 an amendment gave engineering the status of a self-regulating profession. Successive amendments in 1947 and 1950 provided for the formulation of a code of ethics and for its enforcement.

The by-laws of the association, enacted within the terms of *The Professional Engineers Act* of 1968–9, placed the management of the affairs of the association in the hands of a council. There was provision for five regions: the Western Region, the West Central Region, the East Central Region, the Eastern Region, and the Northern Region. Each of these had a regional congress consisting of regional councillors, the chairman of each component chapter, and one other member of each chapter's executive committee. The chapters constituted the basic units of the association. In 1968 the membership of about 26,400 professional engineers made the Ontario association by far the largest in the country.

The association assumed a major responsibility for the establishment and maintenance of standards of knowledge and skill among its members. It also undertook to influence academic and professional requirements for registration. Its influence was exerted through the accreditation of engineering undergraduate courses in Ontario universities. A graduate of such a course, after two years of acceptable engineering experience, was granted the full privileges of a professional engineer. Recognition was also granted to accredited courses in other Canadian universities and to those accredited by the Engineers Council for Professional Development in the United States. A thorough study was made of universities in other parts of the world; graduates of those considered to meet Ontario standards were admitted without further requirement while others had to write prescribed examinations. Those who had completed only a part of an engineering course might also be registered to practice by passing examinations.

As a means of maintaining standards of practice the APEO encouraged its members to participate in a number of educational programs. Among these were university-related courses, including full-time graduate courses, evening classes, and workshops or seminars. Of considerable importance also were technical society programs which disseminated information on new technology through periodicals such as the *Engineering Journal*, published by the Engineering Institute of Canada, the *Engineering Digest*, the official organ of the APEO, and other publications of Canadian, American, and British origin. Educational objectives were also pursued through technical meetings, evening classes, workshops, and seminars. Among seminars co-sponsored by the APEO were two dealing respectively with Law for Engineers and Managing Engineers. Until recently the association was involved in home study courses offered in co-operation with the Department of Extension of the University of Toronto. In 1969 the responsibility for such courses was transferred to the Engineering Institute of Canada. Subjects offered in 1969--70 were mathematics, applied mathematics, technical subjects, accounting, administration, economics, education, English, law, political science, psychology, and statistics.

THE CHEMICAL INSTITUTE OF CANADA

The Chemical Institute of Canada became the national professional and scientific organization for chemists and chemical engineers. The membership consisted of professional and university student members organized in sections across the country. The work of the institute was conducted nationally by the Council and Board of Directors and by local executive officers. Educational activities affected senior high school students, university undergraduates, and members of the profession.

As of 1969 educational service to high school students was largely in the form of vocational information and guidance. Brochures dealing with chemistry and chemical engineering were published in English and French, and continually revised and re-issued. Copies were distributed widely without charge to the recipients. Local sections maintained liaison with high schools in their areas to ensure that they were adequately provided with information about chemistry, chemical engineering, and associated professions. The institute published a journal for high school teachers of chemistry called *Canadian Chemical Education*.

Among the sixteen or so organizations supporting the Youth Science Foundation, the institute was one of the most active. Through this foundation it supported the Science Fair program, which was designed, along with other measures, to interest high school students in careers in science. The foundation published a periodical called *Science Affairs* for senior high school students.

The institute demonstrated considerable interest in the quality of teaching in secondary schools. In the late 1960s it carried out two surveys of teachers' qualifications and science teaching facilities. It was hoped that these would make a significant contribution to the improvement of standards in high school chemistry teaching.

The influence of the institute in university circles was exerted mainly through its Student Chapter program. There were approximately fifty of these chapters located on the campuses of practically all Canadian universities and at a number of technical institutes. Their activities touched on all fields of science and the scientific professions. Tours were arranged on a trial basis for representatives of the Canadian chemical industry to speak on careers of a non-research nature. The institute published the *Student Chapters Bulletin*, a quarterly which contained material of particular interest to the undergraduate.

Nearly all the scientific and technical programs of the institute might be classified as continuing education. Among those of particular note were professional development courses offered for a number of years at annual conferences. These were designed to update individuals who had graduated some years earlier and wanted a concentrated course in recent developments. Similar courses had also been presented for some years at the Annual Canadian Chemical Engineering Conference. The institute was contemplating the extension of the professional development course program to serve areas that were remote from normal facilities. Another contribution in the field of continuing education was a series of correspondence courses offered in conjunction with a number of universities. These ranged from highly specialized scientific courses to those of a more general and cultural nature. Interest was being shown in the possibility of developing some of these courses so that they might carry credit toward certain graduate degrees.

There were several miscellaneous activities with a fairly direct bearing on education. 1 / Each year from 1961 on, the Chemical Education Award was presented to a person who had made an outstanding contribution in the field. 2 / The Chemical Education Division of the institute prepared a major brief on scientific education in Canada for submission to the appropriate federal and provincial authorities. 3 / The institute participated in the two Canadian Conferences on Education and in the UNESCO Commission Forum on Continuing Education for Engineers in 1966.

THE CANADIAN MEDICAL ASSOCIATION
From the time of its incorporation in 1867 the Canadian Medical Association (CMA) had an active role in promoting medical education and continuing medical education for its members. Most of its educational objectives were accomplished through the organization of autonomous bodies with specific roles, such as the Medical Council of Canada, the Royal College of Physicians and Surgeons, the College of Family Practice, the Canadian Council on Hospital Accreditation, and the Canadian Hospital Association. All of these originated as committees of the CMA.

The association took an interest in the preparation and recruitment of well-qualified candidates for the university medical schools. In this cause it urged adequate secondary school courses in the physical and biological sciences, and called attention to deficiencies in English expression among students. In order to attract a share of the best minds to the medical profession, it published various brochures, included educational material in the *Canadian Medical Association Journal*, and encouraged physicians to participate in careers day programs in secondary schools.

In 1930 the General Council of the association, recognizing the need to standardize intern training and to raise the quality of such training in Canadian hospitals, authorized the Department of Hospital Services, and later the Committee on Approval of Hospitals for Internship, to establish and enforce a set of standards. A booklet was prepared containing an outline of the requirements for approval. An arrangement was also made with the American Medical Association for the reciprocal recognition of approved hospitals in Canada and the United States. New scientific developments and changing social conditions called for continued attention to the specifications. Similar to the program for approval of internship programs was that for schools of physical and occupational therapy, the responsibility for which was assumed by the Committee on Rehabilitation. The CMA was also involved in other paramedical education programs such as those for medical laboratory technologists and radiological technicians. Bases for approval of these programs were outlined in the appropriate documents, prepared in co-operation with various other associations.

THE ONTARIO MEDICAL ASSOCIATION

The Ontario Medical Association (OMA) was formed through the initiative of physicians in Toronto and Hamilton in 1880. The organization was incorporated under provincial law in 1921. Its major objectives were defined as follows: to cultivate the sciences of medicine and surgery, to promote public health, to raise the standard of medical education, to assist in the advancement of medical legislation, to improve and standardize hospital services, and to serve humanity and the medical profession by investigation, study, and research in all matters in which the profession could properly interest itself. Membership was open to all medical graduates resident in Ontario, and in 1970 the total of about 9,500 represented approximately 75 to 80 per cent of all practising physicians in the province. There were special membership provisions for those aged sixty-five and over, for those unable to practise for health reasons, and for those leaving Ontario. There might be up to twenty-five living honorary members.

One of the earliest achievements of the association was the formation of a medical library for the province in 1885. At the end of the 1960s this library, operated by the Academy of Medicine, Toronto, had 70,000 volumes and 900 current journals. In 1898 a study was conducted leading to a recommendation to the Ontario government that lighting and ventilation of classrooms be improved. Later studies led to pressure to end child labour, which was prohibited by the Factory Act of 1905, and to medical inspection of school pupils.

Activities having a bearing on education in recent years included a survey of handicapped children in 1960, which provided a basis for official and voluntary agencies to attempt to improve the co-ordination of services, including rehabilitation and education, for such children. The same cause was furthered in later years by rehabilitation conferences sponsored by the OMA. Briefs were presented to the Ontario government with respect to public health, education, traffic safety, taxation, youth, aging, civil rights, workmen's compensation, ambulance services, the healing arts, the incorporation of the professions, and medical services insurance.

An OMA postgraduate education program was begun in the 1920s to keep the members up to date, particularly those in areas without convenient access to teaching centres. Clinical speakers were supplied for branch society, district, and section meetings. Grants were made, amounting to $15,000 in 1967, to assist the continuing education programs of medical schools. An OMA medical librarian contributed to medical library services. The annual meeting in Toronto, the largest of its kind in Canada, included three days of scientific sessions and section meetings.

Members were provided with regular issues of the *Canadian Medical Association Journal* and the *Ontario Medical Review*. The latter, published by the OMA after 1922, featured legal opinions and information on legislation, medical economics, investment and estate planning, and other matters of interest. Public information services were maintained to disseminate information about the medical profession and to build up support for causes which it attempted to promote.

THE ROYAL COLLEGE OF PHYSICIANS AND SURGEONS OF CANADA

The Royal College of Physicians and Surgeons of Canada was incorporated by act of the federal Parliament in 1929 to establish qualifications signifying training and competence in special branches of medicine or surgery. The educational interests of the college were thus particularly in the field of graduate medical education. One of its functions, as indicated in a brief submitted to the Commission on the Relations between Universities and Governments in December 1968, was to set fellowship examinations in fourteen medical and nine surgical specialties.[9] At that time there were 4,389 fellows of the college, over 94 per cent of whom were resident in Canada. In many teaching hospitals fellowship in the college was a requirement for an appointment to the staff. For the previous twenty-five years the college had also set examinations leading to specialist certificates. As compared with the fellowship examinations, these demanded a lesser knowledge of medicine or surgery and of the basic sciences. The brief reported that there were 13,207 holders of certificates in Canada, including fellows of the college, who qualified for them automatically.

A major function of the college was to establish standards of graduate training. According to the brief to the commission, graduate programs had been prescribed in twenty-four specialties. The usual program was of four years' duration beyond the internship, and was the same for both fellowship and certification examinations where both were conducted. In fulfilling its responsibility for maintaining educational standards, the college began a program in 1947 for the accreditation of hospitals offering graduate training.

The college held the view that the best arrangement for graduate training in the medical and surgical specialties was to have teaching hospitals closely affiliated with medical schools. It therefore encouraged the universities to expand their training programs. Recognizing the high costs of university participation in graduate medical education, it urged adequate financial provision for the establishment of the necessary facilities. For example, it presented a brief to the Canadian Universities Foundation in 1964 on the financing of higher education in Canada.

There was evidently some feeling at one time that the relationship between the college and the Canadian medical schools left something to be desired. Matters were said to have been improved by the establishment of the Association of Canadian Medical Colleges, an affiliate of the Association of Universities and Colleges of Canada. Liaison was effected through the exchange of representatives at certain meetings. Co-operation with various national professional specialty societies was also regarded as being of increasing importance.

In January 1968 the college began the publication of a quarterly journal, the *Annals of The Royal College of Physicians and Surgeons of Canada*, which was intended primarily as a house journal to inform fellows of the college and certificated specialists about college affairs. It also included a certain amount of scientific material derived from the major lectures delivered at the annual scientific meeting and the prize-winning research awards.

THE COLLEGE OF FAMILY PHYSICIANS OF CANADA

The College of Family Physicians of Canada, as it was renamed in 1968, was founded by general physicians in 1954, and incorporated by federal legislation in 1960 as the College of General Practice of Canada. It was seen as a means of improving the competence of family practitioners through education, paralleling the contribution of the Royal College of Physicians and Surgeons of Canada to practitioners specializing in a restricted field of medicine or surgery. Its work was said to be based on two assumptions: that family practice was an important field in its own right and not merely the absence of a specialty, and that the physician who elected to cover the broadest spectrum of services could not be satisfied with the minimum amount of training. The major functions of the college were considered to be to help bring about an increase in the availability of training facilities and to encourage family practitioners to make greater use of these facilities. Another important objective was to influence medical educators to improve curricula and the quality of instruction at the undergraduate, residency, and graduate levels.

The annual scientific assembly, held in different parts of the country and sometimes abroad, was regarded as an important educational experience for the participants. One feature of these meetings was the daily continuous showing of the best available medical films. Financial assistance from donations and lectureships from various scientific organizations made it possible to provide qualified speakers. Provincial chapters also held annual assemblies lasting from one to four days, with an academic program providing local opportunity to earn study credits.

The college claimed some credit for the establishment of a family practice section at a number of medical colleges across Canada, with general practitioners as instructors. It also exerted pressure in favour of a second year of internship for those anticipating family practice as a career. Recognizing the inadequacy of the basic undifferentiated training of the undergraduate program, the college undertook in 1965 to study the concept of advanced or graduate training in family practice. Several pilot projects were undertaken, involving a three-year period of training after graduation.

As a service to members, the college created a Medical Recording Library consisting of tape-recorded lectures by Canadian authorities. The original tapes were continuously revised and updated, and new ones added. To provide for those who did not own tape recorders, disc recordings were made and sold on an annual series basis at very low cost.

In discharging its major function of promoting continuing education, the college co-operated with university departments of continuing education, hospitals, and other medical organizations to provide up-to-date, practical, and attractive courses of particular value to family doctors. An annual fund was administered by the college to enable provincial and regional chapters to organize clinical days and other formal teaching programs at local hospitals. A monthly periodical, the *Canadian Family Physician*, was provided free of charge to all general practitioners in Canada. It constituted a means of keeping members informed of college activities and of publishing technical articles with a bearing on the needs of the family physician. As a means of encouraging contributions an annual literary award of $500 was instituted for the best submission. Further contributions to the encouragement of continuing education were made in the form of awards for graduate study. Certain grants were offered to help defray expenses incurred in attending refresher courses lasting two weeks or more, while others were available for study periods of six weeks or longer. As part of a Commonwealth program, one member of the college was granted a Nuffield Travelling Scholarship in each three-year period. This award was intended to defray the cost of travel and maintenance and the expense of a replacement during the recipient's absence from his practice.

The conditions of membership were such as to exert pressure in favour of continuing education. An active member had not only to be a graduate of a recognized faculty of medicine and to have been in general or family practice for five years, but also had to submit satisfactory evidence of having completed one hundred hours of postgraduate studies in each two-year period in order to remain in good standing. A medical graduate engaged in general or family practice, approved internship, or approved residency, but without the five years of experience required for full membership, might be admitted as an associate member provided that he met the same requirements of postgraduate study. Study credits could be obtained by attending the annual Scientific Assembly of the college or the annual assembly of a provincial chapter, by attending the annual convention of the Canadian Medical Association, l'Association des médecins de langue française du Canada, and provincial medical societies, by taking courses initiated, sponsored, and approved by a university, by taking courses conducted by recognized medical teachers, by taking courses initiated, sponsored, or approved by the College of Family Physicians of Canada or its provincial and regional chapters, or by engaging in other formal training judged acceptable by the national or provincial education committees of the college.

THE ROYAL COLLEGE OF DENTAL SURGEONS
OF ONTARIO

From the time of its establishment in 1868 the Royal College of Dental Surgeons exercised its main responsibility for standards of dental practice by examining candidates for admission to the profession. It exerted a strong influence in favour of the establishment of a Faculty of Dentistry at the University of Toronto. In later years it supported the extension of training facilities to the University of Western Ontario. The nature of its powers and responsibilities gave it a powerful voice in dental education. In addition to its involvement in programs for dental practitioners, it ruled on applications by colleges of applied arts and technology to establish courses for dental assistants.

There was a growing interest during the 1960s in providing an opportunity for continuing education for members of the college. For example, a Centenary Seminar was held at the University of Toronto in the summer of 1968. The Faculty of Dentistry provided the necessary facilities and assisted with the organization. The success of the project led to a similar event in 1969 at the University of Western Ontario called the Royal College of Dental Surgeons Memorial Seminar. Plans were made for the third conference in the series to be held at Toronto in 1970. Local seminars in various parts of the province were also held with the assistance of funds from the Ontario Department of Health.

The Board of Directors of the college, meeting in 1969, took note of the new interest on the part of legislators in the requirement of proof of continued competence in dentistry. There was a considerable range of points of view on this issue among members of the profession. The Executive Committee made four recommendations applying to the Continuing Education Committee: 1 / that it review the existing system of extramural and extension lectures, considering such factors as need and attendance, and give further attention to administration and co-ordination; 2 / that, as part of its review, it arrange to consult the deans and heads of departments of continuing education; 3 / that it do some long-range planning with respect to the Memorial Lectures, and 4 / that it study the future role of study clubs and of the Academy of General Dentistry.

THE ONTARIO DENTAL ASSOCIATION

The Ontario Dental Association has a very long history, having been founded in the year of confederation. Its early efforts, like those of so many other professional associations, were devoted to the establishment of standards for practitioners, based on certain educational requirements. At the third meeting, held in Toronto in 1868, the members approved the wording of a proposed bill, which they succeeded in having passed through the Legislature during the same year. This bill required that all those practising dentistry in the province must be examined by a Board of Examiners. In incorporating the Royal College of Dental Surgeons of Ontario, it covered procedures for electing members of the Board of Examiners, authority to establish and control a dental college, the granting of certificates of licentiate of dental surgery, and provision for prosecuting those not holding licences who practised dentistry. Despite amendments, the substance of the legislation remained the same for the next century. It was the first measure of its kind in the world, and the forerunner of many similar acts in other provinces and countries.

The second major achievement of the organized profession was the upgrading of educational standards for the licence. In 1925 the college agreed to turn over its property to the University of Toronto, except for an equity of $50,000, and a Faculty of Dentistry was created. Further information about this development is given in volume IV, chapter 3, of this series.

At the organizational meeting of the Canadian Dental Association in 1902, each province was urged to set up a formal education committee. The Ontario association responded in 1909 with what was at first called simply the Education Committee, and later the Dental Public Health Committee. Among other achievements, it began the publication of *Oral Health* in 1911, prepared subject matter for booklets distributed by the Department of Agriculture, sponsored lectures at normal schools and public meetings, had dentists appointed to sanatoria staffs, outlined lectures for nurses, appeared before municipal councils urging the provision of dental services in schools, and encouraged local societies to form education committees. By 1912 Toronto had the first free government-sponsored dental clinic for the poor in North America.

An unsuccessful effort was made in 1935 to persuade the government to attach a dentist to the health unit opened with financial support from the Rockefeller Foundation in Prescott-Russell-Glengarry-Stormont. The first appointment of this kind was made in Welland-Crowland in 1950. Another of the major activities of the association during the postwar period was the encouragement of studies of the effects of fluoridating drinking water and the promotion of such a practice once its value had been established.

The relative reduction of the rural population, combined with a demand for higher standards of dental care, was a problem which the Dental Public Health Committee tackled with vigour. Since it was a well known fact that a boy who was brought up in the country or in a small town was more likely to set up a practice there than one brought up in the city, a campaign was organized to identify promising recruits for the profession while they were still in high school. These young people were brought to Toronto, shown the facilities for dental training, given information about the possibilities of dentistry as a profession, and entertained at an annual dinner.

There was a major restructuring of the association in the 1960s, arising partly out of confusion in the minds of many members about its functions in relation to those of the Royal College of Dental Surgeons. The two bodies formed a liaison committee in 1961 to study the situation. Two years later a firm of management consultants was engaged to conduct an investigation and recommend changes. Its chief proposal was that the Royal College of Dental Surgeons should relinquish to the Ontario Dental Association all its activities except those relating to training, examination, licensing, certification, and the regulation of the profession. Local societies would become branches of the Ontario Dental Association and elect representatives to serve on the governing body. The Ontario Dental Association in turn would become the corporate member of the Canadian Dental Association for Ontario. Nearly all of the recommendations of the management consultant firm were accepted, and the association was thus put in a stronger position to serve the interests of its members in educational and other respects.

A major educational activity of recent years was the holding of a three-day annual convention, attended by approximately 1,500 dentists, at which clinicians from Canada and the United States presented papers on all aspects of dentistry. In 1969 there were thirty-six component societies which held evening meetings or all-day clinics where a clinician presented a paper. This type of program was offered by the Academy of Dentistry, an association of dentists in Metropolitan Toronto. At both the provincial convention and the academy winter clinic there were also programs for dental hygienists and dental nurses. As a further service to members the *Journal of the Ontario Dental Association*, containing scientific articles and items of general interest, was published monthly.

THE CANADIAN DENTAL ASSOCIATION

The Canadian Dental Association was recognized as the national body for organized dentistry of which the Ontario Dental Association was the corporate member. It maintained a Council on Education, appointed by the Board of Governors, to deal with educational questions. As defined in material prepared for the Second Canadian Conference on Education in 1962, the council's duties were 1 / to study, to develop policies on, to evaluate, and to review dental educational programs, 2 / to support reciprocity in provincial dental practice licensure through a national examining board, and 3 / to encourage recruitment of desirable candidates for the study of dentistry.[10]

Considerable credit was given to the council for the improvement of facilities for dental education in the six Canadian universities which offered such a program by 1960, including one newly established at the University of Manitoba. The accrediting committee was said to have reinforced the council's efforts by using gentle but effective persuasion on the universities concerned. As a means of encouraging research in university faculties, the association spent several thousand dollars each year to support studentships, fellowships, and equipment grants.

A major educational contribution of the association was in the field of publication. It produced a monthly journal, a *Governors' Letter*, a *Dental Economic Newsletter*, pamphlets, and films. Some of these were designed to keep the membership aware of new developments and trends. Others provided information about careers in dentistry: for example, a brochure called *Dental Officer Training Plan, The Canadian Armed Forces*. Still others promoted dental health habits and dental care. Among these were pamphlets and leaflets entitled *Care Following Dental Surgery*, *Facts Favour Fluoridation*, *How to Brush Your Teeth*, and *Broken and Infected Teeth Can Be Saved*. Films produced by the association came in two classifications: those for lay audiences and those for the profession.

In conjunction with its program of providing candidates for dental education with information about the dental profession and about courses of study leading thereto, the association assisted dental schools with the selection of students. To this end it maintained, in co-operation with the American Dental Association, a program of aptitude testing. As of 1970 participation in the program was either recommended or required by every Canadian dental school. There were test centres in nine widely dispersed centres in Ontario. The tests were designed to measure the applicant's ability to read scientific material with comprehension, to demonstrate manual dexterity, to reason with numbers, manipulate numerical relationships, and deal intelligently with quantitative materials, to use and understand the meaning of words, to visualize the reconstruction of two- and three-dimensional patterns, to demonstrate knowledge in the field of elementary biology and chemistry, and to apply principles and solve problems in the fields of biology and chemistry.

THE CANADIAN PSYCHIATRIC ASSOCIATION

The Canadian Psychiatric Association was established as the national organization for physicians working in the field of psychiatry. According to the by-laws approved in 1963, active membership was open to any duly qualified medical practitioner licensed to practise in one of the provinces who had specialized in psychiatric practice for at least three years before applying. There was also provision for associate, inactive, and corresponding membership for those who could not qualify for active membership.

The objects of the association were stated in the same by-laws:

1. To further the increase of psychiatric knowledge and to encourage and develop research into the causes, treatment and prevention of mental disorders.
2. To establish an organization on behalf of the psychiatrists of Canada for their mutual benefit, for the exchange of scientific information and for the promotion of their professional welfare and usefulness.
3. To represent the members of the Association in their relationships with the Government of Canada, provincial and municipal governments, universities, medical associations, and other associations, organizations and bodies with which the psychiatrists of Canada from time to time may have relationships.
4. To encourage psychiatric education in universities, hospitals and related institutions and the establishment of mental health clinics, demonstration units and other facilities for the advancement of psychiatric education, and for the improvement and extension of the treatment of mentally ill persons.
5. To publish journals and other literature for the dissemination of psychiatric knowledge to medical practitioners and others.
6. To receive bequests, donations, grants of money and to raise monies by membership fees, public subscription or in any other manner that is not contrary to the laws of Canada or any of the provinces for the carrying out of the objects of the Association.[11]

Although these objectives had a large educational component, the association did not itself make a practice of providing educational programs. The various provincial associations, all affiliated with the national organization, were active in offering refresher courses for their members. The Canadian Psychiatric Association published a scientific journal called *Canadian Psychiatric Association Journal.*

THE ONTARIO COLLEGE OF PHARMACY
The Ontario College of Pharmacy made a practice of sponsoring regular series of lectures in various centres around the province such as Ottawa, London, Toronto, Kingston, and Brantford. These were ordinarily held once a month between September and May, and have attracted about 10 per cent of the potential audience. The speakers were members of the

Faculty of Pharmacy in the University of Toronto, pharmacy residents in various hospitals in the province, community pharmacists, and members of the Ontario College of Pharmacy itself. Topics varied from problems facing the profession to sophisticated presentations on drugs and drug therapy.

The college also made a practice of conducting a three-day seminar in Toronto every two years for pharmacists from across the province. The papers presented there usually dealt with drug therapy. All lectures were reproduced and copies made available to any pharmacist in the province, along with such other printed material as might be considered worth distributing. The series of twenty lectures conducted by the Faculty of Pharmacy of the University of Toronto every fall and spring on some aspect of drug therapy were well attended by members of the college. Educational material was distributed through a monthly newsletter and a bulletin published five times a year.

As of 1969 the college was considering a substantial expansion of its program of continuing education. One possibility was that centres might be set up in various places around the province to which all pharmacists might have convenient access. A pharmacist in each centre would be trained as a speaker and supplied with prepared lectures on drug therapy for presentation to his audience, with maximum assistance from existing audio-visual aids.

Interest was also being shown in an experiment begun in Minnesota in 1966, where there was a problem of supplying up-to-date information to over 2,200 pharmacists in a widely scattered area, many of whom were unable to attend seminars and short courses at the Minneapolis campus of the University of Minnesota. The medium adopted to reach them was closed circuit television. In an experimental try-out half-hour video tapes were secured, each attempting to cover an entire disease category and presenting the drugs considered useful in its treatment. An expert delivered an additional thirty-minute presentation on the same topic on live television, followed by questions posed over the telephone and answered on live camera. The response was sufficiently enthusiastic that an expanded program was planned.

Another interesting technique involving the employment of amplified telephone calls (the tele-conference technique) was used by extension services in pharmacy at the University of Wisconsin. The network linked more than 115 hospitals, university centres, and courthouses in the state. All points on the circuit had a loudspeaker and handset. To hear the proceedings a participant turned on the loudspeaker, and by using the handset he could make himself heard at all the listening points. The technique was used mainly to conduct formal and informal classes followed by discussion periods. A trial of the system in 1966 produced an overwhelmingly favourable response. As a result a fourteen-week course covering all aspects of institutional pharmacy was offered. Each lecture, carefully prepared beforehand, was accompanied by slides, reading references, and other materials which were distributed to the listening centres in advance.

THE REGISTERED NURSES' ASSOCIATION OF ONTARIO

A brief account of the development of nursing education in Ontario is given in volume VI, chapter 19, of ONTARIO'S EDUCATIVE SOCIETY. A good many references are made there to the development and the educational contributions of the Registered Nurses' Association of Ontario (RNAO). This section attempts to focus attention more directly on the organization as such.

The organization began as the Graduate Nurses Association of Ontario in 1904. From the early stages its members devoted their efforts to the establishment of standards of education and practice for nurses. Realizing that desired improvements in nursing service would be achieved only through legislation providing for the registration of those who met recognized standards, they presented a series of draft bills to the Ontario Legislature. In 1922 *The Nurses Registration Act* was passed, meeting many of the conditions requested by the association, but denying it the responsibility for enforcement, which was left in the hands of the Department of Health. Continued pressure was exerted for the passage of an act that would grant rights of self-determination to the profession. Finally in 1951 what had, since 1925, been called the Registered Nurses' Association of Ontario was authorized to establish minimum standards for entrance to schools of nursing, to determine the content of the curriculum followed in the schools, to set qualifying registration examinations, to register successful candidates, and to discipline members of the profession. For the time being the government retained the right to approve schools of nursing.

During the 1950s the association acquired office space, equipment, and a large staff to carry out its new functions. In 1959 a request was made to the Minister of Health for the remaining statutory power. The minister, reluctant to see a voluntary association given so much authority, proposed instead the formation of a new statutory body called a college. The RNAO gave this suggestion a good deal of consideration before bestowing its approval, subject to the principle that the profession had the right to determine its standards of education and practice, and to the condition that the governing body consist of elected representatives of every member of the profession residing in Ontario, who would constitute the voting majority, along with the appropriate cabinet minister.

In 1960 the executive of the RNAO called a conference attended by the Minister and Deputy Minister of Health and representatives of the Ontario Medical Association, the Ontario Hospital Association, schools of nursing, the Ontario Hospital Services Commission, and other interests.

Agreement on the principles and policies formulated by the association paved the way for the latter to prepare a draft bill governing all the legal aspects of nursing, including those at that time covered by *The Nursing Act* and *The Nurses Registration Act*, for both registered nurses and nursing assistants. After consideration by the minister, this bill was submitted for the approval of members of the profession at a general meeting. A *Nurses Act* was subsequently passed by which the Ontario College of Nurses took over the statutory powers in question, including the right to inspect nursing schools. After that date the RNAO continued in various ways to exercise its diminished powers in the cause of professional improvement.

The RNAO consistently campaigned for the highest possible qualifications for teachers of nursing. A series of six three-week institutes held between August 1966 and July 1967 might be considered indicative of some of the tangible steps taken in pursuit of this goal. A total of sixty-nine Ontario schools of nursing were represented, with each school contributing between one and six participants. At the first four institutes topics dealt with included the role and responsibilities of the teacher (with emphasis on interpersonal relationships), teaching methods, the selection of learning experiences, and evaluation. The teaching was done largely through discussion, with some use of audio-visual aids. It became evident during the sessions that many of the participants needed more opportunity to work out the practical implications of the theory with which they were dealing. A desire for assistance in curriculum planning was also evident. The last two institutes, restricted to nurses with at least one year of university preparation and two years of teaching experience, were devoted to this topic.

A resolution approved by the members at the annual meeting in 1966 led to the adoption of a program, formally known as the Plan of Action, to provide advanced training in such clinical and specialty areas as medical-surgical, obstetrical, pediatric, and psychiatric nursing. An *ad hoc* committee was appointed to determine how such a program could be carried out. According to the plan, accepted at the annual meeting the next year, the association offered a considerable range of services: 1 / assistance in identifying community needs, resources, and possible locations for formal programs; 2 / consultation with respect to planning and initiating programs; 3 / provision of information about short courses currently available within the province; 4 / provision of assistance to educational institutions, agencies, and course directors in preparing for and conducting programs; 5 / referral of identified learning needs of nurses to appropriate institutions or agencies within the province; 6 / provincial co-ordination of clinical programs for registered nurses; 7 / suggestions of areas for needed research relating to continuing education for nurses.

The program was designed to cover a five-year period consisting of two phases. During Phase I, to be carried out in 1969–70, the main efforts would be devoted to 1 / the development of minimum curricula, 2 / the conduct of pilot projects in educational institutions such as regional schools of nursing and colleges of applied arts and technology, 3 / the formulation of criteria for approving programs, 4 / the conduct of area studies in various locations to determine the suitability of clinical, educational, and community resources for training programs, 5 / the assembly of a list of resource people and potential teachers in each area of nursing practice, 6 / the development of a central information service indicating opportunities for formal continuing education available through the RNAO, 7 / the formation of an advisory group, consisting of representatives of allied professions, to assist the co-ordinator of the program, 8 / the identification of needs for training programs and the establishment of priorities, and 9 / the referral of program proposals not coming under the plan to the appropriate educational institutions. Phase II, lasting from 1970 to 1973, would involve 1 / the continued development of training programs, 2 / the drawing up of a roster of graduates and the maintenance of contact with them, 3 / the conduct of a study to determine the best means of ensuring recognition for nurses pursuing further education, 4 / the development of programs to update practice, to offer a means of qualifying for registration, and to assist nurses in functional areas, and 5 / measures to encourage follow-up studies of graduates. One such study would involve the construction of profiles of continuing learners with which participants in various programs might be compared.

A list of post-diploma clinical nursing programs in non-university settings available at various times and in various locations was as follows: psychiatric nursing at Ryerson Polytechnical Institute in May and September 1969 and in September 1970; pediatric nursing at Ryerson in September 1969 and September 1970; operating room nursing at St Michael's School of Nursing, Toronto, in September 1969 and March 1970; operating room technique at the Hotel Dieu Hospital in Kingston in May and November 1969.

A campaign conducted in Metropolitan Toronto in 1967 to attract inactive nurses back into part-time service at a time of serious shortage indicated the association's concern for providing the best possible service to the public. The project was carried out co-operatively by the RNAO, the Ontario Hospital Association, and the Ontario Hospital Services Commission, which formed a joint co-ordinating committee with a full-time director. To counteract the reluctance of many former nurses to return after a lengthy break, the RNAO and the hospitals of the area offered six-week refresher courses. The Ontario Hospital Services Commission contributed a substantial sum to finance the program.

Preliminary steps involved sending a letter to each of nineteen thousand registered nurses residing in Metropolitan Toronto and the counties of York, Peel, and Ontario. An attempt was made to determine the local response to refresher courses and to identify the factors influencing the return of inactive nurses to professional service. Among the most common problems mentioned by the respondents were the need for day care centres for children and the need for flexibility in the hours of work for part-time nurses with children. Some saw as an obstacle the low rate of pay for part-time nurses and the effect of income tax regulations.

Through the refresher courses an attempt was made to provide a basis for continued learning in the form of orientation and in-service education. The program was designed to provide knowledge of current trends in health services and nursing and an awareness of the relationship between these and the health needs of society, to re-establish the ability and confidence of the participants, and to teach them to make effective use of available resources for continued learning. An effort was made to deal with each participant on the basis of individual need.

The courses aroused considerable enthusiasm among many of the participants. Toward the end of 1968, after nine courses had been offered, a waiting list of applicants began to develop for the 1969 schedule. Some of those enrolling were in active service but considering a change in their area of employment. Other centres in the province expressed an interest in offering the courses for local residents. While many of those who completed the courses found it difficult to locate part-time work that met their requirements, there was evidence of some change in the attitude of hospital officials toward this type of service.

A major aspect of the work of the RNAO was the holding of conferences for various groups of members and other participants. The topics for discussion commonly included various aspects of nursing education such as admission requirements and curriculum. Some of the best illustrations of this type of activity were to be found in conferences for directors of schools of nursing.

Plans for meeting the shortage of nurses announced by the Minister of Health in 1965 caused a number of difficulties and some confusion. In certain schools enrolment outdistanced the available facilities and teachers. There were problems in adapting instructional programs to the two-plus-one pattern. The meaning of the internship year was unclear in many minds. Proposals to establish new regional schools caused anxiety about the adequacy of clinical facilities. As a result of repeated requests by directors of schools of nursing for assistance in planning changes, in interpreting the criteria for different types of programs, and in clarifying the role and authority of the College of Nurses and of the Ontario Hospital Services Commission with respect to granting approval for changes in programs, a conference for these officials was held in January 1966.

A series of resolutions, mostly carried unanimously, indicated considerable dissatisfaction with the program for the expansion of nursing training outlined by the Miinster of Health the previous year. The group favoured the principle of the two-year program for the preparation of nurses at the diploma level – an alternative to the two-plus-one scheme – and went on record as supporting the establishment of schools offering such a program provided that they satisfied the criteria established by the College of Nurses. The group also felt that, if the Ontario Hospital Services Commission wished to finance the cost of nursing education and the maintenance of students by providing bursaries and loans for those requiring assistance, the resulting indebtedness should be met in the same way as that incurred for other student loans available in Ontario. In sponsoring the meeting the RNAO was performing its function of focusing the dissatisfaction of a group of its members with certain actions of officialdom. Some of the discussion indicated the feeling that the nursing profession was not in fact nearly as close to self-determination as the theory suggested.

The next conference involving the same group was held two years later. A series of meetings preceded it, leading to the formation of a Planning Committee for a Conference for Directors of Schools of Nursing. The objectives of the conference were to enable the participants to discuss recent changes affecting nursing education and plans for health services in Ontario and to provide a forum for a discussion of ways and means of accelerating recruitment into the nursing profession. Contrary to the implications of the title, assistant directors of nursing schools attended in addition to directors.

Many of the resolutions passed at the conference had a direct bearing on education, as a selected list will show. 1 / A universal application form should be adopted by diploma schools of nursing, and an *ad hoc* committee should be appointed to co-operate with the staff of the College of Nurses in developing the necessary form. 2 / Consideration should be given to the establishment of pre-entrance tests to assist schools of nursing in the selection of students. 3 / The recently amended regulations of the College of Nurses with respect to minimum entrance requirements to schools of nursing (involving the relaxation of some conditions) should be supported. The reasons given for this stand were that current society acknowledged that every individual should have the maximum opportunity for self-development, that schools of nursing should have flexibility in meeting objectives, and that an increased number of graduates was required to meet the health needs of the people of Ontario. 4 / Directors of schools of nursing should accept a responsibility for providing and interpreting information about the requirements for admission and career opportunities in nursing to school guidance officials and others working in the same area. 5 / The conference reiterated the resolution of 1966 that the two-year program for the preparation of diploma-level nurses be supported, and that a school proposing to offer such a program be permitted to do so, without undergoing an interim period as a two-plus-one school, provided that it met the criteria established by the College of Nurses. 6 / The directors of schools of nursing should become involved in initiating regional planning for nursing education. 7 / Continuing conferences and workshops should be held for nursing service personnel to define the various positions required to provide nursing care and for faculty personnel to plan curricula to prepare people for these positions, to plan for the implementation of such curricula, to participate in programs of continuing education, and to improve their techniques in guidance, counselling, and interviewing applicants and students. 8 / The Council of the College of Nurses and the RNAO should be encouraged in their efforts to develop nursing programs in colleges of applied arts and technology.

Another type of conference was held in March 1969 for those involved in public health nursing. The objectives were to enable the participants to examine the needs of public health nursing practice, to share information about studies being conducted in public health nursing, and to receive up-to-date information about current preparation of graduates of basic nursing education programs in Ontario. It was intended that the delegates, who were in charge of large and small health programs throughout the province, would return to their units with information and ideas and discuss them with their colleagues. At a later stage a second conference would be held and recommendations made.

There were several factors leading to the organization of the conference. With the expansion of health services and the change in their emphasis which had been marked in the immediately preceding period, there had been an enlarged role for public health nurses and a demand for an increase in their numbers. Pressure was being exerted on agencies employing them to fill their vacancies. At the same time there was a tendency among universities to phase out their certificate programs in public health as well as in other branches of nursing. It seemed particularly desirable to define the respective roles in public health nursing of the university graduate, the holder of a diploma, and the holder of a certificate. Several groups of public health nurses were meeting independently in various parts of the province to consider the direction that public health nursing would take in the future. The RNAO recognized its responsibility for co-ordinating these initiatives.

The schedule of conferences for the year beginning in September 1969 included the following, some held in co-operation with other associations: Conference for Nurses in Health Services in Colleges of Applied Arts and Technology; Nursing Conference of the American College of Obstetricians and Gynaecologists; 13th Annual RNAO Conference on Personal Growth and Group Achievement; Conference for Directors of Nursing; Conference on the Nurse's Reactions and Patient Care; Institute of Nursing Home Care; Conference for Public Health Nurses; Conference for Faculties of University Schools of Nursing; Conference on Our Role in the Hospital Emergency Department; Conference on the Staff Nurse and Her Leadership Role; Conference for Directors of Schools of Nursing; Conference for Nurses in Staff Education and Staff Development. In addition, individual chapters of the association held conferences and workshops.

THE CANADIAN NURSES ASSOCIATION

The educational concerns of the Canadian Nurses Association, as described in 1969, were as follows. 1 / It sponsored workshops with such topics as social and economic welfare, nursing service, and nursing education, usually in co-operation with provincial nurses' associations. Reports were prepared on some of these workshops. 2 / It provided assistance in the form of senior resource people for workshops organized by provincial associations. As an example, institutes for non-professional personnel in nursing libraries were held in 1968. 3 / It published two journals, the *Canadian Nurse* and *L'infirmière canadienne*, to keep members informed of association activities and of matters of current interest in the profession, including new developments. 4 / It provided a library service to all its members across Canada and abroad, involving loans of books and documents, reference service, and free bibliographies. 5 / Consultant services were offered to institutions, provincial associations, and other groups in the areas of administration, nursing education and service, economic and social welfare, public relations, and library services.

THE CANADIAN ASSOCIATION OF OCCUPATIONAL THERAPISTS

The establishment of provincial societies of occupational therapists preceded that of the national organization. One was founded in Ontario in 1920 and, when granted a provincial charter in 1921, already had branches in Hamilton, Kingston, London, and Ottawa. Although plans for a Canadian organization had been largely completed by 1928, and a slate of executive officers elected, a government charter was not granted until 1934.

As listed in its submission to the Committee on the Healing Arts in 1966, the objectives of the association were as follows:

(a) To maintain an organization on behalf of the occupational therapists of Canada for their mutual benefit; for the exchange of scientific information and for the promotion of their professional welfare.
(b) To represent the members of the Association in their relationship with federal, provincial and municipal governments, universities, medical and other national and international associations, organizations and bodies with which the occupational therapists of Canada from time to time may have relationship.
(c) To establish and maintain proficient standards for occupational therapists in Canada.
(d) To provide a consulting service for its members; for schools of occu-

pational therapy, hospitals and other institutions which employ occupational therapists.

(e) To assist in the planning of occupational therapy departments and programmes.

(f) To operate a placement service for the benefit of occupational therapists and organizations which require personnel.

(g) To recommend salary scales and personnel policies.

(h) To provide publicity material and exhibits for the recruitment of students and the provision of information regarding occupational therapy to allied organizations and the general public.

(i) To promote an understanding of the value and use of occupational therapy among all treatment and rehabilitation groups and to promote its further development.

Much of the association's effort to ensure standards of proficiency had a direct bearing on education. For example, it defined minimum levels of education, advised on the development of new schools, examined the curricula of such schools, assessed programs for adequacy of clinical experience, and provided a consulting service to hospitals and members of the profession. It published the *Canadian Journal of Occupational Therapy*, a quarterly designed to exchange scientific information, to disseminate knowledge about occupational therapy, to keep the members up to date on the activities of the national and provincial associations and of the World Federation of Occupational Therapists, and to promote an understanding of the value and uses of occupational therapy. An active recruitment program was conducted through the distribution of literature, a careers booth exhibit at the Canadian National Exhibition, participation of members in career days at secondary schools, and the provision of recruitment kits for speakers. Annual conferences and study courses were conducted to exchange scientific information, to advance and develop the profession, and to promote the cause of occupational therapy.

In an effort to ease the shortage of occupational therapists, the association established a school at Kingston in 1959. It benefited from federal-provincial rehabilitation grants and from the services of members of the Faculty of Medicine at Queen's University, who lectured on medical subjects. Admission to the course, of eighteen months' duration, required a university degree or diploma or a registered nurse's qualifications. The course was continued until 1967.

Short courses were provided through the national or the provincial organizations before the annual conference in October. Consideration was being given in 1969 to the offering of a refresher course for occupational therapists desiring to return to practice after a prolonged period of absence. The lack of sufficient training facilities had, up to this time, been a factor in preventing the idea from being implemented. There seemed a possibility that short courses might eventually be conducted in hospitals.

THE CANADIAN ASSOCIATION OF SOCIAL WORKERS

Although the concepts involved are as old as deliberate and conscious efforts on the part of one human being to promote the welfare of his fellows, social work as a profession is of comparatively recent origin. The first Canadian school of social work was established in Toronto in 1914. When the Canadian Association of Social Workers was formed twelve years later, the only other such school was in Montreal. Among the objectives of the founders of the organization were to interpret professional social work to the board members of agencies and to the public, to recruit young people to the profession, and to influence the direction of social services.[12] The original organization had committees on membership, placement, publications, and service standards.

During the first few years of the association's existence, there was insufficient agreement among the members to enable them to formulate a policy on social work education.[13] The problem was that a large number of them were executives of agencies whose status might have been threatened by too much emphasis on education. For the time being, the association concerned itself chiefly with the distinction between trained and untrained workers. Uncertainty among social workers themselves reinforced doubts in the university community that social work properly belonged there.

A number of activities with some bearing on education characterized the period of the 1930s and 1940s. Publication of *The Social Worker* began in 1932. A report on professional training for social work in Canada was produced in co-operation with what was then called the Canadian Council on Child and Family Welfare. Association branches encouraged the opening and expansion of university schools of social work, and exerted pressure for the improvement of the content and quality of instruction. Efforts were made to persuade young people to prepare for careers in social work. Concern with educational facilities for social workers led to the holding of conferences on social work personnel in co-operation with the Canadian Welfare Council and the Canadian Committee of Schools of Social Work in 1943 and in 1948.

In 1952 the association produced a statement of standards to be met by medical and psychiatric social service departments in hospitals, clinics, and sanatoria. This statement specified that the content of an educational and training program for social work staff and students should be determined by the social service department in conformity with administrative policy. Sufficient staff members were to be provided to carry out regular social work duties as well as to conduct the educational program. Affiliation with an accredited graduate school of social work was recommended. It was suggested that the social service department, with the approval of the hospital or clinic administrator, initiate or participate in courses or conferences about the social aspects of illness with doctors, interns, medical students, nurses, students, and other professional groups within the hospital. The educational process was said to continue outside the formal teaching program of the department. Each member of the staff was to assume a reesponsibility for interpreting the social aspect of illness in everyday work.

In 1956, following a series of local and regional workshops, a national workshop on social work education was held in co-operation with the National Committee of Canadian Schools of Social Work and the Canadian Welfare Council. The Canadian Welfare Council subsequently formed a Commission on Education and Personnel for the Social Services, which pressed for the expansion of social work education at all levels. During this period efforts were made to secure official action on a number of other social causes. The position of the association was strengthened in 1956 by federal incorporation. Action was also taken to establish provincial organizations in Ontario and other provinces.

During the 1960s the association was active in sponsoring conferences in co-operation with federal government departments, schools of social work, the Canadian Welfare Council, the Canadian Medical Association, and the Association of Universities and Colleges of Canada. Delegate conferences were held every two or three years. Policy statements were issued on such matters as undergraduate education and promoting enlarged opportunities for social work education, as well as on a considerable number of non-educational issues. A particularly comprehensive undertaking in 1969 was a series of highly structured and intensive workshops for the purpose of defining competence in the social worker.

In 1969 a committee was engaged in devising a plan to implement an earlier report on the development of criteria for recognizing programs of university education for social work. In view of the rapid development of educational programs in the community colleges, it had been asked to consider the entire spectrum of education for the social services. Membership included representatives from graduate, undergraduate, and community college programs.

THE CANADIAN INSTITUTE OF CHARTERED ACCOUNTANTS
AND THE INSTITUTE OF CHARTERED ACCOUNTANTS
OF ONTARIO

The Canadian Institute of Chartered Accountants became the co-ordinating body for the institutes of chartered accountants in the ten Canadian provinces. These provincial institutes had complete authority over the educational requirements and standards of their members. Thus the development of a national policy was possible only to the extent that they could be persuaded to co-operate. The first effort to perform this function was undertaken by what was then designated the Dominion Association of Chartered Accountants in 1902. In 1909 it was agreed that provincial institute members would automatically become members of the national association. At the same meeting the principal role of the national association was defined as that of assisting the provincial institutes.

The desire for greater uniformity in standards among provinces led in the same year to the establishment of a committee to investigate the matter. Over a number of years this committee recommended that only qualified chartered accountants manage practising offices, that only matriculants be permitted to study for admission to the profession, that there be a minimum of two professional examinations, and that a uniform code of ethics be adopted. The association also exerted pressure on the federal government in favour of the accounting profession.

Publication of the *Canadian Chartered Accountant* began in 1911. Beginning as a quarterly, it included proceedings of the institute's annual meetings, reports from provincial institutes, and members' listings. In successive stages the journal became a bimonthly and then a monthly publication. Other forms of publication constituted an increasingly important and valuable aspect of the work of the institute. A catalogue for 1969–70 lists a large number of items ranging from small booklets to substantial books consisting of hundreds of pages, some of them in both English and French.

Before 1921 the Institute of Chartered Accountants of Ontario had a system of qualifying examinations, but no comprehensive system of instruction. Students prepared themselves by a variety of different methods such as private tutoring, cram courses, and correspondence courses, mostly originating in the United States. Dissatisfaction with this situation led in 1921 to the introduction of an official correspondence course. While such an approach left a good deal to be desired, it was the only practical way to reach the scattered body of students in the province, many of whom were outside the university cities of Toronto, Kingston, and London. Because of its experience with correspondence courses as a chief instrument for extension work, and because it was the only university in the province with some full-time accounting staff, Queen's University was asked to assist with the program. Its accounting staff, with part-time assistance for non-accounting lessons and those on specialized accounting subjects, wrote the original course. Their work received the approval of the Board of Instruction of the institute.[14]

The institute course became compulsory for all registered students in Ontario except for those granted partial exemption because of university standing. It was also widely adopted for use in other provinces. Although it remained the chief instrument of instruction, it was gradually supplemented in varying degrees by lectures and discussions organized by the institute or by student associations. After 1964 Ontario students with a university degree were eligible to take the correspondence course in three years along with full-time summer courses of four weeks' duration. Graduates holding a Bachelor of Commerce degree with introductory work in accounting were granted exemption from the primary examination, and were required to have only three years of service instead of four. Unlike most other provinces, Ontario gave no special recognition for a BCom degree with an accounting major.

In 1955 the Education and Examinations Committee of the Canadian Institute of Chartered Accountants commissioned a study as a basis for long-range educational planning. The main recommendation of the resulting report was that university graduation be made a requirement of admission to the profession. After further study by a subcommittee of the Interprovincial Education Committee, the councils of all provincial institutes agreed to this proposal, with implementation at some indefinite date. A report prepared for the Ontario institute in 1962 reaffirmed support for the principle, but suggested that the change not be made until the proportion of university graduates undertaking training had reached the 70 or 75 per cent level.

The Mackintosh report of 1967 recommended that the provincial institutes adopt as their target for the future the transfer to approved universities of all instruction required for qualification as a chartered accountant, ultimately on a full-time basis, except such limited instruction as might be judged to be more effective when the student had some practical experience in public accounting. Mackintosh noted that it had hitherto been impossible to achieve any consensus among institute committees and university representatives as to the subjects in which advanced instruction should be postponed until the period of practical experience. He apparently believed, however, that the difficulty was subject to resolution. As to the minimum period of practical service required after the award of a BCom degree with an approved accounting major, he felt that two years was preferable to one year, the only alternative he thought worthy of consideration. He was unequivocal in his recommendation that provincial institutes should continue to set a uniform final examination, and that their appointees should continue to grade the answer papers. The universities should accept no responsibility in the matter. University staff members who contributed their special knowledge and the benefits of their experience should do so as members of an institute.

At the annual meeting of the Ontario institute in June 1969 a by-law was approved by which, after the close of registration in the fall of 1971, all registered students would have to be university graduates. An educational program was introduced by which instruction was to be taken primarily in university credit classes. Forty-five semester hours were required in a group of subjects consisting of financial accounting, management accounting, auditing, taxation, computer science, quantitative methods, finance, economics, law, and management. The student could meet the academic requirement by taking credit courses 1 / in a regular undergraduate program or as a special full-time student after graduation,

2 / as a registered student of the institute at a university summer school or in a part-time evening program, 3 / through a correspondence program conducted by one of a number of universities, or 4 / under certain circumstances, by participation in a program offered by specified universities under institute sponsorship. In accordance with the recommendations of the Mackintosh report, an additional institute program was to be maintained in the areas of advanced auditing, taxation, and specialized and advanced accounting, where a more practical approach would be followed than in the university courses. This program would require approximately ten semester hours.

For students with the necessary qualifications who resided near York University or McMaster University, it was possible to work simultaneously for credit in the chartered accountancy program and for the degree of Master of Business Administration. Both these universities offered MBA classes in the evening on a trimester basis. It was expected that an additional year of study would be needed for the MBA after the institute requirement had been met.

A special plan was arranged through the University of Waterloo whereby a student could meet the chartered accountancy requirement in a degree program in the Faculty of Mathematics and simultaneously meet a considerable part of the practical experience requirement through the university's co-operative program. The two types of requirements could be met in little more time than it would take to obtain the degree alone.

Despite the new regulation the institute proposed to continue to accept some grade 13 graduates on the basis of conditional registration in order to avoid undue hardship to prospective candidates and to the firms that would otherwise have hired them. Such students might register if they were employed by a practising firm while studying on a part-time basis in a degree course. The practice they obtained while studying would be recognized once they had obtained a degree. The period of experience required for registration as a chartered accountant continued to be three years for all university graduates in spite of the Mackintosh recommendations.

The new program ended the primary and intermediate examinations after the students preparing for them were accommodated. No matter how the program of forty-five semester hours was taken, the sole examinations required were those set by the university. The same arrangement covered special classes sponsored by the institute. The only remaining institute examination applied to the ten-semester period of instruction for which the institute retained responsibility.

The Canadian institute established a Continuing Education Committee in 1960 to maintain and increase the competence of its members. The educational program had two aspects: 1 / evening seminars of one to three days' duration to acquaint members with new techniques and current trends in a wide range of taxation, professional practice, and management topics, and 2 / in-depth courses for specialists covering an extended period, such as the Canadian Institute of Chartered Accountants Tax course, made up of four in-residence periods, home study assignments, and periodic examinations. The three-day annual conference ordinarily included a number of technical sessions on topics in accounting, auditing, consulting, management, and taxation. Other sessions were devoted to research and education.

In 1968 two intensive five-day computer courses were offered. The inspiration for this initiative was provided by a report of the Computer Committee, which warned that planned developments in the computer field would make a large part of the profession obsolete unless the members made a strong effort to meet the challenge. The first course was designed to provide a basic understanding of the concepts, applications, and techniques of data processing and to break down the psychological barriers surrounding the computer. The second course was intended to prepare the participant to evaluate major internal control functions in a computer-based system and to audit a medium-sized system. The instructional approach used involved a combination of video tape and hands-on experience. Periods of fifteen minutes of taped talk were alternated with work periods of thirty to forty-five minutes.

A Committee on Public Relations of the Canadian Institute of Chartered Accountants attempted to increase awareness of the profession among the business and academic communities, the general public, governments, and foreign accounting bodies. To this end it issued promotional booklets and brochures, as well as recruitment films, and conducted a program to publicize newsworthy activities of the profession. Provincial institutes, including the Ontario institute, also maintained public relations programs.

THE GENERAL ACCOUNTANTS ASSOCIATION OF CANADA
AND THE CERTIFIED GENERAL ACCOUNTANTS
ASSOCIATION OF ONTARIO

What was at first designated the Canadian Accountants Association was formed in 1908 with these objectives:

(1) To unite fraternally and socially, for mutual benefit, those engaged in accounting.
(2) To promote amongst its members the study of the science of accounts, the knowledge of the principles of credit and commercial law, the science of finance, applied economics and other objects of practical value, and to encourage the interchange of ideas and experiences by the reading of original papers, discussions, debates and lectures, and by other means calculated to arouse interest and cause research.

When the organization was incorporated by an act of the Canadian Parliament in 1913, the name was changed to the General Accountants Association of Canada.

An abortive attempt was made in 1913 to form a branch of the national association in Toronto. It was not, however, until 1921 that there were sufficient members to meet this objective. In 1931 the Toronto branch formed a study group which had the benefit, during the winter months, of lectures by outstanding lawyers and accountants as well as by some of its own members.

As time went on, local organizations sprang up in Oshawa, Ottawa, St Catharines, Sault Ste Marie, and Windsor. In 1954 the Toronto branch approved the formation of an Ontario Council, consisting of five representatives of the Toronto branch and two of the Ottawa branch, with full power to apply for Ontario letters patent, with educational privileges. The council was duly authorized to appoint Legislation and Education Committees and to arrange for an Ontario university to use the University of British Columbia course with adaptations to meet Ontario requirements. The name Certified General Accountants Association of Ontario was adopted in 1955. Arrangements were made at the same time for affiliation with the national organization and for the amalgamation of the Ottawa and Toronto branches. A provincial charter was granted in 1957.

During the rapid growth period after 1958 working arrangements were made with universities and community colleges, and new lecture centres were opened in various parts of the province. In 1966 the association introduced a program of continuing education courses, which were open to any graduate or to any member of the public at any time of the year, and to students during the summer months. The first of these courses was called Basic Computer Concepts and the second the Human Side of Management.

The study program introduced in the 1950s covered a five-year period for applicants admitted with grade 12 standing. Those with a Bachelor of Commerce degree usually enrolled in the third year of the course. The student (later called undergraduate) was required to have the kind of employment in accounting or finance that enabled him to obtain acceptable practical experience concurrently with his studies. Subjects in the course were accounting, mathematics of finance, statistics, business law, information systems, financial analysis, economics, office management and systems, advanced cost accounting, auditing, income tax, and controllership. The successful candidate was entitled to use the initials CGA after his name. The National Coordinating Council on Education and the Dominion Board of Examiners had the responsibility for the courses of study, for maintaining standards, and for setting, reviewing, approving, and marking the examinations.

The continuing education course in basic computer concepts, also offered by correspondence, was designed to teach the student the terms commonly used to describe the components and operation of an electronic computer system, to provide him with examples of elementary computer programming, to enable him to recognize the desirable features of a good computer system, to help him understand or install system controls and audit trails, to tell him what he should expect from a computer system and how the system should assist him in his work, to enable him to employ standard techniques and tools in problem solving, to teach him how computers could be used as problem-solving tools, to give him a glossary of computer terms and a data-processing bibliography, and to give him the entrance prerequisite to advanced computer system courses. The course in management covered such matters as motivation, leadership, communication, interviewing, employee orientation, management by objectives, planning and work measurement, formal and informal organization, group behaviour, the process of change, discipline and control, and the resolution of conflict.

THE CANADIAN INSTITUTE OF ACTUARIES

The original organization of actuaries, the Actuaries Club, was formed in 1907 in Toronto "to promote in a social way actuarial knowledge of assurance among its members." Membership was at first sharply restricted, but the requirements were gradually relaxed. The slightness of the program was indicated by the fact that an attempt to charge an annual fee of $2 was voted down in 1936. By 1946 the membership had grown from the original twenty-four to over two hundred, and is said to have included all the well known names in the actuarial profession in Canada.

While the activities of the club were largely social, it was given credit for considerable influence on the development of actuarial thought in Canada. Its committees were involved in calculating rates and in drafting clauses for the total disability and double indemnity benefits adopted by most companies. Members prepared a schedule of occupational ratings which were regarded as useful for many years. The most important activity was considered to be that of assisting members and students to prepare for the actuarial examinations. Lectures were initiated in 1923, and study circles were organized six years later.

In 1946 a committee, established to examine the status of the club, recommended that it be reorganized on a national basis. This committee proposed that a bound and indexed report on the proceedings of each meeting be produced and that there be an annual membership fee. The Canadian Association of Actuaries was accordingly formed and a constitution adopted. The new organization absorbed the Toronto club as well as a comparable one in Winnipeg.

The association gave way to the Canadian Institute of Actuaries, which was incorporated by federal legislation in 1965. The change was said to have reflected the desire of actuaries to have a more professional, or perhaps stronger, organization than the association had been. There was also pressure to establish formal standards of qualifications for the profession that would be recognized in federal and provincial legislation for accreditation purposes, and possibly as a basis for licensing. The role of the actuary seemed to be increasing rapidly in importance because of the growth in insurance and pension funds.

Requirements for fellowship in the Canadian Institute of Actuaries were in the late 1960s attained by passing ten examinations set by the Society of Actuaries, a North American organization. Although not absolutely essential, a university education was regarded as a highly desirable prerequisite to an actuarial career. Courses in actuarial science were offered in such Ontario universities as Queen's, Toronto, Waterloo, and Western, as well as a few in other parts of Canada. The student was urged to take the first two examinations, which covered basic mathematics, while still in university. Later examinations were usually written after graduation when the candidate was employed. They tested him on the more advanced mathematical and business aspects of insurance and pension programs, preparation for which required practical experience. It ordinarily took four or five years after graduation to complete the entire examination program.

As of 1968, the Canadian Institute of Actuaries co-operated with the Society of Actuaries in preparing and administering correspondence courses to help candidates prepare for some of the examinations. These courses consisted of questions designed to give the student a means of checking his grasp on the work. They were not considered to be a desirable substitute for lecture courses where a local instructor was available. The course was handled by tutors, who were ordinarily employed by local firms. The fee of $25 was often paid in whole or in part by the firm employing the student.

THE AGRICULTURAL INSTITUTE OF CANADA

The Canadian Society of Technical Agriculturists brought together professionals in the field of agriculture in a voluntary association for the first time in 1920. The Canadian government granted the organization a charter in 1928. As a means of achieving legal status for the profession, steps were taken in 1945 to establish agrologist institutes under provincial statutes as the provincial divisions of the association, which was renamed the Agricultural Institute of Canada. The Quebec organization, la Corporation des agronomes, maintained independent status rather than operating as a provincial division of the institute. The basic operating unit within the provinces was the branch, to which those registered as agrologists in a provincial agrologist institute might be admitted as members. These people included research scientists, educators, resource use advisers, management consultants, service representatives, administrators, and farmers. Some were engaged in professional practice, while others were professional employees of government, other public agencies, universities, schools, commercial enterprises, and associations.

The general objectives of the organization were to increase the knowledge, skill, and proficiency of the members in the practice of agrology, to enhance the usefulness of agrologists to the public, and to ensure to the public the proficiency and competency of agrologists. The particular functions of the national organization included representing agrologists at the national and international levels on matters of concern to the food and agricultural industry, the profession, and the general public; co-ordinating and standardizing the agrologists' acts in the various provinces; improving professional standards and practices; co-ordinating and stimulating the exchange of information and views between various scientific disciplines and agricultural science by holding national meetings and by publishing in the scientific and professional fields; sponsoring Canadian speaking tours by internationally prominent agricultural authorities; promoting official recognition of the profession of agrology in national and international circles; administering nationally recognized honours and awards for members and other outstanding Canadians; promoting the growth of professional solidarity; and improving remuneration, working conditions, and employment benefits for the agrologist. Provincial activities were of a similar nature, with appropriate modifications to suit the different sphere of operations. Much the same might be said of the work of the branches. Obviously a good deal of the work could be included under a broad definition of education.

The chief publications of the institute were the bimonthly *Agricultural Institute Review* and three scientific journals: the *Canadian Journal of Soil Science*, the *Canadian Journal of Plant Science*, and the *Canadian Journal of Animal Science*. The organization also made a practice of publishing the proceedings of scientific societies affiliated with it: the Agricultural Pesticide Society, the Canadian Agricultural Economics Society, the Canadian Society of Industrial Engineering, the Canadian Society of Agronomy, the Canadian Society of Animal Production, the Canadian Society for Horticultural Science, the Canadian Society of Rural Extension, and the Canadian Society of Soil Science. Provincial and national news letters were also issued.

During much of its history the institute maintained committees to study various aspects of agricultural education. Among the topics considered were the teaching of agricultural science in elementary and secondary schools, the qualifications of teachers of agriculture, curricula and academic standards of agricultural schools and colleges, scholarships, teaching and research fellowships, agricultural extension, and the development and maintenance of professional standards and ethics. A substantial amount of money was raised and awarded in the form of scholarships. Accompanying this program were efforts to encourage young people to proceed with their education, particularly in agriculture or biological science courses.

THE ONTARIO FEDERATION OF AGRICULTURE

The Ontario Federation of Agriculture, an association including most of the agricultural organizations in the province, attempted to help farmers to understand the social and economic factors that affected them and to seek favourable legislative and administrative arrangements. The organization was closely associated with certain adult education movements in co-operation with governmental and other agencies. Outstanding among these was Farm Radio Forum, which was taken over by the Rural Learning Association. Other activities included conferences on community development, insurance, marketing, assessment and taxation, expropriation and property rights, and farm accounting. All these conferences were designed to build up a group of informed farm people with a capacity for leadership. Certain matters were considered by an education committee, including curriculum, the costs of education, teacher training, and community colleges. At the end of the 1960s this committee devoted a considerable proportion of its efforts to the manpower retraining program, particularly as it affected those concerned with agriculture.

THE ONTARIO INSTITUTE OF AGROLOGISTS

The Ontario Institute of Agrologists, an organization of professional workers in agriculture, was established by provincial legislation in 1960. Under terms of affiliation with the Agricultural Institute of Canada, all members belonged also to the national organization. In a submission to the Provincial Committee on Aims and Objectives of Education in the Schools of Ontario in 1965, the association defined its interest in education in this way:

1) to assure that every person has an opportunity to [sic] the maximum development of his or her intellectual and personal abilities:
2) to assure that rural youth, and particularly the children of families engaged in agriculture, should have educational facilities and programs at least equal to those for urban youth,
3) that there should be sufficient and appropriate educational facilities and programs for students preparing themselves for professional service as agrologists.

The brief contained a number of recommendations with respect to rural education. It proposed that the consolidation of rural elementary schools be carried out as quickly as possible, without endangering the quality of instruction, in order to equalize educational opportunity between rural and urban areas. It urged that rural school boards be given such financial assistance as would enable them to compete successfully with urban boards for the best teachers. The restricted scope of libraries in the smaller (usually rural) schools might be overcome by a basic grant for library books to all boards, regardless of size, with an additional per pupil grant. The integration of the guidance programs in the high schools with those of the elementary schools associated with them was said to be particularly important in rural areas. Special provincial grants were suggested as a means of speeding up the establishment of kindergartens in rural schools. A particular plea was made for studies relating to the educational opportunities available to rural youth.

At the end of the 1960s the association was initiating an educational program with classes on specific subjects. As a result of the response to a questionnaire mailed to the members, a one-week course called the Science of Weed Control was offered at the University of Guelph. The first effort created such a demand that a second session was held a few months later, and arrangements were made for a repetition of the course in other parts of the province. Plans were also made to hold courses on other topics of current interest.

THE ONTARIO VETERINARY ASSOCIATION
The Ontario Veterinary Association became the licensing body for Ontario, and all veterinarians practising in the province were members. Although it had existed for many years, it began to show an active interest in education only toward the end of the 1960s. Many of the initiatives were taken by the local academies, which were loosely tied to the provincial organization. For more than a decade some of these offered one-day refresher courses for practising veterinarians in various fields.

The association formed a Continuing Education Committee with a number of specific responsibilities. 1 / It was to have control over the planning of scientific sessions sponsored by the association or by subsidiary groups. 2 / It was to organize a minimum of two major courses each year, to be sponsored by the association and supported financially by the participating veterinarians. 3 / It was made responsible for publicizing programs in order to ensure the maximum attendance. At a meeting held in June 1969 it was agreed that a list of possible speakers on various subjects should be compiled by the central committee. Each local association would report a planned meeting at least two months in advance, and the committee would suggest an appropriate speaker. There was a feeling that the interest of members might be increased if some of the presentations were less sophisticated.

At the same meeting there was agreement that four types of courses should be made available. 1 / In-depth courses of several days' duration might deal with one subject such as swine diseases or bovine surgery.

2 / Courses extending through Saturday afternoon and Sunday or Sunday only might be offered by local associations. Where this practice was already established, the courses were reported to be very popular. 3 / Unstructured short sessions offering practice tips might be given during evening or weekend meetings. In some cases different views on a certain topic might be offered at the same meeting or at different meetings held two or three weeks apart. 4 / Demonstration courses might be offered for a limited enrolment – ordinarily at the Ontario Veterinary College. These might be arranged as a follow-up to some of the one-day meetings held locally.

THE ROYAL ARCHITECTURAL INSTITUTE OF CANADA

The desire for closer association and united action on the part of provincial organizations of architects led to the formation in 1907 of the Architectural Institute of Canada. Incorporation followed in 1908, and permission to use the term Royal was granted the next year. According to a revised act of incorporation passed in 1955, the objects of the institute were as follows:

(a) to establish and maintain a bond between the societies recognized by the Royal Institute as component associations and to promote the welfare of the architectural profession in Canada;
(b) to establish and maintain a bond between the Royal Institute and societies or institutes having similar objects;
(c) to promote a knowledge and appreciation of architecture and of the architectural profession;
(d) to promote and make available to the members of the Royal Institute knowledge pertaining to the practice of the architectural profession;
(e) to promote encouragement and recognition of worthy aspirants to the profession.

Provincial legislatures granted powers to the architects' association or registration boards to define principles of professional conduct and to examine the qualifications of applicants for registration as architects. An applicant with acceptable qualifications became a member of the national body, and could use the letters MRAIC after his name. The institute consistently exerted pressure to have the standards of admission raised and to have them made uniform across the country. Support was given to schools of architecture in various universities, including Carleton, the University of Toronto, and the University of Waterloo in Ontario. A recommended standard minimum syllabus was prepared for use by those entering the profession without a university education, with annual examinations based on it. By 1970 this syllabus had been adopted by seven of the provinces.

Two Royal Architectural Institute of Canada College of Fellows

Scholarships, valued at $3,500 each, were offered to qualified candidates beginning in 1968. Their purpose was to enable the recipients to improve their knowledge of architecture through travel, study, or research. A candidate had to be a Canadian citizen with at least three years' residence in Canada and to have graduated within five years of the award from a Canadian school of architecture recognized by the institute. In earlier years a single award of a lesser amount was made for the same purposes every two years.

THE ONTARIO FORESTRY ASSOCIATION

The Ontario Forestry Association originated in 1949 as the Canadian Forestry Association of Ontario, a branch of the Canadian Forestry Association, which had been active since 1900. In the early days the primary purpose was to inform the general public about the values of forest resources and about the need to protect them from forest fires and other destructive agents. The meetings took the form of large public gatherings. As time went on, promotional efforts were made through an increasing range of media such as radio, films, and slides, and through the publication of pamphlets and the journal *Forest and Outdoors*.

Eleven purposes were listed in the charter incorporating the Canadian Forestry Association of Ontario:

(a) TO advocate and promote the full development, protection and utilization of the forest resources of the Province of Ontario for maximum public advantage;

(b) TO advocate and promote a complete stock-taking of the forests of the Province of Ontario comprising location, condition of growth and accessibility;

(c) TO support measures safeguarding the forests from preventable loss, and to encourage public co-operation;

(d) TO urge and encourage all phases of forest research;

(e) TO support the work of Schools of Forestry and Ranger Schools, and to stimulate public education and interest in all phases of forestry;

(f) TO promote restocking of areas where natural regeneration is inadequate and where watershed protection or other sound purposes justify tree planting;

(g) TO promote understanding of the basis of sound land use and of the importance of maintaining under timber growth those areas more useful for tree crops;

(h) TO stimulate, through methods of demonstration and local instruction, a wider knowledge of how farm woodlots may be profitably developed;

(i) TO encourage the development of a balanced programme of national and provincial parks and the improvement of wild life resources for the public welfare;

(j) TO urge the establishment of areas of woodlands about settled communities; and

(k) TO support forest legislation based upon the rights of the public and the needs of forest industries.

When the name the Ontario Forestry Association was adopted in 1958, the purposes were stated thus: "To promote sound land use and the full development, protection and utilization of Ontario's forest resources for maximum public advantage."

At the first meeting of the Ontario association, which was chaired by the dean of the Faculty of Forestry at the University of Toronto, it was decided that the educational program in the province would be devoted to an attempt to sustain and direct public conviction on resource management. Among the topics suggested for the attention of the association were fire prevention, woodlot management, and forest research. One of the first concrete actions was taken in 1950 when a lecturer was employed to visit schools, service clubs, and other agencies to speak on the importance of forestry and on forest fire prevention. This program, similar to those maintained by forestry associations in other provinces, was made possible by a grant of $4,000 from the provincial Department of Lands and Forests. This department lent a truck, a motion picture projector, and a screen to assist with the project. A second tour, begun at the end of the same year, had support from the Toronto Anglers and Hunters Association. In 1952 the program consisted of 950 lectures which were heard by an estimated 150,000 people. Tours continued to be a major part of the work of the association until 1959, after which they assumed lesser importance. While, at its best, the program was considered to be very effective in arousing interest in conservation, it was difficult for a voluntary association to sustain because of a rapid increase in salaries and other expenses, and because of other demands made on the budget. It was felt, further, that there was undesirable duplication of effort in some areas as district staffs of the Department of Lands and Forests increased their lecturing activity. In addition, television made audiences more critical and more difficult to attract.

The Ontario Forestry Association became involved with conservation schools in 1958 when the manager of the association was invited to act as chief instructor of the Dryden High School Conservation Camp. His duties, which he continued to fulfil in succeeding years, consisted of acting as master of ceremonies, giving some instruction, and suggesting modifications in the program. The camp was operated for a three-day period for thirty-six boys and girls from grade 10. In 1960 the manager assumed a similar role in a conservation camp program for all grade 8 boys at Espanola. During the next and subsequent years all grade 8 boys and girls were accommodated in two or three sessions of the three-day program running concurrently. Assistance was provided in a third area with the introduction of the Marathon Conservation School program in 1964. Although such service could not be extended indefinitely, it provided experience that could be used to advantage in other Ontario Forestry Association activities.

The annual report of the president for 1968 included this list of activities under the heading Forestry Education: the publication of four issues of the *Ontario Tree Farmer*, a journal then in its tenth year; continued participation in the Dryden High School Conservation Camp and the Espanola Conservation School; the development of a course in natural resources management to be offered by the Extension Division of the University of Toronto; the sponsoring of an exhibit at the Canadian National Sportsmen's Show; the sponsoring of Forests Week; the provision of assistance in the development of a course in environmental science for grades 9 and 10, and the delivery of addresses to teachers of the course; the sponsoring of a Tree Bee Competition, a tree identification and conservation quiz for grade 6 children in Toronto schools; the organization of a three-day Pine to Prairie Tour for twenty-nine resource rangers and leaders, an interprovincial travel project carried out in cooperation with the Canadian Forestry Association and the Citizenship Branch; the securing of approval for the use of land for a Forest Resource Centre and the preparation of a suggested program for the centre; the distribution of thousands of pamphlets, charts, posters, and stickers to schools, youth, and adult groups.

In an informal statement in 1969 J.D. Coats, secretary-manager of the association and a participant in its work from the early years, suggested that the organization had been chiefly successful in encouraging others to take an interest in its causes. Government departments were much more active than formerly in forest fire prevention, and the public in general had become aware of the Smokey the Bear symbol. There had been a great increase in concern about the litter problem, which the association had tackled when little was being done. There were grounds for the feeling that an influence had been exerted on school curricula, particularly as shown in the recent interest in natural resources and in outdoor education.

THE CANADIAN ASSOCIATION OF BROADCASTERS

The Canadian Association of Broadcasters was established in 1926 to foster, develop, and protect the interests of broadcasting. It eventually claimed as its members an overwhelming proportion of privately owned stations. Members have been expected to adhere to a code of ethics beginning with this statement.

The purpose of this Code of Ethics is to document the realization by proprietors and managers of broadcasting stations that, as publishers and an integral part of the press of Canada, their first responsibility is to the radio listeners and television viewers of Canada for the dissemination of information and news, the supply of entertainment varied to meet the various tastes of viewers, and the necessity for ethical standards in dealing with advertisers and their agencies.

In the realm of providing information the association maintained such projects as Report from Parliament Hill to enable members of Parliament to report regularly to their constituents at no cost to themselves. This program was carried by scores of stations throughout the postwar period. Another information service, offered through the association's Program Exchange in Toronto, was the gathering of Canadian and some foreign programs of high quality and their distribution to member stations. A similar service involving programs in French was performed by the Montreal office.

The association took some pride in the co-operation between member stations and universities. The stations welcomed panels, hot lines, documentaries, news, news analysis, and musical presentations, as well as instructional programs by professors and lecturers. Many of these programs were considered attractive far beyond a student audience. Broadcasters indicated an occasional scarcity of sufficient material of high quality from the universities, and suggested that staff assistance and recording facilities could be made available on a larger scale.

In 1958 the association became concerned about the lack of enough trained people to keep pace with the accelerating growth of radio and television broadcasting in Canada. A committee was accordingly established to explore ways of meeting the shortage. As a result of this committee's deliberations, a special one-month concentrated course for newcomers to broadcasting was offered in 1961 in co-operation with Ryerson Institute of Technology. Any member radio or television station was authorized to enrol full-time or part-time junior employees or individuals known to be interested in entering the broadcasting field. The sponsorship of trainees was considered to be advantageous to the station in terms of a saving in time and salary costs and in the increased efficiency of graduate personnel. There was, of course, an upper limit to the number who could be accommodated.

It was claimed that the Basic Training for Broadcasting course, as it was called, was one of the most complete of its kind ever offered in North America. There were two distinct sections, one for radio and one for television. During the first half of the course the emphasis was on the historical and general aspects of the subject, and during the latter half on the practical. While certain topics, such as broadcast regulations, the network, research, ratings, and administration were common to both sections, most of the subject matter applied specifically either to radio or to television. The outstanding quality of the equipment and facilities at Ryerson was considered to be a vital factor in the success of the course.

A further venture in the field of training began in 1963 when the association first provided in-station training for overseas students in Canada under the Colombo Plan and the Commonwealth Technical Assistance Program. The activity began with a single student, who was in his second year at Ryerson Institute of Technology in the Radio and Television Arts program. The association appealed to its members to provide training opportunities for this student who, as a result, enjoyed a variety of experiences at five different stations. By 1967 the program had expanded to the point where a total of 208 weeks of training were provided for a substantial number of students.

THE INVESTMENT DEALERS' ASSOCIATION OF CANADA
The Investment Dealers' Association of Canada was founded in 1916 as a national, non-profit organization. Its declared objectives were to educate and protect the Canadian investing public and to foster and sustain an environment favourable to saving and investment in Canada. It pursued these objectives by offering correspondence courses and by issuing certain publications.

A home study course, entitled How to Invest Your Money, was developed from questions submitted over a period of several years to investment houses and the Investment Dealers' Association. Topics covered included reasons for investing, a glossary of investment terms, sources of investment information, interpreting financial statements, bonds and debentures, preferred shares, appraising common shares, how to buy bonds and stocks, building an investment portfolio, and managing investments soundly. What was called the Canadian Securities course, in English and French, covered a list of topics that were somewhat too detailed for listing in the present context. Course II of Principles and Practices of Investment Finance in Canada, as offered in 1968–9, covered financial statement analysis, corporation finance, the Bank of Canada, the money market, provincial finance, municipal finance, salesmanship, investment policy, and selling to institutions. This course was intended mainly for directors, partners, and employees of certain firms with access to a wide variety of reference material and to experienced counselling. It was planned as a sequel to the Canadian Securities course.

FOURTEEN

Adult education

It is somewhat anomalous to isolate a small group of associations for identification with adult education, since a majority of the associations dealt with in this volume were concerned directly or indirectly with the education of adults. Those dealt with in this chapter were distinctive in that they either attempted to promote the cause of adult education in general (e.g., the Canadian Association for Adult Education and the Ontario Association for Continuing Education) or else provided educational programs for particular groups of adults. Some concentrated on promoting a specific educational approach or medium of instruction.

THE CANADIAN ASSOCIATION FOR ADULT EDUCATION
The impulse that led to the establishment of the Canadian Association for Adult Education (CAAE) in 1935 was described by W.J. Dunlop in an editorial in *Adult Learning* in 1936.

The Canadian Association for Adult Education was organized because most, probably all, of those who have been engaged for years in the sphere of adult education in Canada felt the need of a definite means of inter-communication, a forum for the discussion of common problems, a source of inspiration for the maintenance of ideals. To labour alone, to wrestle with knotty problems unaware of the means used by others to solve these problems, to plod along unassisted by the advice or the experience of others travelling the same road, is wasteful effort. For one's own peace of mind and for one's encouragement, it is essential to know that others have had the same difficulties and probably, the same triumphs.[1]

These words would be appropriate to the founding of many organizations in addition to the CAAE.

By Dunlop's account a large number of individuals and organizations in Canada known to be engaged in any type of adult education were invited to attend a meeting at the University of Toronto in May 1934. Arrangements were made by a committee of interested individuals in the city of Toronto. The response to the invitations was said to have been overwhelming, with almost everyone demonstrating a desire to tell what had been and was being done in his own special field. There were expressions of keen interest from the American Association for Adult Education and the World Association for Adult Education. The chief problem at the meeting consisted in giving everyone a chance to speak without prolonging the proceedings beyond the scheduled two-day period. The eighty-six delegates and the many visitors were said to have been amazed at the extent and diversity of adult education activities in Canada. They had no difficulty in agreeing that a national organization should be formed and a government charter sought. A survey of adult education in Canada was to be undertaken, a project that was made possible by the benevolence of an interested man who insisted on remaining anonymous.

By the time a second meeting was held in June 1935 the survey had been completed and published in mimeographed form and a charter had been obtained. Most of the meeting was devoted to organizational work. A short time later E.A. Corbett began an energetic and productive career as director of the association. Financial assistance was given by the American Association for Adult Education and the Carnegie Corporation of New York. Dunlop's appraisal was extremely favourable.

The movement for adult education has caught the imagination of Canadians generally. We are on the threshold of important developments. Rarely, if ever, has an organization shown in such a short time the necessity for its existence as has the Canadian Association for Adult Education.[2]

One of Corbett's successors, J.R. Kidd, summarized the functions of the organization for the second Canadian Conference on Education, held in 1962.[3] 1 / It maintained a clearing house, a national library, and an office to provide information about continuing education. 2 / It interpreted the principles and values of continuing education. 3 / It undertook research and arranged demonstrations of new methods and techniques. 4 / It initiated needed services. 5 / It represented Canadian adult education abroad.

The organization's role as a clearinghouse was discharged actively through regional and national conferences, study seminars, special committees, and commissions on various subjects. The Joint Planning Commission discharged a major responsibility in this area by bringing together 1 / such government departments as Labour, Agriculture, and Citizenship and Immigration, which provided educational services, 2 / national services of information and culture such as the Canadian Broadcasting Corporation, the National Film Board, and the National Gallery, 3 / functional groups such as the Canadian Chamber of Commerce, the Canadian Labour Congress, and the Co-operative Union of Canada, and 4 / miscellaneous organizations such as the United Nations Association, the Canadian Film Institute, the Canadian Jewish Congress, and the National Council of the YMCA. Representatives of these organizations met regularly to exchange information and to identify problems that needed attention. They also gave consideration to broader themes such as education about human rights, means of increasing cultural exchanges between East and West, and the uses of broadcasting in education. Their discussions were considered useful in preventing overlapping, focusing effort, and encouraging the joint planning of projects.

In his report on adult education facilities and services in Metropolitan Toronto, published in 1960, Kidd described the chief instruments by which the CAAE attempted to achieve its objectives.[4] Through Citizens' Forum, maintained jointly by the CAAE and the CBC, half a million Canadians listened to weekly presentations on vital national and international problems on radio and television. Study pamphlets were distributed beforehand, and lively and productive discussions often followed the broadcasts. Similar techniques were used in the National Farm Radio Forum to deal with topics of importance to people living in rural areas. The management of the enterprise was shared by the CBC, the Canadian Federation of Agriculture, the Co-operative Union of Canada, and the CAAE. *Food for Thought*, an adult education journal published eight times a year, contained articles on citizenship, community activity, education, social science research, and the mass media. A Commission for Continuous Learning, a department within the association, conducted research into the methods and content of adult education and served as a national centre for experimental work in informal adult education. The staff were prepared to give advice and assistance to business firms, government agencies, labour unions, voluntary associations, and individuals, both inside and outside the country. They also participated in training programs offered by farm, business, and labour organizations, community groups, school boards, departments of education, and universities. The publication *Continuous Learning* appeared shortly after this list was compiled. By 1969–70 the list of publications also included *Accent*, an occasional newsletter for administrators of adult education programs in local school systems, community colleges, and other institutions; *Meeting Poverty*, a newsletter dealing with the economic, social, and educational aspects of poverty; *Trends*, a publication for adult educators appearing at irregular intervals and dealing with subjects such as educational television, creativity, and adult basic education; information service sheets giving a monthly listing of recently produced materials in various areas of adult education; a directory of residential adult education centres; and a directory of chief administrative officials in school board organizations for adult education.

In the annual report made in April 1969 an extraordinary list of donors and organizational members was supplied. It included three federal government departments, eighteen provincial government departments and branches, forty-two schools and school boards, nine other federal and provincial government agencies, fifty-six universities and colleges, fifteen co-operatives, twenty-five labour organizations, eighty-eight business corporations, thirty-three "other national organizations," and seventy-one provincial and local organizations. Total revenue, contributed by these agencies and by individuals, amounted to $241,374 for the year.

Reference to the activities of some of the committees of the CAAE as described in the 1969 annual report will give some idea of the paramount concerns of the association at that time. This treatment is intended to be illustrative rather than exhaustive. The report itself makes no pretence of mentioning every detail that might be of interest to a reader.

The School Board Adult Education Committee had not been particularly active because of the difficulty of getting members from distant parts of the country to attend meetings. A successful workshop had, however, been held at Glendon College, York University, where thirty-five participants had dealt with the theme "Involvement in Adult Education." A keynote address had been followed by presentations by a "reaction panel" and by discussion and comments by the audience.

During the year the Communications Committee had concerned itself with federal government policy on the availability of channels for educational television. While negotiations with the Canadian Radio and Television Commission to obtain the use of one of the UHF channels in Toronto by a consortium of educational agencies had not been fruitful, some progress had been made in obtaining partial use of a VHF channel in Edmonton for the Metropolitan Edmonton Educational Television Association. The latter would share the channel with the CBC for a three-year period. Among the committee's interests was that of providing the greatest possible access to television materials for non-broadcast purposes.

The committee dealing with poverty and adult basic education had had an active and productive year. Among its contributions was a seminar on adult basic education held at Elliot Lake, leading to a request that the CAAE and the Institut canadien d'éducation des adultes co-operate in providing a professional service organization for adult basic educators. Several issues of *Meeting Poverty* had been or were in the process of being published, and demand for them was keen. The committee was taking advantage of the activities of the Special Senate Committee on Poverty to present a brief.

A new committee on human relations training had been formed in 1968, and was considering the kind of organizational structure needed to ensure adequate support for such training. Some direct financial assistance was being received. Consultations were planned for late 1969 and early 1970.

With the aid of a Kellogg grant the Canadian Commission for the Community College, acting as a committee of the CAAE, was investigating the feasibility of a national organization of community colleges. A year's investigation had revealed a disturbing lack of communication and of exchange of information among the colleges. Members of the CAAE saw in the colleges an important opportunity to further the cause of adult education.

An *ad hoc* Committee on Consumer Education, formed in 1968, had devoted five lively meetings to the discussion of consumer affairs and to the planning of an action research project in consumer education. Steps had been taken to establish an Industrial Liaison Committee to assist in planning and organization of the project and to help gain the financial support of the national business associations. The objectives of the first stage of the investigation were to discover what was being done in consumer education, what needed to be done, and how consumer education could be carried on most effectively. These objectives would be pursued through direct contact with consumers at all economic and social levels, by a study of research projects carried out by business and industry, and through discussion with knowledgeable people in the field. In the second stage a number of task forces consisting of people who were well informed about consumer matters and skilled in communication would develop experimental informational-educational programs, conduct courses, prepare curricula, and design effective ways of carrying on consumer education. In the third or action stage the proposed programs would be implemented. It was hoped that financial assistance would be provided by federal and provincial governments and by business and industrial organizations. At the time the report was released, action was being delayed while an attempt was being made to secure the co-operation of the Canadian Association of Consumers.

The Public Affairs Committee, with financial support from the Citizenship Branch of the Department of the Secretary of State, had been involved in the publication of a summary of volume 2 of the Report of the Royal Commission on Bilingualism and Biculturalism. Separate versions had been issued in English and French. It was hoped that the availability of these summaries at low cost would encourage public discussion of the commission's recommendations. The committee had been very concerned over what it saw as the inadequacy of treatment given by the media to the work of royal commissions. There was particular dissatisfaction with the performance of the broadcast media, and pressure was being exerted to improve matters.

The Voluntary Action Committee had been engaged in an intensive study of the relationship between government and voluntary agencies in Canada. The aspects of this relationship under investigation were 1 / legal relations between voluntary associations and government, 2 / the advisory board or council, 3 / grants, contracts, and subsidies, 4 / delegation of government powers and responsibilities to education, 5 / the structure of voluntary associations, 6 / voluntary associations in the political process, community action, and planning, 7 / the situation in Canada as compared with that in other countries, and 8 / new approaches to citizenship participation. The approach used to deal with each topic involved the commissioning of a competent person to prepare a background paper, the holding of a small seminar at which interested individuals reacted to the paper, and the compilation of a pamphlet synthesizing the paper and the views of participants in the seminar. The Citizenship Branch of the Department of State was providing financial assistance for publication.

THE ONTARIO ASSOCIATION FOR CONTINUING EDUCATION

At a meeting at Windsor in April 1964 the Ontario Conference on Continuing Education recommended the formation of an Ontario Association for Continuing Education (OACE) to assist in the provision of a more thorough and co-ordinated service to adult education in the province. As a result, the Canadian Association for Adult Education appointed an organizing committee to establish an Ontario division, which would at the same time constitute the Continuing Education Section of the Ontario Educational Association. Provision was made for existing members of the CAAE residing in Ontario to assume automatic membership in the OACE. Members of the OEA could transfer to the new section if they felt that they had a pronounced interest in adult education.

The OACE offered the following services to its members: 1 / for those involved in informal education, a means of meeting and conferring with others with similar concerns and interests, 2 / an opportunity to broaden the scope and influence of continuing education, 3 / information about resource materials and people, 4 / seminars on matters of continuing education, and 5 / newsletters. Arrangements were made for the distribution of publications produced by other agencies.

According to a calendar of events for 1968–9 leading members of the OACE participated in the following activities: a National Seminar on Basic Education at Elliot Lake in September and October; a seminar at Atkinson College, York University, on "Continuing Education in Metropolitan Toronto" in October, leading to the production of a Metropolitan Toronto Adult Education Directory; a school design workshop sponsored by the Youth and Recreation Branch of the Ontario Department of Education in November; a seminar on "the College in the Community" organized by the colleges of applied arts and technology in November; a workshop on "a Metropolitan Exchange for Continuing Education" held at Forest Hill Centre for Continuing Education in November; a workshop on "the Adult as a Learner" held in December; a meeting of the Ontario Association of Departments of Extension and Summer Schools in February; a meeting of the Executive Committee with L.M. Johnston, Assistant Deputy Minister of Education, held in February; a workshop on consumer education in March; meetings in association with the OEA convention in March; a seminar at the Hamilton Education Centre on "How Adults Learn," held in March; a meeting of community agencies held at Humber College in May.

THE WORKERS' EDUCATIONAL ASSOCIATION

The by-laws of the Workers' Educational Association (WEA), as amended in 1962, indicated the following purposes:

(a) To promote cultural education among working men and women, to enable them to obtain the benefits of a University education and to assist them to acquire the knowledge which is essential to intelligent, full and effective citizenship;

(b) to promote the organization of local branches or district associations in various parts of Ontario;

(c) to call attention to, and to spread knowledge of the facilities for education among all working people;

(d) to publish and to assist in publishing journals and other literature;

(e) to hold conferences and to participate in conferences;

(f) to promote the work of other workers' organizations interested in education;

(g) to serve as a clearing house for information;

(h) to sponsor and initiate researches and studies on education;

(i) to supervise and conduct experiments and demonstrations in co-operation with other local, provincial and federal agencies.

The WEA was founded in Great Britain in 1903 as a result of the efforts of Albert Mansbridge. Under the original title, the Association for Promoting Higher Learning Amongst Working People, its purpose was to interest working men and women in university extension classes, and to promote university extension work of interest and value to working people. The early years were marked by a determined and in some ways a successful effort to break down the barriers between university representatives and labour spokesmen. At a convention in 1906 the principle was established that the tutorial work of the WEA would be administered by an equal number of university and workers' representatives, thus assuring to workers the subjects, the type of instruction, and the tutors they wanted.[5]

Mansbridge visited several of the British dominions, including Canada, in 1917, where he encouraged the extension of his movement. The Trades and Labour Council of Toronto was inspired to petition the University of Toronto for classes of a nature similar to those being offered in Britain, and the university responded by providing an experimental class in political philosophy, which ten trade unionists attended. At a meeting held in Central Technical School in 1918 an association was brought into being. Six classes were offered during that year, and an increasing number in subsequent years. An appeal to the premier of the province, E.C. Drury, in 1922 resulted in a decision that the government would henceforth reimburse the university for the cost of the program.

The association was soon forced to confront a serious problem in terms of the nature of its membership. By 1926 it was claimed that only fifty-six of the eight hundred members attending classes in Toronto were manual workers, and that the rest were white collar workers. In that year the university decreed that the classes would henceforth be limited to "working men and women." These were defined as including all those who were engaged in occupations similar to those followed by trade unionists. This action met with protests on the part of the membership, but to no avail. The number of members in Toronto promptly dropped to 135.

The Carnegie Corporation assisted in the expansion of the association throughout the province by making a grant of $5,000 in 1929. At a convention held in London steps were taken to form an Ontario WEA, and a general secretary was appointed as full-time organizer. A further Carnegie grant of the same amount in 1931 resulted in a growth in the number of district associations from one in each of Toronto and Hamilton to a total of fourteen. Despite the financial difficulties of the depression the members found means of raising the funds needed to maintain the provincial organization. Further Carnegie grants, now paid to the university, made an important contribution to the program. By 1935 there were twenty-two district associations in Ontario, and forty-three classes were offered with an enrolment of 2,012.

The first summer school classes were offered in 1932. In the absence of any permanent quarters these were at first held in private schools in different parts of the province. A building was finally acquired at Port Hope in 1942, and occupied after the necessary renovations had been made. The WEA slogan applying to the summer school was "a holiday with a purpose." The operation flourished for a number of years until lack of interest on the part of trade unions led to a decline in attendance. In 1963 the school was sold and the funds were used to pay the salary and expenses of a full-time provincial organizer.

The WEA introduced the Agricola Study Clubs in 1936. These groups based weekly discussions on lecture notes as well as radio presentations. They evolved into a separate organization, the forerunner of Farm Forum. Another radio series, Labour Forum, dealt with economics and labour problems. The successor to this program was Citizens' Forum, offered as a CBC service.

The existence of the Agricola Study Clubs led to the publication of bulletins and other materials, which were supplied to interested individuals and groups all across Canada. As a result, there was an accelerating move to form district associations in other provinces. A resolution of the Ontario convention in 1936 led to the establishment of a Canadian association, which benefited from a Carnegie grant of $3,500. In 1937 district associations were set up in Winnipeg, Calgary, Edmonton, Vancouver, and Victoria.

Despite the usual reluctance of the Canadian government to provide financial assistance for educational programs, even in the field of adult education, grants of $5,000 were made from that source in 1938 and in 1939 to assist with the education of the unemployed. The WEA admitted to its classes anyone who was unable to pay fees because of lack of employment. When the situation changed during the war, however, the grants were discontinued. The period just before and during the war was one of considerable financial uncertainty, since there was no assured and dependable income from any source.

During the war the emphasis of the work of the WEA shifted from academic matters to trade union concerns. The association set up a research department, appointed a research director, began the publication of *Labour News*, and undertook the writing of briefs for union negotiations and the keeping of records on wages and working conditions for the benefit of unions. These services were of a type that most unions were unable to maintain on their own initiative.

Another financial crisis occurred in 1949 when the Ontario government withdrew its annual grant. In an attempt to continue its regular program the association incurred substantial debts. When W.J. Dunlop, who had earlier represented the University of Toronto on the WEA Board of Directors, became Minister of Education, he arranged to have the grant restored. The final termination of the Carnegie grants a decade earlier had, however, made it impossible to continue to maintain a full-time general secretary, and the association had to depend on the voluntary efforts of the incumbent, D. Wren.

The Toronto group has in recent years sponsored new types of activities. It arranged for a series of lectures on the Citizen and the Law, dealing with the legal implications of certain everyday problems in the life of the average citizen. These lectures, given by experts in their respective fields, were followed by periods of discussion. Another series, conducted in co-operation with the Academy of Medicine in Toronto, was called the March of Medicine. The academy planned the lectures and supplied the speaker, while the WEA was responsible for the organizational work and promotion. Still another series, Investment and Money Management, was offered in co-operation with the Canadian Mutual Funds Association. The provision of classes in oral French produced a very enthusiastic response.

An important contribution to the trade union movement was the organization of classes for trade union leadership. These classes dealt with the regulations governing trade union activities and the principles of trade unionism. During the 1968 winter term, for example, the topics covered were Automation and Collective Bargaining; Collective Bargaining and Public Services; Collective Bargaining, Municipal and Federal; Taxation and Labour; Social Services of the Future; Trade Unions and the International Scene; Women in the Canadian Labour Force; and Trade Unions Role – Tomorrow.

Brief references to the remainder of the Toronto program of adult evening classes for the same year will convey some impression of the nature and scope of this aspect of WEA activities. 1 / A course in philosophy for those who took a serious and sustained interest in the subject was given in the form of guided reading and discussion under a tutor. 2 / A course in psychology involved an experimental approach to problems of everyday interest. A few of the topics dealt with were Freudian psychoanalysis; persuasion: from advertising to brainwashing; social classes and social problems; the development of intelligence and morality; and the limits of psychology as a science. 3 / A course in public speaking covered such items as the proper use of words, stance and delivery, and the preparation of material. 4 / A course in parliamentary procedure dealt with all aspects of the rules of order and the procedure for conducting a meeting. The ten lessons included practice sessions in the form of model meetings. 5 / A course in amateur photography was provided for adults only. 6 / A series on the New Left consisted of ten titles by different speakers: The New Ferment Within the Catholic Church, What's Cooking in the Theological Pot?, Student Power and the Universities, The Anti-Professional – New Approaches to Social Work, The New Visual Environment and Its Impact on the Lively Arts, The New Left and the Welfare State, The New Psychiatry, The New Thinking Within the Labour Movement and Its Role in Human Society, Is the Classroom Obsolete?, and The Changing Status of Women. All these series lasted for a period of ten weeks, and were open to members for a nominal fee. There were no examinations and no formal course credits.

FRONTIER COLLEGE

Frontier College originated in 1899, and received a charter by an act of the Canadian Parliament in 1922. Its special mission was to bring education to men working in isolated parts of the country, often in unskilled seasonal jobs. Many of these men were completely or functionally illiterate, or barred from access to Canadian culture because of unfamiliarity with either official language. Long evenings in camps and bunkhouses were conducive to dissipation and demoralization. At the same time, unfilled hours presented an opportunity for participation in educational activities, given the existence of sufficient motivation and the necessary opportunity.

Men who take pride in their ability to engage in hard physical labour are often contemptuous of those involved in other types of occupations. The crucial concept behind Frontier College was that those who would teach such men must win their respect by matching their efforts on the job. The university students who spent their summer vacations in this way were expected to avoid the temptation of acting as time-keeper or water boy, or of accepting a soft job in the office. Having demonstrated that they needed no special favours, they might hope for a receptive class during spare hours, when they were prepared to teach the simple skills of literacy or whatever else the men demanded and they felt qualified to offer. Further, the very presence of individuals with cultivated minds was supposed to exert a salutory influence on those around them. Whether or not such a result was achieved naturally depended very much on the personality and character of the students selected for the task. A vital aspect of the Frontier College program was to choose labourer-teachers with care.

When the program began, most of the men found in the camps were native-born Canadians with an affinity for a rootless existence or with an impediment to success in the settled communities in the more populated parts of the country. A few years later a large proportion consisted of new arrivals from foreign countries. The function of many of the classes then became one of facilitating assimilation into the prevailing culture. Many of the men had learned to resent authority, and resisted its appearance in any form. Winning them over posed a major challenge to the patience and sincerity of the would-be teacher.

Although the students received some extra remuneration in addition to their wages as labourers if their income otherwise failed to reach a level guaranteed beforehand, the main appeal was to their desire for service. The college consistently had far more applicants from teachers than it had places to fill, and was able to fill many of the available positions with graduates. In 1924 the principal, E.W. Bradwin, estimated that only about 10 per cent of those accepted in any particular season might be expected to fail, and an additional 15 per cent to produce indifferent results.

The basic program retained its essential features for decades, despite changes in the composition of the labouring group the classes were intended to help. In the 1960s, however, the college adopted a scheme to promote adult education in community settings. While field workers continued to offer special classes, they also assumed a responsibility for assessing the needs and aspirations of communities, for encouraging the reinforcement of positive values already existing, and for supporting greater participation by residents in local affairs. They acted within guidelines established in co-operation with various levels of government or with organizations in the community.

Frontier College has used its well earned credentials to promote the cause of better education for adults at the bottom of the educational ladder. In 1969 it submitted a brief to the Special Senate Committee on Poverty in which it claimed that 43 per cent of Canadians had less than a complete elementary education. This level was labeled as the lowest of

312 Educational contributions of associations

any industrial nation. Occupational training programs were said to be defective because those who most needed them could not meet the admission requirements. Preparatory courses were held to be too short to bring them up to the minimum standards.

According to a report in early 1970 the college operated a small office and maintained a field staff of one hundred on an annual budget of $130,000. For a six-month term the average cost of maintaining a volunteer was $1,300. A full year of service during the same period cost the Company of Young Canadians ten times as much. It was estimated that the expenditure of the college would be much less than doubled if it could keep its workers in the field for a full year, since recruiting and transportation costs would be substantially reduced. Despite the comparative efficiency of the program, grants and donations were not keeping up with the need. In fact in 1969 the federal government reduced its annual contribution from $10,000 to $5,000. Even though the original amount was restored, the *Globe and Mail* denounced this action in a scathing editorial on April 9, 1970, entitled "Cruel penny-pinching".

A look at the financial books of Frontier College suggests very strongly that the federal Government is never more hypocritical than when it is professing concern for the problems of Canadians in remote areas.

The relationship between poverty and lack of education, training and work opportunities is certain enough. The need for a form of rescue operation was touched upon in the Commons three years ago by Jean Marchand, who was then Minister of Manpower and Immigration: "We want to provide a second chance to the people who need it most. These are the men and women who missed the chance to acquire a skill during their youth or whose skill has been made obsolete by technological change."

Bravo! But how does one reconcile this with the chilly facts and figures presented by Frontier College, an organization (chartered, incidentally, by an Act of Parliament) dedicated to promoting adult and community education services in outlying parts of Canada? In 1960 its grant from Ottawa climbed to $10,000 and has not grown since then – a claim that cannot be made of the cost of living during the same period. Its services are admitted to be among the most effective in Canada.

Until recently the college grant came from the federal Department of Labor, which embraced manpower policy. In the 1969–70 fiscal year the department cut the grant, without warning, to $5,000. After sustained appeals to the Department of Manpower and Immigration, a grant of $5,000 for 1970–71 was obtained – an amount which will restore the level of federal help to 1960's $10,000.

All of which is pitiful and shameful. Surely all sense of proportion must have been lost in Ottawa if an organization with the objectives and credentials of Frontier College must struggle and argue this way in order to extract peanuts from the Treasury. The amount in question is less than one-millionth part of total federal spending.[6]

THE CANADIAN SOCIETY OF RURAL EXTENSION

The Canadian Society of Rural Extension (CSRE) was formed in 1960 as a means of improving the lines of communication among workers in rural extension. Its status was that of an affiliated society of the Agricultural Institute of Canada. It was designed to meet the needs of people in extension, adult education, and advisory work in the same way that other affiliated societies of the Agricultural Institute of Canada represented agricultural economics, agricultural engineering, agronomy, annual production, horticulture, and soil science. Objectives stated in its constitution were 1 / to advance the standards of research and education in rural extension, 2 / to encourage professional improvement among extension workers, 3 / to provide an opportunity for reporting, exchanging, and evaluating information about rural extension in Canada, and 4 / to publish a *Canadian Journal of Rural Education*.

The organization has presented programs at its annual convention held in June in conjunction with that of the Agricultural Institute of Canada. Among its themes were Research in Extension, Extension's Changing Role, Rural Development – a Challenge to Extension, and Meeting the Needs of the Community. CSRE representations to the Special Committee of the Senate on Land Use exerted an influence on the national Agricultural Rehabilitation and Development Act (ARDA) program by stressing the need for an educational approach to extension in rural development. The cause of extension was pressed on the Advisory Council on Scientific Affairs. The organization co-operated with the Canadian Association for Adult Education in the development of training programs. Publications at the end of the 1960s includedt *Stop Gap* and a president's biyearly newsletter respectively outlining the research and the extension activities of the members.

Membership was open to those who belonged to the Agricultural Institute of Canada or who were graduates of recognized universities. Those who were not university graduates but actively engaged in extension work could become associate members. In 1969 the membership of approximately 450 consisted of agricultural representatives, home economists, adult educators, teachers, writers and broadcasters concerned with farm matters, representatives of business, industry, governments, universities, and voluntary organizations, and private individuals.

THE RURAL LEARNING ASSOCIATION

The Rural Learning Association came into existence in 1965 as a result of the amalgamation of the Ontario Farm Radio Forum, the Ontario Folk School Council, and the Ontario Rural Leadership Forum. All three of these organizations had been concerned with adult education in the rural areas of the province. As early as 1959 a resolution was passed at the annual meeting of the Ontario Farm Radio Forum authorizing the incoming council to explore the possibility of arranging such a merger. It was hoped that a way would thus be found to eliminate existing duplication of services and to bring about a fruitful exchange of information.

The Farm Radio Forum, introduced during the war, provided rural people with an opportunity to discuss their problems in an atmosphere of sociability. The first ten years of the program constituted a period of expansion until, at its peak, it had 875 local groups. UNESCO officials devoted considerable attention to the program, and found it worthy of recommendation to less developed countries. In Canada, however, the number of groups declined, paralleling the reduction in the farm population.

The folk school movement was introduced in Canada by farm leaders in the 1930s and, after a lull, experienced a renewal in the late 1940s. The purpose of the schools was to improve people's understanding of themselves, their community, and the world in which they lived. At first the programs were held in farm homes, but later those organized regionally and provincially assumed the form of leadership training courses.

Formed in 1953, the Ontario Rural Leadership Committee brought together representatives of six farm organizations and two departments of government. At the beginning its main function was to assist with one- or two-day leadership forums at the county level. Its main contribution at a later stage was to hold an annual week-long leadership forum designed to create an awareness of social and economic factors affecting rural life and to teach group leadership techniques for rural leaders.

The new organization, the Rural Learning Association (RLA), considered its main function to be the provision of leadership development programs for the improvement of organizations and communities in rural Ontario. Its most important effort in the personal development field was the annual Provincial Training Course held at Geneva Park. Planned in co-operation with farm organizations, government departments, and co-operatives, it was attended by members of such rural organizations as Women's Institutes, Junior Farmers, co-operatives, federations of agriculture, and the Ontario Farmers' Union. As a means of continuing the work of the parent organizations, the RLA also sponsored and assisted with many regional and local training courses and folk schools. Through the Interprovincial Youth Exchange Project, twelve young people were sent for a two-week visit to Alberta and twelve young Albertans visited Ontario for a similar period as a means of gaining experience that would contribute to their capacity for leadership.

Because of its independent status and its receipt of financial contributions from a wide variety of sources, the association was in a particularly good position to encourage the expression of different points of view. An opportunity for free and frank interchange of opinions was offered at a Design for Tomorrow conference in 1967, where thirty-five young members of the Ontario Federation of Agriculture and the Ontario Farmers' Union discussed the goals and needs of agriculture and the kind of organization needed to achieve these goals.

A major objective of the RLA training courses was to bridge the gap between those who had access to and an understanding of new information in the social and economic fields, including agricultural representatives, ARDA personnel, and teachers, and those who needed such information. Great value was also seen in bringing together representatives of different groups and organizations. An annual marketing conference held in co-operation with the Ontario Federation of Agriculture was attended by over one hundred staff and board members from marketing boards, associations, co-operatives, and government departments. The 1969 conference, held at Geneva Park, enabled the participants to pursue two main objectives: 1 / to learn about marketing boards and the process of marketing, and 2 / to learn how to be more effective on their boards.

With financial assistance from the Indian Affairs Branch, the RLA has sponsored a large number of Indian folk schools. One of these was held at Kenora in March 1969 for the benefit of over sixty young people who had dropped out of school. The purpose of the school was to help them overcome feelings of inadequacy and learn to speak up in a group. They viewed films on problems such as lack of identity and lack of self-respect. There were presentations on the topics "Who am I?" and "What is there to be proud of in being an Indian?" Indians and government officials addressed the group and participated in other ways. At another folk school held the same month at Thunder Bay, the theme was "This Is Where It's At!" The thirty participants were given an opportunity to learn about group behaviour and dynamics and the difference between process and content in a discussion. They debated the child-centred and subject-centred approach to learning. Other sessions were devoted to studies of modern music, dancing, social recreation, and the problems of discrimination, shyness, community co-operation, and publicity. The school was considered so successful that plans were initiated immediately to hold a similar school at the end of the summer.[7]

Some of the same types of objectives were pursued at a provincial training course held at Geneva Park in February 1969. Part of the program consisted of sensitivity training. During the mornings and evenings, groups of approximately ten met to gain new insights into their behaviour, feelings, and reactions, to establish more authentic relationships with other people, and to break down their defensiveness. During the afternoons they joined workshop groups dealing with community development, personal development, and "worthwhile meetings and communications." Before they left for home, they met in regional groups to plan follow-up meetings to assess what they had learned and to decide how their individual and collective talents could best serve the rural community.

THE CANADIAN HOME READING UNION

The movement that eventually led to the founding of the Canadian Home Reading Union began in Great Britain in 1889 with the establishment of the National Home Reading Union. The founder, the Reverend J.B. Paton, was said to be primarily interested in furthering the education of children of people of modest means. The aim of his organization was to guide readers of all ages in their choice of books, to unite them in one comprehensive association, and to bring them together in groups for mutual help and understanding. The National Home Reading Union published a book list each year indicating the best and cheapest books available. It also issued a monthly magazine containing articles on topics from such fields as science, history, theology, poetry, art, and literature.

Branches were established about the turn of the century in such Ontario communities as Peterborough, Norwood, Petrolia, and Ottawa. The Ottawa branch proved to be particularly active, and exerted a strong influence on the development of the movement. In 1930, when the parent body found it impossible to continue meeting the expenses of publishing the book lists and the magazine and dissolved itself, such offshoots were too well rooted to succumb with it. The Canadian Home Reading Union was formed as a result. Since at this time there were only two branches in Canada, the one at Ottawa and another at Toronto, an important aim of the central committee was to stimulate the creation of new circles. These would contribute to the realization of the major objective of encouraging reading and the appreciation of good literature.

Some questions were raised at the annual meeting in 1968 about the future of the organization. A canvass of the members showed unanimous satisfaction with the aims that had been pursued over the years, although it was agreed that there was room for improving the means of attaining them. The possibility of a change of name was given some serious consideration. Of the total of eighteen branches, ten were opposed to a change, while the other eight suggested a variety of possibilities.

THE CANADIAN FILM INSTITUTE

A National Film Society was established in 1935 "to encourage and promote the study, appreciation and use of motion and sound pictures and television as educational and cultural factors." A report produced a few months later by the secretary, Donald Buchanan, urged that the society serve as a national clearinghouse to stimulate public appreciation of film as a cultural instrument and to encourage the use of films as visual aids. Proposals were made for the establishment of regional film libraries and of a film museum to preserve films and newsreels depicting Canadian life and industry. A few years later the society concentrated efforts on the creation of an informed and enthusiastic audience for the films produced by what became of the National Film Board. It also did much to ensure the maintenance of a balance between state and private production.

The primary function of the institute was to establish and maintain a national resource film library for all Canadian borrowers. Emphasis was placed increasingly on the type of films used by audiences with an interest in "the way people live, work, organize, educate and feed their children,"[8] and by those concerned with scientific discovery, travel, and the arts of their own and other nations. There were special collections of the films of a number of diplomatic missions as well as those from the NFB and several government departments. A Science Film Division, affiliated with the International Scientific Film Association and supported by the National Research Council, evaluated and distributed films of interest to scientists, technicians, and educators, and organized festivals of scientific films. Certain films were handled for American universities and organizations without commercial facilities for distribution, such as the National Safety Council, the American Dental Association, and the American Psychiatric Association.

After a UNESCO festival and seminar were held in Ottawa in May 1963, a Centre for Films on Art was set up with the active co-operation of the institute. A collection of films belonging to the National Gallery of Canada was handled by the institute as part of a larger collection, and provided the basis for screenings and festivals in all parts of the country. Provincial departments of education and other bodies previewed items from the collection as a means of deciding what to purchase.

In 1952 Canadian film societies undertook to organize themselves into a federation which constituted a division of the Canadian Film Institute. By 1966 the number of member societies had exceeded one hundred, with about 27,000 individual members. In the same year the institute was assisting this federation to provide an index of seven thousand feature films available in Canada, with sources and rental charges. The federation supplied information for the preparation of program notes, published a quarterly bulletin, and occasionally bought rare and unusual films. It thus offered a means by which Canadian audiences could view important films with no great commercial promise.

The Canadian Film Archives were established as a division of the institute in 1963 to formalize the activities carried on by volunteers over the previous decade. The following year the unit became one of the forty-five members of the International Federation of Film Archives, and thus became eligible to borrow from other national archives in order to add to the variety of programs available to the National Film Theatre, which held weekly screenings at the National Museum in Ottawa in addition to more frequent screenings in its own theatre.

The Canadian Film Institute received assistance from the Canada Council over a five-year period to set up its Information Service. For regular operations, however, it depended for its funds on membership fees and payments for services, including those to government departments. Its existence depended on the enthusiasm of its voluntary supporters. According to a recent brochure, associate membership at $1 a year, individual membership at $5 per year, institutional membership at $25 per year, and corporate membership at $50 per year entitled the members to a considerable number of informational and other services.

FIFTEEN

Community cultural and recreational associations

Only two associations are dealt with in this chapter: the Young Men's Christian Association (YMCA) and the Young Women's Christian Association (YWCA). They were unusual, although not unique, in terms of the range of educational, cultural, and recreational services they provided in many communities across Canada. Despite the word "young" in their title they appealed to all age groups, and despite the word "Christian" they ceased to place any great emphasis on creed.

THE YMCA

Origin and early development in Canada[1]

The YMCA originated in England around 1844 as a religious fellowship to exert a constructive influence on rootless young men in industrial cities. From the beginning education was one of its chief objectives. The educational interest was shown in the Toronto branch, established in 1853, by the provision of a reading room, a library, and rooms for conversation, lectures, classes, and religious meetings. Weekly meetings were held for the mental and moral improvement of the members; at these some topic of interest was discussed and a member read an essay or a short lecture.

When a new building was opened in Toronto in 1872, the association offered classes in shorthand, bookkeeping, elocution, and drawing, followed soon afterward by special classes for Chinese and Italians. During the subsequent years there were courses leading to matriculation, dropped in favour of those offered by the Toronto Board of Education in 1933, and advanced university-level courses, eventually transferred to the University of Toronto. At various times courses were offered in life insurance, fire insurance, credits and collection, traffic management, accounting, real estate, and foremanship.

The waves of immigrants entering Canada during the early years of the twentieth century provided a demand for various kinds of service programs. It was said that every branch established one or more classes for the foreign born. A comparable need appeared and was met in a variety of ways during the years of heavy immigration following the Second World War.

Interest in meeting the needs of men serving in the armed forces was demonstrated as early as the time of the Fenian raids around 1870. During the First World War a reading and lecture program was conducted in all Canadian military camps. YMCA initiative helped to establish Khaki University, a project which served as an example for many other countries.

Organization
As of 1968, the constitution defined the purposes of the National Council as follows:

1. To foster a cohesive National Canadian Movement and a sense of belonging to a world-wide Christian fellowship.
2. Assist and co-ordinate the work of member Associations in the fulfilment of the purposes of the YMCA as set forth in the following historical statements.
    (a) *The Paris Basis* – a basis of the affiliation of the World Alliance of YMCAs adopted at the first World Conference at Paris in 1855:
    "The Young Men's Christian Association seeks to unite those young men who, regarding Jesus Christ as their God and Saviour, according to the Holy Scriptures, desire to be His disciples in their faith and in their life and associate their efforts for the extension of His Kingdom amongst young men."
    (b) *The Preston Basis* – adopted by the Fourth National Convention of Canadian Young Men's Christian Associations at Preston, Ontario, November, 1924, and later by the International Convention of Canada and the United States at Washington, 1926:
    "To lead young men to faith in God through Jesus Christ; to promote their growth into fulness of Christian character; to lead them into active membership in the church of their choice; to make the extension of the Kingdom of God throughout the world the governing purpose of their lives."
    (c) *The Cleveland Basis* – adopted by the Forty-third International Convention of Canada and the United States at Cleveland, 1931, and as amended at the Annual Meeting of The National Council of YMCAs of Canada, February, 1958:
    "The Young Men's Christian Association is a world-wide fellowship united by common loyalty to Jesus Christ for the purpose of building Christian personality and a Christian society."
3. To co-operate with other national and international agencies with purposes consistent with the YMCA.[2]

The National Council worked for the achievement of the purposes of the organization by sponsoring and leading conferences and assemblies, interpreting the history, philosophy, and program of the movement at home and abroad, carrying on study and research at the national level, and developing standards and goals. It provided direct services to member associations by correspondence and by personal visits in connection with administration, personnel, program, financial and membership campaigns, surveys and studies, leadership conferences, selection and training of secretaries and volunteer workers, and other matters. It maintained a personnel department to assist in the selection, training, placement, transfer, and retirement of secretaries. It operated a clearinghouse for significant ideas in various fields of association work and prepared and distributed bulletins and other publications relating to these ideas. It collected, organized, and interpreted records and reports of member associations.

Each local association was under the independent direction of its own board of directors, with complete responsibility for raising its own funds. Boards of directors were elected by the local members, and have employed their own staff within guidelines suggested by the national organization. They contributed to the support of the National Council, which gave them the advantage of a definite identity and broader associations, as well as providing opportunities for members to participate in projects organized on a regional, national, or international basis.

Approach to education

A statement prepared for the second Canadian Conference on Education in 1962 indicated what goals the YMCA attempted to pursue and how it sought to attain them.

No more important educational method for developing Christian personality has been used in the Association than that of assigned responsibility, carefully made, widely distributed, graded as to ability, protected by supervision. It has been used in the YMCA from the very beginning. The use of this principle is seen today in such things as the general practice of organizing all groups with officers chosen for various duties, in the Leaders Clubs of the Physical Department, in the universal use of committees, in the multitude of ingenious devices for putting men and boys to work, not only for the purpose of getting the work done, but even more for the purpose of developing the attitudes and competence for doing work. It is seen in the practice of involving persons of all ages in the experience of decision-making, of planning, of evaluating. By this means they learn how to think and to do.

The exercise of responsibility in thinking, planning, and acting leads to growth in a Christian direction, when it involves the search for the Christian way of thinking, the Christian attitude, the Christian solution, the Christian relationship, the Christian standards of value. The leader thus builds up in his "followers" an understanding of the Christian way of life and the habit of applying it in all situations. Without this direction-giving, growth through the carrying of responsibility may be entirely unrelated to Christian goals for persons and society ...

The heart of the theory of the experience-centered program is that literally everything entering into one's experience becomes part of him. The way in which he responds to experience determines its educational effects on him. A fight at camp may be as much a part of the day's educational program as a lesson in swimming. Experience can be educational in a bad sense as well as in a good sense. It becomes educative in a good sense when one thinks about what has happened; reflects on it; evaluates it (preferably along with other people, and with the help of mature persons); considers what was good in it, what not good, what to leave, what to keep ...[3]

Current continuing education activities
An impression of the daytime and evening classes offered under the heading of continuing education may be obtained from a brief review of the program of the North Toronto YMCA in 1968–9. The courses carried no academic credit, but were designed to "enrich the lives of the participants and to stimulate them to further study and community service." They were particularly intended to appeal to the adult who liked to read, who secretly yearned to paint a picture, or who sought a real understanding of music, to the stay-at-home, to the career girl on her way up, to the housewife or couple who sought rewarding activity for a precious evening out, and to the mother who needed morning relief from daily chores with provision for supervised play for her pre-school children. There were no educational prerequisites. Courses typically involved ten or fifteen participants meeting for a weekly two-hour session for ten weeks. It was claimed that the students selected the area of interest, set the pace, directed proceedings to attain their goals, and evaluated themselves.

The list of courses included 1 / Human Relations I, dealing with "emotional learnings and the ways in which they can affect our behaviour when we are with other people"; 2 / Human Relations II; 3 / Developing Personal Potential, offering the student "an opportunity to identify and assess his or her personality resources and capacities, and to relate these to personal values and goals"; 4 / Child Psychology, emphasizing the social, emotional, and intellectual development of the child from infancy through the elementary school years; 5 / General Psychology, concentrating on the experimental approach to the study of growth and development, learning, perception, and motivation, as well as on such topics as the sensory basis of response, individual and group differences, mental testing, attitude formation, personal adjustment, and the historical aspects of psychology; 6 / God and the Good: a Skeptic Looks at Religion; 7 / Frontiers of Thinking, dealing with "the nature of philosophy as a basic type of inquiry" and centring on questions about the nature of life and the meaning of reality; 8 / Learning to Live with Leisure; 9 / The Problems of Freedom in a Democracy, covering such topics as the "clear and present danger test" as a measuring rod for free speech, free speech and the obscenity problem, the growth and gradual nationalization of the concept of justice, loyalty and security provisions, freedom of the press, religious freedom, academic freedom, the place of the minority in the Canadian pattern of life, and the relationship between military policy and freedom; 10 / Personal Financial Planning, dealing with economic forecasting, types of investments, stock market functions, appraisal of stocks, bonds, and mutual funds as investments, insurance, the home as an investment, and opportunities for borrowing money; 11 / The Banks and Society; 12 / Environment and Design, analyzing the social, political, and economic heritage influencing the existing condition of the environment, and focusing on possible solutions of problems of function and aesthetics; 13 / What Does Urban, Regional and Local Planning Mean to Me?; 14 / Contemporary Issues as Shown in Films and Literature, including topics such as prejudice, war and violence, youth in crisis, pop culture, trends in satire, and designs for an ideal society; 15 / Sex, Love and You, exploring facts, attitudes, behaviour, sex roles and problems, and current issues, with attention to all stages of childhood and young adulthood; 16 / Crises of Life through the Mirror of Literature; 17 / Your Creative Writing I; 18 / Creative Writing II; 19 / Creative Practical Photography – Beginning, consisting of discussion of composition, lighting, camera angle, subject possibilities, special effects, and basic principles, with practical application through field exercises and critique; 20 / Painting with Oils, Water Colours and Sketching; 21 / Colour Design and Space in Interior Decorating, designed to develop each student's awareness of beauty, ability to be selective, personal style of expression, and "sensitivity to imaginative design possibilities in the commonplace"; 22 / Dancing; 23 / Invitation to the Arts, involving a study of the stylistic, aesthetic, and social aspects of painting, sculpture, drawing, and graphic art; 24 / Sculpture; 25 / Effective Speaking and Listening; 26 / Great Ages of Music: 17th, 18th, and 19th Centuries; 27 / A Taste for Music; 28 / Beginning on the Downbeat, a song session; 29 / Getting the Most out of Married Life; 30 / French without Tears I; 31 / French without Tears II; 32 / Spanish for Beginners; 33 / Intermediate Spanish; 34 / Italian; 35 / Russian for Beginners; 36 / Introduction to Journalism, covering the function of the editorial department and the "inside man," and the techniques and problems of reporting, newswriting, and researching, with substantial practice in rewriting news stories; 37 / Women's Rights: Unfinished Business; and 38 / Dilemmas in 20th Century Life.

The So-Ed program

So-Ed, a name derived from Social-Education, appeared first in Canada with the organization of a group in Vancouver in 1940. The program originated with the YMCA in the United States, and groups were sponsored in Canada not only by that organization, but sometimes also by the YWCA, by the YMCA and the YWCA together, by churches, or by other community groups. The purposes of the movement were to provide young people with opportunities to make new friendships, to develop their understanding of the meaning of Christian living, to become more knowledgeable about their community and the world, to improve their understanding of human relations, to enjoy social recreation, to grow personally, and to develop leadership abilities. All these goals were consistent with those of the YMCA and the YWCA in general.

So-Ed groups made a practice of meeting one night a week for periods of six to twelve weeks in the autumn, winter, or spring, and sometimes in the summer. Each evening's program customarily consisted of three parts: lecture-discussions, skill training, and social activities. The educational program was not intended to provide thorough training in any subject, but rather to present basic information and to stimulate thinking. Meetings were held in YMCA buildings or in other community facilities. The groups commonly had a membership of between sixty and four hundred.

The So-Ed movement flourished in the 1940s and 1950s. The YMCA recognized its performance of a special adult education function, and regarded it as a means of interesting new members and as a testing ground for new program ideas. It underwent a period of decline in the 1960s, and by the end of the decade was considered to be on the way out.

Industrial management clubs

Industrial Management Clubs, which existed within YMCAs as well as in communities without Y organizations, were flourishing at the end of the 1960s. The chief function of these clubs was educational, with emphasis on management training. In 1968 there were reported to be forty-five chapters with nearly five thousand members. Courses were held annually at the University of Western Ontario and Laval University, and seven centres offered a three-year evening course in supervisory management designed by the University of Windsor.

Scholarships and bursaries

Before 1962 small awards were made to worthy candidates for further study. During the previous year there was said to have been a heavy demand for bursaries and for grants from the loan fund. The yearbook mentioned the presentation of the Inter-Provincial Women's Auxiliary Scholarship to a student at the University of Toronto, the Toronto Y-Wives Bursary to a student at Sir George Williams University, the Board of Directors Bursary to another student at the same institution, and two General Secretaries' Bursaries to students at the University of New Brunswick and George Williams College in Chicago. Mention was made of assistance to students by the Montreal Association, other local associations, the International Y's Men's Movement, and George Williams College. Much the same list of awards was reported for 1961.

After the establishment of the Canadian Youth Fund in 1961, assistance was provided on a much larger scale. Thirty-three undergraduate bursaries and three career development grants were awarded from this fund in 1962, while the established scholarships and bursaries were continued. In 1963–4 the National Committee on Financial Aid decided to concentrate on aid to students in their second or third year of university who were in financial need. Twenty-one students received bursaries in January to enable them to complete their year, while twenty-eight were assisted during the subsequent autumn term. These bursaries amounted to a total of $14,415. A further sum of $6,200 was granted to career secretaries to enable them to engage in graduate study.

In 1966–7 there was a thorough appraisal of the results obtained from career grants to secretaries. As a result it was decided that top priority should be given to those associations which identified specific job openings and assisted particular secretaries to obtain the specialized training to fill them. Career grants were also to be available to enable secretaries to participate in short-term, non-academic training sessions as well as in specialized studies at the graduate level. Because of the rapid depletion of the Canadian Youth Fund, it was obvious that further endowment funds would be needed to continue the assistance program.

Staff training

It was established in 1934 that the minimum educational requirement for employment in the YMCA would be a college degree. Two years later it was suggested that the most appropriate content areas for undergraduate study leading to Y work might include religion, philosophy, history, psychology, biology, economics, sociology, political science, modern literature, and education. These suggestions, without constituting formal requirements, were used as a guide by students and their advisers and as a basis for assessing the adequacy of a candidate's educational preparation.

The National Councils of the United States and Canada decided in 1943 that professional personnel employed on or after May 1, 1945 should complete thirty semester hours of professional education as one of the requirements for certification as YMCA secretaries. The six basic areas covered in this program, as revised in 1954, were 1 / history, philosophy, and organization of the YMCA, 2 / Christian leadership and interpretation, 3 / administration, 4 / leadership and supervision of program and groups, 5 / guidance of individuals, and 6 / community organization and relationships. It was assumed that the course requirements in each basic area constituted a minimum common core for all secretaries, that there should be further specialized study beyond this minimum for particular positions involving boys' work, young men's work, physical education, the business secretaryship, student work, and other activities, and that further specialization might be pursued within the six basic areas.

According to a booklet prepared by the Committee on Professional Education in 1954,[4] the first basic area covered the nature of the YMCA, the working principles of its organization and program, the forces that brought it into existence, the influences that determined its existing character, the directions in which it was moving, the problems it confronted and its ways of meeting them, and its place in the organized pattern of religion, recreation, education, social service, government, and community life. The student was expected to become acquainted with the formative ideas, events, and personalities associated with the movement from its beginning. He was supposed to understand how the original motivation had been modified by the changing cultural and religious climate. The study of the current organization included such aspects as lay control, membership participation, the basic nature of boards, committees, and membership groupings, and local, national, and world structure.

In the area of Christian leadership and interpretation, the secretary was supposed to be knowledgeable about four topics: 1 / the Hebrew-Christian heritage, including the Old and New Testaments, with special emphasis on the life and teachings of Jesus and the main events in Christian history since his time; 2 / current religious trends, with particular attention to the varied ways in which religious thought and experience were expressed in North America; 3 / ways of helping people to grow in religious insight and experience; and 4 / the application of Christian ethics to such social problems as intercultural relations, labour, and war. The secretary was expected to have integrated his own thinking and experience around a Christian philosophy of life.

Administration, the third basic area, involved planning, allocating resources of personnel and material, stimulating and directing people to carry out plans, co-ordinating the efforts of such people, and evaluating the results in the light of the original purposes. The principles of the course were derived from the fields of psychology, sociology, anthropology, and human relations, supplemented by practical contributions from business, government, education, social work, the church, military life, and the YMCA itself. Reference was made in the booklet to the substantial body of knowledge and technique relating to the application of democratic principles to administration.

The fourth area was intended to help secretaries provide leadership in the formulation of program policies and in the processes of recruiting, training, and supervising program leaders. The settings in which groups operated and required guidance covered a very wide range. "These [groups] include staffs, boards, committees, and leadership groups; program groups, classes, teams, and special interest groups; groups of different age levels and of different ethnic, religious, and cultural backgrounds; groups engaged in health education, religious education, parent education, public affairs education, and community efforts of many kinds."[5]

The secretary was expected to understand the group experience both as a means of developing people and of getting things done. More specifically, he was expected to have adequate knowledge of sound grouping practices in organizing committees, the effect of group experience on individuals, the process of decision making, ways of guiding discussion, methods of determining objectives, and procedures for making and carrying out plans.

The secretary required supervisory knowledge and techniques to formulate qualifications for leaders, to recruit them, to conduct programs of pre-service training and orientation for them, and to improve their competence by in-service training and other means. He had to be familiar with the standards for various types of programs and the criteria for evaluating them. It was considered particularly important that he exercise his responsibilities in such a way as to give program leaders a sense of satisfaction in their work and a feeling of enthusiasm.

The fifth basic area, guidance of individuals, was described as a phase of leadership. The goal of this aspect of the program was to promote the growth of the individual toward values implied in the YMCA's Christian orientation. Some of the local associations maintained guidance centres where counselling was conducted by specially trained secretaries. In others the function was performed on a less formal basis. Every secretary was supposed to have a minimum competence in the field. It was expected that his general education would have given him a reasonable background of psychological knowledge relating to such work. His professional training included such topics as 1 / the objectives of a counselling relationship, 2 / dynamic factors in the counselling relationship, 3 / methods of counselling, 4 / the value and use of psychological tests and other instruments used for guidance purposes, and 5 / the relationship between the counselling point of view and other expressions of leadership such as teaching, salesmanship, and evangelism. Particular attention was given to those aspects of counselling that were significant in the YMCA setting, such as fair play and good sportsmanship, boy-girl relations, family life, religious uncertainties, and attitudes toward adherents of other faiths.

The sixth area, community organization and relationships, covered both the general process by which individuals associate to identify and meet certain needs and the characteristics and contributions of specific agencies such as schools, churches, recreational agencies, social work agencies, and others. Study in this area included a review of the historical background of such concepts as community, community organization, social need, social process, social tension, and social disorganization, as well as an examination of the historical development of efforts to co-ordinate social welfare in urban and rural communities. The secretary was expected to be familiar with modern methods of studying the community. For this purpose, he needed some understanding of the way in which a town or city developed, how natural areas were formed, and how business and industrial enterprises were distributed. He needed to be aware of the socio-economic factors at work in a community, the class structure, and the power groups competing for control. He was expected to learn to view community organization as a means of meeting personal needs, for which it had to be in a process of continuous change. In studying the structure of the community, he was to give particular attention to community chests and councils, YMCA–church relations, YMCA–YWCA relations, YMCA–school relations, YMCA–university relations, relations with other organizations serving youth, relations with agencies in the social work field, and relations with civic, economic, and racial groups.

For many years the National Council operated a training and conference centre at Geneva Park on Lake Couchiching, which came to be used all year round. In 1968 the premises occupied a 120-acre site with two miles of shoreline. The buildings included dormitories, an auditorium, a gymnasium, a lounge, and seminar, conference, and catering facilities for large groups. There was also full provision for summer sports activities. The centre was available, not only for Y use, but also for conferences and seminars held by other organizations.

Summer school was conducted on an annual basis after 1960, when a four-week session was held at Geneva Park. The courses offered for junior secretaries seeking to meet certification requirements were accredited by Sir George Williams University. The course topics were substantially those just described. A total of fifty-nine people were enrolled in 1960, including twenty-eight from the United States. In 1961 the University of Waterloo entered the field by offering one of the courses.

The YMCA *Yearbook* for 1964 reported that the National Personnel Services Division had organized five staff development programs during the previous year, giving every professional secretary in the Canadian movement at least one training experience. There had been a seven-day orientation course for new secretaries enrolling seventeen participants, seven summer school courses for junior secretaries enrolling thirty-four Canadian and thirty-one American participants, a six-day leadership lab for program staff enrolling twenty secretaries, a ten-day executive training workshop for younger executive secretaries enrolling twenty-six participants, and an organization development project for experienced secretaries enrolling eleven highly placed officials. Additional training programs and skill schools were sponsored by other departments of the national organization.

A highlight of the staff development program in 1964 was a workshop on organization change attended by twenty-seven experienced secretaries from Class A associations. The purposes of this workshop were to re-examine, evaluate, and implement association goals, to produce a clearer understanding of the social forces affecting the association and of ways of coping with them, and to increase the participants' sensitivity and self-understanding so that they might relate more effectively to staff associates and members. Various other projects, seminars, and workshops attracted additional groups of officials.

Each year there was some new initiative to expand the program further. In 1966 271 staff members participated in some type of training experience away from the job. A total of $4,970.74 was spent from the Canadian Youth Fund to finance these activities. Members of the Personnel Services Committee became convinced that expenditures for staff recruiting and development should be part of the operating budget of the National Council.

In 1966 a task force was established to propose measures for upgrading the competency of YMCA and YMCA–YWCA officers with responsibilities in the areas of program and administration. Concern had been expressed over the increased turnover during the previous five years, which left the median period of staff service at only four years. It appeared that the policy of internal training for management positions would have to be supplemented by bringing in trained people. Further problems revolved around the increasing diversity of positions in the organization and the need for more highly qualified specialists. Adequate training programs had also to be devised for program and administrative aids, local leaders, and specialists without university training. The one-stream approach to training, serving both junior and senior levels, no longer seemed satisfactory. A basic challenge was that of devising a program that would motivate people to strive for continuous self-improvement.

The new training policy involved the retention of the existing program as a possible pathway to YMCA work along with a variety of additional routes to the achievement of maximum professional development. Entry was made possible at every level of job responsibility. Orientation was regarded as essential for all new employees, with a special program required for senior personnel. Changes pointed to a need for a clear definition of all positions in the organization and for definite specifications for each position.

According to the recommentations of the task force, local associations, in discharging their responsibility for the selection of all their own personnel, were expected to be as clear as possible about the competencies required for each job. A university education was still to be regarded as a crucial qualification for the majority of YMCA positions, particularly for those anticipating long-term employment in the association. Those associated with policy formulation and development were expected to demonstrate "a quality of spiritual awareness based on religious belief." Naturally, also, those accepted for employment were supposed to have substantial capacity for further growth.

Orientation was to include familiarization with the job, the local community, the Canadian YMCA movement, the world movement, and the Society of Association Personnel. The national organization would be expected to assist local associations to carry on the necessary activities,

There were to be separate orientation programs for 1 / "indigenous" leaders, program and administrative aids, and technicians, 2 / staff members with a general university background but little work experience or professional training, and 3 / highly qualified professionals and managers entering the YMCA from allied fields after substantial professional experience.

Extent
In 1968 there were more than 125 YMCAs and YMCA–YWCAs across Canada with a total membership of 220,000. About thirty communities had combined YMCA–YWCAs. Total investment in plant and equipment in 1967 was estimated at more than $73 million dollars.

Finances
A complete Y program could be operated only at substantial cost. An attempt was made to keep membership fees as low as possible to enable those with modest means to participate. In many cases of need fees were waived altogether. Sources of revenue other than direct charges included civic, county, and provincial governments, contributions from business and industry, personal gifts, and bequests.

Relationship with the YWCA
In 1960 the National Council gave serious consideration to the possibility of amalgamation with the National Council of the YWCA. In view of the continued growth in the number of YMCA–YWCAs, some form of union seemed inevitable. A resolution of the annual meeting urged that immediate discussions be undertaken to determine the form and time of such a union. Later events indicated, however, that there were much greater problems in the way of this development than many had supposed. In some respects it appeared that the trend was toward a strengthening of the independence of the two organizations.

Evaluation
A survey reported in 1963 revealed many important facts about the nature of participation in YMCA activities.[6] The following selection includes those judged to be of most interest. 1 / While the number of young adult participants between the ages of eighteen and twenty-nine had increased since 1942, the proportion of that age group had decreased. The number of young men members between eighteen and twenty-four had declined, while the number of men between twenty-four and twenty-nine and of women over the whole young adult age span had increased. Young adults constituted one in seven of the total membership, as compared with one in four in 1942. 2 / About 80 per cent of the members were enrolled in groups. 3 / Physical education groups comprised nearly 40 per cent

of all groups, with half the members consisting of young adults and registered non-members. 4 / Informal education classes made up about 35 per cent of the total groups, with one-third of the participants being young adults. 5 / Social recreation groups constituted slightly less than 10 per cent of the total, with one in ten participants being a young adult. 6 / Special interest groups comprised 3 per cent of the total, with about 3 per cent of the membership consisting of young adults and registered non-members. 7 / Less than 1 per cent of the young adult members served on YMCA boards. 8 / About 2 per cent of young adult members served on official committees of boards, and somewhat more as members of councils. 9 / About 5 per cent of young adult members served as officers of Y clubs, teams, councils, or committees. 10 / About 25 per cent of young adult leaders were involved in training programs. 11 / The proportion of Protestant members had been increasing somewhat in the young adult category, while the proportion of Roman Catholics and Jews had declined slightly. 12/ About 40 per cent of young adult male members were college graduates.

In 1968 the annual meeting assumed the form of a York University Conference, where about five hundred people spent five days discussing the future of the association, with emphasis on priorities among issues and goals. The enthusiasm and optimism expressed by the participants were said to have left no doubt about the continued existence of the Y. Facilities had been renewed, and membership, leadership, program participation, and numbers of staff had reached record levels. There were, however, serious questions about the adequacy of the program to meet the social needs of Canadian communities. A number of conclusions were distilled from the discussions. 1 / There was a need for increased involvement of youth, women, and members of various ethnic and religious groups, both in policy-making groups of the associations and the National Council and in the total life of the movement. Things had evidently reached the point where the word "young" in the title appeared to be almost a misnomer. The participants at the conference, including the young people, were not at all certain that they knew the best means of involving youth. There was, however, little support for the view that there was a genuine generation gap. 2 / There should be a new statement of purpose for the association which would be more widely accepted and which would reflect a new concept and understanding of membership. What was meant was that the rigorous Christian position should be modified to reflect a more humanistic point of view. There was also a strong feeling that less emphasis should be placed on members and membership growth, and more on contributions to the life of the community as a whole. 3 / A related suggestion was that the association should extend its scope to work with more people and organizations in the community. Among the examples mentioned were university students, ethnic groups, and alienated youth. Experimental programs might be undertaken, with associated research to test their validity. 4 / There should be stronger professional leadership, involving the selection and retention of more competent staff, improved training, and increased job satisfaction. 5 / The process of attracting, training, and involving lay program leaders and board and committee members should be improved through orientation and training programs and clear job descriptions. 6 / The organization should develop agreed-upon methods of expressing itself on social issues where it had concern, interest, and competence. There was considerable uncertainty about the exact meaning of this proposal, and about how it could be implemented. 7 / The National Council and the member associations needed greater financial resources. 8 / The role of the National Council should be strengthened, and the effectiveness of its communication with local associations and members increased.

THE YWCA

Origin and early activities
The YWCA developed in Great Britain in the mid-nineteenth century as a result of the formation of two movements which ultimately merged. One consisted of prayer circles or unions, composed mostly of young women from the leisured classes who were interested in such social service activities as visiting workhouses and offering scripture classes for girls of the working class. Emma Robarts, originator of the movement, used the term "Young Women's Christian Association" as a parallel to "Young Men's Christian Association," an organization that was building a favourable reputation. The second organization, inspired by Lady Kinnaird, provided housing and supervision for young women who gathered in London on the way to join Florence Nightingale in her nursing mission during the Crimean War, and later for those seeking employment in the city.[7]

The first YWCA in Canada was organized in Saint John, New Brunswick, in 1870. Its statement of objectives placed strong emphasis on the promotion of religion, both among its members and among those with whom they worked. The Toronto association, the second in the country, appeared in 1873. Among its first projects was the opening of two boarding houses for girls immigrating from Britain and for those moving into the city from the rural communities of the province. By the end of the century, associations had been formed in Kingston, Hamilton, London, Peterborough, Ottawa, and Brantford. Most of them encouraged women and children to come to their rooms where the former were offered classes in sewing and Bible study and the latter were taught reading and penmanship as well as engaging in Bible study and play.

By 1920 most colleges and universities, as well as many private schools, had student YWCAs. These groups typically held weekly meetings, with some additional Bible classes. Returned missionaries frequently gave addresses, helping to raise money for work in foreign fields. Members also read papers dealing with various aspects of Christian life as applied to students. The Student Christian Movement, formed in 1920, took over this type of activity.

The first conference in which Canadian associations were involved was held in 1875. Conventions, at which delegates of the members assembled to determine goals and define policies, began in 1893. It became established practice to hold these every four years. The dates of these four-year conventions, 1961, 1965, and 1969, constituted highlights of the development of the organization during the 1960s. Each year between conventions the National Council, including the National Board, the presidents of local associations, and World Council members, assembled in Toronto to look after interim business.

There were several noticeable trends in the work of the YWCA in the 1950s and the 1960s. 1 / Government action was urged in various areas affecting the welfare of Canadians. 2 / A strong effort was made to improve communication and understanding between Protestants and Roman Catholics. 3 / Similar interest was shown in encouraging harmonious relationships between French- and English-speaking cultures.

Recent consideration of purposes
As in the YMCA, serious consideration was given in the late 1960s to the real purposes which the YWCA actually served and ought to serve. It had become increasingly evident that the organization was involved in a broad spectrum of community service, and not, as early statements implied, with reinforcing the beliefs and practices of an interdenominational but nevertheless specific Christian group. In 1967 a survey conducted by the Montreal association uncovered a widespread feeling that a new statement of purpose was needed. While awaiting official action, this association used an excerpt from *When Women Work Together* by Josephine Perfect Harshaw.

The YWCA is a voluntary membership organization with a Christian purpose. It works consciously to include in its membership women and girls from different economic, racial, occupational, religious, cultural and age groups. As a local, national and world movement the YWCA develops program and services which take into account the needs and concerns of its members in the changing community.

Members take part in developing the life of the Association through the democratic process of shared responsibility and co-operative effort. Through group experience, opportunities are provided for individuals to grow and become responsible leaders and citizens.[8]

It was agreed at the 1969 convention that consideration should be given to the matter for possible action in 1973.

Educational functions
In a statement prepared for the Second Canadian Conference on Education, held in 1962, the educational concerns of the YWCA were expressed in this way:

... the YWCA carries on a continuing educational program in Citizenship, the broad principles of Christianity, in Health Standards, Public Affairs, and a variety of social and cultural interests. These programs are adapted to the special interest of the younger age groups with which the Association works as well as with the other age groups.

The primary focus of all work in the Association is the growth and development of each individual member and the group work and educational methods used take into account the varying abilities and potentialities of individuals.

Profiting from affiliation with the World YWCA, the Association carries on an educational program in international understanding and encourages Associations to be alert to, and to take social action on, matters on which through careful study they are competent to speak.[9]

The World YWCA Council, at its meeting in Melbourne in 1967, produced a statement of policy on the responsibilities of the organization in the field of education. Specific recommendations were preceded by some observations on the growing importance of education in modern society, on the characteristics of a good education, and on the desirability of ensuring equality of educational opportunity for both sexes. Proposals for YWCA action were given under four headings: influencing governments, work with parents, establishing institutions, and developing out-of-school education. Action at strategic points of governmental decision making was to be preceded by intensive studies of educational aims and policies, of problems, and of plans for the future. Work with parents was to involve efforts to encourage parental interest in children's education, ensuring that all children were enrolled in school, developed sound vocational aspirations, and understood the relation between education and employment. The task of establishing educational institutions for pre-school, primary, and vocational education might fall to the YWCA in the interval before governmental educational institutions had been built up. The main contribution of the organization was said to be in the area of out-of-school education, where people required help to meet the new demands of daily life, to keep up with advancing frontiers in their professions or occupations, to readjust to and retrain for new situations, and to use their free time constructively. The statement of policy elaborated on the responsibilities of the YWCA in these terms.

It is in this field that the YWCA has a special duty to explore the boundaries of education, and to discover the meaning of Christian illumination of all its educational efforts. By originality and competence and readiness to serve groups whose educational needs are not being met, it can assure the acceptance of the work of the voluntary organizations.

The YWCA, as well as the churches, has a role to play in education for Christian unity and in making efforts to relate our religious faith and spiritual values to the world of technology, scientific thought and social attitudes.

The YWCA has an opportunity to invent new ways of preparing citizens to make a contribution to national life and the world order. Such education should lead to an appreciation of the cultural values of other peoples. It should help in developing the courage, patience and ability to approach, with an attitude of openness and reconciliation, those who hold opposing opinions.[10]

Staff training

Like the YMCA, the YWCA demanded much more from its professional employees than good intentions. The first training course for volunteers and staff was offered in Toronto in March 1914. The thirty participants came from the city and from eight other Ontario communities. In 1920–1 a training school was held in co-operation with the University of Toronto. After that time close co-operation was maintained with universities, particularly with their schools of social work, and staff members were encouraged to avail themselves of opportunities to combine study with their work, as well as to engage in graduate study.

In 1931 the first summer school for secretarial study and training was held at Lake Couchiching. An annual orientation course of one week's duration for secretaries was held regularly from 1945 on. Although it went under different names, this course continued to deal with the history, structure, procedures, purposes, and implications of the movement. A further initiative was an in-service training plan, instituted in 1955, when a four-month pilot course on finance was held for executive directors.

Leadership training received strong emphasis in the 1960s. A manifestation of this development was the establishment by the national organization in 1963 of a Co-ordinating Committee for Leadership Development, with the responsibility for developing and interpreting policies and standards related to the training of volunteer and regularly employed staff. It instituted training programs in co-operation with various departments and helped to promote and carry out leadership development activities in local and regional settings.

The idea of training camps for Y teen leaders was advanced in 1961, and accepted with enthusiasm. In 1965 a two weeks' leadership training camp was held under the joint sponsorship of the national councils of the YMCA and the YWCA for older teens who carried responsibilities in the physical education program of local associations.

What was called "the most inclusive and significant leadership training project with which the Canadian YWCA has ever been privileged to participate"[11] was an International Training Institute assembled in Pennsylvania in 1965. Fifty-eight specially selected staff and volunteers from thirty-one countries and four continents, representing an age range from thirty to sixty, took part in the three-month program. The main objective was to explore the opportunities for Christian women to exert leadership. Members exchanged ideas, plans, programs, and convictions. Considerable attention was devoted to recruiting and training of staff and to ways in which communities could be stirred to provide needed services. At the end of a one-month seminar the participants dispersed to various parts of the United States and Canada, where they spent a month working with local associations. At a closing session at the Banff School of Fine Arts they analyzed and evaluated their experiences.

Student assistance
Modest funds were made available in the 1940s for suitable staff members to take approved courses in universities or other accredited schools. Recipients of certain awards were expected to give at least two years of service to the YWCA at the end of the period of study. An allocation of $4,000 provided assistance for thirty-one individuals between 1943 and 1948, and a total of $13,180 was granted to the same number between 1949 and 1952. In 1959–64 the expenditure on scholarships and bursaries amounted to $16,052. At the 1969 convention it was reported that, during the four-year period since the previous convention, somewhat less than half the study grants from the Development Fund were used to assist experienced staff to take short refresher courses and about one-fourth to enable experienced staff to complete undergraduate work. The rest was spent for graduate courses in social work, for pre-employment training experiences, and for subsidies to associations to enable them to employ prospective staff for summer projects in advance of permanent employment.

SIXTEEN

Youth groups

The associations designed primarily or exclusively for the benefit of young people usually attempted to combine educational with social and recreational activities. They placed heavy emphasis on the development of character and sometimes on training for leadership. Some were associated with religious organizations, while others were purely secular.

THE BOY SCOUTS OF CANADA

The Boy Scout movement spread to Canada shortly after its introduction in England in 1907 as the result of the efforts of Lord Baden-Powell. Provision was made for younger boys through the Wolf Cub program in 1916, and for young men through the Rover Scout program in 1917. Venturing was initiated in 1966 for those between Boy Scout and Rover Scout age. The movement in general has been regarded as a major supplement to formal education. According to a recent statement, the aim was to help boys become resourceful and responsible members of the community by providing opportunities for their mental, physical, social, and spiritual development. The programs, each adapted to a specific age group, were designed to encourage boys to love and serve God, to respect the dignity and rights of the individual, and to recognize the obligations of the individual to develop and maintain his potential to the utmost.

The Wolf Cub program, for boys between the ages of eight and ten, emphasized work and play with others in groups, the growth of a sense of responsibility, and the development of skills in hobbies and handicrafts. Boy Scouts between eleven and fourteen participated in a program featuring membership in small friendship and interest groups called patrols, challenging patrol activities based on the principle of learning by doing, the development of good health and physical fitness, experience in and appreciation of the community and the out-of-doors, and the development of hobbies, interests, and skills. The Venturers program, for boys between fourteen and seventeen, offered opportunities for meeting people, going places, and doing interesting things, including involvement in a wide range of co-educational activities. Members were encouraged to become involved in the life of the community. Rover Scouts, between seventeen and twenty-three, were given opportunities for individual development and self-discovery and for the exploration of vocational opportunities.

The movement operated through a system of local sponsorship. The sponsor might be a church of any denomination; a service club such as Kinsmen, Kiwanis, Lions, Optimists, Rotarians, the Canadian Legion, Elks, or Women's Institutes; a professional or business association or institution; the Canadian Armed Forces at their bases in Canada and overseas; public and private schools and school associations, including schools for the blind, deaf, handicapped, mentally retarded, and hospitalized; and groups of citizens. The sponsor provided the meeting facilities, the administration, and the leadership, while the national organization supplied the program. This arrangement made it possible for the movement to maintain its position as by far the largest youth organization in the country.

The *Canadian Boy*, a magazine for Cubs, Scouts, and Venturers, was made available to members on registration. Its nine yearly issues contained stories and useful information. The *Scout Leader*, the official organ of the Boy Scouts of Canada, contained notices of policy changes, information about scouting events, and articles and suggestions about the different aspects of scouting. The *Canadian Scout Executive* served the group referred to in its title. Many scout councils have also published their own news bulletins providing information about local events.

A major responsibility of national, provincial, regional, and district scout councils was to maintain a volunteer staff to organize and provide service for the movement in their areas. These people assisted with the offering of adult education programs for scout leaders and non-members. The programs involved such themes as learning how to work with people, developing leadership skills, examining values and the way in which values develop, learning and gaining skill in the use of instructional techniques, developing programs for groups and individuals, discovering and using community resources, exploring the programs and methods of the Boy Scouts of Canada, and gaining skill in specific program activities. Educational purposes were pursued by means of face-to-face consultation and counselling, small-group discussions and workshops, training courses, seminars and conferences, on-the-job training, the production of handbooks on scouting, and the publication of magazines and bulletins.

Members of local councils were prepared to encourage people demonstrating an interest in serving the movement by providing information on the aims and principles of scouting. Once a person had been given an assignment, the local council members might help him plan a suitable training program. Training was offered in small units of about three hours each, to be taken singly or combined in a course. Three levels of training were recognized: initial, intermediate, and advanced. The first was of fifteen hours' duration, the second of about forty hours, and the third a continuing process with no terminal point.

National training institutes were held for the benefit of trainers and other leading members of the scout movement. Toward the end of the

1960s there was a strong emphasis at these week-long meetings on human relations training and the development of self-awareness. The program for 1969 consisted of courses on the themes of 1 / training trainers in human relations training, 2 / human relations training, 3 / training techniques, and 4 / assessing needs and planning and evaluating training experiences.

In 1969 the national office had over eighty professional executives whose responsibility it was to prepare the outlines and documentary material for use at the local level and to administer national training programs. These executives were encouraged to continue their own education through the provision of time off and financial assistance. The national office began to operate a training centre near Acton, Ontario, in 1937.

The Boy Scout movement underwent a thorough internal examination in the late 1960s to provide the basis for an adaptation of its programs to meet current needs. The essence of the changes made as a result consisted of a shift from a "program-centred" to a "boy-centred" approach. Whereas there had formerly been a tendency to try to mould boys to fit a predetermined model, attention was henceforth to be concentrated more on discovering and developing the unique talents of each individual. It was recognized that this change in emphasis would require a substantial modification in the outlook of many adults who were involved in the scout movement. The adult training program would be counted on to help leaders break down a dominant, authoritarian attitude toward young people. There was no intention, however, of abandoning the adult role of positive leadership.

GIRL GUIDES OF CANADA

The Girl Guide movement, paralleling that of the Boy Scouts, was founded in 1909. The first Canadian Girl Guide company was organized at St Catharines in 1910, a Canadian headquarters was established in 1912, the Canadian Council was incorporated by an act of Parliament in 1917, and the Canadian government began the payment of an annual grant in 1919. A World Association of Girl Guides and Girl Scouts was established in 1928 to provide liaison among the many national organizations that had been established by that time. At the end of the triennial conference held in 1966 there were forty-three full member countries and thirty-eight associate member countries.

According to a recent statement, the aims of the movement were to assist girls from seven to eighteen in the formation of character by encouraging them to be responsible citizens of the country and of the world, by introducing them to adventure and the out-of-doors, by training them in skills which would help them to become good homemakers, and by teaching them to experience the joy of giving service to others. The program for achieving these objectives, like that of the Boy Scouts of Canada, underwent a thorough reappraisal during the 1960s. As a result, less emphasis was placed on the perfection of practical skills such as knot tying and on ceremonials and more on assisting the leader to get to know the girls and to further their personal and individual development.

As of 1969 every adult leader was expected to take a training course before her position in the movement was officially recognized. As a first step she had an orientation session with the local commissioner, who explained the local organization and the basic set-up. She might then proceed to basic training in sessions with other new leaders or take a correspondence course if active training sessions were not accessible. There were further courses to provide knowledge of specialized aspects of guiding such as music, camping, new games, and approaches to the various tests in the program. It was reported that almost every adult member of the movement received some type of training each year in the form of an evening, an all-day, or a weekend session with groups varying in number from ten to forty. The instructors were experienced leaders who had been trained in methods of teaching adults.

In 1968 the total Canadian membership reached 116,439. It was categorized as follows: 58,944 Brownies in 2,484 packs; 41,783 Guides in 1,798 companies; 2,167 Land Rangers in 228 companies; 620 Sea Rangers in 48 crews; 272 Air Rangers in 31 flights; 122 Cadets in 8 companies; 9,502 Guiders; 756 Commissioners; 595 secretaries; and 1,678 committee members.

BOYS' CLUBS OF CANADA

Boys' Clubs of Canada began as a local movement which organized informally in 1929 and obtained a federal charter in 1948. The general purpose of the clubs was "to promote the health, social, educational, vocational and character development of boys" and to provide "wholesome leisure time activities and guidance under trained leadership." While service was provided for boys from all income levels, there was a particular focus on the needs of those from low-income families. Fees were kept very low to ensure that potential participants were not excluded because of economic factors.

The national organization was under the general direction of the National Board, with a National Advisory Council of prominent citizens. Support came from government, service clubs, and fraternal, civic, veteran, labour, business, and women's organizations. Each local club was expected to have a non-sectarian board of directors, a qualified full-time executive director, full-time and part-time assistants, volunteer leaders, a diversified program of activities, a club building or quarters open to all members during its hours of operation, and an adequate operating budget.

Full-time professional workers in most clubs were expected to have a recognized university degree with courses in sociology, psychology, education, and other social sciences. Graduate work was regarded as a decided advantage for promotional purposes. A work study program conducted jointly by Sir George Williams University and Boys' Clubs of Canada enabled promising candidates to obtain the desired training. The program included part-time field work experience of at least twelve hours a week in a club under the supervision of a professional worker. Candidates were expected to commit themselves to at least a year of service in a club affiliated with Boys' Clubs of Canada. The national organization was also prepared to pay half the cost of tuition, under certain conditions, for a professional boys' club worker wishing to continue his formal education.

It was the practice to hold three regional leadership training seminars with the support of the Fitness and Amateur Sport Directorate of the Department of National Health and Walfare. In 1969–70 a fourth seminar was held in Newfoundland to look after the special needs of Boys' Club workers and volunteer leaders in that province. At these seminars new methods and techniques of working with young people were introduced, and participants exchanged information and ideas about successful youth work programs. At the end of the 1960s the association was in the process of organizing a junior leadership development program to take advantage of the leadership contributions of older club members. Such programs had been appearing in an unco-ordinated fashion at the local level.

THE CANADIAN GIRLS IN TRAINING

The origin of the Canadian Girls in Training (CGIT) owed a good deal to the ideals of service aroused during the First World War. The name of the organization reflects the predominance of military concerns at that time. Much of the stimulus for the founding of the movement came also from the success of church-centred programs being established for boys. The broad outlines of the CGIT program were prepared by the Advisory Committee for Co-operation in Girls' Work, later called the National Girls' Work Board, which included representatives of the Boards of Christian Education of the Anglican, Baptist, Presbyterian, and Methodist churches, and of the YWCA. For a number of years the YWCA provided the budget for the new organization, including salaries of national and provincial girls' work secretaries, office space, and travelling expenses.

After the preparation of a small booklet, *Canadian Girls in Training*, in 1917 the national leaders organized a campaign to assemble girls' conferences in population centres across Canada. The sponsorship of local church, YWCA, and other community organizations was solicited in advance. A typical conference began on a Friday evening and lasted through religious services on Sunday. The program on Saturday consisted of talks, demonstrations, and group discussions, with emphasis on four slogans: "Cherish health," "Seek truth," "Know God," and "Serve others." The intention was to arouse enough interest to ensure the formation of a local group. The late war and immediate postwar period saw the organization of provincial and city girls' work boards, leaders' councils, girls' cabinets, and leaders' and girls' camps across Canada. When the YWCA ceased to maintain financial responsibility for the movement in 1920, the churches proved ready and able to take its place.

As outlined in informal literature produced by the CGIT organization, the program was based on several main principles. 1 / Whatever the importance of the school and the home, the ultimate responsibility for the Christian education of teen-age girls rested on the church. 2 / On the assumption that the small group, consisting of eight or ten girls, was the most effective organization for this age level, and that this group should be associated with the church, the Sunday school class, already in existence, was chosen as the CGIT unit. 3 / In accordance with the belief that the leaders of a program of Christian education should be women of Christian faith and character, the appointment of leaders for CGIT groups became the responsibility of the congregation. 4 / The holding of a mid-week session of the Sunday school class was considered an essential means of implementing the CGIT program. It was thought highly desirable to ensure that the Sunday and mid-week sessions were closely related. 5 / The ultimate aim of the program was to have every girl committed to and established in the Christian way of life. Great stress was therefore placed on personal and group Bible study and prayer and courses in the meaning of church membership and missionary education. 6 / The scope of the program was all-inclusive, emphasizing the completeness or wholeness of the Christian life. There was an attempt to offset the tendency to separate the spiritual from the secular.

There is said to have been resistance at an early stage to the concept of the leader as the controller of the group, who chose and directed its program. The leader came to be expected, instead, to lead through participation in a democratic group where the girls made their own decisions. Her role was to enrich the program they chose so that their later choices would reflect deeper and more serious interests. The use of tests, badges, and awards according to regular practice among Boy Scouts and Girl Guides was consciously rejected, since it was considered more desirable to learn to enjoy and value an experience for its own sake than to strive to excel others. Tests were held to be inappropriate because the things that mattered most in a Christian education could not be objectively measured.

Arrangements were made for co-operation with various other agencies maintaining programs with objectives similar to those of the CGIT. In 1923 it was agreed that, where responsible authorities in a local church felt that the needs of the girls were being met by a Girl Guide company, organized under the church's auspices, the policy of the National Girls' Work Board would be one of avoiding duplication. Where Girl Guide programs were being carried out in church groups, joint community rallies would be held. About the same time the YWCA "warmly endorsed" the CGIT, and declared that it would refrain from introducing any other program which might interfere with one established by that organization. The CGIT decided to endorse and promote Junior Red Cross courses for girls aged twelve to sixteen and the St John Ambulance course for girls aged sixteen to eighteen. Co-operation with the Student Christian Movement took the form of encouraging girls to go to university and of endeavouring to enlist the services of university students for summer camps and for permanent leadership after graduation.

The formation of the Religious Education Council of Canada (RECC) in 1919 had major implications for the CGIT movement. At a meeting the following year the National Advisory Committee for Co-operation in Girls' Work, which changed its name to the National Girls' Work Board, asked the RECC to recognize it as the medium through which it would carry on its girls' work. In 1932 arrangements were made for constituent units of the board to name their intended board members as representatives of the RECC, which would then designate them for membership on the board. As members of the RECC, they would thus participate in its deliberations. Other council boards looked after boys', children's, and young people's work.

During the 1940s there was increasing interest in adolescents on the part of other agencies. Many of the competing groups were junior branches of adult organizations which were intended as an assurance of future membership. The YWCA rapidly extended its work with teenage girls, many of whom were not being reached by church groups. Young people's groups increasingly included adolescents, and the formation of junior young people's groups was accelerated.

When the RECC gave way to the Department of Christian Education of the Canadian Council of Churches, the organizational status of the CGIT movement underwent an important change. According to regulations adopted in June 1961 there was provision for a Canadian Girls in Training Committee of the council with the following responsibilities:

1. To provide an agency for conference, consultation, common planning and policy-making by the co-operating bodies concerning the Canadian Girls In Training program.
2. To prepare material suitable for the promotion and program of the Canadian Girls In Training Movement.
3. To make financial provision for executive leadership for the Canadian Girls In Training Movement. These persons shall be available to the co-operating bodies and shall give direction to such projects as may be agreed upon by the Canadian Girls In Training Committee.[1]

An important feature of recent CGIT activities was a leadership program maintained under the direction of a Leadership Education Committee. An example of this type of work was a six-day leadership seminar for volunteer organizational workers held at Geneva Park in 1966 with the assistance of the Ontario Department of Education. Most of the participants, who included a group of Canadian Indians, were interested in community recreation, Home and School affairs, and committee work. Pre-session preparation, demanding an estimated twenty hours of study, was obligatory. One individual whose homework was demonstrably not done was in fact refused admission. At the first session the participants were divided into small groups of six or seven members, where they remained for the greater part of the seminar. At a preliminary session they were given an outline of their assigned task, which involved reaching an agreement on each question before going on to the next. Some of the sessions lasted until two or three o'clock in the morning. As a result of the seminar it was hoped that similar projects might be encouraged in the future.

A related aspect of CGIT programs was a correspondence course, which was first introduced in the mid-fifties. Designed for group leaders, it carried no formal credit toward a certificate or diploma. The respective themes of the five lessons were "The Group," "What is CGIT?," "Leadership," "Program Planning," and "Growing as a Leader."

The official publication of the CGIT was the *Torch*. Over the years it carried information on the activities of the organization, inspirational articles, book reviews, suggestions for programs, and other such material.

THE CANADIAN COUNCIL ON 4-H CLUBS

The Canadian Council on 4-H Clubs was formed in 1931 to co-ordinate the provincial manifestations of the movement and to provide some national direction. The significance of the name of the organization is found in the pledge:

I pledge –
My HEAD to clear thinking,
My HEART to greater loyalty,
My HANDS to larger service, and
My HEALTH to better living for my club, my community and my country.

The program was devoted to a number of educational and other objectives. It attempted to help young people engaged in a wide variety of farming, homemaking, community service, and other activities to 1 / acquire the knowledge, skills, and attitudes necessary for a satisfying personal, family, and community life, 2 / develop leadership talents and abilities, 3 / promote the study and practice of good citizenship, 4 / develop a knowledge of and appreciation for agriculture and home economics and their relationship to the national economy, 5 / recognize the need for continuing education and explore career opportunities, 6 / broaden communications and relations with other countries, and 7 / develop a sound philosophy of life based on lasting and satisfying values.

Clubs were organized and maintained under the guidance of extension officials of the department of agriculture in most provinces, including Ontario. Senior club members and community volunteers gave voluntary service as adult and junior leaders. Assistance was also provided by service clubs and other organizations. The national organization served as a headquarters for the exchange of information among provinces and other countries, conducted studies on current problems and future programs, and utilized the assistance of co-operating agencies. Its specific services included the holding of national 4-H Club conferences, the maintenance of a national 4-H supply service, the organization of national and international exchange programs, the issuing of publications, and the conduct of publicity and public relations.

Communities with several 4-H Clubs often had club leaders' councils for activities such as judging classes which were common to all community clubs. In some such areas there were also club members' councils, with possibly two delegates from each club. These councils looked after such matters as recreation and publicity.

Many of the typical 4-H Club projects exemplified the motto "Learn to Do by Doing." A member might raise a calf or sew a suit, conduct meetings, keep financial records, or display project material. Incentives were provided through local and regional competitions, demonstrations, rallies, tours, camps, and conferences. Among awards offered by the National Council were opportunities to attend 4-H Club conferences held in Washington and Chicago, as well as the privilege of participating in 4-H travel exchanges. Regional incentive awards included participation in rallies, tours, camps, and training courses. Individuals and business firms offered numerous prizes and trophies for conspicuous achievement at the local level.

Despite the relative decline of the farm population in comparison with that of many other occupational groups in the country, the 4-H Club movement continued to flourish. In 1968 there were 75,044 members enrolled in 5,831 regularly organized clubs. This enrolment, higher by 2,352 than that of the previous year, represented a new record. There was also an unprecedented number of local volunteer club leaders – 18,037 as compared with 16,535 in 1967.

THE NAVY LEAGUE OF CANADA

There were several branches of the Navy League of England in Canada during the period between 1895 and 1917. In general that organization was devoted to the maintenance of a powerful British navy. When representatives of Canadian branches met to plan the formation of a Canadian organization, they expressed faith in the importance of sea power as a means of safeguarding the commercial and financial interests of a peace-loving empire. The policy of the new organization was defined in this way:

That the Navy League should help, so far as Canada can help, in strengthening the bases of this protection by promoting popular appreciation in this Dominion of Naval history, traditions, functions and duties.

That it should influence national action and policy along maritime lines by a wider knowledge of what the Royal Navy and a Merchant Marine mean to each and all of us at home, when travelling abroad, or when shipping or receiving merchandise from overseas.

That it should give sympathetic support to the men who man these fleets and who have borne the long-sustained burden and stress of the great war which has recently ended ...

That it should help at the proper time any naval policy that our Government may evolve which is based upon naval strategy as applied to the Empire, and should support Imperial trade and the real freedom of the seas, while exercising through the franchise of its members an influence on Members of Parliament so that never again shall this vastly important subject be made a political football.[2]

The plan of action adopted in the early stages consisted of three aspects: 1 / an educational campaign to spread information about the Navy and the Mercantile Marine through lectures, the circulation of literature, and the placing of readers in public schols, 2 / a drive to raise funds for the relief of British and Canadian sailors and their dependents, and for sailors' homes, institutes, and hospitals in Canada and throughout the British Empire, and 3 / an effort to encourage the establishment of volunteer Naval Brigades for boys and young men in which they might receive practical and theoretical instruction in seamanship to prepare them for service in the Mercantile Marine. The first and third of these aspects of the plan had obvious educational implications.

The League began the publication of a journal called *The Sailor* as its official organ. This journal was used as a means of keeping members informed of the activities of the organization and of helping to educate the community about the value of sea power. It was said that, although every Canadian who operated a factory, exported or imported goods, raised grain, or engaged in mixed farming had a direct interest in the merchant service, many people gave little thought to its importance. As another medium of education, the Educational Committee of the Ontario Division sponsored the preparation of a Naval reader, which was intended to give young people a real appreciation of the work of the Navy and the Merchant Marine and of the importance of sea power.

The three organizations for children and young people were Royal Canadian Sea Cadets, for boys between thirteen and eighteen; Navy

League Cadets, for boys of eleven and twelve; and Navy League Wrenettes, for girls between thirteen and eighteen. The programs for these organizations included instruction to develop such skills as swimming, life-saving, first aid, signalling, and seamanship. For Sea Cadets there were courses during the summer in Canadian Forces training establishments and training cruises in ships of the Canadian Forces. In 1969 the Navy League offered fifteen university scholarships for Sea Cadets, ex-Sea Cadets, and Wrenettes. Among the intangible privileges of membership were companionship with other young people of similar interests and the opportunity to gain recognition according to one's ability and effort.

A new and expanding program in Ontario in 1969–70 involved informal camps organized by local corps in various resort areas where cadets spent a weekend or in some cases an entire week. A particularly successful one was attended by about seventy cadets from seven corps. Two other five-day camps elicited the co-operation of five corps.

Youth training programs cost about $160,000 per year at the end of the 1960s. These funds were obtained from private and public sources such as Community Chest agencies, tag days, Navy League membership fees, and federal and provincial grants. Drives for funds were carried out on a local basis, and most of the funds raised in a particular community were spent in the same place. The Armed Services provided supervision for the summer training program of the Royal Canadian Sea Cadet Corps, as well as necessary equipment, transportation, medical care, and victualling in Royal Canadian Navy ships and establishments.

At the end of the 1960s organizations for young people were in a reasonably flourishing condition. As of December 31, 1969, the Ontario Division reported the existence of fifty-one branches serving eighty-six individual units. These units, consisting of forty-nine Royal Canadian Sea Cadet Corps, twenty-four Navy League Cadet Corps, and thirteen Wrenette Corps, had increased by seven over the previous year. The total number of boys and girls enrolled was about five thousand – approximately the same as in 1965 and twice the membership reported in 1954.

SEVENTEEN

Religious organizations

In the broad sense of the term the churches regarded a large part of their work as educational, including regular religious services. Most of them had programs designed to reach all age groups from infancy to old age. This chapter deals with only a small number of the organizations that were active in the field, and covers their work only briefly. In terms of the number of people reached, the churches must be considered in the forefront of voluntary educational agencies.

THE ANGLICAN CHURCH OF CANADA

The Social Action Unit of the Anglican Church of Canada, formerly called the Council for Social Service, has been responsible for much of the work which might, in a somewhat less than completely comprehensive sense, be called educational. The creation of this department of the General Synod as a result of a motion passed in 1915 did not indicate any radical new policy, but represented a desire to continue certain activities in an expanded and more effective form. Soon after its formation, the council undertook studies on immigration, gambling, alcoholism, and moral questions. In 1917 publication of the *Bulletin* was begun to educate the clergy and the laity on social and moral questions. Some of the topics dealt with in the early years were "Industrial Unrest," "Alien Immigration," "Mothers' Pensions," and "Infant Mortality."[1]

During the ten or twelve years immediately after the First World War the work of the council consisted mainly of assisting with the problems of postwar re-establishment, migration, and unemployment. Co-operation was established with a variety of other agencies in the social welfare field. One of these was the Child Welfare Council, later called the Canadian Welfare Council, with which studies, field trips, and other educational projects were conducted jointly. During the 1930s the council participated in a committee with the Missionary Society, the General Board of Religious Education, and the Women's Auxiliary to establish travelling libraries for families in remote areas with no access to public libraries. Newly established diocesan councils distributed a large amount of information and educational material to clergy and church members by means of bulletins, pamphlets, slides, and books on economic, sociological, and theological topics from a lending library. There were increasing efforts to pressure governments into taking more responsibility for social welfare to alleviate the effects of the depression.

An activity of an indisputably educational nature was begun in 1950 with the creation of a Committee on Marriage Counselling. This committee emphasized service to the clergy to enable them to become more aware of resources and new skills in marriage counselling. A National Institute on Marriage was organized, followed by some regional institutes. Much of the social service work of the 1950s had to do with the reception of immigrants and their integration into the life of the community. Part of the program involved the offering of English language classes.

During the 1960s Anglican Church agencies showed a great deal of interest in family life education. Material was provided for parish, diocesan, and regional use in the organization of programs in this area. These programs were designed to demonstrate the more positive side of the church's ministry to families, as compared to services to those in trouble. The basic premise was that, despite the rapidity and nature of social change, the family still provided the best opportunity for the healthy growth of the human personality. The family-life education program was said to have three essential elements: 1 / comprehensive background knowledge of how individuals grow and develop within the modern family, 2 / understanding of how groups function, and 3 / increasing awareness of one's feelings and reactions in a group setting. Various sessions and courses differed in their specific objectives. Examples were a course for couples contemplating marriage, an eight-to-ten-week program for parents of preschoolers and their children, a four-night session for parents of school-age children, a four-night session of exchanges between parents and their teen-age offspring, and a program dealing with issues of concern to young adults. These were sometimes offered in a series of morning or evening sessions or in a full-day or weekend workshop.

In 1966 Anglican and other Canadian churches co-operated with Ortho Pharmaceutical (Canada) Ltd in the planning and conduct of a one-day symposium on all aspects of family planning. The papers and proceedings were said to have been distributed to every doctor and clergyman in the country. As a result of the success of the project a further symposium on family life education was held the following year, attracting almost three thousand physicians, clergymen, educators, social workers, and interested parents.

THE UNITED CHURCH OF CANADA
The Presbyterian, Methodist, and Congregational Churches in Canada were combined on June 10, 1925, to form the United Church of Canada. Educational matters were the concern of the Board of Religious Education, which was to provide for each age group in the church through

programs of worship, instruction, service activities, and recreation. Special attention was to be given to the development of religious knowledge, the promotion of Christian attitudes, and the encouragement of Christian conduct. The board was to provide leadership for the following agencies: Sunday schools; young people's societies and similar organizations; groups of older boys and girls meeting between Sundays; junior groups such as Junior Departments, Junior Christian Endeavor, and Junior Leagues; the public schools; church vacation schools; summer and winter training schools and training institutes; and leadership training schools. This list excluded regular Sunday church services, a major educational influence which was considered to be the responsibility of the whole church.

The Board of Christian Education was formed in 1932 to replace the Board of Education and the Board of Religious Education, both of which had existed far back in the history of the uniting churches. In addition to the responsibilities mentioned in connection with the Board of Religious Education, the Board of Christian Education administered the Marriage Guidance Council, which was to help clergymen through seminars, training institutes, and literature to perform their pastoral functions relating to marriage more effectively; to adopt programs in co-operation with other departments and agencies; and to produce literature to help in preparation for marriage and family life and in marriage counselling. The board was to make an annual review of its activities and to report to the General Council through the Division of Congregational Life and Work.

Programs for the Christian education of boys were conducted as follows: Tyro for juniors between the ages of nine and eleven, Sigma-c for intermediates between twelve and fourteen, and Tuxis for seniors between fifteen and seventeen. These organizations offered opportunities for recreation, sports, handicrafts, and instruction at the appropriate level. For older boys there was increasing stress on discussion of problems and guidance.

An Explorer program, begun in 1927, evolved into the recognized weekday program for junior girls. Other churches sponsored it as a program for both boys and girls. During the late 1950s an inter-church committee developed suitable program materials, which were produced by the United Church Publishing House. The purpose of the Explorers was to learn through participation in activities and projects, to engage in play, and to worship.

During the 1960s a comprehensive new curriculum was planned, tested, authorized by the General Council, and produced. Based on the Bible, it had three main themes: God and His Purpose, Jesus Christ and the Christian Life, and the Church and the World. Each theme was to receive emphasis in turn during successive years of a three-year cycle. About 95 per cent of the church's pastoral charges became to some degree involved in the plan.

Considerable efforts were made to prepare teachers for educational work in the church. Between 1961 and 1970, 185 demonstration schools were held for 10,477 teachers and staff members, and 36 observation practice schools for 1,932 trainees. The latter schools, of one week's duration, were mostly for teachers of kindergarten, junior, and intermediate children. These activities were widely scattered across Canada.

The Board of Christian Education submitted a set of recommendations and proposals for consideration by the commissioners to the Twenty-Fourth General Council with respect to education in the church in the 1970s.[2] There would be efforts to meet the needs of three 'constituencies": 1 / the people, including adults, parents, youth, and children in about 755,000 households, plus single adults and older persons; 2 / about 80,000 volunteer lay teachers and leaders in congregations and communities; and 3 / about 3,000 ministers, deaconesses, and other full-time professionally trained leaders. Curriculum resources appropriate for each group would continue to be produced and made available at the lowest possible cost.

THE RELIGIOUS SOCIETY OF FRIENDS

Much of the original impulse that led to the founding of the Religious Society of Friends, or the Quaker movement, by George Fox in seventeenth-century England manifested itself in recent years in social service and educational activities, often closely intertwined. The members, individually and collectively, attempted to bear witness to their faith by helping the unemployed, sponsoring improved care for the mentally ill, and working for prison reform, racial equality, and social justice. In accord with their emphasis on the importance of an educated membership they founded many schools and colleges in Great Britain and North America. A renowned example in Ontario is Pickering College at Newmarket.

The well known Quaker antipathy to the settling of international disputes by force, and the objection of adherents of the faith to military service, manifested themselves in efforts to promote the cause of peace. This motive was evident in the founding of the Canadian Friends Service Committee in 1931 "to unify and expand the concerns of Friends in Canada for peace witness and peace education, international service and social concerns." A major means of promoting international understanding consisted in holding conferences and seminars for diplomats and other leaders. At these gatherings small groups of individuals from various religious, national, racial, and political backgrounds lived together for several days, studying and discussing common experiences. As an aspect of the program of peace education in Canada, the Grindstone Island Peace Centre was established in 1963. At this centre students, teachers, journalists, diplomats, and others could consider such topics as disarmament, economic and social justice, and alternatives to violence in settling disputes. The peace education program involved such Canadian matters as relationships between the French- and English-speaking groups and international problems such as the war in Vietnam and the status of China.

The distribution of efforts on the part of the Canadian Friends Service Committee in 1968 was indicated by the annual report. 1 / International services and relief work, including community development at Friends Rural Centre, Rasulia, India, leadership training through service in Mexico, help to refugees in Egypt, support of a day nursery for Arab refugee children in Jordan, and the development of social services in Pakistan cost $19,153. 2 / Shipment of drugs and surgical first aid kits to the Democratic Republic of Vietnam (Hanoi), the National Liberation Front, and the Republic of Vietnam (Saigon), and support for the Quaker Prosthetics and Rehabilitation Centre in Quang Ngai, South Vietnam, cost $66,262. 3 / Services in Canada, such as support of the Canadian Urban Training Program, leadership development through services to underprivileged youth, and support of community development programs for Canadian Indians cost $1,556. 4 / The peace education program, including a conference with mass media and university representatives, year-round contact with diplomats, peace literature and films, the development of training in non-violence, addresses and discussions on current national and world issues, the promotion of dialogues between French- and English-speaking Canadians, contacts with groups and individuals abroad, support of the Quaker program at the United Nations, and Quaker conferences and seminars in southern Asia cost $27,767. This information indicates the overwhelming concern of the organization for international relief work.

The interest of the society in combatting prejudice and promoting positive feelings among different social groups was demonstrated in the 1960s through seminars on biases in teaching. At one of these gatherings, held at the Education Conference Centre in Toronto in February 1964, a prominent speaker dealt with the many ways in which prejudice entered the schools. A panel of well known educators pursued the same topic during the afternoon. The participants were said to have clarified their thinking and to have recognized many areas of subtle bias of which they had not previously been aware. The Teaching Problems Sub-Committee, which had made the arrangements for the seminar, was encouraged to continue its activities. The same cause was promoted through encouragement of the Ontario Human Rights Commission.

EIGHTEEN

Service clubs
and associations

In varying degrees service clubs and associations combined social purposes with efforts to further various worthy causes. The raising of money to assist young people with scholarships and bursaries was an activity that often had a particular appeal for them. They sometimes enriched the atmosphere of schools by providing books, radios, television sets, musical instruments, and other equipment. Some of their programs were designed to further the education of various groups of adults. Not least important were activities intended for the enlightenment of their own members.

THE ASSOCIATION OF CANADIAN CLUBS

Canadian Clubs had as their theme the building of respect for Canada as a nation and the fostering of pride in Canadian identity. The move began in the 1890s when the need for these qualities, never considered to be in abundant supply at any time in the history of the country, was particularly marked. The first club resulted from the passing of a resolution at Hamilton in 1893.

It is, in the opinion of this meeting, a fit and proper time to take definite steps, however humble, to deepen and widen the regard of Canadians for their land of birth or adoption and to increase their interest in matters affecting the welfare of their country.
Be it, therefore, resolved that this meeting proceed to the organization of a society to be known as *The Canadian Club*, having for its objects the encouragement of the study of the history, literature, and resources of Canada, the recognition of native worth and talent, and the fostering of a patriotic Canadian sentiment.

There was press support for the hope that the movement might speedily assume national proportions. During the succeeding decade, however, only two additional clubs made their appearance, one at Toronto and another at Ottawa. Some apprehension was expressed at Toronto at what was seen as a threat of disloyalty to the Empire, but the club managed to flourish. The movement rapidly gained momentum in the first few years of the twentieth century, and by 1907 there were nearly thirty clubs in various places across the country. The Association of Canadian Clubs was organized in 1909. Thirty years later it was incorporated by Act of Parliament with the declared purpose of fostering throughout Canada an interest in public affairs and of cultivating an attachment to Canadian institutions.

The clubs attempted to achieve their objectives chiefly through lectures. In the earlier years there was a great demand for good public speakers, and very large audiences were often assembled to hear them. Later decades, however, witnessed the development of a large number of cultural, sports, recreational, and educational activities which, along with radio, and later television, offered increasingly successful competition. Changes of this kind affected the clubs' methods of operation. They tended to undertake such activities as prodding other organizations to help further their objectives, marking local historic sites with national significance, offering free classes in basic English for new Canadians, participating in citizenship ceremonies, and sponsoring exhibits of Canadian art. In the face of competition for people's time, they reduced the number of their meetings and concentrated on securing speakers of the highest quality.

The focus of attention shifted over the years. Colonial-mindedness gave way to cultural influence from the United States as a threat to Canadian identity. Besides attempting to counteract such influence, the clubs identified for themselves a major role in combatting provincialism and regionalism. There was also an interest in Canada's position and reputation among the nations of the world. An alert and informed public opinion was seen as a vital element in the solution of problems in all these areas.

THE IMPERIAL ORDER DAUGHTERS OF THE EMPIRE

The Imperial Order Daughters of the Empire (IODE) came into existence in 1900 as a "patriotic, non-sectarian, non-partisan and philanthropic" organization for Canadian women. It operated on a number of organizational levels: junior chapters for those under eighteen years of age, primary chapters, municipal chapters with jurisdiction over primary and junior chapters within a locality, provincial chapters, and a national chapter. Its interest in education was demonstrated by the fact that it spent $330,515 on activities in that field in 1969, a slight reduction from the expenditure of the previous year.

The best known service of the IODE to education to the end of the 1960s was the provision of scholarships, bursaries, grants, and loans. In 1959–60 1,262 students received such awards from provincial, municipal, and primary chapters, the total financial assistance amounting to $144,821.90. The recipients were enrolled in the widest variety of university, teachers' college, and other post-secondary courses. In numerous instances, high school students were assisted to complete their program. Members occasionally contributed to the effort to keep promising students from remote rural areas in school by taking them into their homes.

By 1961–2 the total amount spent on student assistance reached $172,178.55, benefiting 1,810 individuals. The number of the latter rose to 1,994 the following year, although the total expenditure declined slightly. The trend toward more and somewhat smaller awards was again in evidence in 1963–4. The awards then consisted of 249 scholarships, 732 bursaries, 144 grants, 150 loans, and 899 prizes. It was estimated that the IODE gave 4 per cent of all student awards made in Canada. Some of the assistance was directed toward such fields as music, art, ballet, drama, and creative writing in prose and poetry. One chapter offered a bursary for summer study in oral French; another established a fund to assist in the training of teachers for work in the Canadian Arctic; another provided a scholarship for an Indian or Eskimo student residing in the Northwest Territories; others assisted blind and handicapped students. Special awards listed in the report for 1964–5 included a bursary fund for negro students, another for Indian and Métis students, a fellowship in social work, a grant to a ward of a Children's Aid Society to enable him to attend an Institute of Technology, and awards to a deaf student and a blind student attending a college of education, to a deaf student to go to Washington, DC for laboratory science, to a French-speaking student from western Canada for further study in Quebec, to a student for advanced study in radiological technology, and to an Eskimo student.

By the mid-sixties the establishment of student loan funds by the Canadian and several provincial governments was exerting an influence on the IODE student assistance program. Consideration was given to the possible expansion of awards to students in certain specific categories: 1 / the bright student from a low-income home, proceeding to an advanced degree, who feared the burden of future loan replayments; 2 / the student with specific technical skills who needed additional courses in academic subjects; 3 / the student who desired special training in another province; 4 / the graduate student; 5 / the student needing support for study of the creative arts; 6 / the Eskimo or Indian student needing financial encouragement to complete a secondary school education; 7 / the student who left school early and wished to resume his education. The IODE saw no reason to withdraw from the field of student assistance because of increased government activity.

The report for 1965–6 indicated an increasing interest in continuing education. Bursaries were awarded for teachers to continue oral French studies, for teachers of retarded children to attend summer school, and in one instance for an ex-serviceman to take a correspondence course. Student assistance was complemented by the sponsorship of night school classes. In many cases IODE members acted as instructors.

In 1967–8 there was strong emphasis on assisting students at the secondary level to meet the costs of transportation, fees, and extra tutoring. One chapter encouraged family interest by presenting the bursary

certificates to the mothers of the recipients. Another assisted the graduates of its adopted Indian school to proceed to secondary education. A
number of chapters maintained emergency funds for secondary and post-
secondary students. Prizes and awards were given for outstanding achievement in every subject, as well as for improvement shown.

Work with schools
According to the 1959–60 report, 70 per cent of the chapters adopted or
assisted schools during he year. A total of 2,264 schools were sent
librairies, library refills, recreational equipment, handicraft equipment,
visual aids, flags, and pictures. The yearly IODE calendar, designed primarily for the classroom, was produced, and 17,382 copies were placed
in schools. Prizes for school achievement included 2,418 books, as well
as cups, plaques, and cash awards. Representatives of chapters visited
their schools on Remembrance Day and Commonwealth and Citizenship
Day and special programs were prepared to make students aware of the
significance of these days. In some provinces copies of the programs
were distributed with the assistance of the Department of Education. The
total amount spent on assistance to the schools during the year was
$63,018.97.

The annual report for 1961–2 mentioned the continuation of similar
activities. Many gifts were said to have been intended to stimulate interest
in art, music, drama, and literature. Particular attention was directed
toward children with physical handicaps. The campaign to arouse patriotism involved the distribution of four hundred pictures of Queen
Elizabeth II to schools, civic buildings, a university, and an Atlantic ice-
breaker. In the same cause, 358 flags and 35,715 calendars were donated
to schools and other agencies. A major increase in concern for the welfare of Indian and Eskimo children led to the adoption of all fifty-six
schools in the Arctic and Mackenzie education districts. These schools
received 1,700 prize books and other gifts valued at $3,657. Similar
interest was shown in the forty-two schools of northern and southern
Labrador. In subsequent years there was a further expansion of assistance
programs in remote schools in Newfoundland.

More specific information was given in the 1962–3 report about
donations to schools. Unique gifts included a reference library of the
National Geographic magazine covering a period of thirty-one years, a
model of the solar system, provision for special outings to local industries
and historical sites, a royal family scrapbook contest, and a conservation
contest. There were donations of outdoor sports equipment of every
type, as well as games, crafts, sewing materials, band instruments, film
strips, and other items for indoor use. Some of the more costly gifts were
projectors, microscopes, electric typewriters, and pianos.

The report for 1965–6 noted that, although in some areas integration
and amalgamation had closed Indian schools, there had been a marked

increase in assistance to those remaining. Besides sending books and supplies, adopting chapters encouraged further education by giving prizes to all Indian students graduating from high school, taking students by bus from their reservation to visit museums and other places of interest, and giving awards to students for perfect attendance, as well as providing the scholarship and bursary assistance already mentioned. One chapter made a practice of sending clothing and other goods to the school, where they were sold and the proceeds used for school supplies. For the first time achievement awards for various subjects in the school curriculum were offered on behalf of the National Chapter to students in the five secondary schools in the Mackenzie educational district. The IODE secured the co-operation of provincial Departments of Education to evaluate the effectiveness of its work and to increase the number of Indian school adoptions.

The program for 1967–8 naturally reflected the centennial theme. Tours were arranged to Expo, to the Confederation Caravan, and to museums and historical sites. There were presentations of special centennial medallions, silver dollars, stamp collections, and spoons. Many of the customary programs of the IODE were adapted in such a way as to draw attention to the significance of the celebrations.

Special projects

The IODE engaged in a variety of activities called "special educational projects," which were mentioned in the minutes of annual meetings. Reference was made in the report for 1959–60 to the Commonwealth Correspondence program, called in earlier years the Young Comrades correspondence. Students, particularly those attending rural schools, were said to be deriving great benefit from contacts with boys and girls in other provinces and countries. They were finding the information from their letters useful in social studies and citizenship discussions. Another special project emphasized in the same year was the sponsorship of cultural activities. Many students were given tickets to attend lectures, concerts, and music and drama festivals, and were provided with the means to visit the Stratford Shakespearean Festival and the capital, as well as to participate in United Nations seminars.

Under the heading of special educational projects the 1961–2 report mentioned the donation of $2,000 by one chapter to help a university establish an Arts Centre. Among the many community interests of the IODE were music and drama festivals, art exhibits, public-speaking contests, and physical fitness classes. Educational equipment was purchased for schools for the blind, cerebral palsy clinics, and schools for the retarded. Local libraries were staffed and partially supported. Many members, either as representatives of the order or as individuals, made contributions to education by attending provincial conferences, serving on curriculum committees, appearing on radio and television on behalf of educational causes, and standing for election to school boards.

The total contribution to special educational projects in 1964–5 amounted to $45,321.54. The report for that year listed safety and health classes, assistance to music, art, drama, public-speaking, and skating festivals, the cataloguing and repairing of books and the staffing of local libraries, the establishment of a Library Endowment Fund and a free lending library, a summer school for Indian and Métis girls, student trips to the United Nations, special training for physically handicapped children and adults, the purchase of a mace and flag pole for a new university, and the provision of a rare book collection for another university. One municipal chapter organized a drop-out project designed to prevent early school leaving. The members worked after school hours with students who were encountering difficulties in basic school subjects. Educational authorities were reported to have been "amazed" at the results and to have requested an expansion of the program.

The report for 1966–7 mentioned many of the same activities listed in previous years, but gave particular attention to the broadening of work in special education. There was an increase in assistance to sheltered workshops and to schools for the handicapped, retarded, and emotionally disturbed. Books were translated into braille, a gift of special resonant instruments was made to a school for the deaf for use in the band, supplies were purchased for a kindergarten for Indian and Métis children at Slave Lake, and assistance was provided for an orientation class for Indian children having difficulty at school. Both the 1966–7 and 1967–8 reports referred to help for Head Start classes in depressed areas of cities.

In 1959–60 the organization took cognizance of the extreme lack of books and other educational supplies in West Indian schools. Eleven chapters scattered across the country established links with the same number of secondary schools in St Kitts, Nevis, Anguilla, Montserrat, and Dominica. An initial library was sent to each school, followed by magazines, records, and novels. Eight chapters sent sets of the *Encyclopaedia Britannica*. Because of the success of the project, it was extended during the next year to what was then the Federation of the West Indies and to British Honduras. Twenty-five schools became involved, and a great many more applied for adoption. In 1961–2 the number participating reached a total of forty-five. For a number of subsequent years the program remained fairly stable, although the range of items sent increased to include microscopes, tape recorders, language records, and art supplies.

THE FEDERATED WOMEN'S INSTITUTES OF ONTARIO
The first Women's Institute in Ontario was formed at Stoney Creek in 1897 on the initiative of Adelaide Hoodless. Affiliated with the Farmers' Institute, it was designed to assist women to minister to the health, comfort, and general welfare of the family in the rural home. A second institute was soon formed at Saltfleet, and the movement spread quickly, not

only to other provinces of Canada, but also to Great Britain, the other dominions, and various European countries. The Ontario Department of Agriculture encouraged the movement in Ontario with financial grants and other forms of assistance.

Mrs Hoodless worked through the Women's Institute to persuade the provincial government to make provision for a women's department at the Ontario Agricultural College. A contribution of $200,000 by Sir William Macdonald led to the establishment of Macdonald Institute. One of the earliest direct contributions of the Women's Institute to education was a lecture service, called the summer series, dealing with various aspects of homemaking. Some years later demonstration lecture courses of ten days' duration were introduced. These courses dealt with such topics as cookery and food values, sewing, nursing and first aid, and homecrafts. The Women's Institute Branch of the Department of Agriculture set up a packet loan service to supply information for the preparation of speeches, debates, and other programs. Free bulletins dealt with nutrition, water supply, poultry, and related matters. Local leader-training schools were organized, beginning in 1935, accommodating one or more leaders from each branch. These leaders then took the information back to the members of their local groups.

The programs of the monthly institute meetings were educational in purpose. Papers and addresses were presented on a great variety of subjects, and visiting speakers included doctors, lawyers, clergymen, and other informed individuals. Their presentations were typically followed by discussions among the members.

A certain number of Junior Women's Institutes were organized, often as a sequel to month-long courses held by local branches of the institute in co-operation with the agricultural representative. Considerably more numerous were the Homemaking Clubs, which enrolled 2,500 girls in 1942. These clubs gave girls an opportunity to learn how to entertain, how to choose materials for dressmaking, how to prepare foods economically and tastefully, and how to deal with other household matters. Gardening and canning clubs achieved some of the same purposes. The names of the various clubs were eventually abandoned in favour of "4-H Girls' Homemaking Clubs." In 1968–9 there were 2,918 of these clubs with 12,986 members. In many cases local Women's Institute branches acted as sponsors and institute members participated as leaders.

Part of the institute educational program involved direct help to schools. Institutes encouraged and sponsored the provision of medical and dental inspection, hot lunches, musical instruction, libraries, first aid kits, and playground equipment. Their members served as trustees, secretaries of school boards, teachers, and janitors. They formed school committees to co-operate with teachers and trustees in beautifying school grounds. Prizes and medals were given for attendance, punctuality, entrance examinations, essays, and contests.[1]

A scholarship fund was introduced immediately after the Second World War as a memorial to the founders of the Women's Institutes half a century earlier. The money was used for Ontario Women's Institute Entrance Awards of $100 each for students entering the degree course in home economics at Macdonald Institute. Two awards were made in 1948 and five annually in subsequent years. Additional contributions made possible the establishment of the Dorothy Futcher Ontario Women's Institute Scholarship for members of the Junior Women's Institute and the 4-H Girls' Homemaking Clubs. In 1970 there were twenty-six county, area, and district scholarships of $100 each. The recipient could use the money to further her education in any way she saw fit through courses or for instruction in music, drama, literature, or art, subject to the approval of the Ontario Women's Institute Scholarship Committee.

As a member of the Associated Country Women of the World, the Ontario organization participated in an international scholarship program in honour of Lady Aberdeen, which originated in 1959. The scholarship was used for training women in home economics, nutrition, and rural community welfare. The awards were made in close consultation with the Food and Agriculture Organization of the United Nations. Another effort in the international scholarship field was begun in 1961 when the Federated Women's Institutes of Ontario agreed to raise $50,000 for a fund to help educate young women in the developing countries.

In 1940, on the suggestion of Lady Tweedsmuir, the Women's Institutes undertook to compile histories of local communities. By 1970 about 90 per cent of the Ontario branches, numbering over 1,300, had become involved in the work. Curators were appointed at branch, district, area, and provincial levels to act as custodians of the books and to co-operate with historical societies. The material was of interest to students conducting research in local history and to history teachers.

A change in central administration was made after the Second World War when the Women's Institute Branch became the Women's Institute Branch and Home Economics Service. The services of this branch were made available to all rural women in the province and to Women's Institutes applying for assistance. In 1964 the branch became the Home Economics Branch of the Department of Agriculture and Food. In 1969 26,000 women participated in programs designed to improve homemaking skills and management. The program of the Home Economics Branch in 1970 included short courses, training schools, and workshops in crafts, clothing and textiles, food and nutrition, and parliamentary procedures.

THE NATIONAL COUNCIL OF JEWISH WOMEN
OF CANADA

When the National Council of Jewish Women was founded in the United States in 1893, sections of the organization were established in various parts of Canada. A Canadian Division was formed in 1939, and a charter obtained in 1947. By-laws of the Toronto Section, as revised in 1965, stated that the National Council was "dedicated to furthering human welfare in the Jewish and general communities, locally, nationally, and internationally. Through an integrated program of education, service and social action, it provides essential services and stimulates and educates the individual and the community toward their responsibility in advancing human welfare and the democratic way of life." Six specific purposes of the Toronto Section were listed:

To promote the program of the National Council of Jewish Women of Canada;
To further unite efforts on behalf of Judaism by making available means of study;
To bring about a closer fellowship among all Jewish Women;
To furnish a medium of interchange of thought through working together with other organizations in pursuit of common interests and goals;
To encourage and furnish efficient volunteer service through personal commitment;
To cherish and preserve those values which contribute to the dignity, understanding and equal rights of every human being.

In its early stages the council devoted much of its attention to newly arrived immigrants. Many of these people felt a sense of bewilderment, and were very much in need of friendly assistance. The council held English and citizenship classes, organized summer camps, and provided recreation for working women and children. Among the highlights of the contributions of the Toronto Section in the early years were the operation of a Red Cross centre during the First World War, the provision of care for the sick during the influenza epidemic of 1918, and the opening of Community House on St George Street in 1922. The formation of Jewish welfare societies was promoted to take over the financial burden of philanthropic work, and the council turned its attention in other directions.

The council's educational program was said to have been designed to create local, national, and international awareness of public issues. Among the activities of this type were study groups, general meetings, stands on public issues, and representations to government authorities through letters, interviews, resolutions, and briefs. Some of the service projects had a major educational component: for example, such programs for the elderly as Golden Age Clubs, Creative Living, and Second Careers, as well as enrichment programs for preschoolers and their mothers, and tutorial services for older students. A certain amount of assistance was provided to students with good academic records and demonstrated financial need. Travelling fellowships were granted to those interested in studying the problems of older people. Short courses were sponsored for nurses to enable them to participate in rehabilitation programs for the aged. The education of the council's own members were promoted through institutes and seminars on general aspects of organizational work and on specific projects. Examples included an institute on community services, an institute on social action, area conferences, and leadership and human relations seminars.

A number of projects were carried out to assist educational causes overseas. An Israeli Fund, administered through the Ministry of Education, enabled a substantial number of Jewish and Arab teachers to improve their qualifications for teaching in Israel. Ship-a-Box projects involved supplying kindergartens in Israel and Morocco with toys and other materials. The Israeli Foundation for Handicapped Children received assistance in providing special equipment such as wheel chairs, sports equipment, and machinery for the rehabilitation of the handicapped.

THE CANADIAN FEDERATION OF UNIVERSITY WOMEN

Individual university women's clubs existed in various centres before the establishment of the national federation in 1919. They were encouraged to unite so that Canada might have a vehicle for representation at the International Federation of University Women, which was then being planned. Delegates to the organization meeting, held in Toronto, came from Ottawa, Winnipeg, Regina, Edmonton, and Victoria. From the beginning the new federation made all phases of education its first interest, as reflected in some of the resolutions passed at the meeting. One proposed an annual scholarship of $1,000 for graduate study outside the country. Another urged members to work for more women members of governing bodies of universities and colleges and of school boards. A committee was formed to report on the condition of libraries in Canada.

The implementation of the resolution regarding scholarships was a prominent feature of the federation's early achievements. A number of women who benefited from these scholarships went on to occupy important professional and other positions. In the late 1920s one of the presidents of the organization listed a number of other educational concerns: helping university women to find work for which they were adapted, working for higher salaries for teachers, securing the appointment of deans of girls in secondary schools, and providing opportunities for the gifted child, education for leisure, and adult education. A Vocations Bureau was set up in an office in Toronto in 1930, but was forced to close little more than a year later because of a lack of funds. During the same period two investigations were conducted by the education committee: a study of the standards and curricula in the secondary school system of the various provinces and a study of experimentation in radio in relation to formal education. A few years later the Vocations Committee prepared a summary of professional courses of study in Canada and arranged for the publication of a series of monographs on occupations.

Interest in the occupational field was heightened during the depression years because of the increase in discrimination against working women which accompanied it. An exhaustive study was made of women in administrative positions in Canada in the mid-thirties.

The interests of the federation during the Second World War were largely concerned with relief work, which was particularly directed toward university women. In the early war years the number of members remained fairly static, but a period of rapid growth followed. During the late war and early postwar period high school teachers were provided with information about various women's professions in Canada to be used for vocational guidance. There was also provision for a grant for experimental children's library work in thinly settled rural areas. The number and value of scholarships and bursaries awarded were gradually increased.

In 1950 the federation adopted the practice of supporting its resolutions with submissions to agencies that might be in a position to further its causes. It presented a Brief to the Royal Commission on National Development in the Arts, Letters and Sciences in which it made recommendations in the areas of scholarships, research in education, a National Library, UNESCO, radio, and television. Later resolutions requested the establishment of a Canada Council, the formation of a Canadian Commission for UNESCO, and the provision of adequate funds for the National Gallery and the CBC. The federation's views on the educational possibilities of radio and television continued to be presented at intervals during the next few years.

By the early 1960s women were being welcomed into the economy much more readily than they had been two or three decades earlier. Attention was shifted toward support for refresher courses and continuing education, with growing recognition of the need for research in this area. There was solid support from the federal and provincial governments and consultants from academic and government circles, as well as the members themselves, for the study leading to the report *Women University Graduates in Continuing Education and Employment*, published in 1967. This study demonstrated the high degree of interest in further education among women graduates of universities.

The wide variety of activities of local clubs in 1969–70 was illustrated in the Golden Jubilee issue of the *Chronicle*, a federation publication.[2] Many Ontario clubs sponsored meetings on the Hall-Dennis report, at which members of the Provincial Committee on Aims and Objectives appeared to address the audience and answer questions. Some study groups discussed the status of women in Canada. A great deal of concern was shown over the problems of Canadian Indians, and one club made a grant of $400 for the continuing education of a non-treaty Indian. There were also studies of other minority groups, including Hutterites, Doukhobors, and Canadian negroes. Projects of a specifically educational nature included efforts to alleviate the difficulties experienced by emotionally disturbed children, the establishment of a day care centre, and the organization of volunteer tutoring under school board supervision. In one community the proceeds from several art shows were used to provide art instruction for grade 3 pupils. Other groups supported preschool programs for disadvantaged children. There was a strong effort to promote bilingualism, with French conversation groups flourishing everywhere. These and many other activities demonstrated the vitality of the movement.

The triennial conference held in March 1970 featured three study seminars dealing with topics chosen by the members through a questionnaire: environmental pollution, disadvantaged Canadian Indians, and unrest in education. Associated with the first of these topics was a preview of a film on the pollution problem in cities, with Toronto as an example. The seminar had the benefit of the experience of people from industry, the federal and provincial governments, universities, and private practice, among whom were physicians, biologists, lawyers, chemists, physicists, engineers, and economists. The study seminar on Indian problems was addressed by Harold Cardinal, president of the Indian Association of Alberta and author of *The Unjust Society*, as well as by a number of other Indian participants. All these sessions had broad implications for education as well as contributing to the enlightenment of the members themselves.

KIWANIS

Kiwanis, an international service organization, had clubs in nineteen countries in 1969. At that time there were approximately 130 clubs in Ontario in thirteen divisions. Each club enjoyed a considerable degree of local autonomy so that it might adapt its services to meet the needs of its own community. It was common to find in each club five standing committees dealing with areas of service which impinged on education: youth services, public and business affairs, vocational guidance, key clubs, and Circle K clubs.

Youth services committees were involved in activities for boys and girls of elementary and secondary school age. There was also a special effort to reach adolescent youth, particularly those who were not engaged in formal education. Among major programs for youth were the Kiwanis music festivals conducted annually in many Ontario communities. The Metro Toronto Music Festival in 1969 attracted more than 29,000 participants, and those in Orillia and Owen Sound about 2,000 each. The participants had the benefit of evaluation and advice from competent adjudicators of national and international prominence. Considerable sums of money were distributed each year in the form of scholarships and bursaries for further study in music. Another type of service to youth was the provision of supervision and financial support to boys' and girls' clubs. The North York Kiwanis Club owned a 142-acre farm near Brooklin with a building and facilities for year-round use to which teacher-supervised groups from North York schools made almost daily field trips.

An example of an educational service provided through club committees on Public and Business Affairs was the publication of a booklet *You and the Law*, which was used as a supplement to addresses given on the subject in secondary schools. Speakers were selected with attention, not only to their professional competence, but also to their experience in communicating with adolescents. Information and advice were offered to encourage young people to obey the law. They were also given some suggestions on procedure if they should find themselves in conflict with the law.

Kiwanis vocational guidance committees offered counselling sessions in co-operation with school administrators. Through these sessions individual students and groups were made aware of various scholarships and bursaries offered by the club.

Key clubs and Circle κ clubs were formed in secondary schools and post-secondary educational institutions with the purpose of developing leadership. Each club was organized with the co-operation of the principal, and was supervised by members of the Kiwanis Club in association with the principal or a designated staff member. There were said to be particularly active key clubs in secondary schools in Barrie, Owen Sound, and Kitchener, and Circle κ clubs at Ryerson Polytechnical Institute and the University of Waterloo in 1969.

The organization had an internal leadership program which ensured that leaders received training "from the time they become club presidents to the time they are ready for the International president's gavel." The program began in late October of each year with the International Council meeting, a four-day orientation session where governors-designate and new district secretaries assumed the role of students, and international board members, international committee chairmen, and past international presidents acted as instructors. The "students" received information and advice on administrative and community service matters. On their return home the governors held training conferences for the benefit of lieutenant governors, who headed the divisions into which districts were subdivided, and for district committee chairmen. Lieutenant governors in turn held training sessions for club presidents, and the latter did the same for club officers, directors, and committee chairmen. At each level the training program was designed to indicate what could be done in the service field and how it could be done most effectively.

NINETEEN

Social welfare organizations

The small group of associations classified here as social welfare organizations range from the Canadian Red Cross, with worldwide connections, to St Christopher House, an agency serving local community purposes. During the period under review they customarily recognized that education had a good deal to do with their ultimate prospect of alleviating the undesirable conditions they attempted to combat. They might engage directly in educational work or assist with programs undertaken by other agencies.

THE CANADIAN RED CROSS SOCIETY

The Red Cross, one of the best known and most highly respected of international organizations, was founded in 1859 on the initiative of the Swiss, Henri Dunant, who had recently observed the horrors of the Battle of Solferino. The immediate purpose was to provide more satisfactory care for the wounded on the battlefield and to protect non-combatants in time of war. Educational aspects of the program developed incidentally during the years that followed.

The international organization came to be governed by the International Conference of the Red Cross which attempted to meet every four years. This conference was made up of representatives of all recognized national Red Cross, Red Crescent, and Red Lion and Sun Societies, the International Committee of the Red Cross and the League of Red Cross Societies, as well as diplomatic representatives of countries adhering to the Geneva Conventions. A Standing Commission of nine members handled matters during the intervals between sessions.

The first Red Cross flags to be flown in Canada appeared during the Riel Rebellion in Saskatchewan in 1885. A Red Cross corps, consisting of a hospital surgeon and six others trained in medicine and surgery, served as volunteers during the fighting. In 1896 the first overseas branch of the British Red Cross was formed in Toronto under the unwieldy name, the Canadian Branch of the British National Society for Aid to the Sick and Wounded in War. This organization undertook active service during the Spanish-American War by raising a small amount of money for sick and wounded soldiers. When the Boer War broke out in 1897, branches were formed in the larger cities and in more than fifty smaller centres, and clothing, blankets, food for invalids, and money were collected and sent to South Africa.

The Canadian Red Cross Society Act of 1909 established the Canadian Red Cross Society as a corporate body to provide volunteer aid according to the Geneva Conventions. The organization, under its first president, General G.S. Ryerson, remained for the time being part of the British Red Cross Society. When the First World War broke out, a period of vigorous activity and growth began. During the war the society raised over $35 million for the relief of suffering, shipped 341,325 cases of supplies overseas, established and maintained five hospitals in England and one in France, provided numerous facilities for recreation, maintained ambulance convoys and trucks for transporting goods in Europe, and set up an information bureau in London.

A decision was made after the war to use the organization for peacetime work according to the principles of the League of Red Cross Societies, established in 1919. The program of service in Canada included the establishment of nursing stations and outpost hospitals, the organization of the Junior Red Cross to help make Canadian children aware of the problems and needs of children in other parts of the world, and the development of disaster services for the assistance of those afflicted by fire, floods, and other calamities. In 1927 the international committee recognized the Canadian Red Cross as an independent national society.

At the beginning of the Second World War there were 374 branches of the society in nine provincial divisions. Contributions during the war included goods and funds amounting to about $125 million as well as volunteer services the value of which it would be impossible to estimate. About 16.5 million parcels were sent to prisoners of war. After 1945 more emphasis was placed on international assistance for refugees, displaced persons, and victims of natural disasters. The educational element began to appear in such programs as the water safety service. The Junior Red Cross, more recently known as Red Cross Youth, devoted its efforts to health, service, and international understanding.

After its origin as the Junior Red Cross in 1922, Red Cross Youth became part of the school program in all Canadian provinces. In recent years membership included children and young people at the elementary, secondary, and post-secondary levels ranging from six to twenty-five years of age. From the beginning an educational purpose was recognized. When the idea of mental health began to be propounded actively in the 1930s, the organization recognized the importance of education in terms of its influence on the child's mental health.

During and after the Second World War youth membership, which had previously been concentrated mainly in elementary schools, began to grow quickly in secondary schools. Students conducted campaigns to have entire school populations vaccinated, assisted as clerks and attendants at blood donor clinics, organized x-ray surveys to identify cases of tuberculosis, and worked as volunteers in hospitals. After early campaigns to promote health education within the school system had largely succeeded, the organization continued to provide material such as posters, booklets, visual aids, and a magazine for elementary school children. It also continued to pursue the objective of converting health knowledge into action.

Volunteer services in hospitals and assistance in the blood donor program remained important. Most of the provinces organized War on Poverty programs in which Red Cross Youth members tutored younger children, took them to parks, museums, and libraries, and in general acted as big brothers and sisters. High school student members helped with swimming programs for blind, retarded, crippled, or arthritic children; organized and staffed reading enrichment programs; worked on Indian reservations during the summer; developed a translation service, volunteering translations in more than a dozen languages; provided funds for portable pools to be used where there were no other swimming facilities; and raised funds for speech classes for deaf and hard of hearing children. In the process, the young participants had an opportunity to develop and apply ideals of good citizenship and to acquire leadership skills.

Members of the organization were encouraged to examine the peculiar needs of their own communities and to organize appropriate projects. In addition to services already mentioned, they organized carol singing and similar entertainment in hospitals and homes, collected toys and books for children's hospitals and Indian and Eskimo schools, provided treats and made favours for homes and hospitals, made therapeutic and other toys for children's hospitals, knitted sweaters, socks, and mittens, sewed clothing, made health kits, school supplies, games, Christmas or birthday presents for children and adults, organized poster competitions, exhibits, and displays, and made "happiness kits" for children in families that had lost their homes through fires or other disasters.

There was an increasing tendency to look outward as many of the original Canadian causes began to seem less urgent. Even more emphasis was placed on cultural exchanges, which had been important from the beginning, as arts, crafts, tapes, and albums were sent abroad and similar items received from other countries. Relief and assistance for the deprived and disadvantaged abroad were regarded as a contribution to international understanding. One project of the organization which had both national and international applications involved the production of a manual called *Teen Care in the Home*. Thousands of copies of a Spanish edition of this manual were distributed in Latin America to assist Red Cross societies there with health education programs.

Among specific international service programs was a Sudan School Gardens Project, for which members raised more than $200,000 to provide the services of a nutritionist and a horticulturist, garden equipment, seeds, poultry, tools, and wells. The recipients of this assistance were taught how to grow vegetables and raise poultry, how to use the foods judiciously, and how to save seeds for future crops. The program continued after Canadian Red Cross Youth phased out its support. Another international project involved the assignment of a field worker to Pakistan to help set up a Junior Red Cross program in the schools as a means of promoting health education.

Members at the post-secondary school level were regularly sent to leadership centres organized on an international, national, regional, or provincial basis. As a centennial project in 1967 the Canadian Red Cross Society arranged for more than four hundred young people from Canada and other countries to attend a two-week seminar called Rendezvous 67. For the foreign visitors this seminar was preceded by a period of home hospitality. At times Canadian delegates were sent to study centres in other countries; in 1968 two went to the Philippines and two to Czecho-slovakia, while two young people and a staff member visited Peru; in August 1968 two attended a study session in Upper Volta.

Among a wide range of activities, the Nursing Service offered instruction to a variety of groups, a large proportion consisting of young people. Some recent examples of this type of program were as follows: instruction in nutrition, economical buying, and basic sewing for welfare recipients, mostly deserted wives; work in a school for the retarded and in correctional institutes for teenage girls; adult courses for coloured residents in communities with a high rate of illiteracy; classes for school dropouts of both sexes; and courses for residents in a home for unmarried mothers. Much of the instruction was given by volunteers. The society contributed to the improvement of nursing services by providing a number of fellowships and bursaries.

The annual report for 1968 indicated that 639,293 children had enrolled in training courses under the Water Safety Service, and that 15,439 had taken leadership training. There seemed to be good grounds for assuming that the program had contributed to the reduction of drownings in Canada. Despite a continuous and substantial increase in activities on or near the water, the number of drownings declined by 5.5 per cent as compared with the previous year. The use of portable pools promised to give all Canadian children an opportunity to learn to swim.

THE CANADIAN WELFARE COUNCIL

The Canadian Welfare Council (CWC) was established shortly after the First World War to work for the improvement of welfare services throughout the country. It proclaimed its uniqueness with the assertion that it was the only non-government, citizens' body in the Western world providing both co-ordinating and research facilities over the whole range of the welfare system. It was a kind of federation of national associations in both the voluntary and government fields. During the 1960s its role underwent considerable change in response to the introduction of many new welfare programs by the federal and provincial governments. Its educational activities were primarily in the fields of social welfare education and staff and management development. The Library and the Information and Publications Branch were active in providing service for members, other social workers, and the public. Reports of studies were widely distributed.

Recognition of the growing problem of staffing the social services led the council to establish a Commission on Education and Personnel in 1960. This commission undertook to gather and disseminate information, to promote a clearer recognition of the problem, and to create interest in remedial action. It accepted the idea that educational opportunities needed to be provided and expanded for professional and non-professional workers at several different levels. Two years after its establishment the federal Department of National Health and Welfare recognized the validity of this position by introducing a National Welfare Training and Research Grants program, which entailed substantial financial support for training and research. The Department of National Health and Welfare also responded to cwc urgings in undertaking a manpower survey to determine the number of welfare workers required and the level and types of qualifications they would need. The cwc itself maintained a research committee which studied some of the same questions.

During the 1960s the council conducted an increasingly ambitious program of in-service staff training at various levels. For example, the Committee on Non-Graduate Training arranged for a workshop in 1964 with these objectives: 1 / to gain a clearer understanding of the issues involved in welfare training in Canada, 2 / to identify and assess the practical questions and problems arising from these issues and to assess their implications for and in a sound training program, 3 / to exchange ideas about the content and content organization of training programs in the light of agency service goals and learning theory, 4 / to exchange experiences in using various training techniques and to consider some devices for their evaluation, and 5 / to consider plans for further deliberations and exchanges on welfare training. Some of the addresses and discussions at this workshop revealed a good deal of uncertainty about the amount and nature of the training needed by non-professional workers performing a variety of tasks.

In response to the demand for training in modern management theories and techniques, the Canadian Women's Army Corps sponsored a one-week seminar for senior and intermediate executives in March 1967. The instructors were recognized authorities from the universities, business, and social welfare. Financial support was given under the provisions of the Welfare Grants Program of the Department of National Health and Welfare. The sixty-three students were from public and voluntary welfare agencies in various parts of the country.

A study by Mukhtar A. Malik, Associate Director of Research for the cwc, demonstrates how directly some of the council's interests impinged on matters of concern to the schools. The report, entitled *School Performance of Children in Families Receiving Public Assistance in Canada*, appeared in 1966. Among the major findings were that children of public assistance families performed at a lower level in school than did their close friends of similar social background. Their educational and occupational aspirations and expectations were also lower than those of their friends. These and other conclusions provided the basis for a number of policy recommendations.

Recognition of the significance of certain economic and occupational trends led the council to give increasing attention to the problems and implications of manpower training and retraining, along with related issues of accelerated migration within the country. A project entitled Employability and Public Welfare: an Assessment involved an examination of attitudes toward work among employables on public assistance. Proposals were made relating to training programs for unskilled immigrants.

ST CHRISTOPHER HOUSE, TORONTO

St Christopher House, which began operations in west central Toronto in 1912, provided an example of the way in which educational work could be interwoven with other services offered by a community centre. The area had a strong and continuous need for assistance to immigrants to adjust to an unfamiliar linguistic and cultural environment. Great stress was placed on the necessity for positive co-operation among different racial and religious, as well as linguistic, groups. The organization had characteristics that made it an important training ground for social workers.

The Board of Directors, which became incorporated in 1963, had representatives of neighbourhood interests, including the major religious groups. Most of the operating funds came through the United Appeal of Metropolitan Toronto. Other funds, some for specific purposes, were received from the Metropolitan Corporation, the provincial government, the Board of Home Missions of the United Church of Canada, service clubs, and foundations. Contributions in terms of service were made by large numbers of volunteers. In 1967 there were about three thousand active participants in the organized activities of the house.

Programs of several different types were offered for various age groups. Among those with the most direct bearing on education were the following: for preschool children, nursery school and a Head Start program; for school-age children, an art centre; for youth, teen clubs and classes, homework dens, tutoring, and counselling; for all ages, a music school; for adults, evening and daytime English classes, community development meetings, a homemakers' club, a nutrition club, a Portuguese mothers' group, and a nursery mothers' group.

In an article in *Canadian Welfare* in 1965, Eleanor Reesor told of a number of activities being carried on at the house, including some of an educational nature. As early as 1913 the staff and volunteers had offered instruction in elementary English. The existing need was for basic English instruction for a number of immigrant groups, especially Portuguese, who constituted over half the people visiting the house. A new Portuguese-speaking staff member had been added the previous year to improve service to this group. Along with formal instruction, many of the newcomers sought the help of an interpreter when applying for jobs, paying their taxes, obtaining medical and legal services, and translating official mail from schools and government agencies.

Free English-language classes were of course being offered by the Board of Education. Many preferred the house, however, because they knew more of the other participants, they worked in small groups, and the atmosphere was comparatively intimate and friendly. The board classes, in contrast, were large and formal and the approach seemed unduly bookish. The house was in a better position to make adaptations to deal with particular problems. Daytime classes catered to shift workers, housewives, and the seasonally unemployed. A special afternoon class for Portuguese women met the objection of their husbands to their attending co-educational classes. There was home instruction, as far as possible, for invalids and housebound mothers of preschool children.

A family life course was being offered for mothers of preschool children of a variety of racial origins. These children were looked after in a colourful play area full of interesting toys and materials while their mothers sat in a conversation circle in another part of the auditorium. Under the guidance of a trained leader, they gradually shifted their attention from a desultory discussion of everyday problems to various aspects of child raising such as the value of sound and sufficient sleep. The program was designed to help the mothers understand their children better and to develop some good foster homes in the area.

The annual report of the house for 1969 told of an increase in the nursery school staff and a drive to bring the proportion of immigrant children up to its normal level. As a result, the school was overflowing with eager pupils. In a joint project the music and nursery schools had undertaken to teach children of preschool age to play the violin, and some very promising musical talent had been uncovered in the process. Performances by older pupils of the music school in various parts of the city had contributed to the development of a sense of community pride.

During 1969 the house continued to provide leadership opportunities for students from the School of Social Work and the Public Health Course at the University of Toronto, from Ryerson Polytechnical Institute, and from Centennial College. As many as twenty students from such courses were accommodated at any one time. These students reciprocated by providing various kinds of services to the members. In addition to offering opportunities for direct experience, the house supplied information on its services to large numbers of students.

TWENTY

Associations concerned with health

There were several associations concerned with the welfare of victims of specific diseases or health handicaps. Their educational efforts were directed partly at improving the capacity of these people to deal with their emotional, social, and economic problems, and partly at increasing public understanding of their particular needs. In some cases the issue was one of dispelling prejudice and misconceptions about what the handicapped were capable of doing. If there was a possibility of preventing or postponing the onset of a specific disease, the association was usually concerned with publicizing the necessary measures. Support might be given for research designed to improve methods of prevention or treatment.

THE CANADIAN PUBLIC HEALTH ASSOCIATION AND
THE ONTARIO PUBLIC HEALTH ASSOCIATION

The Canadian Public Health Association (CPHA) concerned itself with the professional training and educational standards of public health workers. Certain activities in Ontario resulted from an expansion of the health unit plan between 1948 and 1950, and from new legislation on sanitation, particularly in the fields of food hygiene, recreation, and pest control, which called for a higher level of technical competence on the part of inspectors. The association introduced one-day refresher courses for these inspectors, and at the same time began to produce technical bulletins on a variety of relevant topics. In 1953 an Ontario Sanitary Inspector's Training Course was initiated with the assistance of federal health grants.

The correspondence courses previously offered by the CPHA were withdrawn from Ontario in 1953, thus forcing the candidate for the certificate to attend school. The Ontario Department of Health administered the course until responsibility for it was accepted by the Ryerson Institute of Technology in 1963. At the same time provincial and local health personnel continued to participate in the teaching program. Within a comparatively short time the nine-month academic course was lengthened by three further months of practical field work.

In 1946 the CPHA established a Committee on Salaries and Qualifications of Public Health Personnel which, at the request of the Dominion Council of Health, carried out a Canada-wide survey of official public health agencies. The report of this committee indicated the salary ranges applying to different categories of professional and technical personnel, and also recommended educational and experience requirements for the majority of jobs in health agencies, as well as a minimum salary for each type of position. This report was revised and updated every few years after its first appearance. The document was apparently not sufficiently influential to prevent the development of a serious shortage of adequately trained people, which members of the association attributed, at least in part, to poor starting salaries and a more limited salary range than those received by people with equivalent training and experience in other fields.

The Ontario Public Health Association, acting as the Ontario branch of the CPHA, made a practice of holding an annual three-day conference for the benefit of members. These members included medical officers of health, public health nurses, public health inspectors, veterinarians, dentists, public health educators, and administrative staff from the provincial Department of Health and the local health units in the province. The program at the conferences was designed to bring the delegates up to date on recent advances and more efficient practices in community public health programs.

THE CANADIAN CANCER SOCIETY

The Canadian Cancer Society regarded the education of the public about cancer as one of its major responsibilities. The program was planned and executed by an autonomous organization within each province. Ontario's association won the reputation of being the most active of these. The national office had the main responsibility for defining purposes and policies, and also produced and disseminated material.

One of the society's programs, centred on Canadian workers, was called the Employee Education Programme. It drew attention to the number of man-years of work lost and the annual loss of earnings attributable to cancer. Information was supplied through films, pamphlets, posters, speakers, and interviewers. Workers were urged to form committees to set up displays of relevant written material, to arrange for the showing of films, to organize demonstrations and talks, and to keep in contact with the local cancer society in order to be in a position to supply the latest information to interested fellow employees.

Similar devices and procedures were used with various other groups such as service clubs, women's organizations, and students. In the schools particular emphasis was placed on the dangers of smoking, although it was realized that other factors must not be neglected. Stress on safety precautions in handling various substances was considered of special importance for industrial workers. Women were urged to avail themselves of the Pap test.

At one time almost the only objective of the educational program was to promote early diagnosis and treatment of cancer. A great many people were distressed that sufferers from the disease often sought treatment only after it was impossible to do anything for them. It seemed desirable to try to persuade them to watch for suspicious symptoms and report them at once. Over the years, however, it became clear that such an approach was not very effective. The result of arousing apprehension was that many people illogically avoided facing the possibility that they had the dread disease. When surveys demonstrated the weaknesses in the program, educational campaigns were redesigned to place more stress on the elimination of irrational fears, and to persuade people to face the hazards of cancer in perspective. As information accumulated about factors which contributed to the development of various types of cancer, it became possible to place increasing emphasis on prevention.

The Canadian Cancer Society showed an unusual degree of awareness of the importance of evaluating its educational programs. Recognizing the inadequacy of relying on such procedures as counting the number of pamphlets distributed in a year or the size of the audience viewing films on cancer, it undertook the more difficult task of conducting surveys to determine the knowledge and attitudes of people toward cancer. Questions were asked to find out how people rated cancer as a cause of death, the types of cancer they thought were most frequent, their ability to identify warning signs of cancer in various body sites, the reasons for delay in diagnosis and treatment, and attitudes about cancer information. One study, the purpose of which was to determine the relative value of various forms of communication, indicated that the most productive educational medium was television, followed by newspapers and magazines. Pamphlets were regarded as much less effective, and films were rated still lower. Findings of this kind had a good deal to do with shaping the programs of the society.

Part of the educational program of the society was aimed at medical practitioners. A certain proportion of these were reached through the publication of a monthly journal, which was supplied to general practitioners on request. Films dealing with types of cancer and their diagnosis and with recent research findings were made available to medical schools. Opportunities for discussions under the leadership of specialists were provided at conferences held every two years. Research conferences were also held from time to time for highly specialized groups.

THE CANADIAN HEART FOUNDATION

The Canadian Heart Foundation was incorporated in 1956 "to co-ordinate and correlate the efforts of organizations and individuals interested in heart diseases, with a view to reducing the morbidity and mortality therefrom." It constituted a federation of provincial heart foundations, of which there were seven in 1969 – one in each of the provinces from British Columbia east to Quebec and one in Nova Scotia.

In the late 1960s the national and provincial heart foundations spent some 85 per cent of their budgets on research and education, which were regarded as inseparably linked activities. The research was conducted by qualified people in university faculties and hospital staffs with the support of foundation grants awarded on the basis of recommendations by committees of academics. The total value of this type of support in 1969 was about one million dollars. Among the advances made in Ontario from the time the national foundation was formed were the devising of certain diagnostic techniques and surgical treatments, the attainment of a better understanding of rheumatic fever, increased knowledge of the process of thickening of the arteries and the blood clotting mechanism, and the development of the heart pacemaker.

Information about these and other advances was disseminated by means of scientific meetings inside and outside Canada. In Ontario the provincial foundation sponsored an average of one symposium a year beginning in 1961, and published the proceedings of some of them in monograph form. A number of professional education films were acquired for distribution on a free-loan basis to nursing groups and medical schools. Informational material was also provided for other health professions as well as for the general public.

An extraordinary amount of educational material was made available by the foundation for use in schools. For the junior public school there was a diagram showing the direction of blood flow through the heart chambers to the body and lungs; a brief explanation of the action and function of the heart and the bloodstream; an educational activity project in leaflet form called *Heart Puzzle*, designed to reinforce the textbook explanation of how the blood circulates through the heart; and a leaflet presenting five helpful facts about heart disease. For the senior public and junior high school grades there was a diagram of the circulatory system showing the relationship of heart, lungs, kidneys, and the network of larger arteries and veins in the body; a cigarette quiz, consisting of twelve true-false statements enabling the reader to discover his "IQ in smoking"; a heart quiz giving questions and answers about heart conditions and diseases; and an illustrated booklet showing how the doctor examined the heart. For secondary schools there was a circulatory system diagram; a diagram on the heart and how it works; a leaflet explaining the action and function of the heart and the bloodstream; a booklet entitled *Decision for Research*, describing research opportunities and outlining steps to be taken by students interested in research careers; a leaflet explaining how emphysema damaged the lungs and ultimately affected the heart; a booklet presenting information on the cardiovascular diseases; a leaflet providing facts about physical exertion and employment in relation to heart disease; a leaflet, with cartoon illustrations, showing how exercise might be beneficial to the heart; a leaflet presenting information about the relationship of cigarette smoking to cardiovascular and other serious diseases; and a number of other items. Materials for the use of teachers included wall charts illustrating the circulatory system and the functioning of the heart.

For the general public there were many items explaining the functioning of the heart and blood vessels, the nature of circulatory diseases and ailments, and the best types of treatment for those afflicted. A number of booklets and leaflets were designed to help parents recognize certain defects and diseases in their children and to deal with them as effectively as possible. A good deal of the material was devoted to preventive procedures.

Other promotional activities involved the production of material for the news media, including newspapers, radio, and television. Posters were made for display in public transit vehicles and other public places. Education kits on a number of subjects were produced for use by Heart Foundation chapters at the community level. Among topics dealt with were Smoking and Heart Disease, Risk Factors, and Diet and Heart Disease.

THE CANADIAN DIABETIC ASSOCIATION

The Canadian Diabetic Association, chartered by the federal government in 1953, resembled the Canadian Heart Foundation in that it focused its attention on a particular aspect of health. Because of the nature of diabetes, however, it was little concerned with prevention, but instead devoted most of its efforts to helping the victims of the disorder to cope with it successfully. As a lay-medical organization affiliated with the Canadian Medical Association, it established an active chain of branches across the country. In 1969 there were estimated to be about seven thousand members.

In its program to "help diabetics to help themselves through a program of encouragement, education, and services," the branches of the association employed films, literature, and lectures by doctors and dietitians. Members of the association received the *CDA Newsletter* as well as bulletins issued by a number of branches. A particular effort was made to assist with the adjustment of diabetic children. Camps were organized where such children learned to control their condition through the proper balance of diet, drugs, and exercise, as well as to enjoy the pleasures of normal camping experience.

THE CANADIAN ARTHRITIS AND RHEUMATISM SOCIETY

The initiative of a small group of academic physicians was responsible for the establishment of the Canadian Arthritis and Rheumatism Society, which was incorporated in 1948. The founders hoped that research would contribute to the ultimate control and conquest of rheumatic diseases. More immediate results might be expected from the application of existing methods of treatment. The first steps toward the formation of the society were taken at a conference convened by the Minister of National Health and Welfare and attended by representatives of medical schools, health departments, and the medical and health professions.

An article published in the *Journal of the Canadian Physiotherapy Association* in 1968[1] examined the situation in that year in the light of some of the original objectives. The first of these objectives was to increase the number of rheumatologists, of whom there were fewer than six in 1948. Twenty years later the total of such specialists in Canada had reached more than one hundred. One of these was to be found on the staff of almost every teaching and main regional hospital. A second objective was to foster research in the rheumatic diseases. Between 1950 and 1968 the amount spent for this purpose in Canada rose from about $4,000 a year to more than $500,000. The society recognized research, not only as a means of adding to the existing fund of knowledge, but also as an essential contribution to the improvement of medical education, the preparation of teachers of medicine, and the maintenance of high standards of patient care. A third objective was the establishment of arthritis clinics and public outpatient departments. By 1968, thanks in part to the improved supply of rheumatologists, such specialized resources were available in almost every community which enjoyed organized public outpatient services. A fourth objective was to develop sufficient resources for physiotherapy and other paramedical services as a means of helping to correct and prevent disability due to arthritis. In 1948 there were 248 physiotherapists in practice, and 58 hospitals with physiotherapy departments. By 1948 the comparable figures were 2,000 and 434. The number of schools of physiotherapy at Canadian universities had increased from two to eleven. One of the society's particular contributions was to provide fellowships for the training of teachers of physiotherapy.

The society provided seed money for the establishment of rheumatic disease units in various universities, first at Queen's in 1960 and later at McMaster and Western. By 1968 these units offered accommodation for 1,924 clinical patients. Their contributions to education were to provide standards of exemplary patient care, settings for clinical research, and a teaching base for medical and paramedical students proceeding to their degrees at the universities where the units were located. Once begun, the units were maintained by university funds and by contributions from the Ontario Hospital Services Commission.

Professional education was assisted by the establishment of associateships designed to provide support for fully trained people with a major interest in medical teaching or research, and who proposed to follow full-time careers in academic medicine. Each associate engaged in a program of research, teaching, professional development, and leadership in the field of rheumatology. Fellowships were offered for graduate training in internal medicine, with special emphasis on rheumatology, for candidates preparing themselves as specialists in physical medicine in a centre where rheumatology received special emphasis, and for candidates preparing themselves as specialists in orthopaedic surgery, particularly in the surgery of rheumatoid arthritis. There were ordinarily between four and eight of these available in Ontario each year for training at home or abroad. One or two fellowships were also offered annually for the training of teachers of physiotherapy. In a less formal field seminars were held from the earliest days of the society in association with various communities to enable specialists in rheumatology to engage in discussions with local medical practitioners.

Although a large proportion of its educational efforts appear to have been devoted to furthering professional education, the society also engaged in an extensive program of public education. Several hundred thousand people in Ontario were estimated to have been reached each year by educational material, films, and other devices. In 1968 the society introduced what was called an arthritis forum, a widely advertised public meeting at which a specialist in rheumatology presented an illustrated lecture on arthritis and engaged in a question-and-answer session with local physicians. During the first year such forums were held in twelve communities and attracted about three thousand people.

THE CANADIAN MENTAL HEALTH ASSOCIATION
The Canadian Mental Health Association grew out of the National Committee for Mental Hygiene. Credit for the foundation of the new organization in 1918 is given to C.M. Hincks, who was also responsible for such initiatives as the founding of an outpatient clinic at the Toronto General Hospital, the first of its kind in Canada, the opening of the first forensic clinic at the Toronto General Hospital, and the introduction of intelligence testing in the schools.

As defined for the Canadian Conference on Education in 1962, the objectives of the association were as follows:

(1) To work for the development of adequate facilities for the treatment of mental and emotional illness, both in hospitals and in community mental health services.
(2) To change the attitude of the public toward mental illness so that adequate support will be available for the provision of necessary treatment facilities, and so that the mentally ill will be assured that they are not friendless and forgotten, that their fellow citizens want them back well and healthy, and that the community will provide assistance in their social and occupational rehabilitation.
(3) To work by all possible means, and especially through research and education, toward the prevention of mental and emotional illness.
(4) To inform and educate citizens in the facts about mental health and mental illness and to plan practical programmes designed to stimulate the development of positive mental health.[2]

The educational activities of the association were said to be designed to change attitudes, motivation, and behaviour. People were to be educated toward a better understanding of the principles of mental health so that they would think, feel, and act to strengthen their own mental health and that of others. The educational program was carried out through radio, television, newspapers, magazines, pamphlets, films, plays, posters, and public meetings. It was considered necessary to supplement approaches through the mass media with programs directed at target groups, the most important of which were 1 / professionals working with children and adults, such as clergymen, teachers, nurses, police officers, and others; 2 / groups sharing the same experience, such as parents, relatives of mentally ill patients, and the aging; and 3 / groups with a common humanitarian interest, such as parent-teacher associations, women's institute's, labour and industrial organizations, and service clubs. Workshops and conferences were held for teachers, principals, vice-principals, clergymen, public health nurses, police officers, family doctors, industrial and personnel officers, teenagers, adults, and CMHA volunteers.

An early postwar venture of the organization was the establishment of a committee in 1947 to determine the extent to which mental health factors were taken into account in selecting candidates for teacher training in Canada and in recommending candidates for teachers' certificates. The three committee members, consisting of S.R. Laycock of Saskatoon, R.O. Jones of Halifax, and J.R.K. Seeley of Toronto, canvassed the departments of education in all provinces. In a report made in 1949 they indicated that academic standing was the most important factor in selecting teacher candidates, and that, because of the acute shortage of teachers, the level of achievement required was very low. For the same reason, it was proving impossible to take into account personality and mental health factors, even where officials were convinced of the desirability of doing so. The committee suggested that the existing shortage of teachers was related to their low prestige and to the unfavourable view of the function of the schools. It recommended a campaign to educate the public in mental hygiene and to promote a view of education as the guiding of pupils in emotional and social development, as well as the imparting of information and the development of skills. There seemed to be an urgent need for the staffs of teacher-training institutions to acquire further training in mental health principles so that they would be better able to recognize and deal with mental ill-health. These and other recommendations had little chance of being adequately implemented for the time being because the teacher shortage, bad as it was, grew still worse during the next decade.

The crucial importance of the teacher in the building of mental health was recognized in 1948 when the CMHA assisted the University of Toronto in planning a special one-year training course. This project began as an aspect of the Forest Hill Project, which was subsidized by federal mental health grants. The course constituted, in particular, a manifestation of the ideas of Professor William Line. The participants engaged in academic work in child study, psychiatry, psychology, social work, and education, at the same time obtaining practical experience applying mental health principles in the schools of Metropolitan Toronto. After it had been in operation for almost two decades, the course was defined in an informal statement in this way.

Its aim was to equip the trainees with skills and insights which would increase their value to their school systems through a greater understanding of the problems which children experience and the behaviour patterns which they exhibit. It was founded on the belief that the school itself, through its regular teachers, could handle *most* childhood problems with a little help from someone with an enriched understanding of children's needs, and that, where the problems were beyond the scope of the educational system, earlier referral to clinical facilities would result if the school system included someone who was specially trained to recognize symptoms of clinical disorders in their early stages. It was hoped that the presence of such a specially-trained teacher would enrich the understanding of the mental health needs of children among the other teachers and that in this way the mental health of school children generally would be enhanced.

The Forest Hill project was regarded as one phase of a much larger plan to attain higher levels of mental health throughout the country. The main focus of attention was the child, although the study necessarily dealt with adults as well. A particular effort was made to determine how mental health could be promoted and mental illness prevented and cured through the school and other agencies. An extraordinary range of individuals and groups co-operated in conducting the project. These included university staff from a number of departments, the school board, the Director of Education and school principals, teachers, school children, parents, Home and School associations, religious agencies, physicians, the National Committee for Mental Hygiene, the Department of Education, departments of education and school boards in other provinces through liaison officers, and miscellaneous others. The purposes of the project and the values obtained from it were seen in different ways by those observing it from different points of view. The report *Crestwood Heights* which emerged from it was an extraordinary document, and is thought to have had a considerable influence on the mental health and social welfare fields since that time.

In a brief to the Provincial Committee on Aims and Objectives, the Ontario Division of the CMHA emphasized the damaging effects of the pressures that often accompanied school examinations. While the association advocated the abolition of examinations in the first three grades, it did not take an extreme position for more advanced levels, but suggested rather that there be more provision for tests and other forms of evaluation throughout the year. The brief proposed greater recognition of individual differences through more flexible courses of study and a wider range of textbooks to allow for a greater range of reading ability. Stress was placed on the importance of providing kindergartens and junior kindergartens.

To the Select Committee on Youth of the Ontario Legislature, the Ontario Division recommended that all educational authorities employ a school psychologist with training in educational psychology. His function would be to support, guide, and collaborate with teachers, supervisory personnel, and parents rather than to provide clinical diagnosis or assessment of individual children. Another recommendation was that the schools provide children with the basic knowledge of the country's legal system, of the purposes of law, and of the penalties for breaking the rules of society relating to conduct and behaviour. This program would presumably help to prepare them to fulfil their responsibilities as citizens in a democratic society.

THE CANADIAN NATIONAL INSTITUTE FOR THE BLIND

An important service for the sightless began at Markham, Ontario, in 1906 with the founding of the Canadian Free Library for the Blind. A short time later this library was moved to Toronto and placed under the administration of a board of directors. A great new demand for services appeared during the First World War, when considerable numbers of blinded soldiers returned home. The Women's Musical Association assisted the board to purchase its own building, to extend the library, and to offer occupational training. When the federal government indicated its willingness to finance the training program, a national charter was obtained and the Canadian National Institute for the Blind (CNIB) came into existence. It was called "a unique mixture of soldiers, civilians, sighted, and blind – a co-operating body of staff, volunteers, and government." Its main objectives were to serve the blind people of Canada and to prevent blindness.

For organizational purposes divisions were formed in Ontario, the Maritimes, the central western area, and the western area. The two latter were eventually subdivided to form the Manitoba, Saskatchewan, Alberta, and BC-Yukon divisions. In the 1930s divisions were formed in Quebec and Newfoundland. The divisions were administered by professional staff assisted by volunteer boards of management. Each division had district offices run for the most part by blind people, with the assistance of district advisory boards and committees.

A Canadian Women's Association for the Welfare of the Blind was formed in 1917 in anticipation of the organization of the CNIB, and later became the Women's Auxiliary to the Toronto branch of that agency. Similar bodies were soon formed in other cities in Canada. One of the early activities of the Toronto association was to provide facilities where blind girls could learn the use of the sewing machine and acquire other skills. A workshop was later established with power machines, making possible the production of women's and children's wear. Materials were supplied to blind home workers all over Canada, and finished goods were bought back at retail prices to be sold at what later became Blindcraft Gift Shops. The Vancouver Women's Auxiliary introduced a summer camp, which constituted the forerunner of such centres across the country.

The training of blinded veterans of the First World War, the first major effort of the institute, consisted at first only of instruction in braille and simple vocational subjects. When more adequate quarters were obtained, courses in basketry, willowwork, and cobbling were offered. As the veterans completed training and returned to civilian life, the Aftercare Department continued to keep in touch with them and to provide counsel and assistance whenever possible. Similar demands were made on the institute during and after the Second World War, when the government again underwrote a program of vocational and educational training. During this period major efforts had to be made to persuade the public that there were many occupations that the blind could handle with skill and competence. As time went on, they proceeded from simple manual operations to the exercise of highly complex skills. By 1965, for example, a pilot course in computer programming was being offered jointly by the University of Manitoba, provincial governments, and the CNIB. The venture was so successful that a one-year diploma course was subsequently offered on a regular basis. By 1968 it was reported that more than 2,200 blind people were employed. They had become an integral part of the labour force, and were no longer considered to be unemployables.

One of the original services of the CNIB was the provision of home teaching, which began in 1918. Two years later prospective teachers were brought to Toronto for a four-month training course in braille, typing, crafts, and academic subjects such as genetics, biology, and psychology. Training sessions continued to be held at regular intervals, with a program adapted to an increasingly complex rehabilitation scheme. Blind people were considered to make the most satisfactory home teachers. At first only women were recruited on the grounds that they were more patient than men, more interested in crafts, and more sensitive to personal difficulties. Eventually, however, some men were admitted.

In later years a Vocational Guidance Department of the CNIB assumed responsibility for the National Vocational Training course for dictaphone typists, home teachers, field secretaries, and employment and public relations officers. Counsellors helped blind graduates to find suitable careers, as well as assisting those who wished to continue their education. The CNIB absorbed the administration costs of home study courses supplied from the Hadley School for the Blind in the United States to Canadian students.

A major achievement of the CNIB during the 1960s was the establishment, with assistance from the federal and provincial governments, of the Arthur V. Weir National Training and Vocational Guidance Centre in

Toronto. During the planning stages the aims of the centre were listed as follows: improved assessment and counselling, more intensive pre-vocational adjustment, more selective career planning, expanded vocational training and retraining, advanced employment research, new courses to prepare blinded youth for higher education, and greater utilization of government training resources. The structure included a residence unit and a training unit consisting of classrooms, lecture rooms, study rooms, an industrial training department, and an administrative area. Some of the educational programs offered in 1969–70 included twelve-week adjustment training courses, three-week travel training clinics, a five-week summer course for high school students, a six-week preparatory course for prospective university students, a forty-week course in dictaphone transcription, and a short program for key service personnel such as field secretaries, home teachers, employment officers, and public relations officers.

The original Free Library amalgamated with the institute in 1918, and became known as the Library and Publishing Department of the Canadian National Institute for the Blind. It obtained printing equipment to produce its own books, but acquired most of its stock from Britain and the United States. In 1935 the introduction of "talking books," which were recorded on discs, began to serve the needs of those who could not read. During the 1960s the library engaged in a major program of converting these books from discs to the more convenient medium of tape, and of producing new books on tape. Publication of the *Braille Courier* was begun in 1919. Other kinds of materials published for the blind included pamphlets, calendars, crossword puzzles, examination papers, and textbooks. Sighted people offered voluntary assistance in this work, either by transcribing in braille or recording on tape.

In the field of prevention of blindness, the institute had as a major objective "to take measures and adopt every possible means for the conservation of sight, to secure adequate legislation for the prevention of blindness, and to provide for the prompt treatment of diseases of, and injuries to, the eye." Part of the program involved the provision of the necessary services. The first sight-saving class in Canada was formed in Halifax in 1918. An eye survey of school children in Toronto led to the establishment of similar classes there, and others soon appeared elsewhere. Many activities in the area of prevention had little bearing on education and need not be mentioned here. Some involved the creation of an awareness of danger, such as the sponsorship of the Wise Owl Club, undertaken in 1961. This club drew attention to the importance of wearing safety glasses while working with certain industrial processes. From 1962 on, the E.A. Baker Foundation for Prevention of Blindness provided scholarships, fellowships, and grants to ophthalmologists for research and for the purchase of equipment and other facilities not obtainable from regular sources.

The CNIB submitted a brief to the Select Committee on Youth of the Ontario Legislature in 1965. Among its recommendations were that the study of physics and chemistry be introduced at the Ontario School for the Blind, and that grade 13 be added to the program there; that a special school be established for the partially sighted; that more intensive vocational guidance be provided at the Ontario School for the Blind and that a similar program be offered at the proposed school for the partially sighted; that provincial funds be allocated for the expansion of CNIB facilities for the recording and braille transcription of textbooks for blind students; that funds be made available for the private tutoring or group education of deaf-blind youth; and that the age of eligibility for the blind persons' allowance be lowered to sixteen as a means of assisting blind students in their education and training. The tendency after that time was for the institute to place less emphasis on the provision of separate facilities for the education of the blind, and to stress the desirability of integrating them with sighted children and young people. This treatment was thought to offer the best means of promoting common understanding and respect.

THE CANADIAN COUNCIL OF THE BLIND
The Canadian Council of the Blind, which was formed under federal charter in 1944, had over eighty constituent clubs by the 1960s, with a membership of approximately 4,500. The clubs were grouped in divisions, which carried on certain activities at the provincial level. The council pursued three main objectives: 1 / to promote the welfare of the blind through higher education, profitable employment, and social contact; 2 / to foster a closer relationship between blind and sighted people; and 3 / to promote measures for the conservation of sight and the prevention of blindness.

Close co-operation was maintained with the CNIB, which also pursued the objective of improving services. The CNIB provided financial support for the council, thus helping to avoid an excessive number of appeals to the public. The two organizations made combined approaches to the government to improve legislative provisions for the blind. They also co-operated in sponsoring White Cane Week, which featured an educational program designed to inform the public of the needs and capacities of sightless people.

The council published in print and braille a quarterly journal called the *CCB Outlook*, containing items of particular interest to member clubs as well as articles of more general interest. Affairs of the council were dealt with in the monthly *Council Commentary*.

Influence on the provision of school education for the blind was exerted largely through the divisional organizations. Suggestions were made to those responsible for the operation of schools for the blind with respect to suitable programs. Governments were urged to provide more adequate educational facilities. One division established a scholarship fund to enable blind students from the area to obtain higher education. Some clubs offered classes in effective speaking, music appreciation, leadership training, and other subjects. Members were encouraged to learn the manual alphabet as a means of conversing with those afflicted with both deafness and blindness.

TWENTY-ONE

Associations for the welfare of special groups

The special groups dealt with in this chapter are based on linguistic, cultural, religious, or occupational factors. The educational activities in which the relevant associations engaged were often designed to enhance the characteristic interests of these groups as well as to promote understanding and sympathy among the general public. In some cases an attempt to arouse public opinion was part of a campaign to bring about favourable legislative changes.

L'ASSOCIATION CANADIENNE-FRANÇAISE DE L'ONTARIO

The organization known until 1969 as l'Association canadienne-française d'éducation d'Ontario was founded in Ottawa in 1910, when a convention of 1,200 French-speaking representatives of local communities assembled to resist the threat that the provincial government would adopt a policy of curtailing the use of French as a language of instruction in the separate schools. As recounted in volume III, chapter 9, the government was not dissuaded from taking the threatened action, and passed the controversial Regulation 17 in 1912. Between that year and 1927 the association's main activity was to fight this regulation. After a new and more tolerant policy was adopted, it continued to work for an improvement in the status of the bilingual schools.

As time went on, the association recognized a growing number of affiliates, of which there were fifteen by 1969. These organizations consisted of trustees, teachers, parent-teacher associations, school inspectors, masters of teachers' colleges, young people, farming people, and others. This arrangement enabled the association to assume the role of the official spokesman of the French-speaking population on public issues. Its main work was carried out through 24 regional councils and 225 local sections.

The association regularly made known the views of its constituents in the form of briefs. Among the agencies to which these were submitted in the late 1960s were the government of Ontario, with respect to the establishment of French public secondary schools and the teaching of French in the elementary schools, the Royal Commission on Bilingualism and Biculturalism, le Comité franco-ontarien d'enquête culturelle, the Provincial Committee on Aims and Objectives of Education in the Schools of

Ontario, and the Royal Commission of Inquiry into Civil Rights. The chief points made in the submission to the Provincial Committee on Aims and Objectives were 1 / that education should emphasize the importance of creative thinking and critical inquiry, 2 / that every child has the right to a religious education if he so chooses, 3 / that a French-speaking child should not be compelled to adapt to a school designed for English-speaking students, and 4 / that Ontario should set up a bilingual system similar to that of Quebec.

The name of the organization was changed in 1969 to reflect a shift in emphasis. After the Ontario government developed the system of French secondary schools, attention was shifted toward the economic and cultural fields. *Centres d'animation* were established by mid-1970 in Ottawa, Hawkesbury, Cornwall, Sudbury, Timmins, Kapuskasing, Toronto, Welland, and Windsor to stimulate local cultural activity. Activities in the economic field were at the planning stage.

THE INDIAN-ESKIMO ASSOCIATION OF CANADA
The Indian-Eskimo Association of Canada originated as a special study group under the auspices of the Canadian Association for Adult Education in the 1950s. At the end of the decade it became incorporated as a separate body, and within a little more than a year had a membership consisting of nearly fifty organizations and four hundred individuals. Although the association was not designed explicitly for educational purposes, there was a realization from the outset among its Indian, Eskimo, and white members that education would be a prime factor in the realization of its objectives.

The specific purpose of the organization was to support Canadian Indians and Eskimos in their struggle to gain economic, social, cultural, and political equality with other Canadians. According to the report of the executive director to the ninth annual meeting of the members in 1968, the program of the association rested on seven assumptions.

(a) The present low attainment of persons of Indian and Eskimo ancestry is due to identifiable factors which include isolation, deficiencies in the education programs, cultural matters, lack of access to capital, poor housing, the long period of paternalistic treatment, discrimination, prejudices, etc. Conversely, Indians and Eskimos have the innate potential for growth and development equal to that of any other ethnic group.
(b) Indian and Eskimo people must identify their problems and give the leadership needed in their resolution. This task cannot be done for them.
(c) The Indians and Eskimos need sympathetic support from Canadians in general, but this must be done without usurping the leadership.
(d) Indians and Eskimos need to develop their own organizations and I.E.A. should facilitate such development.
(e) Indian and Eskimo communities need to receive development services

equal to those given other Canadian communities in order to develop economically, socially and politically.

(f) Indians and Eskimos must be encouraged to cherish their cultural heritage and work to ensure that it has an honourable place in the Canadian mosaic of cultures.

(g) I.E.A. will be dissolved when native communities and people have opportunities equal to those afforded other Canadians.[1]

The first of these assumptions recognized the importance of educational deficiencies as an explanation for the depressed condition of Indians and Eskimos. The sixth might be considered a declaration of opposition against any educational program designed for the complete assimilation of these groups into one or other of the dominant cultures.

The same report indicated a desire among Indians to have school texts revised to remove the "savage" image. They were said to feel that the history of Canada should begin with the story of the original citizens, and that it should show their role and contribution in the building of the nation. They favoured an educational program related to their environment and needs, with their own language used, where practical, in the early grades.

In general, the association attempted to further the interests of the Indian, Métis, and Eskimo people by providing a platform for them to express their views on what was needed and how it could be supplied, by offering a medium to rally public support for their cause, and by providing factual information for use by their organizations in their struggle for equality of opportunity with other Canadians. The association was said to be reaching many millions of Canadians through members of affiliated organizations. There were over 140 of these organizations and agencies by 1968.

In 1968 the Ontario division reported a number of activities with educational implications. 1 / A conference, attended by over four hundred delegates, was held at the Ryerson Polytechnical Institute on the theme of Indian youth and cultural dimensions. 2 / There was a special study of problems in the Moosonee area. 3 / A Thinkers' Conference on Indian Education was held in May 1968 at Aurora. 4 / The division was co-operating with the Union of Ontario Indians in a field study relating to proposed amendments to the *Indian Act*.

THE CANADIAN ASSOCIATION FOR INDIAN AND
ESKIMO EDUCATION

What were at first called Schools in The Forest Conferences began to be held in 1963 in different parts of the country. At the sixth such conference, which assembled in Toronto in 1968, a constitution was approved for the Canadian Association for Indian and Eskimo Education. This association consisted of people involved in the education of Indians and Eskimos who felt the need for co-ordination of effort, for discussions, and for dissemination of ideas among regions and among government agencies.

The constitution listed five aims:

(1) To promote and improve the educational development of people of Indian and Eskimo ancestry.

(2) To foster maximum co-operation between federal, provincial, and local agencies involved in the education of these people and to function as a co-ordinating agency.

(3) To collect and make available information on pertinent educational developments.

(4) To foster educational research and to publish reports of selected research studies.

(5) To sponsor an annual conference to facilitate the sharing of developments and programs among all member agencies.

At the conference where the constitution was adopted, the keynote address was delivered by the Honourable Arthur Laing, Minister of Indian Affairs and Northern Development, who spoke on the future of Indian and Eskimo Education. Topics dealt with by other speakers included The Layman Looks at Indian Education, Trends in American Indian and Eskimo Education, and Current Research and Studies on the Indian Community. Reports of the discussions reveal uncertainty about the best kind of educational provision for the groups on which attention was focused, and a consequent recognition of the need for research into many questions. A suggestion was made that there should have been more Indian and Eskimo participation at the conference.

THE CANADIAN JEWISH CONGRESS

The Canadian Jewish Congress was established in 1919 to represent the interests of the Jewish community in Canada. Its general objectives were to safeguard the status, rights, and welfare of Canadian Jews, to promote understanding and good will among all ethnic and religious groups, to co-operate with other agencies for the improvement of social, economic, and cultural conditions, and to assist in the establishment of community organizations. It considered education one of its major priorities.

Although the congress was not necessarily directly concerned with all aspects of Jewish education, it is perhaps relevant to consider some of the basic facts about such education in the present context. In the mid-sixties four types of Jewish schools were found in Ontario: day schools, of which there were eight in Toronto and one in each of Hamilton and Ottawa, offering between twelve and twenty-five hours a week of Jewish subject matter; Hebrew afternoon schools, mostly under congregational auspices, offering between four and one-half and ten hours of instruction a week spread over three to five days; Sunday schools, mainly Reform Temple schools, offering two or three hours of tuition a week; and Yiddish schools, of which there were three in Toronto and one in Windsor. It was estimated that 8,208 of the 14,000 Jewish children aged five to twelve in Toronto were enrolled in some type of Jewish school in 1965; the comparable figure for Hamilton was 480 out of 600; and for Ottawa, 650 out of 900. Others were receiving instruction from private tutors or in shorter periods of attendance at schools. Only a comparatively small proportion were continuing their Jewish studies at the high school level; the figure of 16 per cent at Toronto was considered relatively high. By 1968–9 there were estimated to be 10,200 pupils enrolled in day, afternoon, and weekend or one-day schools in Metropolitan Toronto.

The Canadian Jewish Congress subsidized a teacher training institution, the Midrasha L' Morim, established in 1953, and supervised by the Board of Jewish Education. This was one of a number of such schools maintained in various cities across Canada. There were estimated to be 169 professional teachers in Jewish schools in Toronto in 1965, and 75 in other parts of Ontario.

The Educational and Cultural Committee of the congress took an active part in the preparation of curricula for Jewish schools. An outline in use in the Hebrew afternoon schools in Ontario had as its objectives the transmission of the following:

1. A sense of respect for Jewish traditions and an acceptance of Jewish observances, ethical values and Jewish beliefs; the Jewish conception of universal human values, of justice and peace, charity in the wider sense of Tzedakah, honesty and love of your fellow man; reverence for God (Yir'ath Shomayim) as the creator of the universe and eternal force in shaping the destiny of man.
2. A basic knowledge and an appreciation of the Jewish past.
3. A thorough feeling of identification with the Jewish people and its destiny.
4. A willingness to give of oneself actively and constructively to Jewish life and Jewish causes.
5. A basic ability to read, write and understand Hebrew and, wherever possible, Yiddish, and a love for both languages.
6. A basic knowledge of the T'nach (Bible), and its teachings.
7. A deep sense of spiritual and cultural kinship with Israel and its people.[2]

A special issue of the *Newsletter*, issued in June 1968 by the Joint Adult Education Committee of the Canadian Jewish Congress and a number of other agencies, gave two samples of programs for study groups. These programs were actually offered by local associations. The first consisted of a series of presentations on the following topics: Living under Freedom, Ingredients of a Good Jewish Education, Jewish Customs and Ceremonies Throughout the Year, the Jewish Home, the Relevance of Jewish Ethics for Modern Times, Jewish-Christian Relationships, Ideological Trends and Movements in Jewish Life, Israel Today, and the

Place of Religion in our Lives. The second program was in four parts, the first two requiring two sessions each and the last two, three sessions each. The first part, entitled the Jewish Community of Canada, dealt with statistical data, religious groupings, religious versus secular Judaism, the stage of acculturation in relation to the general community, dangers of assimilation, and Jewish life in the suburbs. The second part, Jewish Education, dealt with educational facilities available to children and youth in the community, the type of Jewish education parents desire, the Jewish day school movement, the problem of continuity of Jewish education beyond the Bar Mitzvah age, alienation among the Jewish college youth, and adult education programs in the community and their assessment. The third part, Intergroup Relations, dealt with religious education in the public schools, discriminatory practices in employment, housing, service organizations, clubs, and other situations, anti-semitism in Canada, inter-dating of high school and college youth, and social contacts with non-Jews on the adult level. The fourth part, Ideas for Strengthening Jewish Self-Identification, dealt with the role of the synagogue, the Jewish community centre, Jewish service organizations, adult education programs, organizational affiliation, Jews as Canadians, and the role of Israel in strengthening Jewish life in the Diaspora.

The congress took advantage of opportunities to present briefs to study commissions and committees. Its submission to the Provincial Committee on Aims and Objectives stressed the extent of the Jewish community's interest in public education. Passing reference was made to its opposition to the sectarian teaching of religion in the schools – the main case being left for presentation to the Mackay Committee. Stress was placed on the need for developing tolerance and harmony among the varied racial, religious, and cultural groups which made up Canadian society. The brief urged that the school system emphasize receptivity to the best in all cultures, and prepare the child for life in a multiracial society and world. Specific references were made to the importance of teacher education in facilitating the achievement of such goals. Various suggestions were offered for handling the curriculum so as to foster the desired ideals and attitudes.

A contribution to adult education in particular was the *Newsletter*, issued regularly in Toronto to provide the public with a list of Jewish cultural events and educational programs. Among the activities regularly announced were Hebrew classes, drama group meetings, Talmud lessons, Bible lessons, community forums, youth study groups, YM and YWHA programs, library tours, and meetings of fraternal organizations.

THE CANADIAN LABOUR CONGRESS
The existence of labour unions in Canada dates from the early nineteenth century. At first these were small, isolated groups of printers, shoemakers, stone-cutters, and carpenters. They gathered strength with an influx of

tradesmen with union experience in Great Britain and the United States. Frequent movement across the border led to the establishment of close associations with American unions and the development of the "international" union. As in other countries, a clearcut distinction emerged between craft unionism and industrial unionism. Although the two forms of organization have persisted, the distinction between them has become blurred.

An important move toward central organization was made in 1873 when the Toronto Trades Assembly called the first national convention of Canadian unions. Representatives from thirty-one unions, all in Ontario, attended, and the abortive Canadian Labour Union was formed. A more successful effort made in 1883 resulted in what became known three years later as the Trades and Labour Congress. During this period labour councils were being organized, and at a later stage provincial federations of labour began to co-ordinate unions on the provincial level. American organizations with activities extending into Canada which flourished for a time and then disappeared were the Knights of St Crispin and the Knights of Labour. A Canadian movement, also of short duration, was the One Big Union, which attempted to include all workers in one organization. Between 1901 and 1921 small unions appeared in Quebec under the guidance of the Roman Catholic clergy, and in 1921 they formed the Canadian and Catholic Confederation of Labour.

The Canadian Labour Congress (CLC) was formed in 1956 as a result of a merger of the Trades and Labour Congress of Canada and the Canadian Congress of Labour. In the late 1960s it claimed more than 75 per cent of the total union membership in Canada. Its responsibilities included the development of policies, the organization of programs, and the provision of services needed to further the interests of the members. General policy guidelines were established at biennial conventions, while service departments looked after policy implementation. Apart from those with educational implications, the nature of such services need not concern us here.

As of the end of the decade an Education Department dealt with five regions of the country, each under a regional director who was answerable to the national director. Where a union affiliated with the CLC had an education program, with a department and staff to carry it out, the central department provided co-ordination and co-operation; where it did not have such a program, the central department provided the necessary services.[3]

The most common type of educational activity was the weekend institute, of which over two hundred were held in various parts of the country each year in co-operation with local labour councils. Topics covered at such institutes included methods and procedures in local union administration, collective bargaining, grievance procedures, and related matters. Since most members participated during their free time, these institutes did not involve any great expense. All of the unions affiliated with the council could be involved. A more intensive and sometimes more advanced program on the same topics was offered at residential schools, which lasted up to a week. Known as winter or summer schools, they were regarded as more effective than weekend institutes. They cost more, however, because of lost wages and the necessity of providing the participants with room and board while they were away from home. A third type of educational program was the special course for labour council officers, full-time staff, and financial officers. It covered such topics as safety, welfare, unemployment insurance, labour legislation, and kindred matters. There were also instructor-training programs to develop teaching ability among those who formed the main teaching body in the education program.

The Department of Research had certain functions impinging on education. For example, its staff provided information on collective bargaining and on economic questions for officers and staff of the CLC and for affiliated and chartered unions. They drafted briefs and memoranda for presentation to governments, royal commissions, parliamentary committees, and advisory councils. They represented the congress at conferences sponsored by universities, business groups, unions, government, and other organizations, and co-operated in the educational program. They prepared articles and published booklets and pamphlets on various subjects in the field of economic conditions and economic policy. An *Economic Bulletin* was issued three or four times a year outlining trends in the economy. A monthly bulletin, *Notes on Publications,* issued for the benefit of research directors of affiliated unions, contained information on current data released by various government departments and other material of interest to labour.

The Political Education Department was expected to co-operate with affiliated organizations of the CLC, with provincial federations of labour, and with labour councils, in promoting an understanding of the influence of politics in the daily lives of the members and in acquainting them with the individual and group action they might take to improve conditions. Specifically, it sought to give them a knowledge of 1 / the parliamentary system of government and its historical background and development, 2 / the procedures for enacting legislation and the operation of pressure groups and lobbies which influence the actions of governments in introducing legislation, 3 / the theory of party government and the role of political parties, 4 / the philosophy of the existing political parties and the sources of their power, 5 / the role of the cabinet and of the members of Parliament, 6 / the functions and influence of the opposition parties in Parliament, 7 / a knowledge of how elections are conducted, and the part that unions and their members can play in election campaigns, and 8 / an appreciation of the importance of the other levels of the governmental system, such as provincial legislatures, municipal councils, boards of education, parks and recreation boards, boards of health, hospital boards, and public commissions. This program was carried out at evening classes, weekend institutes, and winter and summer schools, and through the use of textbooks, leaflets, and articles in union publications, through a study of the records of legislatures, and through participation in election campaigns. Local unions were urged to set up political education committees, and the major affiliates to designate someone to co-ordinate their political education program. Each labour council was expected to have a political education committee. Provincial federations of labour were urged to take responsibility for the program at their own level and, if financially possible, to appoint a full-time political education director. The Political Education Department encouraged unions to affiliate with the New Democratic party and to participate in its activities.

A Publications Department assisted in the preparation of material for leaflets and other publications and worked on CLC campaigns to enlist support for its position on current issues. News releases were prepared and circulated as a means of maintaining day-to-day contact with the press and with radio and television stations. Assistance was provided for the organization of Labour Education Week programs, which were designed to give people in local communities a better understanding of the labour movement and its objectives.

Canadian Labour began publication in 1956 as the official journal of the CLC. A bilingual monthly, it carried official statements of the organization, records of the decisions of the Executive Council and conventions, reports on activities of affiliates, articles on matters of interest to the labour movement, texts of addresses by prominent labour spokesmen, and articles on industries employing organized workers. The journal was circulated throughout Canada and in a considerable number of foreign countries as well.

The Labour College of Canada, chartered in 1963, was operated in Montreal through the co-operation of the CLC, the University of Montreal, and McGill University. Its teaching staff was recruited from these two and other universities, from the labour movement, and from government. It attempted to develop competent leadership by providing unionists with basic studies in the social sciences and specialized instruction in the theory and practice of trade unionism. An eight-week intensive course of instruction included courses in economics, history, sociology, political science, and trade unionism. The residential course led to a diploma for the successful candidate. There was also a correspondence course leading to a diploma.

In 1969 there were sixty-nine students enrolled at the college, forty-six English-speaking, and twenty-three French-speaking. Candidates were accepted only after a careful screening process. The college granted a number of scholarships which in 1970 amounted to $1,000 each, and bursaries of lesser amounts. It also paid transportation costs in excess of $50. Various other organizations also made awards which averaged about $1,200 in value.

THE TEXTILE WORKERS UNION OF AMERICA

A great many individual unions had educational programs designed at least to further their own specific objectives, and in many cases also to promote the education of their members in a broader sense. The Textile Workers Union of America (TWUA) is mentioned here by way of illustration. The clause in the objects of the union, as listed in the constitution, which most clearly demonstrates an educational interest, reads thus: "To advance their [the members'] economic, social and cultural interests; to disseminate information among them regarding economic, social, political, and other matters affecting their lives and welfare."

Although the first textile unions in the United States were formed in 1793, the workers in this field were not effectively organized until 1937, when a Textile Workers Organizing Committee (TWOC) of the Congress of Industrial Organizations took the matter in hand. Two years later hundreds of new TWOC locals joined forces with the United Textile Workers. After that time membership increased rapidly and working conditions for the members were greatly improved.

The TWUA maintained an Education Department which offered courses, seminars, and conferences dealing with such topics as the conduct of meetings, collective bargaining, grievance handling, and the purpose and history of the labour movement. Such programs were of particular value to those who assumed the responsibility of organizing and running a new local. A political education and action program involved co-operation with the New Democratic party. A Legislative Department held conferences and workshops on political education to help members exert an influence at the national, provincial, and municipal levels. The Publicity Department was responsible for the union's official publication, *Textile Labor*, and for communication with the press, radio, and television.

One of the publications of the Education Department was a booklet called *Rules for Union Meetings*. As the title implied, it offered an explanation of parliamentary procedures, and indicated how group objectives might be expeditiously achieved. Its production demonstrated a realization of the importance of orderly meetings as an aspect of union activity, and of the necessity for a union leader to be thoroughly acquainted with protocol.

THE JOHN HOWARD SOCIETY OF ONTARIO

What was at first known as the Citizens Service Association was established in Toronto in 1929 on the initiative of General D.C. Draper, the Toronto Chief of Police, with the primary purpose of helping released convicts to rehabilitate themselves in society. The name of the organization was changed to the Prisoners' Rehabilitation Society in 1935, and to the John Howard Society in 1946. A national organization, the John Howard Society of Canada, united all the provincial associations except that of Quebec in 1963.

The charter of the Ontario society mentioned two main objectives: 1 / to provide a social casework service with limited financial assistance to ex-inmates of correctional institutions, and 2 / to press for penal reform through a study of the causes and prevention of crime and all phases of the correctional process from arrest through imprisonment to discharge and after-care. At the annual meeting of the National Society in 1963, the president, Monsignor Joseph E. Le Fort, mentioned the importance of developing, through educational activities, an enlightened public opinion with respect to correctional programs and problems.

The work of local branches was carried out in a variety of ways according to the size of the community and the extent of the need. In the larger centres, such as Toronto, Windsor, London, Hamilton, Kingston, Ottawa, St Catharines, and Thunder Bay, services were provided by professionally trained workers aided by volunteer counsellors. In smaller cities groups of business and professional men and women offered counselling and assistance on a voluntary basis. In still smaller communities the limited number of released prisoners were helped by individual John Howard associates, social workers, clergymen, lawyers, and magistrates. The work was maintained financially by contributions from Community Chests, United Appeals, corporations, and individual citizens.

It was the policy of the society to employ a staff with an orientation toward social casework, community organization, and administration, and to provide them with the more specific training required by social workers in correctional after-care. In 1953 the first formal staff conference was held to develop common policies, practices, and procedures relating to service to released prisoners. Later conferences emphasized the need to integrate and interpret what the society was doing. An outgrowth of group discussions and the presentation of case histories was a document called "Practices of Assistance." As time went on, there was an increasing trend toward the use of outside consultants at the conferences. Institutes were held on such topics as Social Group Dynamics, Psycho-Pathology of Crime, and Casework in Corrections. Other procedures for in-service staff training included 1 / an agency orientation program, involving visits to correctional institutions and social agencies, 2 / summer institutes at American centres, 3 / study tours, 4 / attendance at the Canadian and American Congresses of Corrections, 5 / the maintenance of a library containing journals and books on social work and correctional subjects, 6 / formal supervision at the provincial and branch levels, 7 / staff meetings involving formal and informal group discussions, 8 / educational leave with or without financial support, 9 / the provision of practical field work experience for social work students, and 10 / participation in committee work.

In 1966 the Ontario association employed an officer to engage in public education by preparing materials, working with newspaper reporters, and speaking on request. Other activities with educational implications included the maintenance of liaison with university schools of social work, the provision of opportunities for students to work on projects, and the award of bursaries and training grants to enable employees to secure more advanced education. Internal staff training included two-day development sessions held twice a year and an institute held once a year.

A report of the highlights of the Ottawa branch in 1968 will indicate the extent to which the activities of local societies might be considered educational. This branch continued work with the Elizabeth Fry Society on the Carleton County Jail project, involving the construction of the first regional detention centre in the province; began an educational program in Ottawa high schools; re-established a committee of the board and the community to obtain expanded forensic services for Ottawa; established a pre-release service at Rideau Industrial Farm on behalf of the Provincial Office; contributed to the Marijuana Brief to the Minister of Justice proposed by the Provincial Office; was given representation on the Ottawa Mayor's youth committee; participated in student instruction at the Centre of Criminology of the University of Ottawa; and provided field placement for two students from the School of Social Work at Carleton University.

TWENTY-TWO

Associations for the promotion of social, economic, and cultural causes

Associations designed to further social, economic, and cultural causes usually depend to a considerable extent on education to fufil their objectives. They rely on publications, the media, meetings, and sometimes formal courses. The organizations covered in this chapter were concerned with a great many different matters such as art, conservation, recreation, safety, community planning, and family affairs. They had in common the desire to improve some aspect of society.

THE CENTRAL ONTARIO ART ASSOCIATION

Before 1954 three organized art groups operated in the five counties of Halton, Peel, Dufferin, Wellington, and Waterloo. Evening classes were offered in Guelph, Kitchener-Waterloo, and Fergus for ten or twelve sessions each year. The groups had no opportunity for stimulating contacts or joint exhibits. In an effort to improve the situation twelve art teachers met at Macdonald Institute in 1964 and organized the Five Counties Art Association, later renamed the Central Ontario Art Association in order to indicate that members from a wider geographical range were welcome. In 1957 the teacher participants withdrew to form their own organization, leaving the operation of the association to amateur artists. The new organization, the Teachers' Council of the Five Counties Art Association, continued to assist by providing instruction on sketching trips, by judging entries in exhibitions, and by giving awards.

As time went on, the association set up three regional exhibitions enabling members to exhibit their paintings. Sketching trips, of which there were about four each year, were hosted by members in the area. The Youth and Recreation Branch of the Department of Education provided assistance for workshops and weekend seminars, and the Ontario Council for the Arts made grants for the education program. According to a report in early 1970 the membership of the association was approaching three hundred, and still growing.

THE THEATRE ARTS GUILD

The initiative for the organization of the Theatre Arts Guild came from graduates of the Theatre Arts Option at the College of Education, University of Toronto, in 1967. This group felt that, as a result of increasing participation in theatre arts courses in the secondary schools, there was a need to provide a link between developments in all forms of professional theatre and new approaches to drama in education.[1] During 1967–8 a constitution was adopted and a program of meetings was devised by a planning committee. According to the constitution, the aims of the guild were 1 / to bring together the arts and skills of the theatre and the needs and potentialities of education, 2 / to exchange information, to hold meetings, seminars, workshops, and lectures, and to engage in other similar activities, 3 / to promote, by all available means, the highest standards of theatre arts in the educational process, and 4 / to promote the use of theatre and the dramatic form in education at all appropriate levels.

An attempt was made to hold meetings in locations of special interest to members and to ensure that presentations avoided excessive formality, but rather provided opportunities for personal discussion and the exchange of ideas. Among other activities which the guild promoted were short visits to other parts of Canada and to the United States. It was hoped that a program called Operation Meeting-ground would result in the development of new ways to bring theatre and education together.

THE QUETICO FOUNDATION

The objective of the Quetico Foundation was to preserve wilderness areas in Ontario for recreation and scientific use. Its activities were educational in the sense that it needed a strong body of public opinion in order to further such an objective. One means it used to promote its cause was the publication of the *Quetico Newsletter*, which included articles describing the attractions of various parks, recounting successes and failures in the constant struggle against the encroachments of mining and industrial interests, and telling of the specific activities of the foundation.

The formation of the foundation was related to a movement that began as early as 1885, when Alexander Kirkwood, an employee of the Department of Crown Lands, began to express concern about the lack of foresight being shown in the exploitation of the forests of the province. His efforts were instrumental in the establishment of Algonquin Park in 1893. Another major step was taken in 1909 when the area in north-western Ontario later known as Quetico Park was set aside for similar purposes. At the same time the state of Minnesota was persuaded to establish a comparable reserve on its own side of the border, known as the Superior National Forest. Unlike the Canadians, who had acted before the problem of restoration had arisen, the Americans had to purchase many resorts, cottages, and camps and return them to the wilderness, a task in which public spirited citizens assisted. Inspired by this example, a group of Canadians eventually decided that a protective program was needed to retain what they had gained. In the 1930s a Canadian Committee was set up under the chairmanship of the Right Honourable

Vincent Massey. This committee became the Quetico Foundation in 1954. Four years later, as a result of a request from the Minister of Lands and Forests, the foundation amended its charter to extend its activities to all wilderness parks in Ontario.

A leaflet produced by the foundation presented the objectives of the latter in this way.

The Foundation believes that the recreation that comes from living in our wilderness country more or less as a pioneer with a tent and a canoe and fishing tackle is gaining greater significance than ever before ... For the young, recreation of this kind builds character; for the mature, it brings the kind of peace that tends to restore the wear and tear brought about by speed, noise and pressure. The Foundation also believes that greater use of our wilderness areas will bring greater appreciation of their many scenic, historical, recreational and scientific values, and that this appreciation is the most effective way by which these values may be preserved.

The foundation developed a program consisting of four essential elements: 1 / the promotion of public appreciation of the value of the wilderness assets of the province and of the need to conserve them intelligently; 2 / efforts to secure effective zoning of wilderness areas to include adequate points of access, peripheral areas for resorts, outfitters' establishments, and summer cottages, and, in particular, areas of substantial size to attract the venturesome; 3 / support for a clear, comprehensive, and positive provincial government policy with respect to wilderness parks; 4 / continuing scientific research in the field of conservation leading to the accumulation of knowledge that might be applied to the preservation and wise use of natural resources.

In addition to publishing its own newsletter, the foundation assisted writers for nationally circulated magazines to obtain material on the wilderness conservation and recreation movement. News and advisory services were placed at the regular disposal of radio and television broadcasters. The 16-mm colour film "Quetico," which won a Canadian Film award in 1958, remained in continuous demand. The foundation financed the publication of a number of monographs based on the work of specialists and written in a popular style. It was a common practice for the foundation to support field work during the summer in co-operation with other institutions. In 1969, for example, a grant of $450 was part of a larger fund spent on an archaeological survey of the Trent Valley.

THE CONSERVATION COUNCIL OF ONTARIO
Concern about the use and management of natural resources in Ontario led to the calling of a conference of agriculturalists, foresters, naturalists, and sportsmen in 1951. Recognizing the need for a forum for the exchange of information and ideas, these individuals took steps to form the Con-

servation Council of Ontario, which held its first official meeting in 1952. Serving as a co-ordinating body, the council began with eleven provincial associations and groups involved in some way in conservation. By 1969 there were twenty-three of these: the Canadian Institute of Forestry (Southern Ontario Section), the Committee of Conservation Authority Chairmen of Ontario, the Community Planning Association of Canada (Ontario Division), the Consumers' Association of Canada (Ontario), the Federation of Ontario Cottagers' Associations, the Federation of Ontario Naturalists, the Junior Farmers' Association of Ontario, the Northern Ontario Tourist Outfitters Association, the Ontario Association of Landscape Architects, the Ontario Camping Association, the Ontario Chamber of Commerce, the Ontario Council of Commercial Fisheries, the Ontario Educational Association, the Ontario Federation of Agriculture, the Ontario Federation of Anglers and Hunters Inc, the Ontario Forestry Association, the Ontario Institute of Agrologists, the Ontario Medical Association, the Ontario Professional Foresters Association, the Ontario Soil and Crop Improvement Association, the Quetico Foundation, the Soil Conservation Society of America (Ontario Chapter), and the Town Planning Institute of Canada (Central Ontario Chapter).

The original charter of the council listed seven aims: 1 / to provide a continuing forum for the exchange of information vital to conservation, 2 / to discuss and test ideas that may benefit resource interests, 3 / to plan and encourage research concerning any phase of conservation, 4 / to provide the public with accurate information about the main issues of conservation in Ontario, 5 / to co-ordinate the activities of the major organizations in Ontario concerned with resource use and management, 6 / to advise and co-operate with government agencies and others entrusted with the proper use of natural resources, and 7 / to carry out a broad educational program to encourage the wisest use of Ontario's renewable natural resources.

The educational efforts of the council were directed chiefly toward community decision makers, whom it attempted to reach through a quarterly bulletin, periodic briefs and reports, and annual conferences. Much of the same material was sent to high schools in Ontario. Student participation at conferences was encouraged by special rates. A standing committee on conservation engaged in two main types of activities: making submissions to government agencies on aspects of conservation education and studying methods of educating the public on the theme of environmental quality. The council as such did not sponsor formal courses, although many of its members were engaged in conservation education.

Between 1955 and 1966 the council submitted briefs to twelve government agencies and government-sponsored study groups such as the Provincial Committee on Aims and Objectives of Education in the Schools of Ontario. It attempted to influence the appropriate levels of government to pass legislation on several matters, some of them having a direct bearing on formal education. 1 / It urged the federal and provincial governments to develop a comprehensive water policy. 2 / It advocated the preservation of the province's twelve million acres of prime farm land by new zoning and taxation laws. 3 / It pressed for a survey of Ontario's existing and future needs for outdoor recreation and the adoption of a program for the acquisition of enough provincial parks in southern Ontario to meet these needs. 4 / It recommended the establishment of an accredited training course in conservation principles for elementary school teachers. 5 / It supported the provision of natural science schools.

Some of the council's educational concerns were brought out in its submission to the Provincial Committee on Aims and Objectives. It made five recommendations:

1. That suitable courses be taught in a manner that will emphasize the principles of conservation[,] e.g. social studies, natural science courses; and geography, economics, history, and biology later in the school programme.
2. That students be introduced to the outdoors through one or more weeks of continuous participation in a natural science school program.
3. That Boards of Education be made fully aware of the legislation under the Schools Administration Act (Section 66a) providing for the formation of natural science schools, and encouraged to take advantage of these provisions.
4. That provision be made under the Schools Administration Act for groups of boards to combine to form a natural science school, where individual boards do not meet the present average daily attendance requirements as defined in the act, or when they would find it prohibitively expensive to provide a school by themselves.
5. That a training course for elementary school teachers be designed and operated to equip them with the knowledge to present conservation topics as part of their teaching programs. A proposal for such a course has been outlined in the Conservation Council's "Proposal for an Ontario Elementary School Science Field Study Course," which was submitted to the Minister of Education in January, 1964 ...[2]

In a brief submitted to the Select Committee on Conservation Authorities in August 1966, the council made recommendations regarding public information and education:

1. That a comprehensive public information programme be undertaken, both to provide definite information on the broad aims and objects of Conservation Authorities generally, and to give specific details, with objective analysis, on each authority's programmes.
2. That Authorities place more emphasis on educational programmes, particularly those directed towards encouraging the application of sound

conservation principles in renewable resource management. These programmes should be made available to the general public, and especially
to students, contractors and landowners. Information media of all types
could be used, including film shorts, inexpensive published material and
advisory services.

3. That Authorities participate with local boards of education and others in
establishing more natural science schools, on property adjacent to land
owned by Authorities, to enable suitable Authority lands to be used as
outdoor laboratories.

4. That all Conservation Authorities have access to the services of a trained
field officer and a competent conservation education officer. Provision is
made for this in the Act, and it is particularly desirable that these be provided adequately in all cases. Specialist staffs should be available as consultants to Authorities and Municipalities whose operations do not justify
full time specialists in all fields.[3]

THE CANADIAN ASSOCIATION FOR HEALTH,
PHYSICAL EDUCATION AND RECREATION

What was at first called the Canadian Physical Education Association
was founded in 1931 and incorporated as the Canadian Association for
Health, Physical Education and Recreation (CAHPER) twenty years later.
It attracted as members those who were active in one or more of three
fields: health education, physical education, and recreation. They were
employed for the most part in schools, universities, and public and private
recreation agencies and organizations. Among the objectives of the association were 1 / to work for the improvement of the standard of competence of those working in its major fields of interest, 2 / to promote the
establishment of adequate programs of health and physical education and
recreation, and 3 / to stimulate interest in these programs.

The association attempted to attain its goals by co-operating with
departments of the federal government and with other organizations, including the Canadian Medical Association. It joined with the Parks and
Recreation Association of Canada for the improvement of recreation
programs and leadership training. With the assistance of the National
Advisory Council on Fitness and Amateur Sport, it developed the
CAHPER Fitness-Performance Tests. From time to time it published Canadian sports rule books in English and French. Its journal, distributed
widely to libraries as well as among the members, reported new developments at home and abroad. A research committee attempted to influence
interest in health through the publication of its findings in reports such as
The Physical Work Capacity of Canadian Children, which was used in
schools. Financial contributions enabled Canadians to publish material
about sports which commercial publishers would not handle. Provincial
departments of health and education were given assistance in the preparation of course outlines for health education.

THE NATIONAL SAFETY LEAGUE OF CANADA

The National Safety League of Canada was given its original charter in 1918. It was active after 1963 in promoting accident control in the fields of home, child, water, recreational, and farm safety. Its objectives were 1 / to provide a national clearinghouse for all matters relating to its interests, 2 / to publish or arrange for the publication of safety materials, 3 / to develop and maintain close liaison with all safety organizations, 4 / to disseminate and promote the use of safety information through the various communications media, 5 / to assist in the organization of workshops for the training of professional and volunteer workers in safety, 6 / to encourage the production of technical information for use in accident prevention procedures and programs, 7 / to enlist the co-operation of research and other agencies in testing safety procedures and devices, 8 / to exert influence on manufacturers and designers to encourage the production of safer materials and equipment, 9 / to collect and disseminate up-to-date accident statistics, and 10 / to provide incentives for leadership and achievement in safety.

The campaign for home safety was conducted through publications and broadcasts on the prevention of falls, the promotion of water safety, fire prevention, warnings about the hazards associated with discarded refrigerators and ice boxes, the dangers of plastic film, safe handling and storage of poison in the home and outdoors and the value of poison control centres, safety precautions involving electrical wiring and appliances, safe storing and handling of firearms and ammunition in the home, and rural community and farm safety. Child safety was promoted through the recognition of a Child Safety Day, focusing attention on the importance of looking out for children's safety throughout the year. A baby-sitters' training course, dealing with safe child care and sitter and parent responsibilities, was promoted across the country. Information was compiled and disseminated on the dangers associated with poorly designed and inferior materials. As part of its water safety program, the league produced a better boating course based on a booklet issued by the Department of Transport, and distributed it to associations and organized groups across Canada. Publicity stressed the importance of learning to swim well and of using life-saving equipment. Recreational safety was promoted through the preparation of a draft safety code for amusement devices and temporary structures at carnivals, fairs, and amusement parks. The league co-operated with the Canadian Ski Patrol Systems in promoting accident control. With the co-operation of the Dominion Bureau of Statistics, data on fatal accidents were compiled annually, with information on the causes, location, and age groups involved. Such material proved of value to provincial governments and safety organizations.

The National Safety League of Canada merged with the Canadian Highway Safety Council in October 1968 as the Canadian Safety Council. The Canadian Industrial Safety Association joined in January 1969. Programs of the new organization were identified with engineering, enforcement, and education. Under the first of these headings were improvements in the design of highways, signs, signals, road markings, and motor vehicles. Enforcement included the support of safety legislation by the federal and provincial governments and the encouragement of public support for education. The public education program involved outlining the accident problem and suggesting ways to help reduce accidents and accidental deaths and injuries and encouraging the development of a positive attitude toward public safety.

Emphasis was placed on the importance of beginning safety education as early as possible. A national campaign associated with Elmer, the Safety Elephant, was carried out to teach children from kindergarten to grade 3 the safety rules of traffic. In 1969 this program involved about 800,000 children in over 2,500 schools. It was considered to have been successful in reducing traffic accidents involving school children by as much as 50 per cent. An Elmer Summer Safety Contest was carried out with the co-operation of daily newspapers and television as a means of keeping children's attention on safety rules during the summer.

With assistance from the Insurance Bureau of Canada, the council conducted a program to qualify teachers for driver-education instruction in Canadian high schools. These courses were usually carried out during the summer vacation. Between 1961 and 1968 over two thousand Canadian teachers completed this course.

Other programs initiated or continued by the council included a defensive driving course, which was funded by a special grant from the Motor Vehicle Manufacturers' Association. In 1968 this program produced 36,000 student graduates, 627 qualified course instructors, and 131 qualified instructor trainers. A committee involving the railway industry and the Railway Section of the Federal Board of Transport Commissioners produced a brief on accidents occurring at the intersection of highways and level crossings. It placed strong emphasis on the desirability of a joint program of public education by the two major railways. The council co-operated with the Joint Fire Publicity Committee in publishing a paper entitled *Canada Safety Council Presents Fire Prevention News*. A correspondence course consisting of twelve lessons was prepared to help safety supervisors to do a better job of accident prevention. A small plant safety package showed how to install and conduct a sound accident prevention program. Consultation services were available to assist industry to set up programs and to solve problems. *Safety Canada*, a news bulletin, was published eleven times a year in English and French. Among safety films produced were two entitled respectively "Are You Warm to the Touch?" and "Be Safe – Be Seen." Efforts were made to supplement compulsory and selective car check maintenance by campaigns to focus public attention on the importance of regular checks by competent mechanics. Thousands of kits were distributed containing a car check list, a diagnosis list, a "Check Your Car, Check Accidents" poster, and a press release. The same campaign involved spot announcements on radio and television. What had originated as Child Safety Day became National Child Safety Week, and Farm Safety Week and Safe-Boating Week were added.

THE ROYAL LIFE SAVING SOCIETY

As its name implies, the Royal Life Saving Society was formed to promote the preservation of life. An early statement of its purposes, which continued to be pursued by various means in successive years, was as follows:

(a) To promote technical education in life saving and the resuscitation of the apparently drowned;
(b) to stimulate public opinion in favour of the general adoption of swimming and life saving as a branch of instruction in schools, colleges, etc.;
(c) to encourage floating, diving, plunging and such other swimming arts as would be of assistance to a person endeavouring to save life;
(d) to arrange and promote public lectures, demonstrations and competitions, and to form classes of instruction, so as to bring about a widespread and thorough knowledge of the principles which underlie the art of natation.

The society originated in England in 1891 as a result of efforts by a small group of citizens who were interested in giving training in the techniques of water rescue. Evidence of long-standing support by royalty and other prominent people was given in 1904 when Edward VII bestowed the present name on the organization. Four years later a branch of the parent society was formed in Ontario, and other provinces gradually followed suit. In 1947 authority was given for the formation of a Canadian Council of Branches, which was permitted to make awards and to adopt organizational and operational procedures suitable for Canada. Under a supplementary charter granted by the Queen in 1960 the society was reorganized with autonomous national branches in the United Kingdom, New Zealand, Australia, South Africa, and Canada under the general direction of a Commonwealth Council. Such dignitaries as George Drew and Lionel Chevrier served in succession as senior Canadian representative on this council. A new constitution for Canada was drawn up in 1962.

After the Supplementary Charter came into force in 1960, the Ontario branch of the society gained new importance. Its heaquarters served also as the administrative office for the Canadian council, with the responsibility of supplying, recording, accounting for, and delivering awards for all provincial branches. Organizational changes in the Ontario branch in the mid-sixties included a limitation on the terms of executive officers to two years and a decentralization of responsibility. Modifications were made in examiners' qualifications and a training syllabus was prepared for those seeking to qualify as instructors.

Qualified instruction for Royal Life Saving Society awards was obtained at municipal pools, in local summer programs at waterfronts, at camps, and in schools. These programs were termed "affiliates" of the national society. Instruction was given by professional aquatics personnel, physical education teachers, and instructors trained by the Canadian Red Cross or the YMCA. Such instructors had their qualifications evaluated at regular clinics held by the society. Services of examiners at these clinics was offered on a purely voluntary basis.

The Royal Life Saving Society of Canada co-operated with the National Council of YMCAs of Canada, the Canadian Red Cross Society, and the Society of Directors of Municipal Recreation of Ontario to establish the National Lifeguard Service, the purpose of which was to train lifeguards. The program was under the supervision of the National Directorate, with a provincial directorate in each province. Courses were held throughout Ontario using course outlines and other materials specially prepared for the purpose. In addition to enlarging their practical experience, the candidates were expected to develop a mature attitude and keen judgment.

THE ONTARIO CAMPING ASSOCIATION
The Ontario Camping Association was formed to bring together camp directors, leaders, and counsellors interested in the development and maintenance of standards for children's camps, and in the study and appreciation of broader aspects of the camping movement. According to a leaflet issued by the organization, members were "fundamentally interested in the growth, welfare, protection and education of children and teen-agers through camping." There was one class of membership for camp directors, who were supposed to be carefully selected by a Membership Committee to ensure that they agreed with and accepted the objectives of the association, that they could provide evidence that their camps and officers enjoyed acceptable status in the community, and that they had a sincere interest in the welfare of children. There were also individual memberships open to counsellors, senior camp staff, camp board members, and others with an interest in various aspects of camping.

The association maintained a camp directory, revised annually, which it distributed to the public free of charge. This publication gave information on each member camp, including its location, the length of its season, its staff, and the fees charged. Public relations activities included the distribution of information to newspapers and radio and television broadcasters. Speakers were furnished to organizations desiring up-to-date, authoritative information on camping. The quarterly *Canadian Camping Magazine* kept members acquainted with the latest news and trends in camping. A newsletter dealt with matters of provincial import, including new or revised government regulations. Members had the use of a library of books on camping and outdoor activities, crafts, skills, and other matters. A counsellor placement service compiled lists of the names of prospective counsellors and staff, indicating their names, camping experience, and qualifications, and distributed it to member camps. An annual conference provided lectures and papers by experts from all over North America, as well as workshops, seminars, and discussion groups.

An Education Committee organized a program for members, including open meetings held several times a year. These featured speakers, panels, discussions, or movies dealing with topics of current interest. "Interest group" meetings were held in the spring for new and experienced camp staff. Directors' seminars were held in co-operation with members from Manitoba and Quebec.

THE ONTARIO HUMANE SOCIETY

The Ontario Humane Society has been active in certain familiar causes for almost a century. Some of the forty-nine local societies existing in Ontario in 1969 carried on what were known as "humane education" programs. The energy and effectiveness with which these programs were conducted depended entirely on the existence of a local volunteer who was interested in the work. The usual procedure was to encourage children to form junior groups of the society, which met from time to time according to their own individual pattern. Literature, mostly produced in the United States, was distributed with the objective of teaching children how to care for different kinds of animals. It was hoped that they would develop reverence for life, tempered by common sense. The provincial organization assisted by supplying promotional materials and junior pins. Other education programs involved sponsoring poster, essay, and film contests with a slant toward the humane treatment of animals.

The Ontario Humane Society formed the Ontario Humane Education Society in 1962. Although the attempt to raise funds for the venture were unsuccessful, the society was kept alive for three years, employing a full-time and later a part-time professional organizer. The Ontario government and the Department of Education gave the movement a distinctly chilly reception. Not only were funds refused, but the society's representative was also denied access to classrooms for the purpose of making presentations. Nor was approval granted for the distribution of the society's periodical in the schools.

An associated development, the Kindness Club of Canada, had more success. A specialist group organized by Mrs Hugh John Flemming in New Brunswick in 1960, it spread to various parts of North America and to other countries of the free world. The essential approach was an appeal to the emotions and humane sentiments of young people. There was some apprehension lest the problems of raising funds prove to be insoluble, and the organization disappear once the initial inspiration died out.

THE COMMUNITY PLANNING ASSOCIATION OF CANADA

The Community Planning Association of Canada, which was formed in 1947, pursued the following objectives: 1 / to encourage, stimulate, and guide citizens' interest in and understanding of municipal and regional planning; 2 / to inform citizens and elected and appointed municipal officials and their advisers of current trends and practices in the planning and development of the community; 3 / to promote education in environmental planning in universities, colleges, and schools and to support programs of continuing adult education; 4 / to provide a forum to enable the citizen and government agencies at all levels to exchange views on planning; and 5 / to urge citizens to exercise their civic responsibilities by participating in the planning process.

The national association was organized into divisions corresponding to the provinces. Policies were formulated by a National Council consisting of representatives of these divisions along with six other members without geographical affiliation. Each division maintained effective autonomy, with control over its own program, finances, and administration. Financial sustenance came from membership fees and donations from private individuals and corporations. The federal government subsidized the national organization, while most divisions received grants from their provincial governments.

The association pursued its informational and educational aims by using every available means of communication. New planning techniques and developments were presented and discussed for the first time at its national, provincial, regional, and local conferences. The association produced the periodical *Community Planning Review*, as well as newsletters, booklets, and pamphlets through which it attempted to increase citizens' understanding of planning principles and processes, and to provide information on local planning issues. Briefs were submitted to government agencies, and suggestions were made for the improvement of legislation. These reflected stated opinions of members and resolutions and recommendations from conferences, public meetings, and seminars. The press, radio, and television were used to reach citizens, professionals, and high school and university groups.

The Ontario Division took particular pride in a number of achievements. 1 / After it presented a brief to the Select Committee of the Legislature on the Municipal Act and Related Acts, the government decided not to proceed with the proposed elimination of planning boards. 2 / It gave leadership from 1961 on in the realm of regional planning by holding a conference on the subject and by circulating the proceedings in booklet form and later as a textbook. 3 / It co-operated with the Norwich Union Insurance Societies to encourage renovation and improvement schemes in many Ontario communities. 4 / A number of branches held contests and competitions to encourage students and citizens to present proposals for community betterment. 5 / The Toronto Region Branch undertook a successful campaign for an overall, integrated plan for the waterfront. 6 / The same branch distributed copies of a digest of the report of the Goldenberg Royal Commission among its members, civic leaders, appointed officials, and community groups in the Metropolitan Toronto area in order to help ensure that the recommendations and implications of the document would be properly understood. 7 / It applied effective pressure on many Ontario municipalities to enact by-laws to establish and enforce minimum standards of occupancy and maintenance of dwellings.

The Ontario Division did not always see its interests as consistent with those of the national association, which it tended to consider too much under the thumb of the federal government. Critics suggested that federal support carried with it a certain amount of pressure to avoid advocating fundamental reforms. Ontario members were somewhat better pleased when arrangements were made in 1959 for a higher degree of decentralization. A feeling remained, however, that the speed of action at the national level was too slow.

THE RETAIL COUNCIL OF CANADA

The Retail Council of Canada was formed in 1963 to represent the interests of retailers to the federal and provincial governments, to supply members with legislative, trade, and statistical information, to work for the solution of common trade problems, and to perform certain educational functions. By the end of the 1960s it claimed to represent most of Canada's medium-sized and larger retailers as well as a substantial cross-section of the smaller units in the industry. There was provision for direct membership for stores actively engaged in retailing; associate (trading) membership for trading firms performing some retailing activities or maintaining close associations with the industry, but with interests primarily in other fields; associate (general and professional) membership for enterprises such as banks, financial institutions, and firms of management consultants; and affiliate membership for Chambers of Commerce and sectional trade associations.

The main educational activities of the council have consisted of a variety of conferences and seminars. Some of these have been designed to serve the needs of specialists of various types, including those in the finance and control fields. An example was a three-day seminar held in May 1969 in co-operation with the Society of Industrial Accountants of Canada, where the following topics were dealt with: Introduction to Merchandise Control, Scope and Nature of Merchandise Inventories, Merchandise Classifications, Inventory Management Systems, Merchandise Control Systems, Merchandise Information Systems, the Role of the Computer, and Selecting the Operating System and Implementation. Another type of program is the one-day seminar on a specific subject. Consideration has been given to offering a merchandising course for those not having ready access to an academic institution where one is available.

THE VOICE OF WOMEN

The Voice of Women organization in Canada was formed in 1960 to pursue the following objectives, as stated in the constitution:

to unite women in concern for the future of the world; to help promote the mutual respect and co-operation among nations necessary for peaceful negotiation between world powers having different ideological assumptions; to protest against war or the threat of war as the decisive method of exercising power; to appeal to all national leaders to co-operate in developing methods of negotiation on matters affecting their national security and the peace of the world; to appeal to all national leaders to co-operate in the alleviation of the causes of war by common action for the economic and social betterment of mankind; to provide a means for women to exercise responsibility for the family of mankind.

A promotional brochure appealed to potential members on the basis that the organization provided a means by which women who were disturbed and concerned about the growing violence in the world could unite for effective action. Among the particular issues and dangers mentioned were Vietnam, radiation, and the threat of nuclear war. An opportunity was offered for learning about these matters and sharing information with others through books, periodicals, tape-recordings, and speakers at meetings. A second sphere of participation involved action such as writing letters to the local member of Parliament and to the press, expressing views on radio opinion programs, and pressing various other organizations to take a stand on issues.

The Voice of Women took the view that atomic war, the supreme danger, could best be avoided by the withdrawal of the Canadian government from military alliances such as NATO and NORAD and the conversion of war industry to industry for peaceful purposes. A particular campaign was conducted against research on weapons for chemical and biological warfare and the accumulation of such weapons. The organization pressed for stronger support for the United Nations and the establishment of Canadian diplomatic relations with China. It gave enthusiastic support to programs of peace research. Opponents with a different viewpoint from time to time accused the Voice of Women of being a Communist or Communist-sympathizing body. This charge met with emphatic denials.

Like so many other organizations, the Voice of Women demonstrated a rapidly rising concern in the late 1960s over the problems of air, water, and soil pollution. Some of the approaches used in the campaigns against war and preparations for war were employed in connection with this issue. Certain groups associated Canadian pollution problems with the use of defoliants in Vietnam, and waged a common campaign against both.

Some of the particular concerns of the organization with respect to the education of children in schools were expressed at the annual meeting in 1966. On that occasion a resolution was passed to the effect that there should be vigorous protests against national, racial, or religious biases appearing at any level of education via teachers or textbooks. It was also resolved that provincial departments of education should "include in their courses of study a description of the moral values of each part of the world." At the same meeting a committee was appointed to draw up a brief for presentation to the Mackay Committee, which had undertaken to investigate the teaching of religion in Ontario public schools. The resulting document took the position that moral, ethical, or religious values could not be taught in a democracy without damage to the individual. Nothing must be done to interfere with the child's right to make his own choice among alternatives. Even learning in school that it was desirable to be a Christian was said to give the child a feeling of superiority, which caused prejudice and division. The brief outlined educational approaches that might be useful at various age levels for the development of a moral sense.

A brief was submitted to the Provincial Committee on Aims and Objectives of Education in the Schools of Ontario, with some recommendations reflecting the special concerns of the organization, and others of a more general nature. Among the propositions in the first category were that education must equip children for world citizenship and that schools should accommodate all children, regardless of social class and level of intelligence.

An education workshop held in 1970 dealt with the question of American influence on Canadian education. Consideration was given to statistics reported in the *Educational Courier* in May 1969, which indicated the number of staff members in Canadian schools attending conferences in Canada, the United States, and elsewhere; the national origin of resource personnel participating in workshops and conferences; the proportion of schools in various provinces using educational television programs produced in the United States; and the origin of textbooks, magazines, films, and filmstrips used in Canadian schools. The participants were concerned with ways in which they could encourage a serious examination and evaluation of the content of educational material.

THE VANIER INSTITUTE OF THE FAMILY
As a result of efforts by General Georges Vanier, Governor-General of Canada, and by Mme Vanier, a Canadian Conference on the Family was held in June 1964 at Rideau Hall and Carleton University. This conference was attended by approximately three hundred invited guests representing a variety of interests from various parts of the country. At the close of the proceedings, the following motion was passed:

That we the participants in the Canadian Conference on the Family are of the opinion that what has been undertaken and accomplished during our sessions now concluding, and the work done in preparation therefor, is of continuing value and importance to all Canadians, and especially to organizations, public and private, and to individuals concerned with the family;

That we express and record the earnest hope that appropriate and adequate provision can and will be made for carrying on the activities initiated by the Conference through some specific organization devoted to maintaining and developing the interest in family life mobilized by the Conference; and,

That the National Council of the Conference be requested to give immediate consideration to the establishment of such an organization with appropriate functions and powers.

In September of the same year a provisional committee was formed to establish the Vanier Institute of the Family. The institute was incorporated under federal charter in April 1965 with membership of approximately one hundred.

The general aims of the institute were to study the environment and characteristics of Canadian families and to promote their well-being. The first of these was to be achieved through a program of research and the second through education, information, and the exercise of influence on social and economic planning through co-operation with governments, educational institutions, religious agencies, and other public and private bodies. It was intended that duplication of effort would be avoided through close collaboration with government and voluntary agencies. The institute planned to use its resources to initiate, commission, and support studies through others working in related fields and to employ the best qualified people from time to time for specific projects.

The main financial resource of the institute was an endowment to which the federal government contributed $2 million and agreed to match contributions received from other sources. By the end of 1968 the total had reached $5,858,000 from nearly eight hundred contributors. The ultimate goal was $10 million.

Study projects planned at an early stage gave evidence of the institute's diverse concerns: 1 / a study of family life education, including preparation for the responsibilities of marriage, parenthood, and responsible citizenship; 2 / studies of the law and the family, involving co-operation with the law reform commissions of the provinces and the attorneys general of most provinces; 3 / a study of the effects on the family of the presence in the home of a handicapped member; 4 / studies of the effects on family life of technological change, including labour mobility and shift work; 5 / studies of the effects of poverty on Canadian families, involving co-operation with the Economic Council of Canada; 6 / a study of a new approach to day care services, with attention to the needs of families and the developmental requirements of children; 7 / a study being supported in co-operation with the Clarke Institute of Psychiatry in Toronto on the dynamics of family life, with the objective of determining the characteristics of the normal, productive family; 8 / a study of specific factors affecting both urban and rural family life and the family life of indigenous ethnic groups in Canada.

The Family Life Education Project began with the compilation of a list of groups and organizations which were presumed to be involved in some aspect of family life education. This effort produced more than 17,000 names, to which questionnaires were distributed. A special questionnaire was sent to schools and other educational institutions, and one with appropriate modifications to universities and community colleges. Some effort was also made to secure a response from the mass media. A total of 29,000 questionnaires were sent to all agencies. A final report on the results was expected to be published in monograph form in 1971, and was counted upon to give a reasonably clear indication of what was being done in the field of family life education in Canada.

Related to this study was a "consultation" held at the School of Fine Arts at Banff to enable about seventy-five participants from government departments and non-governmental associations to examine and clarify the basic definitions and assumptions of family life education and to determine the nature of the needs, how the process should be conducted, who should be involved in implementation, and what training should be provided for people with various backgrounds working in the field. A background paper was commissioned, to be ready for distribution in time for study before the opening session.

The institute sponsored a seminar on Day Care – A Resource for the Contemporary Family at Le Cercle Universitaire d'Ottawa in September 1969. To it were invited twenty-five people representing day care and related services, education, health, welfare, recreation, and social and technological change. These people were expected to formulate "a broad, positive concept of day care related to the needs of the contemporary family." As background material, papers were prepared on The Family in Contemporary Society and Emerging Family Patterns, The Effects of Early Childhood Experience, An Overview of Canadian Day Care Services, and New Directions for Day Care. Recommendations emerging from the discussions were regarded as a basis for a program of public education and as a means of influencing the actions of government and private agencies. The anticipated result was increased public support for those working in the day care field.

The institute produced or supported the production of a number of publications. *The Family in Canada* by Frederick Elkin contains an account of knowledge and gaps in knowledge about Canadian families. *An Inventory of Family Research and Studies in Canada (1963–1967)* refers to over two hundred research projects – projected, in process, or completed – as reported by government agencies, universities, and associations. *The Canadian Conference on the Family: 1964: Proceedings* contains the texts of papers presented at the conference and a summary of the discussions that followed. A *Bibliography on the Family from the Fields of Theology and Philosophy* by Michael McDonald lists over 1,200 works on marriage and family life, including general reference works, official Church documents, and materials on preparation for marriage, sex education, population control, and related topics. The institute also handled a catalogue of 16-mm films on the family prepared and published by the National Film Board of Canada.

TWENTY-THREE

Charitable foundations

Frequent references in different volumes and chapters of ONTARIO'S EDUCATIVE SOCIETY to the contributions of some of the great American foundations make it clear that these agencies have made a major contribution to Canadian education. Canadian foundations have operated on a much smaller scale. However, by dealing in some detail with a single entity, the Atkinson Charitable Foundation, this chapter shows that it has been possible for such an agency to play a crucial role in the development of education.

THE ATKINSON CHARITABLE FOUNDATION

The Atkinson Charitable Foundation was established by Joseph E. Atkinson in 1942 "to receive and maintain a fund or funds and apply the income thereof, in perpetuity, for religious, charitable or educational purposes within the Province of Ontario." The report of the executive administrator in 1950 related the role of this foundation to that of others in Canada in the following terms.

There are about a dozen private foundations with philanthropic aims in Canada, most of them dedicated to a single objective or a limited field. The Atkinson Charitable Foundation is the first to launch an aggressive, active program on a general scale and with support to diversified projects. It is also the first in Canada – indeed far ahead in this respect of many of the older foundations in Britain and the United States – to publish fully the actions it takes as these occur and to state its reasons for such actions.[1]

The intended nature of the foundation was indicated in certain sections of Atkinson's will.

In making the foregoing provisions it is my desire that the ownership and operation of the newspapers known as The Toronto Daily Star and The Star Weekly shall not fall into private hands, and that the shares in the capital stock of The Toronto Star Limited and The Toronto Star Realty Limited held by me shall be held in trust for and ultimately belong to The Atkinson Charitable Foundation ...

This should accomplish two things:

1. The publication of the papers will be conducted for the benefit of the public in the continued frank and full dissemination of news and opinions, with the profit motive, while still important, subsidiary to what I consider to be the chief functions of a metropolitan newspaper;

2. The profits from the newspapers will be used for the promotion and maintenance of social, scientific and economic reforms which are charitable in nature, for the benefit of the people of the Province of Ontario.[2]

The foundation did not try to establish its guidelines too rigidly at the outset, but left them instead to be shaped in the light of knowledge and experience. There were, however, a few obvious principles to be adhered to. The trustees saw little value in investing funds in direct charity, in established forms of education, in routine or well supported research, or in temporary palliatives that promised only to prolong an undesirable situation. Direct assistance was not to be provided for individuals in distress. The task of the foundation was to encourage those who sought new knowledge and new ways to apply it to human betterment, and to publicize their efforts and achievements. It also recognized a duty to examine objectively, as the opportunity arose, areas in which there were demonstrable needs and methods of meeting those needs, as well as a responsibility for making known its findings.

The very first grant, made in 1946, had implications for education. It was an award of $1,500 for the purchase of the nucleus of equipment for a Child Hearing Clinic at the Hospital for Sick Children in Toronto, where research and teaching were to be conducted. The development of the program was interrupted by the death of Atkinson in 1948, and by the lengthy legal processes that lasted for the next two years. The foundation was pushed rather hastily into full-scale activity in 1950 when amendments to the *Dominion Income Tax Act* made it practically mandatory for charitable institutions to distribute 90 per cent of their net annual income during the same year. Fortunately the trustees were in the position of having done a good deal of preliminary work, and were prepared to act promptly.

Some of the grants with the most obvious bearing on education made in 1950 were the following: a grant of $20,000 each year for five years to the Toronto Western Hospital to establish a two-year demonstration course in nursing; $5,000 each year for three years to the Canadian National Institute for the Blind for the discovery and preschool education of blind children in Ontario; $10,000 each year for five years to Queen's University to establish and to maintain for a limited period a chair of pediatrics in conjunction with the children's hospital in Kingston; $20,000 each year for two years to the Ontario Society for Crippled Children for research and for treatment, education, and rehabilitation of child victims of cerebral palsy at Woodeden Centre near London; $4,000 to the University of Toronto, $2,500 to each of Queen's University and the University of Western Ontario, and $2,000 to each of McMaster University, the University of Ottawa, and Carleton College for tests of methods and results of awarding bursaries to deserving students.

Contributions to nursing education remained a conspicuous feature of the program of the foundation. By 1955 the total given to the Toronto Western Hospital, in addition to the original grant, reached a total of $136,625. Among other awards were $33,454 to St Joseph's Hospital in Toronto for equipment for a new nursing school and $27,500 to the Victorian Order of Nurses (VON) for in-service courses and other activities. In later years there were repeated grants for bursaries to enable graduate registered nurses to take training in public health nursing. By 1966 the VON had received a total of $55,500.

The report of the foundation for 1951 indicated that the amounts devoted to general education had not been large in comparison with those invested in medical and social service education, but that the results had been very gratifying. Identified as the most outstanding was the university bursary program, which assisted fifty-four young people to gain higher education in 1951–2. The bursary program was extended to the Ontario Agricultural College to enable ten young Ontario farmers to take the short diploma course in practical agriculture. A grant of $20,000, spread over three years, was made to McMaster to help in the restoration of that university's department of fine arts. The Canadian Association for the Deaf received a grant to finance university-level education of a deaf student for five years at a college in Washington, DC. The foundation classified as educational contributions its assistance to organizations devoted to the advancement of the fine arts and culture, such as the Art Institute of Ontario, the Dominion Drama Festival, the Canadian Ballet Festival Association, and the Opera Festival Association of Toronto. Grants of this type were continued and increased in later years. One of the chief beneficiaries was the Stratford Permanent Theatre Fund.

By 1952 the results of the bursary experiment were judged to have been very successful. The sixty students who had been selected on the basis of merit, financial need, and future promise had nearly all obtained high marks, fifteen of seventeen at the University of Toronto having earned honour standing. The bursary scheme had been demonstrated to have definite advantages over the scholarship system in which awards were commonly made to the recipient of the highest mark, without regard to financial need. In addition, scholarships were sometimes subject to restrictive rules that excluded a large part of the student body. Encouraged by the initial success of the bursary program, the foundation expanded its operations by adding Albert College, Alma College, the Ontario Agricultural College, Kemptville Agricultural College, and the Western Ontario Agricultural College at Ridgetown. In 1954–5 grade 13 graduates of nearly one hundred private secondary schools were made eligible for the grants in addition to those of the three hundred publicly supported secondary schools who were eligible the previous year. At the same time all the degree-granting universities and colleges in the province were brought into the plan. At that time a total of $57,600 was awarded to 167 young people in amounts ranging between $200 and $400. An additional sum of $25,100 was made available for a continuing bursary program applicable to students in any year of their studies. Both aspects of the student aid program continued to expand in subsequent years.

By 1963, when more than 59 per cent of the foundation's total income available for grants was used to support educational projects, $196,000 went for student bursary aid and $265,824 for university expansion and other general assistance projects. An additional $10,586 was used to support five culture and youth development projects and a religious library expansion program. During 1963–4, 488 students entering Ontario universities shared bursary grants totalling $156,000, while $40,000 was divided among about two hundred students already in attendance. From the time bursary assistance had begun in 1951, the total contributed for this purpose had amounted to almost $2 million.

The trustees decided in 1966 that the foundation would have to reduce its allocation for student bursary aid, although help would continue for needy undergraduate students in the form of direct grants to participating universities. The ostensible reason for this decision was that increasing demands were being made on the foundation's limited funds, many of them coming from organizations in fields other than education. The development was understandable in the light of the major increase in government grants and loans at this time.

A major educational venture of 1952, and a new departure in the program of the federation, was the award of $200,000 to Carleton College to establish a graduate school of public administration. The plan had been worked out carefully between spokesmen for the college and officials of the federal government. Courses were intended to be of particular value to those interested in public service at the federal, provincial, or municipal level. The same year saw the beginning of assistance to programs of education in religion in the form of grants for summer schools for clergymen at McMaster University and the University of Western Ontario and a subsidy for the establishment of a library in the new building of the United Church Training School in Toronto.

Further assistance for the development of university facilities and programs was provided in 1957. Queen's University and the University of Western Ontario were each given $25,000 to help them meet the greatly expanded student enrolment foreseen over the succeeding years. The grant to Queen's went toward the purchase of a fifteen-inch reflecting telescope in an observatory at the top of a new engineering building. This observatory was to be used for teaching and research in optical and radio astronomy, and was also to be accessible to school children and citizens of Kingston. The grant to Western was used for furnishings for classrooms, laboratories, and a reading room in the new building for the School of Nursing.

University assistance in 1958 included a grant of $25,000 to McMaster University to cover the cost of high-temperature vacuum equipment for research in metallurgy to be carried on in the new engineering building. A grant of $5,000 was made to Assumption University of Windsor to assist with a five-year expansion program in the modern languages laboratory. The funds helped to pay for thirty-six tape recorders and a control panel for mass production of tapes for individual use. The next year the newly established University of Waterloo received $10,000 for the purchase of x-ray diffraction equipment for the Chemistry Department.

A grant of $782,000, the largest in the history of the foundation, was made in 1961 to help in the establishment of the Joseph E. Atkinson College at York University. This was a novel venture in that the college was the first institution of higher learning in Canada established primarily for evening students. The success achieved within a few years was much greater than anticipated at that time, to judge by yearly increases in enrolment. A still larger grant, this one amounting to $800,000, was made to York in 1965 to expand Atkinson College and to make possible the construction of the Elmina Elliott Atkinson Hall, a new student centre named for Joseph E. Atkinson's wife.

University grants in 1964 included one of $14,651 to the University of Windsor to help expand language laboratory facilities and another of $1,000 to help develop a special library collection in the university's Institute of Canadian and American Affairs. A grant of $10,000 contributed to the expansion of the arts library for graduate students at McMaster University, and one of $5,000 to Waterloo Lutheran University was used for similar purposes. The Centre of Criminology of the University of Toronto received a $5,000 grant toward what was eventually to be a library of thirty thousand volumes. The University of Toronto also received small sums to help sponsor conferences.

Grants to universities in 1966 included one to McMaster University for $10,000 to enable the Department of Metallurgy and Materials Science to purchase an electron microscope. Carleton University received $7,500 to purchase equipment for teaching and research in child psychology; Waterloo Lutheran University received $5,000 to purchase laboratory equipment for its new science building; and the International Forum Foundation of the University of Toronto received $1,500 for a "pre-teach-in" education program. In 1967 a grant of $6,000 helped the University of Western Ontario to undertake a pilot program of academic counselling and testing to help students choose study programs and course options.

The Toronto Metropolitan area of the Boy Scouts' Association received $41,850 in 1953 for assistance in developing what was known as a composite camp, the purpose of which was to provide camping experience for boys whose leaders were unable to accompany them to camp or who were unable to pay camping fees. Although the development of the campsite was delayed, a considerable number of boys were subsidized under the plan.

The Atkinson Study of Utilization of Student Resources was launched by the Department of Educational Research of the Ontario College of Education in 1955 with an initial foundation grant of $35,000. This study exerted a major influence on the directions taken by educational research in Ontario for some years thereafter. An account of its purposes and results is given in volume v, chapters 13 and 14. The reports of the foundation referred to the findings for a number of successive years. An extension of the original plan providing for a longer follow-up of the students involved was made possible by a further grant of $50,000 in 1957.

The foundation became involved in 1955 in improving educational facilities for retarded children by granting $24,453.50 to the Metropolitan Toronto Association for Retarded Children for the enlargement and consolidation of a school unit in the former quarters of the Canadian National Institute for the Blind. The grant was used for the specific purpose of providing equipment for several departments and services of the new school, including equipment for three manual training classrooms, three domestic science classrooms, a power tool demonstration class, an occupational therapy department, a physiotherapy centre, a gymnasium, and other sections.

The Stothers Exceptional Child Foundation Inc of Toronto received $3,000 in 1964 to finance the experimental production of condensed large type school texts for visually handicapped children. The project had been begun five years earlier by Mrs J.E. Moody who, with volunteer assistance, had adapted a substantial number of texts in this way.

Repeated foundation support was provided for the Elizabeth F. Brown Memorial Camp where children from Warrendale Centre at Newmarket combined a vacation with an intensive diagnostic program conducted by the Warrendale staff. The grant for this enterprise amounted to $6,000 in 1965. In the same year $2,000 was awarded to the Ontario Association for Emotionally Disturbed Children.

Assistance for the educational program of the Ontario Temperance Federation was begun in 1958 with a grant of $2,500. A Provincial Youth Conference on the Alcohol Problem was held in Toronto, with about 150 youth leaders from all parts of Ontario in attendance. According to the report of the foundation in 1958, "the conference was aimed at conveying factual scientific information on aspects of the alcohol problem of interest and concern to youth and to offer them a better understanding of the problem through personal observation of the social implications of it." Support for this program was continued in subsequent years.

Among a variety of projects too numerous to mention here, the report of the foundation for 1960 referred to a number of grants for library development. The Canadian Association for Adult Education received $7,500 to enable its library in Toronto to give better and more comprehensive reference and information service. The money was used specifically for the hiring of more staff to catalogue a backlog of books, periodicals, pamphlets, and other documents. The Toronto Public Library also received a grant of $2,500 to enable it to complete and distribute the results of a survey of the educational adjustment and leisure time activities of immigrants. At the same time the University of Toronto received $1,000 to assist it in providing materials for the Edward Johnson Memorial music library. Modest grants for the expansion of library services continued throughout the decade. In 1967, for example, Victoria University was given $5,000 to help expand the library at its Centre for Reformation and Renaissance Studies, thus enriching a major facility for advanced scholars and graduate students conducting research on the period between 1450 and 1660. Library expansion grants of $2,500 were also made to Huron College, London, and Huntington University, Sudbury.

The foundation entered the field of school curriculum study in 1961 by awarding $15,000 to the Joint Committee of the University of Toronto and the Toronto Board of Education to make possible the activities that led to the founding of the Ontario Curriculum Institute. The story of the origin and contributions of this agency is recounted in volume v, chapter 11, and references are made to it in various other parts of ONTARIO EDUCATIVE SOCIETY. The grant made it possible to assemble professors, teachers from all levels of the school system, and other experts, and to publish and distribute the results of their efforts. In 1964 the foundation granted $17,600 to the Ontario Curriculum Institute to support the introduction of a summer program for teachers and the establishment of reading demonstration centres at three locations in Ontario.

Adult education enterprises receiving assistance in the early 1960s included the Parent Education Bureau in Toronto. This agency gave counsel to individuals and, in co-operation with Home and School groups, conducted classes on the problems encountered by parents in dealing with their children. A grant of $21,380 made to the YMCA in 1961 was intended to assist in the reconstruction of its national leadership training centre at Geneva Park. This grant was used specifically to furnish and equip twenty rooms in the new eighty-bed lodging unit. The adult education field benefited further in 1965, when a grant of $5,000 was made to the Canadian Association for Adult Education to facilitate the establishment of the Ontario Association for Continuing Education.

To cite illustrations of support for religious education, two grants were made in 1962. The Salvation Army received $10,933 for laundry equipment for the new William Booth Memorial Training College in Toronto. Cadets came from all over Canada and from Bermuda for training in evangelical work and for tasks in hospitals, youth centres, rehabilitation centres, and other social service agencies. The second grant was made to St Peter's Anglican Church in Toronto to help rebuild and furnish its parish hall, destroyed by fire, thus enabling it to continue its religious and social welfare work.

A strong interest in recreational and welfare projects was shown in the grant program for 1967. Grants of $2,506 and $2,355 went respectively to Olde Davenport United Church in Toronto and St Agatha Children's Village in the Waterloo area to purchase craft and recreational equipment. Rose Avenue Public School in downtown Toronto received $4,500 for after-school supervised recreational programs for children living in high-rise apartments whose parents were both working. St Andrew's Day Nursery in the University of Toronto received $3,315 for equipment and furnishings. A grant of $3,467 assisted the Big Brothers of Metropolitan Toronto in providing group counselling services for mothers of fatherless boys; one of $7,500 to the Community Services Organization, an association of inner-city churches in downtown Toronto, helped to support programs for distressed families, unwed mothers, preschool children, juvenile delinquents, alcoholics, and drug users; one of $4,600 contributed to a pilot project undertaken by the Metropolitan Toronto Social Planning Council to improve communication between young people and "frontier" volunteer adult workers in the Etobicoke area; and one of $7,348 enabled Boys' Village, in cooperation with children's aid societies, to initiate "project recovery" to assess the needs of problem children.

A summary of the amounts granted by area of activity from the establishment of the foundation through 1968 indicates the relative importance of education in the program of the foundation, as well as demonstrating the extent of the foundation's contribution. During that period education, health, and social welfare were awarded $5,928,085, $5,524,096, and $2,151,616 respectively for a total of $13,603,797, nearly all of which was actually paid by the end of 1968. The three categories of educational activity were bursaries and general assistance, culture and youth development, and religious education and other religious activities, the respective shares of which were $5,371,088, $462,219, and $94,778. This amount of money, judiciously spent on carefully selected projects, could not help but have a profoundly beneficial effect on the development of education in Ontario.

TWENTY-FOUR

Associations concerned with international causes

The associations included in this chapter were concerned with two main aspects of international affairs: improving international understanding and rendering services to people in other countries. Objectives in the first area were achieved largely through educational means. Services consisted of educational assistance to or in foreign countries or to foreign students resident in Canada. Activities of voluntary associations in this field commonly received official support.

THE CANADIAN INSTITUTE OF INTERNATIONAL AFFAIRS

The Canadian Institute of International Affairs was founded on January 30, 1928, on the model of the Royal Institute of International Affairs, with which it was affiliated. Its main purposes were to study external policies and developments and to provide sound information about international affairs. When new international organizations such as the United Nations and the North Atlantic Treaty Organization were formed, it sought to create an appreciation of their role among Canadians. Emphasis was placed on the maintenance of close relations with similar organizations within the Commonwealth. The status of the institute was non-official and non-partisan. Its charter prevented it from expressing formal opinions on international questions. Pursuing a policy of objectivity, it restricted itself to providing a forum for the expression of all shades of "responsible" opinion.

Full membership in the institute was restricted to citizens of Canada or other Commonwealth countries. Canadian residents who did not meet this condition could, however, be admitted as associate members without voting rights. There was also provision for honorary members, members-at-large, and student associates. Members were elected by the branches, of which there were twenty-eight in 1968, or by the National Council. Particular value was placed on members whose interest or experience in international affairs enabled them to make a contribution of high quality.

The work of the institute was carried on by research scholars, by study groups in the branches, and in meetings where presentations were made by authorities on international affairs and members engaged in discussions with them. National activities, as reported in 1968, included commissioning research on international affairs and Canadian external relations; publishing books in the biennial series *Canada in World Affairs*, in the *Contemporary Affairs* series, and in collaboration with other publishers; publishing periodicals, including the quarterly *International Journal, Monthly Report on Canadian External Relations*, and six pamphlets a year in the *Behind the Headlines* series; maintaining a reference library of about twenty thousand books, periodicals, and documents for the use of members, scholars, and the general public; providing speakers for branch meetings and preparing material for branch study group programs; creating opportunities for direct communication between government officials and members of the academic, business, and other communities; promoting public education in the form of seminars, conferences, and study sessions, both for members and for non-members.[1]

What the institute has called its public education program perhaps warrants elaboration. In 1959–60 pamphlets in the *Behind the Headlines Series*, designed to provide brief but authoritative treatment of topics of current interest to the general reader, included the following: *Challenge in China* by F.C. Jones (vol. XIX, no. 3); *American Foreign Policy: Ice Moving Out?* by James M. Minifie (vol. XIX, no. 4); *The Soviet Economic Offensive*, by R. Mikesell and D.A. Wells (vol. XIX, no. 5); *Electing an American Government*, by G.M. Craig (vol. XIX, no. 6); *Upsurge in Africa*, by Anthony Delius (vol. XX, no. 1); *Crisis and Change in Latin America*, by John D. Harbron (vol. XX, no. 2). Special memoranda were issued under such titles as *The Indus Basin, The Outer Seven, Antarctica: Claims to Sovereignty*, and *Ghana's New Constitution*. Study kits covered topics such as the Far East, Canada, and the Atlantic Community; Canadian foreign policy; Canadian-American relations; the Middle East; the Commonwealth of Nations; and the Soviets, the satellites, and the West.

The research program of the institute received a good deal of early support from the Rockefeller Foundation. Research funds were used to support the biennial survey *Canada and World Affairs*, each volume of which was written by a different scholar. In 1963 the Ford Foundation committed itself to an annual grant of $40,000 each year for a five-year period, making it possible to commission a variety of studies in four main areas: strategic issues of defence and foreign policy, relations among the North Atlantic nations, the role of the middle powers, and current economic questions. Among the first studies undertaken under this program were a study of Canadian experience in truce control and mediation, and projects entitled Canada and the Arctic: Some International Considerations and Military Force and the Security of Small Nations. The rapid expansion of the research program made a significant change in the balance of institute activities, with the branches declining in relative, although perhaps not in absolute, importance.

By the time the initial Ford grants were exhausted at the end of 1967, the institute had funded approximately thirty major research studies and a large number of seminars. During this period income from normal Canadian sources had more than doubled and there were good prospects that the special programs could eventually be continued from income obtained in this way. The Ford Foundation was, however, prevailed upon to continue the same annual grant for two additional years, and then to contribute declining amounts for three further years. Somewhat increased emphasis was henceforth to be placed on international organization and economic development. Although the grant in question was to end in 1972, the Ford Foundation was prepared to sponsor special projects: for example, a grant of $80,000 was made over a three-year period to stimulate academic and non-academic studies of contemporary China. The institute launched this program by bringing together about fifty people from across Canada, mostly from the universities, to form a consultative committee.

THE UNITED NATIONS ASSOCIATION IN CANADA

The United Nations Association (UNA) in Canada, a successor to the League of Nations Society, began operations under its new name in 1947. Its objectives were to encourage the study of international problems as they related to Canada, to foster understanding, good will, and co-operation among nations, to inform Canadians of the purposes and achievements of the United Nations Organization, to mobilize support for it, and to influence the government to work through it. It placed particular stress on the promotion of world peace, disarmament in all its forms, and respect for human rights.

At the end of the 1960s the association had a central office in Ottawa and thirty-one branches. It raised about 15 per cent of its annual budget of $120,000 from membership fees, somewhat more in the form of a federal government subsidy, and the rest through public campaigns. Expenditures were divided about equally between information and more specifically educational services. The first activity included printing and distributing about eighty thousand copies of the monthly *World Review* for use in high schools; supplying three hundred high school library resource centres with material on the UN and its agencies; printing reference papers on important international issues and distributing them to members of Parliament, the press, and the general public; and responding to thousands of requests for general information. The second type of activity involved sponsoring seminars and model assemblies and organizing meetings, educational tours, lecture series, and conferences designed to promote the ideals and objectives of the UN. At the model assembly, held annually in January, about three hundred Ontario students represented member states of the United Nations and conducted debates on issues of current concern. Another annual event of major importance was a conference at Lake Couchiching where students, resource advisers, and internationally known speakers participated in seminars and informal discussions. One of the educational tours, organized by the Toronto branch, enabled about one hundred students to visit New York and watch the UN in action. An annual university extension lecture series was introduced at Scarborough College.

Despite the aura of pessimism and discouragement that surrounded the UN organization itself on the occasion of its twenty-fifth birthday in 1970, the association launched an enthusiastic campaign to commemorate the event. Certain plans included recognition of 1970 as international education year. The decision was made to hold an international model assembly in Montreal, attended by student delegates from twenty nations and equal numbers of Canadian from all parts of the country. The program included visits to regional seminars by small groups of the participants. Other major events in which the UNA had an interest, if not necessarily a major role, included a Youth Day at the General Assembly on which young people from all member states could sit with regular delegates; a creative art contest held in conjunction with UNESCO, encouraging youth to express in artistic form the aspirations of humanity toward a union of all nations in peace, freedom, and justice; and the provision of bursaries enabling selected Canadian university students to engage in high-level research and training at the UN Institute for Training and Research.

Individual branches had their own special programs. The Metropolitan Toronto branch, for example, undertook in 1970 to establish three educational centres in Senegal to help combat illiteracy and to assist in retraining refugees. A United Nations Festival was intended to enable Toronto's many ethnic groups to contribute to a varied international program and to acquire a better understanding of the character and purposes of the UN.

The association presented a brief to the Provincial Committee on Aims and Objectives in which the point was made that the school had a definite obligation to encourage the development of constructive attitudes toward other peoples and cultures, international co-operation, and the implementation of the principles of human rights. It was said that any classroom devoted to the development of acceptable and worthy members of a society of free men must be oriented toward education for international understanding. Past experiments in education for this purpose were criticized for a lack of continuity and direction.

WORLD UNIVERSITY SERVICE OF CANADA

The World University Service (WUS), formerly known as the International Student Service, originated in efforts on the part of university people in different parts of the world to assist their fellows in Europe after the devastation of the First World War. The organization, founded in

1920, was devoted to the ideal of a university community transcending all barriers of race, nationality, and creed. Relief programs were defined broadly to include international education through conferences, meetings, and study tours. The scope of the organization's activities eventually came to include research into university problems.

The international organization devoted strenuous efforts during the Second World War to helping students in the devastated areas survive the conflict. Camp centres were organized for refugee and internee students, university examinations were arranged for prisoners of war, and books and stationery were supplied to prison camps. The immediate postwar years were devoted to the work of reconstruction. As a means of helping students recover from physically and mentally enhausting experiences, rest centres were set up in France, Switzerland, the United Kingdom, Germany, Greece, Italy, and Austria.

The Canadian organization came into existence in 1939 on the initiative of J.B. Bickersteth, then Warden of Hart House at the University of Toronto. The movement won the enthusiastic support of university administrators and government officials as well as of students and faculty. It was reported in 1955 that more than $200,000 had been raised since 1946 for mutual assistance. A scholarship program was organized to enable refugees and other overseas students to study at Canadian universities. The Canadian government co-operated by supplying travel grants from Colombo Plan funds for students from participating countries.

An annual Canada Seminar was introduced in the early 1950s to provide an opportunity for the discussion of such topics as "this Nation Canada" and "Canada – Community and Communications." Beginning in 1948, Canadians were also involved in international seminars, the first three of which were held in succession in Germany, the Netherlands, and France. In 1951 attention shifted to Asia, and a seminar was held near Ottawa on the theme "the Contributions of East and West." It was attended, not only by European and North American students, but also by the first recipients of Colombo Plan assistance studying in Canada. After a year during which funds were insufficient to support a seminar, assistance from the Ford Foundation made it possible for one hundred delegates from Asia, Africa, Europe, the Middle East, and North America to meet in Mysore, India, to discuss the theme "the Human Implications of Development Planning." A number of study tours were also sponsored to give Canadian students an opportunity to understand the problems of other nations. In 1955 twenty-one students participated in a seminar held in Japan, four students and a leader took part in a study tour of West Africa, as well as visiting Europe, and three students and a leader toured the Caribbean region.

The rapid rise in the number of overseas students in Canada led the National Conference of Canadian Universities and Colleges to appoint a committee in 1960 to consider their problems. As a contribution to this activity, the World University Service of Canada organized a regional conference at the University of Western Ontario the following year. Overseas students from a number of countries and universities assembled to express their views and discuss matters of concern with representatives of government agencies, university administrators, and officials of campus organizations.

Between 1950 and 1970 the international organization, with Canadian contributions, engaged in a number of activities financed from governmental sources or from the proceeds of national fund-raising campaigns. Student centres were established at Seoul, Korea, at Madras, India, and at Ayacacho, Peru, a library in Lesotho, and a hostel at Lusaka, Zambia. In 1961 a book was published in co-operation with UNESCO on *The University Today – Its Role and Place in Society* and a report was published on economic factors affecting access to the university. A workshop on university development was held in Sierra Leone in 1959, work camps in Ghana, Sudan, and Burundi in 1959, 1965, and 1966 respectively, health conferences in Singapore, Ceylon, and Thailand in 1951, 1962, and 1964 respectively, and student mental health conferences in Switzerland and the Netherlands in 1961 and 1970 respectively. The WUS agreed in 1968 to administer a scholarship program for Rwandese refugees in Burundi.

Additional projects were carried out by national organizations. For a time the Canadian service offered graduate scholarships for students from emerging countries. Teachers were provided for Lesotho, Botswana, and Peru. Medicaments were supplied to university or student health services in Asia, Africa, and Latin America. Gifts-in-kind programs involved medical and educational equipment, textbooks, and journals.

In 1969 the WUS of Canada adopted a new constitution with somewhat changed conditions of membership. A membership fee was now exacted, as well as an agreement to support the objects of the service. The rather lengthy statement of objects read as follows:

World University Service aims at promoting international university solidarity, at providing service within and between universities, and at supporting efforts on the part of students, teachers and others to meet the basic needs of universities. It is based on concern for:
A. The sincere and objective search for truth, which implies:
   1) Creative thinking and a critical and many-sided approach.
   2) Resistance to all external pressure liable to hinder freedom of study, teaching or research.
B. The training of men and women with a wide and coherent view of human culture and a sense of their responsibilities within society, which implies:
   1) A proper balance between professional training and true learning.
   2) An active concern for the needs and problems of contemporary society.
C. The achievement of a spirit of community in the university, which implies:

1) That no one be placed at a disadvantage in seeking entrance to the university or in participating in university life on account of race, nationality, sex, social or economic condition, or political or religous conviction, and that within the wider community, every group has the right to establish such educational institutions as are deemed necessary to meet its particular needs.

2) That the fullest development of members of the university community be ensured through promoting and strengthening community life among students, student representatives, teachers and administrators, and between the university community itself and the whole of society, of which it forms a part.

3) That a spirit of real understanding and collaboration be fostered among the university communities of all nations, thus contributing to social justice and international peace.

During the earlier period the organization had concentrated its efforts on providing material assistance to individuals and groups of students and professors in universities throughout the world. Fund raising had thus been an activity of major importance. The new emphasis was on engendering change in the university and, through it, in society. The International Executive Committee recommended that projects be evaluated in terms of 1 / the extent to which they enabled the university community to become involved in the solution of the political, social, and economic problems of the society it served, and 2 / the extent to which they enabled the university community to educate society to understand these problems. In line with these criteria, conferences were held on student health, co-operative enterprises, and community development. Having chosen a more political role than it had originally espoused, the service now began to see itself as a pressure group to promote certain domestic and international causes. There were hopes for an International Exchange Seminar with Cuba in 1971.

CANADIAN UNIVERSITY SERVICE OVERSEAS

Canadian University Service Overseas (CUSO), founded in 1961, did not attempt to make a direct contribution to education in Ontario. Its program, however, had at least two implications that perhaps justify brief mention. 1 / Many of the volunteers whom it sponsored went abroad to teach. After their return home to continue their work in Canadian schools, they commonly demonstrated a breadth of understanding of the human condition that they could not otherwise have obtained. They may thus be said to have experienced the best kind of in-service education. Their background gave them an excellent resource for stimulating the interest of the young people in their charge. 2 / An orientation program for certain volunteers developed at the University of Western Ontario was an actual Ontario educational enterprise.

The service, unlike the later Peace Corps in the United States, was formed through the initiative of private individuals and agencies, including university students and teachers, businessmen, church groups, and service clubs. A small secretariat was set up in Ottawa, and committees were established in most Canadian universities. Initial success aroused government interest, and increasing subsidies were provided to supplement income from other sources. The business of the organization was to recruit and screen university graduates to serve in emerging countries as teachers, nurses, engineers, technicians, and agricultural advisers. They entered a particular country only on invitation and, when the program became established, worked for a minimum of two years at the same salary as their counterparts in the host country. The organization thus had only to finance recruitment, training, transportation, and basic health services. By 1968 there were 825 volunteers working in forty-three countries in the Caribbean, Africa, Asia, and Latin America.

There were strict rules against becoming involved in political affairs in the host countries. The volunteers nevertheless encountered some difficulties along with the satisfaction of employing their skills for the benefit of those who needed them. An Indian critic, for example, declared that his country already had a surplus of university graduates, and that the Canadians were taking scarce jobs. A professor involved in a CUSO orientation program warned that Canadians were entirely too sanguine about their favourable image, and that they were far from immune from arrogance and ignoble motives. They had to take account of the fact that the do-gooder from a developed country was increasingly being regarded as part of the apparatus of colonialism. CUSO volunteers might expect to be blamed for the fact that a good deal of Canada's external aid was associated with the struggle for economic advantage.

Despite these problems the CUSO program was generally regarded as an excellent example of idealism in action, as attested by the continuing requests for volunteers. A considerable proportion of those who served were made to feel that their efforts were appreciated. Even if the benefits ultimately proved to be largely in terms of their own education, the effort might be considered worth while.

THE CANADIAN SERVICE FOR OVERSEAS STUDENTS AND TRAINEES

The Canadian Service for Overseas Students and Trainees was established in 1964 as a response to the needs of the rapidly increasing number of foreigners studying in Canada. By 1969 there were reported to be about twenty thousand of such students. The aims of the organization were to provide services to ensure the general well-being of these students and thus enable them to get the maximum benefit from their experience and to provide opportunities for mutual understanding between Canadians, both in the university and in the community, and the overseas visitors.

The organization undertook a number of activities in pursuit of its aims. 1 / It provided information services to respond to inquiries from overseas about study and training facilities in Canada, the cost of study at Canadian institutions, the cost of living in the country, immigration requirements, and accommodation. 2 / It conducted an annual fall reception service whereby overseas students and trainees were met at all principal points of entry and assisted in reaching their final destination. 3 / Through local organizations, it arranged local reception and orientation, hospitality in Canadian homes, lectures, and other activities. 4 / It offered co-ordination and guidance to community groups and individuals interested in providing services to overseas students. 5 / It published an information bulletin and a newsletter called *Communications*. 6 / It maintained liaison with university personnel, government departments, and voluntary associations concerned with overseas students. 7 / It convened an annual conference bringing together overseas students, Canadian students, university personnel, government officials, volunteer agencies, community workers, representatives of foreign missions, and others with an interest in the welfare of overseas students.

At the end of the 1960s plans were being made to extend service to Canadians going overseas for educational travel and exchange. This service would involve collecting and distributing information on Canadian travel and exchange programs, answering requests from individuals wishing to take part in such programs, publicizing Canadian programs through comparable agencies in other countries, collecting information on foreign programs, and publicizing this information among Canadian individuals and groups.

Notes

CHAPTER 1

1 Edwin C. Guillet, *In the Cause of Education: Centennial History of the Ontario Educational Association, 1861–1960* (Toronto: University of Toronto Press, 1960).
2 *Ibid.*, p. 25.
3 *Ibid.*, p. 222.
4 *Ibid.*, p. 377.
5 Information in this section was largely obtained from F.K. Stewart, The Canadian Education Association: Its History and Role, M Ed thesis, University of Toronto, 1956.
6 *Ibid.*, p. 35.
7 *Ibid.*, p. 49.
8 *Ibid.*, p. 107.
9 F.K. Stewart to W.D.C. Mackenzie, 5 June 1957.

CHAPTER 2

1 Doris French, *High Button Bootstraps: Federation of Women Teachers' Associations of Ontario: 1918–1968* (Toronto: FWTAO, 1968).
2 *Ibid.*, p. 25.
3 *Ibid.*, pp. 45–6.
4 R.A. Hopkins, *The Long March: History of the Ontario Public School Men Teachers' Federation* (Toronto: Baxter Publishing, 1969).

5 *Ibid.*, p. 39.
6 *Ibid.*, p. 145.
7 S.G.B. Robinson, *Do Not Erase: The Story of the First 50 Years of OSSTF* (Toronto: OSSTF, 1971).
8 "Excerpts from O.S.S.T.F. Salary Policy – Revised December 1963," *Bulletin*, XLIV, 1, 31 January 1964, 15–16.
9 D.M. Graham, "Education Committee," in "Our Thirty-Sixth Annual Assembly," *Bulletin*, XXXVI, 1, 31 January 1956, 10.
10 James D. McNabb, "Teachers Shape the Future," *Bulletin*, XLV, 2, 31 March 1965, 76.
11 "Members and Educational Activities," *Bulletin*, XLVI, 4, October 1966, 224–5.
12 Ontario Secondary School Teachers' Federation, Brief to the OTF Commission, December 1966.
13 I.M. Robb, "Some Observations," *Bulletin* XLVIII, 1, February 1968, 12–13.
14 *Ibid.*, 13.
15 J.M. Paton, "Our Ambivalent Profession," *Bulletin*, XLIX, 1, January 1969, 12–16.
16 OECTA, *Your Association: A Handbook for Members* (Toronto: OECTA, [n.d.]), p. 19.

17 OECTA, Executive, Brief submitted to the OTF Commission on the Structure and Functions of the OTF, 23 March 1967.

18 *Pattern for Professionalism*, Report of the OTF Commission to the Board of Governors of the OTF, August 1968, p. 1.

19 *Ibid.*, p. 3.

20 "The Teaching Profession Act, 1944," *Statutes of Ontario, 1944*, chap. 64.

21 *Ibid.*

22 Nora Hodgins, "Memorandum re Educational Television," OTF, June 1964, mimeographed.

23 *Ibid.*, p. 4.

24 OTF, Brief presented to the Select Committee on Youth, 1965, in minutes of meeting of Board of Governors, 9 January 1965, Toronto, mimeographed.

25 *Pattern for Professionalism*, p. A47.

26 *Ibid.*, pp. 27–8.

27 Fred W. Price, ed., *Educational Programs of National Organizations* (Ottawa: Canadian Conference on Education, 1961), pp. 110–11.

28 Factual material for the account which follows was obtained from Gerald Nason, The Canadian Teachers' Federation: A Study of Its Historical Development, Interests and Activities from 1919 to 1960, EdD thesis, University of Toronto, 1964.

29 *Ibid.*, p. 22.

30 *Ibid.*, pp. 33–4.

31 *Ibid.*, p. 77.

32 *Ibid.*, pp. 77–9.

33 *Ibid.*, p. 86.

34 *Ibid.*, pp. 147–8.

35 Price, pp. 111–13.

CHAPTER 3

1 Morley Toombs, "Chairman's Report," in Canadian Association of Professors of Education, *Fifth Annual Conference of the Canadian Association of Professors of Education*, (Saskatoon: Macmillan, 1960), p. 1.

2 Fred W. Price, ed., *Educational Programs of National Organizations* (Ottawa: Canadian Conference on Education, 1961), p. 34.

3 "Canadian Educational Researchers Association / Association Canadienne des Chercheurs en Education," *Communiqué*, I, 1, October 1967, 1-A.

CHAPTER 4

1 CCRE, Report of the Director to the Fourth Annual Meeting of the CCRE covering the period 16 May 1964 to 1 June 1965, p. 3, mimeographed.

2 Fred W. Price, ed., *Educational Programs of National Organizations* (Ottawa: Canadian Conference on Education, 1961), p. 145.

CHAPTER 5

1 Draft of the constitution of the ICIRI [International Council for the Improvement of Reading Instruction], November 1947, quoted in History of International Council for the Improvement of Reading Instruction, p. 3, mimeographed.

2 M.K. MacDonald, "The Metropolitan Toronto Council of the

International Reading Association," *Leadership for Improvement of Instruction*, 13th Yearbook of the Ontario School Inspectors' Association (Toronto: Copp Clark, 1957), pp.81–2.

3 *Ibid.*, p. 82.

4 CSEA, Report of the First Conference, 1955, Quebec City, p. 5, mimeographed.

5 Ontario Educational Television Committee, 1960, Brief presented to the Board of Broadcast Governors on Educational Television.

6 For further information see volume III, chapter 6.

7 *Constitution of the Ontario Alliance of Christian Schools*, Ontario Alliance of Christian Schools, Sarnia, 1957.

8 Ontario Alliance of Christian Schools, Brief submitted to the Provincial Committee on Aims and Objectives of Education in the Schools of Ontario, [n.d.], p. 12.

9 Jacob B. Vos, *The Christian School* (Hamilton: *Christian School Herald*, [n.d.]), p. 3.

CHAPTER 6

1 Margery R. King, "Commission on Emotional and Learning Disorders in Children," *Canada's Mental Health*, XVI, 1 and 2, January-April 1968, 9.

2 *Ibid.*, p. 11.

3 Information in this section was obtained from "Evolution of a Magazine (Special Education in Canada)," *Special Education in Canada*, XXXIX, 4, May 1965, 22.

4 Ontario Federation of Chap-

ters of the Council for Exceptional Children, The First Ten Years, 1967, p. 37, mimeographed.

CHAPTER 7

1 "Benefits of the Ontario School Trustees' and Ratepayers' Association," *Canadian School Journal*, XI, 3, March 1933, 98.

2 "Report of the School Trustees' and Ratepayers' Association," *Ontario School Board Journal*, I, 5, April 1922, 21.

3 "Benefits of the Ontario School Trustees' and Ratepayers' Association," *Canadian School Journal*, XI, 98.

4 Introductory, *Ontario School Board Journal*, I, 1, 12 December 1921.

5 Jean M. Watson, "O.S.T.&R.A. Secretary Reports," *Canadian School Journal*, XXXII, 3, April 1954, 86.

6 "The Urban Trustees' Association," *Argus*, II, 6, June 1943, 189.

7 H.A. Semple, "First Annual Convention of the Associated High School Boards of the Province of Ontario," *Canadian School Journal*, X, 6, June 1932, 215–18.

8 "Urban Trustees' Associations" (by an urban trustee), *Canadian School Journal*, X, 10, October 1932, 354.

9 Ontario Catholic Education Council, Brief submitted to the Provincial Committee on Aims and Objectives of Education in the Schools of Ontario, January 1966, pp. 26–7.

10 Leslie H. Saunders, "A Distinct Public School Trustees' and

Ratepayers' Association," *Argus*, I, 5, June 1942, 2.

11 "Brief of the Public School Trustees' Association of Ontario, Incorporated, presented to the Prime Minister and members of the Legislative Assembly of Ontario," *Argus*, XXII, 3, March 1963, 95.

12 *Argus*, XXIV, 9, September 1965, 314.

13 Information for this section was provided by H.E. Crowder, who served as the first president of the association.

14 J.A. Bain, "Report of Ontario Trustees' Council," *Canadian School Journal*, XXIV, 5, May 1946, 172.

15 Report of meeting called by the Associated High School Boards of the Province of Ontario to discuss the question of a form of central executive committee representing trustee boards in Ontario, Toronto, 2 December 1949.

16 "Constitution: Ontario School Trustees' Council," *Canadian School Journal*, XXVIII, 7, October 1950, 265.

17 "Report on the Advanced Institute for School Trustees and Administrators," *Canadian School Journal*, XLII, 6, September 1964, 26.

CHAPTER 8

1 C.R. Prosser, "The Ontario Secondary School Headmasters' Council," *Bulletin*, XLV, 6 December 1965, 514.

2 J.A. Gummow, "Busy Seminar Season," *Newscap*, II, August 1970.

CHAPTER 9

1 Ontario Association of Art Galleries, OAAG, I, 1, Spring 1969.

CHAPTER 10

1 Information in this section was obtained from Robin Harris, "A Matter of Balance," in *Association of Universities and Colleges of Canada, Proceedings of Annual Meeting*, Montreal, 1967, p. 11.

2 Information from this section is taken from *Universities and Colleges in Canada, 1969* (Ottawa: Association of Universities and Colleges of Canada, 1969).

3 *Ibid.*

4 J. Percy Smith, "Academic Freedom," *Globe and Mail*, 29 April 1969.

CHAPTER 11

1 Edward J. Monahan, "Academic Freedom and Tenure and the C.A.U.T. – The First Twenty Years, *C.A.U.T. Bulletin*, XVIII, 4, Summer 1970, 80–91. Much of the information that follows is derived from the same source.

2 OCUFA, Channels of Communication between the Provincial Government and the Universities, Memorandum to the Minister of University Affairs, 23 November 1965.

3 J.S. Kirkaldy, "Chairman's Comments on Uses and Misuses of Formula Financing," *OCUFA Newsletter*, II, March 1969, 3–6.

4 "Teachers' Colleges," *OCUFA*

Newsletter, II, March 1969, 4–5.

CHAPTER 12

1 "The Royal Society of Canada, 1882–1957," pp. 1–2.
2 *Ibid.*, p. 3.
3 Canadian Authors Association, "What It Is ... What It Does."
4 Information for this section was obtained from Mary E. White, "Phoenix: The First Twenty Years," *Phoenix*, XX, 4, 1966.
5 Information for this section was obtained from a brochure entitled "The Canadian Historical Association," 1968.
6 V.W. Bladen, "A Journal is Born: 1935," *Canadian Journal of Economics and Political Science*, XXVI, 1, February 1960, 1–5.
7 Canadian Sociology and Anthropology Association, 1968–9 Annual Report of the Executive Committee, presented at the annual general meeting of the association, Toronto, 6 June 1969, pp. 1–3, mimeographed.
8 Watson Kirkconnell and A.S.P. Woodhouse, *The Humanities in Canada*, a report prepared by the Humanities Research Council of Canada for the Rockefeller Foundation (Ottawa: The Humanities Research Council of Canada, 1947).
9 R.E. Watters, *A Check-List of Canadian Literature and Background Materials, 1628–1950* (Toronto: University of Toronto Press, 1959).
10 *Union List of Manuscripts in Canadian Repositories* (Ottawa: Public Archives of Canada, 1968).

11 *Humanities Research Council of Canada: Annual Report 1967–1968*, p. 13.

CHAPTER 13

1 *The Ontario Library Association: An Historical Sketch, 1900–1925* (Toronto: University of Toronto Press, 1926), p. 20.
2 *Ibid.*, p. 24.
3 *Ibid.*, p. 26.
4 Ontario Library Association, Proceedings, 1967, p. 19.
5 Information from this section came from Charles Deane Kent, Director, London Public Library and Art Museum, "A Short History of the Institute of Professional Librarians," London, September 1962.
6 *Ibid.*, pp. 4–7.
7 "Continuing Education," *IPLO Quarterly*, Special Supplement, February 1970, p. 111.
8 J.P. Wilkinson, "The Institute of Professional Librarians of Ontario," *Canadian Library Journal*, XXVI, 4, July-August 1969, 277–9.
9 Royal College of Physicians and Surgeons of Canada, Brief to the Commission on the Relations Between Universities and Governments, Ottawa, December 1968, p. 2, mimeographed.
10 Fred W. Price, ed., *Educational Programs of National Organizations* (Ottawa: Canadian Conference on Education, 1961), p. 49.
11 Canadian Psychiatric Association, "Objects and By-Laws," as amended by the 13th annual general meeting, 14 June 1963,

and approved by the Secretary of State for Canada, 19 June 1963.

12 Joy A. Maines, "CASW – The First Forty Years," *Social Worker*, XXXV, 3, September 1967, 225–31.

13 Charles E. Hendry, "Canadian Social Work Looks Back," *Canadian Welfare*, XLV, 2, March-April 1969, 9.

14 Information in this section was obtained from W.A. Mackintosh, *Report to the Councils of the Provincial Institutes of Chartered Accountants in Canada on Educational Plans*, 20 March 1967.

CHAPTER 14

1 W.J. Dunlop, Editorial, *Adult Learning*, I, 1, 1936, 3.

2 *Ibid.*, p. 4.

3 James Robbins Kidd, *Continuing Education*, Conference Study No 6 (Ottawa: Canadian Conference on Education, 1961), pp. 56–7.

4 James Robbins Kidd, *18 to 80: Continuing Education in Metropolitan Toronto*, Report of an Enquiry Concerning the Education of Adults in Metropolitan Toronto (Toronto: The Board of Education for the City of Toronto, 1961), pp. 73–4.

5 WEA, "Golden Jubilee, 1903–1953," Toronto, 1953.

6 "Cruel Penny-Pinching," *Globe and Mail*, Toronto, 9 April 1970.

7 RLA, *Newsletter*, 31st issue, April 1969.

8 Dorothy Macpherson, "Canada's Film Institute," *Variety*, 5 January 1966.

CHAPTER 15

1 The basis for the information in this section is James Robbins Kidd, *18 to 80: Continuing Education in Metropolitan Toronto*, Report of an Enquiry Concerning the Education of Adults in Metropolitan Toronto (Toronto: The Board of Education for the City of Toronto, 1961), pp. 32–4.

2 "New Directions," Fifty-seventh Annual Meeting of the National Council of Young Men's Christian Associations of Canada, 1969.

3 Fred W. Price, ed., *Educational Programs of National Organizations* (Ottawa: Canadian Conference on Education, 1961), pp. 168–9.

4 *Basic Areas of Professional Competence in the YMCA Secretaryship* (an interpretative statement prepared and issued by the Committee on Professional Education – a joint committee of the Association of Secretaries and the Personnel Services Committee of the National Board of YMCAs, approved May 1954 by the Association of Secretaries of North America and May 1955 by the National Council of the United States and the National Council of Canada).

5 *Ibid.*, p. 15.

6 Ellsworth Study, *Young Men & Young Women – New Insights on Becoming Adult*

(Toronto, 1963), pp. 32–3.
7 The story of the early development of the YWCA is recounted in some detail in Josephine P. Harshaw's *When Women Work Together: A History of the Young Women's Christian Association in Canada* (Canada: YWCA of Canada, 1966).
8 "Background Material on Resolution on YWCA Purpose," citing Harshaw, *When Women Work Together*.
9 Fred W. Price, ed., *Educational Programs of National Organizations* (Ottawa: Canadian Conference on Education, 1961), pp. 172–3.
10 Dorothea E. Woods, *The Responsibility of the YWCA for Education* (programme bulletin in the series "The YWCA in Action," for 1968), p. 183.
11 Harshaw, *When Women Work Together*, p. 76.

CHAPTER 16
1 "Body of Regulations: National Canadian Girls in Training Committee," June 1961.
2 "50th Annual Report of Navy League of Canada, Ontario Division, 1 January 1967 to 31 December 1967," Toronto, 20 April 1968, pp. 18–19.

CHAPTER 17
1 For information in this section, acknowledgment is made to *"What's Past is Prologue": A Report to the Church 1915–1965* (Toronto: Department of Christian Social Service, Anglican Church of Canada, 1965).

2 Board of Christian Education, Division of Congregational Life and Work, "Education in the Church in the 70's," Recommendations and proposals from the Board of Christian Education for consideration by Commissioners to the 24th General Council.

CHAPTER 18
1 P. Abercrombie, "The Women's Institute and Education," *Canadian School Journal*, XXI, 11, November 1943, 412–13, 432.
2 *Chronicle* (Canadian Federation of University Women), XLII, 1969–70.

CHAPTER 20
1 Edward Dunlop, "The Canadian Arthritis and Rheumatism Society: The First Twenty Years," *Journal of the Canadian Physiotherapy Association*, XX, 2, April 1968, 84–9.
2 Fred W. Price, ed., *Educational Programs of National Organizations* (Ottawa: Canadian Conference on Education, 1961), pp. 100–101.

CHAPTER 21
1 Indian-Eskimo Association of Canada, Report of Executive Director to the 9th Annual Meeting of Members, 28 September 1968, pp. 2–3, mimeographed.
2 Canadian Jewish Congress, Educational and Cultural Committee, "Revised Curriculum Outline for the Hebrew Afternoon Schools in Ontario," 1967, pp. 2–3.

3 *Departments of the Canadian Labour Congress* (Ottawa: CLC, Education Department, n.d.).

CHAPTER 22

1 Esmé Crampton, "Introducing t.a.g.," *The Stage in Canada*, IV, 3, May 1968, 14–16.
2 Conservation Council of Ontario, Summary of the Brief to the Provincial Committee on Aims and Objectives of Education, Toronto, 9 December 1965, pp. 4–5.
3 Conservation Council of Ontario, "The Conservation Authority Programme," brief submitted to the Select Committee on Conservation Authorities, Toronto, August 1966, pp. 2–3.

CHAPTER 23

1 Atkinson Charitable Foundation, *Annual Report 1950* (for the year ending 31 December 1950, with the period 1942–1950 reviewed), p. 6.
2 *Ibid.*, pp. 7–8.

CHAPTER 24

1 Canadian Institute of International Affairs, *Annual Report 1967–68*, p. 24.

Contents of volumes in
ONTARIO'S EDUCATIVE SOCIETY

General index

Index of persons

DATE DUE

DEMCO 38-297